REFORMING CIVIL PROCEDURE

Drawing on political, social and economic theory, *Reforming Civil Procedure* focuses on the English civil justice system by looking at its history and its processes. The book considers the objectives of civil procedure and how it operates for and against particular societal groups, and what ideas and behaviours impact upon it.

The reform of civil procedure has been beset with difficulties. Some are caused by questions of culture and mind-sets resistant to the changes, some by a confusion and conflict of values, some by overambitious reform efforts, some by a failure to follow through on purpose clauses, and some by swinging from laxity to rigidity with insufficient analysis.

This book makes a strong contribution to the field by synthesising the work of English writers with different views, extending the work in England on the role of philosophy, values, process and culture in litigation, and engaging extensively with American writers who have not previously been the subject of much attention in English civil procedural studies.

Reforming Civil Procedure

The Hardest Path

Dominic De Saulles

•HART•

OXFORD • LONDON • NEW YORK • NEW DELHI • SYDNEY

HART PUBLISHING

Bloomsbury Publishing Plc

Kemp House, Chawley Park, Cumnor Hill, Oxford, OX2 9PH, UK

First published in Great Britain 2019

A catalogue record for this book is available from the British Library.

Library of Congress Cataloging-in-Publication data

Names: De Saulles, Dominic, author.

Title: Reforming civil procedure : the hardest path / Dominic De Saulles.

Description: Oxford, UK ; Chicago, Illinois : Hart Publishing, 2019. | Includes bibliographical references and index.

Identifiers: LCCN 2018058558 (print) | LCCN 2018058984 (ebook) | ISBN 9781509925926 (EPub) | ISBN 9781509925902 (hardback)

Subjects: LCSH: Civil procedure—England. | Civil procedure—United States. | Law reform—England. | Law reform—United States. | BISAC: LAW / Civil Procedure.

Classification: LCC K2205 (ebook) | LCC K2205 .D4 2019 (print) | DDC 347.42/05—dc23

LC record available at https://lccn.loc.gov/2018058558

ISBN: HB: 978-1-50992-590-2
ePDF: 978-1-50992-591-9
ePub: 978-1-50992-592-6

Typeset by Compuscript Ltd, Shannon
Printed and bound in Great Britain by CPI Group (UK) Ltd, Croydon CR0 4YY

FSC www.fsc.org MIX Paper from responsible sources FSC® C013604

For Helen

ACKNOWLEDGEMENTS

I would like to thank the Board of the *Civil Justice Quarterly* and AA Higgins for their agreement to my using *Defending the Civil Justice System*. I also wish to thank the Athens Institute of Education and Research and David Frenkel, of Ben Gurion University, together with RP Craven and A Masood, each of Leicester University, for hosting seminars that formed the basis of part of this work. I should also like to thank Matthew Davies of the Cardiff Law Library for dealing with my endless requests for unusual material.

I have been teaching for over a decade now. Prior to that I was in practice and had the privilege of working with some seriously good lawyers in South Wales and in Bristol – they had a large impact on me. I have taught civil litigation, commercial litigation and personal injury litigation on the LPC and the BPTC here at the Cardiff School of Law and Politics. It is a vibrant place, with excellent staff and hard-working students drawn from all across the common law world. The discipline of having to withstand questioning every lesson keeps me on my toes, and I continue to admire the persistence of students who tackle this difficult subject. We have a tendency in Cardiff to emphasise the team aspect of what we do, but I would be remiss in not thanking Michaela Thomas, Kath Clague and Nicola Harris, who have cheerfully shared the burden of litigation teaching with me.

Over the longer term, Paul Staddon, Matthew Bishop, Jason Tucker, Viv Burfitt, Nicky Priaulx, Annette Morris, Rachel Cahill-O'Callaghan and David Glass have all been greatly encouraging.

Helen, Liz and Matthew have shared with me the highs and lows of writing and teaching. I am very grateful for their love and support: I know how lucky I am.

TABLE OF CONTENTS

LIST OF ABBREVIATIONS

ABA	American Bar Association
ADR	alternative dispute resolution
ALI	American Law Institute (body which created the Restatements of the Law)
ANFP	A New Federal Civil Procedure Part 1 or 2. Articles by CE Clark and JW Moore published in 1935.
AG	Attorney General of the United States.
AndPCP	N Andrews, *Principles of Civil Procedure* (London, Sweet & Maxwell, 1994).
AndECP	N Andrews, *English Civil Procedure* (Oxford, Oxford University Press, 2003).
AndoCP	N Andrews, *Andrews on Civil Processes*, vol 1 (Cambridge, Intersentia, 2013).
Blackstone's Guide	C Plant et al, *Blackstone's Guide to the Civil Procedure Rules*, 2nd edn (London, Blackstone Press, 1999).
BriggsIR	Lord Justice Briggs, *Civil Courts Structure Review: Interim Report* (London, Judiciary of England and Wales, 2015).
BriggsFR	Lord Justice Briggs, *Civil Courts Structure Review: Final Report* (London, Judiciary of England and Wales, 2016).
Bow Rep	Sir Jeffery Bowman, *Review of the Court of Appeal (Civil Division): Report to the Lord Chancellor* (London, Lord Chancellor's Department, 1997).
CivJ Rev	Sir Maurice Hodson, *Civil Justice Review: Report of the Review Body on Civil Justice*, Cmnd 394 (London, HMSO, 1988).
CJ	Chief Justice of the United States Supreme Court.
CPR	Civil Procedure Rules 1998 (as amended).
CsSelP	Homer Cummings, *Selected Papers of Homer Cummings: AG of the United States 1933–1939*, vol 1 (ed Carl Brent Swisher) (New York, C Scribner's Sons, 1939).

England	The legal jurisdiction comprising England and Wales.
FRCP	The Federal Rules of Civil Procedure 1938 (as amended).
JbFabr	Sir Jack IH Jacob, *The Fabric of English Civil Justice* (London, Stevens & Sons,1987).
JnRef	Sir Rupert Jackson, *The Reform of Civil Litigation*, 1st edn (London, Sweet & Maxwell, 2016); Stephen Clark and Sir Rupert Jackson, *The Reform of Civil Procedure*, 2nd edn (London, Sweet & Maxwell, 2018)). The year of publication (2016 or (2018) will be given.
JnReview PR	Lord Justice Jackson, *Review of Civil Litigation Costs: Preliminary Report* (London, TSO, 2009).
JnReview FR	Lord Justice Jackson, *Review of Civil Litigation Costs: Final Report* (London, TSO, 2009).
JoloCP	J Jolowicz, *On Civil Procedure* (Cambridge, Cambridge University Press (2000)).
Lawyers	Judges and all those who practise law.
LegHist	EH Hammond (ed), *Legislative History of the Rules of Civil Procedure of the District Courts of the US* (Chicago, IL, American Bar Association,1938) vols 1 or 2.
RSC (1883)	The Rules of the Supreme Court 1883.
RSC (1965)	The Rules of the Supreme Court 1965.
SorECJ	John Sorabji, *English Civil Justice after the Woolf and Jackson Reforms: a Critical Analysis* (Cambridge, Cambridge University Press, 2014).
Ten Years	D Dwyer (ed), *The Civil Procedure Rules Ten Years On* (Oxford, Oxford University Press, 2009).
WfDR	Lord Woolf, *Access to Justice Draft Civil Proceedings Rules* (London, HMSO,1996).
WfIR	Lord Woolf, *Access to Justice: Interim Report* (London, HMSO, 1995).
WfFR	Lord Woolf, *Access to Justice: Final Report* (London, HMSO, 1996).
White Book	Any edition of *Civil Procedure* (London, Sweet & Maxwell). The year of publication will be identified.
ZoCP	A Zuckerman, *Zuckerman on Civil Procedure: Principles of Practice* (London, Sweet & Maxwell). The year of publication (2003, 2006 or 2013) will be given.

INTRODUCTION

This book looks at the question of why it has proved to be so difficult to reform civil procedure, using the writings of reformers, judges and academics from both sides of the Atlantic to examine the problem in detail. The period covered is roughly 1905 to 2013, with some reference to developments after that date, including the publication of the second edition of *The Reform of Civil Procedure* by Sir Rupert Jackson and Stephen Clark.

The book starts with a sketch of the genuinely gripping story of how the Federal Civil Procedure Rules came to be written.[1] This is a story that is well known in America but not in England. Put briefly, a long campaign for change was brought to fruition during the Great Depression under the newly elected President Franklin D Roosevelt. The demise of the obstructor of change opened the door in a most unexpected way. A stellar group of lawyers wrote a set of rules that proved remarkably successful. Part of the reason for this was that the group's intellectual driving force, Charles E Clark, had his feet kept firmly on the ground by those more worldly-wise than he. Clark is both antagonist (working for himself) and protagonist (working for the forces of change). Readers who like chronologies and cast lists will find them at the outset of the History.

Chapter 1 looks at the issues civil procedure raises for society, and why it is important that the civil procedure system functions properly. The human context of all this is set out and then related to the big questions posed recently by Adrian Zuckerman, Neil Andrew and John Sorabji. The approach is both social and philosophical, in an applied sense. Chapter 1 closes with an attempt to analyse how the process of rule-writing and rule-making can be broken down so that it may be more easily understood. The categories of intention, action and outcome are set out. Those concerned to avoid theory may safely pass over this chapter, save for section XV.

In chapter 2, the reader is taken through a selection of important thinkers from America and England. The connection between the two jurisdictions is fruitful, for it quickly becomes clear that we have common problems and have tried similar solutions. The American writers illustrate the realist, in a broad sense, pragmatic and managerial tendencies. The selection from England starts with Jack Jacob, the grandfather of modern procedural reform, and moves through the waxing and waning of Woolf, the advent of Jackson and the sorry saga of *Mitchell* and *Denton*.

[1] The fuller story is drawn from a number of American articles and original papers cited in this book.

I admit to considerable sympathy for those judges who loyally tried to follow a decision they thought mistaken and were then blamed by the Court of Appeal for doing so. I have taken the opportunity to introduce key writers in field of procedural studies, because they both illustrate the state of knowledge at any given time and show how our understanding has deepened over time. The chapter closes with a discussion about whether Woolf was clear or consistent in his intentions.

Chapter 3 looks at the question of purpose, or goals or intention. The Federal Rules of Civil Procedure (1938) (FRCP) had no explicit interpretation clause like Rule 1.1 of the Civil Procedure Rules 1998 (CPR). Yet the intention behind FRCP Rule 1 was clear. The focus of this part of the study, then, is the first rules of the FRCP 1938 and the CPR 1998 respectively. Each rule has its own strengths and weaknesses, yet the American rule has lasted, with minor change, whereas CPR 1.1's overriding objective had to have a major overhaul in 2013 to increase the profile of proportionality. Judicial treatment of the two rules has been different. In England the Court of Appeal was first enthusiastic, then cooled off and has now renewed its commitment to CPR 1.1. In America, FRCP 1.1 has not played a large role in the case law, partly because of a heightened sensitivity to the constitutional role of the rule-makers. Justice Scalia of the US Supreme Court looms large in this area.

Chapter 4 looks at the delicate question of why Woolf failed (at least in part) and why Jackson has made progress that Woolf did not. This chapter moves Sorabji's argument one step on. The topic is viewed through the categories set out in an important article written by the sociologist Robert K Merton. The article is a contemporary of the making of the FRCP (1938). The chapter then looks at how culture and mind-sets both played a significant role in what happened. The conclusion of the chapter is that Woolf seriously underestimated the human factor, and that the human factor was also the driving force behind why Woolf partly failed. Jackson has been more cautious, yet he too has had to grapple with the rule-drafters and rule-interpreters going off in unexpected directions.

In chapter 5 there is a close focus on the question of what sanctions are and why enforcing them has proved so problematic under the Woolf and Jackson schemes. Here the root of the problems can be traced to a mixture of diverging intentions and too much laxity and harshness in turn. The chapter considers the system's role in all this and why the Jackson reforms were the sign of a serious rot that had to be cut out. There had been an historic unwillingness to say 'no' to those who wanted a second, third or fourth chance.

Chapter 6 ends the book with a look at the appeals system, with some help from Jack Jacob and the Bowman Report in England, and Roscoe Pound and other later American academics. Particular attention is paid to the question of process costs and error costs. The chapter concludes that reducing the number of appeals and rerouting cases of lesser importance was a wise move. For the recent reforms to succeed, judges will have to get used to saying 'no', just as they have had to do under CPR 3.8 and 3.9.

Material relating to David Dudley Field, Jeremy Bentham, Adam Smith, the Codification debate and the Victorian reform of English Civil Procedure has not made it into this book for reasons of space. Another volume on the travails of nineteenth-century civil procedure is projected.

The experienced reader will recognise how I have drawn upon those who have gone before. In particular Zuckerman, Andrews and Sorabji have all contributed to the intellectual foundations of this work, but the direction is my own and I accept the responsibility for that. My principal regret is that I have not found more space for Stuart Sime's work. I draw on him every day that I teach.

Sir Rupert Jackson is a big part of this story. I was lucky enough to be his host for the day when he came to Cardiff as part of his roadshow tour. He looked rather like the 'boy stood on the burning deck'. He has now taken a well-earned retirement. His book, now in a second edition, is required reading. Chapter 28 of it deals directly with the human dimension of the work of the reformers.

Hazel Genn makes the point that there is a danger of 'adopting the agenda and rhetoric of policy-makers, and for conducting research only with the limited objective of discovering how the system could be made to work better within its own terms'.[2] The study of civil justice is a field in its own right: it analyses and critiques civil procedure and the procedural justice it seeks to deliver, creating knowledge that encompasses but goes wider than doctrinal understanding. However, Clifford Geertz[3] offers a warning that it can be difficult to be truly distant from what one is studying for: in some types of study, one has to stay 'rather closer to the ground' than is required for science. Civil justice is such a field of study. There are good reasons for this. We study the rules together with the decisions of judges, which are made in real time in cases concerning real people. I have found that looking at the social world of those working within the civil justice system has helped me to see the process of change more clearly. To approach the subject from this direction is not to say that the work already done in this field is to be devalued – far from it. The challenge is how to question what is already very well known. Just as Woolf was prepared to view ideas from outside the civil justice system as having utility, so I hope that this book may help those within the field to understand its social setting better and, as a consequence, to be able to comment on the planning and implementation of change more effectively.

[2] H Genn, 'Understanding Civil Justice' in M Freeman (ed), *Law and Public Opinion in the 20th Century, Current Legal Problems*, vol 50 (Oxford, Oxford University Press, 1997) 155, 158, fn 3.

[3] C Geertz, *The Interpretation of Cultures* (New York, Basic Books, 1973) 24–25. Geertz is speaking of anthropology, but the study of civil procedure also requires the 'close' approach.

HISTORY: AMERICA TO 1938

I. Governing Legislation

A. Rules Amendment Act 1934

This is the Statute authorising the creation of Uniform Rules of Civil Procedure for the District Courts of the United States:[1]

Be it enacted …

Sec 1.

That the Supreme Court of the United States shall have the power to prescribe, by general rules, for the district courts of the United States and for the courts of the District of Columbia, the forms of process, writs, pleadings, and motions, and the practice and procedure in civil actions at law. Said rules shall neither abridge, enlarge, nor modify the substantive rights of any litigant. They shall take effect six months after their promulgation, and thereafter all laws in conflict therewith shall be of no further force or effect.

Sec 2.

The court may at any time unite the general rules prescribed by it for cases in equity with those in actions at law so as to secure one form of civil action and procedure for both: Provided, however, That in such union of rules the right of trial by jury as at common law and declared by the seventh amendment to the Constitution shall be preserved to the parties inviolate. Such united rules shall not take effect until they shall have been reported to Congress by the Attorney General at the beginning of a regular session thereof and until after the close of such session.

B. Federal Rules of Civil Procedure 1938

Rule 1 Scope of the Rules

These rules govern the procedure in the district courts of the United States in all suits of a civil nature whether cognizable as cases at law or in equity, with the exceptions stated in Rule 81. They shall be construed to secure the just, speedy, and inexpensive determination of every action.

[1] Act of June 19, 1934, c 651, §§ 1, 2 (48 Stat 1064), USC, Title 28, §§ 723b, 723c.

II. *Dramatis Personae*

President Franklin D Roosevelt	US President from 1933 (Democrat).
CJ Charles E Hughes	Chief Justice of the Supreme Court. Appointed to the Court by Presidents Taft (Republican) and Hoover (Republican). A former US Secretary of State.
Attorney General (AG)	
Homer S Cummings	Appointed by FDR.
	Hoover's AG until 1933. Critical figure in securing fusion. Gangbuster.
The Advisory Committee	
William D Mitchell	New York City, (Chairman), (Democrat). Former Solicitor General of the United States, appointed by President Coolidge (Republican). Former Attorney General of the United States, appointed by President Hoover (Republican).
Scott M Loftin	Jacksonville, Florida, President of the ABA. Temporary Senator for Florida.
George W Wickersham (died)	New York City, President of the ALI. Former AG of the United States appointed by President Taft (Republican). Trustbuster. Died 26 January 1936.
Prof Wilbur H Cherry	Minneapolis, Minnesota, University of Minnesota.
Dean Charles E Clark	New Haven, Connecticut, Yale Law School, (Reporter)
Dean Armistead M Dobie	University, Virginia, University of Virginia Law School. Expert on federal procedure.
Robert G Dodge	Boston, Massachusetts. Practitioner. Former Assistant AG for the State of Massachusetts.
George Donworth	Seattle, Washington. Practitioner. Former Federal District Court Judge.
Joseph G Gamble	Des Moines, Iowa. Practitioner.
Monte M Lemann	New Orleans, Louisiana. Practitioner.

Prof Edmund M Morgan	Cambridge, Massachusetts, Harvard Law School
Warren Olney, Jr	San Francisco, California. Practitioner. Former Associate Judge of the California Supreme Court.
Prof Edson R Sunderland	Ann Arbor, Michigan, University of Michigan. Expert on disclosure. Drafted procedural rules for Michigan in the 1920s. Had taught law under Clark at Yale from 1931–33.
Major Edgar B Tolman	Chicago, Illinois. Practitioner. Appointed Special Assistant to AG Cummings to make the drafting of the rules happen. Awarded the ABA medal for 1939.
George Wharton Pepper	Philadelphia, Pennsylvania. Vice Chairman. (Republican) Appointed on 17 February 1936 as replacement for George W Wickersham. Had taught law at Pennsylvania University. Practitioner. Former US Senator for Pennsylvania.

Others

James William Moore	The Committee's Special Research Assistant for Clark. He was teaching law at Yale in 1935. Taught at Yale and Chicago. Went on to write *Moore's Federal Practice* and joined the Rules Committee in his own right in 1954.
Edward H Hammond	Assigned to Committee's staff by the AG, invited by the Committee.
Leland L Tolman	Assistant to Hammond.

III. Chronology

4 March 1929[2]	Mitchell appointed as AG of the United States by President Herbert Hoover (Republican).
October 1929	The Wall Street Crash.

[2] These dates are drawn from the brief but helpful initial compilation of dates in PD Edmunds, *Federal Rules of Civil Procedure* (Chicago, IL, Callaghan & Co, 1938), together with the works on the 1934 Act and the Federal Rules of Civil Procedure (FRCP) (1938) cited in the History. Public events have been verified from the *New York Times* or from the general biographical works cited hereafter. There are good potted biographies of a number of these characters in RK Newman (ed), *The Yale Biographical Dictionary of American Law* (New Haven, CT, Yale University Press, 2009).

28 January 1930	Justices sound out Charles Evans Hughes over post of Chief Justice of the United States Supreme Court (CJ) at the behest of AG Mitchell.
3 February 1930	CJ William Howard Taft retires from office.
13 February 1930	Charles Evans Hughes appointed as CJ by President Hoover (Republican).
8 November 1932	Franklin D Roosevelt (FDR) (Democrat) elected as President. Herbert Hoover is beaten. Democrats gain control of both Houses of Congress.
15 February 1933	Assassination attempt made on President-elect FDR. The Mayor of Chicago is killed.
2 March 1933	Thomas J Walsh, FDR's prospective AG, dies.
4 March 1933	FDR inaugurated.
	William D Mitchell ceases to be AG. Homer S Cummings becomes new AG.
March 1934	FDR begins First 100 Days. Congress passes 15 major bills.
1 March 1934	AG Cummings sends draft bill to Senate Judiciary Committee.
14 March 1934	AG Cummings announces support for uniform federal procedure.
18 May 1934	Senate Judiciary Committee gives favourable report on the bill.
23 May 1934	Bill passed by the Senate.
30 May 1934	House Judiciary Committee gives favourable report on the bill.
8 June 1934	Bill passed by the House of Representatives.
11 June 1934	Letter from AG Cummings to FDR recommending that the bill be signed.
19 June 1934	Rule Drafting Act 1934 signed into law by FDR.
June to October 1934	Supreme Court considers the position.
28 September 1934	Judicial Conference. CJ Hughes takes soundings.
	AG thereafter writes to judiciary to set up committees for consultation.
(?)	AG Cummings proposes appointing Edgar B Tolman as a special assistant.
8 October 1934	Clark aware that fusion may not be pursued.

6 November 1934	Democrats increase their Congressional representation in both Houses in the mid-term elections.
24 December 1934	Clark sends AG Cummings a draft of the article A New Federal Procedure 1.
2 January 1935	Clark discovers that Tolman has been asked to write the new rules and fusion is not to be pursued. Tolman will go to Washington on 14 January 1935.
4 January 1935	FDR's Third State of the Union address marks second phase of the New Deal.
4 January 1935	Message from Clark reaches AG Cummings asking him to look again at the fusion issue.
4 January 1935	Clark writes to Tolman suggesting he, Sunderland, Dobie and Morgan could serve on the rules committee.
14 January 1935(?)	Tolman meets AG and CJ and agrees to chair committee.
	AG proposes to appoint Edson R Sunderland, Roscoe Pound and Charles E Clark to his committee. This committee never meets.
16 January 1935	AG Cummings asks Clark to serve on rules committee to look at common law rules only.
(?) January 1935	Clark accepts proposed appointment.
18 January 1935	Clark complaining about Tolman as 'a babe in the woods'.
Late January 1935	Clark and Moore's 'A New Federal Civil Procedure I' (ANFP 1)[3] published in *Yale Law Journal.*
31 January to 1 February 1935	Clark writes to the judiciary and legal luminaries with a copy of ANFP1, asking them to act.
Early February 1935	Clark meets AG Cummings in Washington. Clark told that if justices are unhappy, matter will end up in Congress.
4 February 1935	Clark complaining about Tolman's appointment making him 'quite sick'.
4 February 1935	Justice Cardozo tells Clark no final decision has been made on appointing Tolman nor on fusion.
6 February 1935	Justice Stone advises Clark to keep fighting.
8 February 1835	Clark informs Mitchell of the issue and says that older judges are getting in the way.

[3] CE Clark and JW Moore, 'A New Federal Civil Procedure I', 44 *Yale Law Journal* 387 (1935).

9 February 1935	Mitchell writes to CJ Hughes (at Clark's request) to call for the uniting of common law and equity procedure.
12 February 1935	Tolman shows some interest in Clark's plan but wonders about its political feasibility.
12 February 1935	Justice Van Devanter tells Mitchell that his mind is open to fusion.
12 February 1935	CJ Hughes tells Clark that no decision has been made, yet reminds Clark that the decision is one for the Court.
13 February 1935	CJ Hughes tells Clark that his views will be put before the whole court.
15 February 1935	Mitchell refuses to allow Clark to publish his (Mitchell's) letter to CJ Hughes.
18 February 1935	Justice Butler encourages Clark to keep agitating.
7 March 1935	CJ Hughes says he has been misunderstood. He wants local bars to participate to reduce opposition.
9 May 1935	CJ Hughes addresses annual meeting of the American Law Institute (ALI). Fusion is to be pursued. There will be a rules committee.
11 May 1935	Clark aware that he and Mitchell would be on the Advisory Committee.
13 May 1935	Mitchell asks Clark for suggestions for academics to go on the Committee.
13 May 1935	Mitchell agrees to Clark publishing 'A New Federal Civil Procedure II'[4] (ANFP 2).
16 May 1935	Clark asked by Mitchell for suggestions as to who should be the Reporter. Clark is less than complimentary about Sunderland, his rival.
17 May 1935	Clark tells Mitchell of his own qualifications for the job.
21 May 1935	Clark sends Mitchell a draft of ANFP 2 and, incidentally, suggests Sunderland involved with problematic Illinois rules.
22 May 1935	Mitchell tells Clark he is not sure what the problem is.
23 May 1935	Mitchell has now grasped Clark's point and writes critical letter to Sunderland. He complains that each district court would conform to local State procedure.
24 May 1935	Mitchell writes to Clark saying that Sunderland is 'entirely off the track'.

[4] CE Clark and JW Moore, 'A New Federal Civil Procedure II', 44 *Yale Law Journal* 1291 (1935).

24 May 1935	Mitchell writes to CJ Hughes on 'personnel and organization'. Sunderland is probably now out of the running for the Reporter's role.
25 May 1935 (?)	Clark suggests to Sunderland that he might deal with summary judgment on the committee and receive a weekly or monthly payment for this.
25 May 1935	Clark writes to Mitchell to prevent Sunderland from being entirely sacked: 'I think he can be most useful.'
31 May 1935	Sunderland writes letter to Mitchell defending himself. It is probably too late.
31 May 1935	Mitchell tells Clark that he wants to keep Sunderland.
3 June 1935	Advisory Committee appointed to draft 'a unified system of rules' by Order of the Supreme Court. Mitchell is to be the Chair, Clark the Reporter.
14 June 1935	Clark suggests agenda for the Committee.
20 June 1935	Meeting of Advisory Committee, Chicago, Illinois.
End June 1935	Clark and Moore's ANFP 2 is published in the *Yale Law Journal.*
21 September 1935	Clark delivers Tentative Draft I. Key wording is in Rule 1.
27 September 1935	Tolman writes to Clark pushing for an interpretive rule.
14–20 November 1935	Meeting of Advisory Committee, Washington, DC.
26 December 1935	Clark delivers Tentative Draft II. The key wording is now in rule A.78.
26 January 1936	Committee member George Wickersham dies.
17 February 1936	George Wharton Pepper appointed to the Advisory Committee by Order of the Supreme Court.
20–25 February 1936	Meeting of Advisory Committee, Washington, DC.
12 March 1936	Draft of Rule 2 contains the key wording.
24 March 1936	Clark delivers Tentative Draft III.
16 April 1936	Meeting of Advisory Committee, Washington, DC(?). Tolman in the chair. Tentative draft III considered.
April 1936	Style Sub-Committee at work. Preliminary Draft of Advisory Committee. Rule 2 moved back to Rule 1 where the key wording now appears.
1 May 1936	Preliminary draft submitted by William D Mitchell to Chief Justice Hughes with covering letter.

7–9 May 1936	CJ Hughes addresses the ALI.
5 May 1936	Letter from Chief Justice Hughes approving circulation of draft rules.
24–28 May 1936	Open forum session at Boston.
Early August 1936	It becomes clear that the rules will not be ready in time to be published as Proposed Rules. CJ Hughes advises Mitchell to make a show of effort so that the Committee is not held to blame.
28 August–2 September 1936	Meeting of Advisory Committee, New Haven, Connecticut.
22–27 October 1936	Meeting of Advisory Committee, Washington, DC.
3 November 1936	FDR defeats Alfred M Landon (Republican). Democrats keep majorities in both Houses of Congress.
20 January 1937	FDR's second inauguration.
1– 4 February 1937	Meeting of Advisory Committee, Washington, DC.
April 1937	Advisory Committee publishes Proposed Rules.
6–8 May 1937	CJ Hughes addresses the ALI.
12 August 1937	FDR appoints Hugo L Black to the US Supreme Court.
29 September–1 October 1937	Open forum session Kansas City.[5]
1 November 1937	Meeting of Advisory Committee, Washington, DC.
November 1937	Advisory Committee publishes Final Report.
20 December 1937	Supreme Court gives notice of adoption of rules. Notice of submittal sent by CJ Hughes to AG Cummings. The submittal noted that Justice Brandeis did not approve.
3 January 1938	AG Cummings' letter of transmittal to Congress confirming rules adopted by Supreme Court.
1–4 March 1938	Hearings on the Rules before the subcommittee of the Senate's Committee on the Judiciary to decide whether or not to postpone the commencement date for the rules. AG Cummings, Mitchell and Tolman make statements.[6]
March 1938	Advisory Committee's Notes to the Rules of Civil Procedure.

[5] Reported at 23 *American Bar Association Journal* 965 (1937).
[6] See PD Edmunds, *Federal Rules of Civil Procedure* (n 2), 7–8.

12–14 May 1938	Chief Justice Hughes addresses the ALI.
19 May 1938	Further hearing before the subcommittee of the Senate's Committee on the Judiciary.
21 July–23 1938	Institute Meeting at Cleveland, Ohio (481 people registered).[7]
16 September 1938	The FRCP (1938) comes into force.[8]
6–8 October 1938	Institute Meeting at Washington, DC (915 people registered).
17–19 October 1938	Symposium at New York City (1,836 people registered).

IV. Narrative

A. Preliminaries

Those who know the English story of fusion and procedural change will be familiar with the Judicature Acts and the Rules of the Supreme Court (RSC) (1883) that followed them. One might be forgiven for thinking that with the famous New York Field Code of 1848 preceding English reform by about 30 years, at the federal level the United States would have followed suit. This was not the case. At the turn of the twentieth century, as Europe moved towards war, the United States was still committed to separate jurisdictions in law and equity, and forward-thinking lawyers looked to the English system of procedure as a model. At this time, there was considerable pressure for procedural reform. The slowness of the pace of legal change compared badly with the rapidity of change in American society as a whole.

This is the story of how before 1933 three bills were brought forward for reform of civil procedure in the federal courts. Each was rejected. The bill of 1912 was aimed at the creation of a set of rules governing procedure at common law; fusion was not on the agenda. The bill of 1916/17 would have required that common law procedure be simplified, speedy and directed towards the merits of the case. The bill of 1923, drafted in part by CJ Taft (a former President), was aimed at both

[7] Each Institute Meeting received lectures from members of the Advisory Committee: see Foreword to *Proceedings of the Institute on Federal Rules*, Cleveland, Ohio, July 1938, in EH Hammond (ed), *Legislative History of the Rules of Civil Procedure of the District Courts of the US* (hereinafter '*LegHist*'), vol 2 (Chicago, IL, American Bar Association, 1938) v.

[8] See CE Clark, 'Fundamental Changes Effected by the New Federal Rules I', 15 *Tennessee Law Review* 551, 555 (1939). The text of Rule 1 was noted in PD Edmunds, *Federal Rules of Civil Procedure* (n 2), vol 1, at 1; and in W Ilse, *Federal Rules of Civil Procedure* (St Paul, MN, West Publishing Co, rev edn, 1944)) 1, with rule and commentary).

procedure and fusion. It set out the lines followed when procedural reform and fusion finally resulted after a change in the law in 1934.

B. 1910 to 1933: A Failed Programme

We can begin our examination in 1906. On 29 August 1906, Roscoe Pound stirred things up with his 'Causes of Popular Dissatisfaction' speech to the ABA's annual meeting in St Paul, Minnesota.[9] An ABA Committee was formed and proposals were put forward. All this had a political aspect. The US President William Howard Taft (Republican), addressing the Virginia Bar Association in 1908, called for 'expedition and thoroughness in the enforcement … of rights'.

In 1910 President Taft[10] was advocating simplicity and expedition, and offering the English experience as a 'model'.[11]

i. *The Clayton Bill*

The following year, 1911, Woodrow Wilson (Democrat) was noting that reform of legal procedure was 'the critical matter'. He was encouraging simplification, the removal of 'technical difficulties', the 'removal of every unnecessary form' and 'the subordination of method to the object sought'.[12] The ABA in the same year passed a resolution calling for 'a uniform system, with the necessary rules of practice'.[13] The mover behind this was Thomas W Shelton, a Virginia lawyer.[14] The topic was

[9] R Pound, 'The Causes of Popular Dissatisfaction with the Administration of Justice' 29 *Annual Report of the American Bar Association* 395 (1906). WH Taft's comments are reported at 49 *Annual Report of the American Bar Association* 519 (1926).

[10] William Howard Taft's experience was a singular one. He was in turn US Solicitor General, a federal judge on the US Court of Appeals for the 6th Circuit, US President, an academic at Yale and then CJ.

[11] Report of the Committee on Uniform Judicial Procedure, 49 *Annual Report of the American Bar Association* 519 (1926). Appendix B contains a topical chronology including helpful extracts from various Presidential addresses. Subrin addresses the role of the chairman Thomas W Shelton in SN Subrin, 'How Equity Conquered the Common Law', 135 *University of Pennsylvania Law Review* 909, 948–56 (1987).

[12] 49 *Annual Report of the American Bar Association* 520 (1926). The speech was given to the Kentucky Bar Association on 12 July 1911. Wilson (Democrat) was elected as US President in 1912 and inaugurated in 1913. Taft (Republican) had stood for re-election against Wilson, but his vote was split by Theodore Roosevelt leaving the Republicans and starting his own Progressive Party.

[13] Report of 27 March 1914 of the Committee on the Judiciary 63rd Congress, 2nd Session, Report No 462.

[14] For the moves and political context, see SB Burbank, 'The Rules Enabling Act of 1934', 130 *University of Pennsylvania Law Review* 1015, 1408–51 (1982); together with J Crowe, *Building the Judiciary: Law, Courts, and the Politics of Institutional Development* (Princeton, NJ, Princeton University Press, 2012) 214. See also JW Moore 'Address of Professor Moore', 44 *American Bar Association Journal* 44 (January 1958); AT Vanderbilt, *The Challenge of Law Reform* (Princeton, NJ, Princeton University

revisited by the ABA again in 1912,[15] the year in which Representative Henry D Clayton (Democrat, Alabama) introduced a bill into the House of Representatives in the following terms:

> Be it enacted … That the Supreme Court shall have the power to prescribe, from time to time and in any manner, the forms and manner of service of writs and all other process; the mode and manner of framing and filing proceedings and pleadings; of giving notice and serving process of all kinds; of taking and obtaining evidence; drawing up, entering, and enrolling orders; and generally to regulate and prescribe by rule the forms for the entire pleading, practice, and procedure to be used in all actions, motions, and proceedings at law of whatever nature by the district courts of the United States.[16]

The bill would have provided for a uniform federal process in common law cases conducted in the district court wherever they were situated in the United States. This would have had the effect of overturning the provisions of the Federal Conformity Act of 1872,[17] which had provided that federal procedure should 'conform as near may be' to the procedure 'at the time in like causes in the courts of record of the State' within whose boundaries the litigation was being conducted. Federal conformity favoured local lawyers and put those with national practices at a disadvantage. No provision was made for fusion because of the Federal Equity Rules of 1912,[18] which had been adopted in the final term of 1912.

The Clayton bill did not pass. On 1 December 1914 Taft joined the ABA's committee. By 1915 a formidable opponent of the bill had appeared. This was Senator Thomas J Walsh (Democrat) of Montana. Walsh was to be the firmest and most effective opponent of the reform movement.[19] The White House nevertheless continued to argue for change; in 1915 President Wilson (Democrat) said 'the speediness of justice, the inexpensiveness of justice, the ready access of justice,

Press, 1955, 2nd printing 1956)) 55; and PG Fish, *The Politics of Federal Judicial Administration* (Princeton, NJ, Princeton University Press, 1973) 22–23.

[15] PG Fish, *The Politics of Federal Judicial Administration* (n 14), 22–23.

[16] See SB Burbank, 'The Rules Enabling Act of 1934' (n 14), 1050. See also SN Subrin, 'Fishing Expeditions Allowed: The Historical Background of the 1938 Federal Discovery Rules' 39:3 *Boston College Law Review* 691, 710 (1998).

[17] Act of 1 June 1872, s 5, 17 Stat 196. See RM Millar, *Civil Procedure of the Trial Court in Historical Perspective* (New York, Law Centre of New York University, 1952) 59–61. The history of this Act can be traced from its root as follows 29 September 1789, 8 May 1792, 19 May 1828, 23 August 1832; see RE Bunker, 'New Federal Equity Rules', 11 *Michigan Law Review* 435, 435–37 (1912–1913).

[18] For good contemporary views, see H Clark, 'The Federal Equity Rules of 1912', 7 *Maine Law Review* 260 (1914); and Bunker, 'New Federal Equity Rules' (n 17). There had been Federal Equity Rules as follows: the English practice was followed until 1822; Federal Equity Rules of 1822; Federal Equity Rules of 1842 (Bunker, ibid, 438–40).

[19] Walsh illustrates nicely the tension between American national party politics, local State politics and individual political conviction. Just because a policy is supported by a party at the national level does not necessarily mean that a Senator will support it in Congress if local feeling or individual conviction point in the other direction. Walsh was not just an opponent of procedural change; he also led the inquiry into the Teapot Dome scandal. This was an oil corruption scandal, which had occurred under President Harding (Republican) in the early 1920s. The investigation made Walsh's name.

is the greater part of justice itself'. He went on to say, 'If you have to be rich to get justice, because of the cost of the very process itself, then there is no justice at all.'[20] Presidential pressure continued: in 1916 President Wilson declared 'we must simplify and reform'.[21]

ii. The Sutherland Bill

As early as 1916–17, another move was made to persuade Congress to vest its rule-making power in the Federal Court. In that year, a draft bill[22] was put forward by Senator Sutherland, but it never reached the statute book.[23] Again, it was opposed by Thomas J Walsh. He may partly have been concerned that new federal rules would mean that Montana lawyers would have to learn two sets of rules.[24] During 1918 Taft was to reflect that Sutherland's bill had not been radical enough.

The Bill provided for the Supreme Court to be given

> the power to prescribe … the entire pleading, practice and procedure to be used in all actions, motions and proceedings at law of whatever nature by the district courts of the United States and the courts of the District of Columbia; that in prescribing such rules, the Supreme Court shall have regard to the simplification of the system of pleading, practice and procedure in said courts, *so as to promote the speedy determination of litigation on the merits.*[25]

[20] 49 *Annual Report of the American Bar Association* 521 (1926).

[21] ibid, 521.

[22] 49 *Annual Report of the American Bar Association* 520 (1926). Appendix B notes that the Clayton Bill of 1912 was in fact the ABA's draft bill.

[23] For the full text, see EM Morgan, 'Judicial Regulation of Court Procedure', 2 *Minnesota Law Review* 81 (1917–1918). That article gives further good background on the early course of civil procedure reform in the US. SB Burbank's, 'The Rules Enabling Act of 1934' (n 14, at 1050–55), covers the detailed background to the 1912 bill. The article then goes on to cover both the political and legal professional sides of a long and torturous process. Burbank addresses the details of the Clayton Bill of 1912 (ibid, at 1050) and the Sutherland Bill of 1917 (ibid, at 1066). The Clayton Bill was a forerunner of Sutherland's, but the language of promotion of objects was not included. Morgan was a contemporary commentator; Burbank offers the benefits of distance in time. Clayton's defence of his position appeared on 5 January 1917 in the *Central Law Journal*. An extract is to be found in DS Holt, *Debates on the Federal Judiciary: A Documentary History*, vol II: *1875–1939* (Washington, DC, Federal Judicial Centre, 2013) 169–71. The Senate Report of 22 January 1917 appears ibid, 172–74. Also helpful is SN Subrin, 'How Equity Conquered the Common Law' (n 11). Further background is given by JB Weinstein, 'The Ghost of Process Past: The Fiftieth Anniversary of the Federal Rules of Civil Procedure and Erie', 54:1 *Brooklyn Law Review* 1 (1988).

[24] SN Subrin, 'Charles E Clark and His Procedural Outlook: The Disciplined Champion of Undisciplined Rules' in P Petruck (ed), *Judge Charles Edward Clark* (Oceana Publications, New York, 1991) 115, 129.

[25] Emphasis added. This draft demonstrates that the RSC's theory of justice was well known. English civil procedure was ahead of the field at this point in time. The English rule-making power is contained in the Civil Procedure Act 1997: s 1 sets out the detail of the power, s 2 specifies in whom the power is vested, and s 3 sets out the process to be followed.

iii. The Cummins Bill

Another head of steam began to build up. In 1922, Taft, now Chief Justice, was calling for a procedural merger of law and equity.[26] An Act of 14 September 1922[27] had enabled the deployment of judges to clear backlogs and permitted the creation of a Judicial Conference to plan for improvements. Taft lobbied hard, behind the scenes, for changes to the law.

The year 1923 brought another attempt to pass a bill. Senator Albert Cummins (Republican), a former ally of Thomas J Walsh, changed his position. He introduced a bill that was in much the same terms as the one that would pass in 1934. Section 1 provided:

> The Supreme Court of the United States shall have the power to prescribe by general rules, for the District Courts of the United States and for the courts of the District of Columbia, the forms of process, writs, pleadings, and motions, and the practice and procedure in actions at law. Said rules shall neither abridge, enlarge, nor modify the substantive rights of any litigant. They shall take effect six months after their promulgation and thereafter all laws in conflict therewith shall be of no further force or effect.

Section 2, drafted by CJ Taft, provided:

> The Court may at any time unite the general rules prescribed by it for cases in equity with those in actions at law so as to secure one form of civil action and procedure for both, provided, however, that in such union of rules the right of trial by jury as at common law and declared by the seventh amendment to the Constitution shall be preserved to the parties inviolate. Such united rules shall not take effect until they shall have been reported to Congress by the Attorney General at the beginning of a regular session thereof and until after the close of such session.[28]

Again the bill did not pass.[29]

The 1926 ABA Report of the Committee on Uniform Judicial Procedure marks another staging post. Appendix A to the Report contained a draft bill. The Report

[26] Noted in SN Subrin, 'How Equity Conquered the Common Law' (n 11), 957. For insight into Taft, see R Post, 'Judicial Management and Judicial Disinterest: The Achievements and Perils of Chief Justice William Howard Taft', 23:1 *Journal of Supreme Court History* 50 (1998). See also KJ Burns, 'Chief Justice as Chief Executive: Taft's Judicial Statesmanship', 43:1 *Journal of Supreme Court History* 47 (2018), noting Republican dominance of the Supreme Court Bench and how Taft wanted more Democratic appointments. Taft was very active in trying to make the judiciary more efficient. Taft's own proposed solutions are clearly set out in WH Taft, 'The Attacks on the Courts and Legal procedure' 5:2 *Kentucky Law Journal* 3 (1916). Taft distinguished between unjust and dangerous attacks, on the one hand, and well-founded attacks on the other (ibid, 3) Picking up on Pound's language (R Pound (n 9)), Taft spoke of well- founded popular discontent, which he put down to delay and to excessive costs caused both by that delay and by excessive legal fees (WH Taft, 'Attacks', 10). Ill-founded discontent he saw as caused by character failings amongst critics (ibid). He noted the impact that the expansion of society was having (ibid, 11) and made six concrete proposals (ibid, 14–15).

[27] 42 Stat 837 (1922).

[28] These drafts are to be found in SB Burbank, 'The Rules Enabling Act' (n 16), 1074.

[29] BD Coleman, 'Recovering Access: Rethinking the Structure of Federal Civil Rulemaking', 39:2 *New Mexico Law Review* 261, 273 (Spring 2009).

indicated that the bill would 'unlock the door to a new era of scientific judicial relations' following the English experience, to enable the judiciary and practitioners to perfect a 'simple, correlated, scientific system' where the judge dealing with a case would see 'to it that the case is brought speedily to issue on the merits'.[30] The same year, Charles E Clark wrote a piece for the *American Mercury* supporting the move for change.[31]

The year 1929 saw Charles E Clark become Dean of Yale Law School and William D Mitchell become AG of the United States. Mitchell took office on 4 March 1929, having been appointed by President Hoover.[32] Although Hoover did not know it, economic disaster lay around the corner. The stock market crash of 29 October 1929 led to the Great Depression, which lasted from 1929 to about 1933.[33]

On the law reform front, by 1930 the ABA had effectively given up on its campaign for change. That year saw change at the top too: CJ Taft retired on 3 February 1930. Just before Taft's resignation, AG Mitchell caused Charles Evans Hughes to be sounded out: Hughes was in office as CJ in less than a fortnight.[34]

On 8 November 1932, FDR beat Herbert Hoover to the US Presidency. Following an attempt to assassinate FDR on 15 February 1933, he became President on 4 March 1933. He was active in trying to get his New Deal Programme off the ground, building upon Hoover's earlier public works programme. During the period known as FDR's first one hundred days, Congress passed 15 major pieces of legislation.[35]

C. Surely the Hour has Struck: The Rule Enabling Act of 1934

The first 100 days having passed, the position on the federal rules was soon to change.[36] It came in the most unexpected way. The process of reform had largely

[30] Report of the Committee on Uniform Judicial Procedure, 49 *Annual Report of the American Bar Association* 513 (1926).

[31] SN Subrin, 'Fishing Expeditions Allowed' (n 16) 710, fn 127.

[32] For good background, see the article on William D Mitchell in RK Newman (ed), *Yale Biographical Dictionary* (n 2), 385.

[33] The classic short book here is JK Galbraith's, *The Great Crash 1929* (London, Hamish Hamilton 1955, reprinted Harmondsworth, Penguin Books,1966), ch 6 of which is especially good on the events surrounding the crash itself. At some point during this period President Hoover offered Clark a federal judgeship but he turned it down – see SN Subrin's entry on CE Clark in RK Newman (ed), *Yale Biographical Dictionary* (n 2), 107.

[34] For the background to all this, see PA Freund, 'Charles Evans Hughes as Chief Justice', 81 *Harvard Law Review* 4 (1967).

[35] See WE Leuchtenburg, *Franklin D Roosevelt and the New Deal: 1932–1940* (London, Harper & Row, 1963) 61. For the early days of Roosevelt's first administration, see JMcG Burns, *Roosevelt: the Lion and the Fox* (New York, Harcourt, Brace & Co, 1986 reprint) ch 9; as well as R Dallek, *Franklin D Roosevelt* (Harmondsworth, Allen Lane, Penguin, 2018)) chs 5 and 6.

[36] For details of two decades of entrenched opposition, see SN Subrin, 'Federal Rules, Local Rules, and State Rules: Uniformity, Divergence, and Emerging Procedural Patterns', 137 *University*

been a Republican political project; Senator Thomas J Walsh (Democrat) had succeeded in blocking change for nearly two decades. Roosevelt's election victory put him in the driving seat as President. For his prospective AG, FDR selected the very same Walsh who had been keeping the reform movement at bay.[37] The hoped-for change looked as far away as ever. This part of the tale concerns how the tide turned in favour of change.

Walsh had just remarried, but within a week, on 2 March 1933, he died of a heart attack *en route* to accept the post:[38] FDR had to find a replacement. Homer Cummings was FDR's temporary choice.[39] Cummings supported change and persuaded FDR to back him. Roosevelt was expecting attacks on the New Deal through the federal courts and could see the benefits of a simplified procedure.[40] It may also be that he could see that a revised rule-making process would offer technocratic efficiency.[41]

Cummings had already written to the Senate Judiciary Committee with a draft bill on 1 March 1934.[42] He publicly announced his proposals at a New York lawyers' Silver Anniversary dinner on 14 March 1934.[43] Cummings warned, 'Our one great enemy is inertia. But surely the hour has struck.' He decided to profile the proposed changes both as part of the New Deal and as part of a long-term Republican project. He was good at making politicians feel that he respected their role. His generally non-ideological profile helped him in his dealings with Congress.[44] Cummings succeeded where others had failed: the proposed changes

of Pennsylvania Law Review 2000 (1989). For general background on the early days of FDR's first administration, see chs 4 and 6 of Dallek, *Franklin D Roosevelt* (n 35); and ch 6 of P Renshaw, *Franklin D Roosevelt* (New York, Longman, 2004).

[37] Walsh was chosen because of his success in the Teapot Dome investigation.

[38] See PC Hoffer et al, *The Federal Courts: An Essential History* (Oxford University Press, Oxford, 2016) 300; J Crowe, *Building the Judiciary* (n 14), 217. Crowe is very helpful on this topic. See also BD Coleman, 'Recovering Access' (n 29), 272; and biographical directory of the US Congress at www.bioguide.congress.gov. A good biography is JL Bates, *Senator Thomas J Walsh of Montana: Law and Public Affairs, from TR to FDR* (Chicago, IL, University of Illinois Press, 1999).

[39] See the article on Homer Stillé Cummings in RK Newman (ed), *Yale Biographical Dictionary* (n 2), 136–37. Cummings was an FDR supporter who was initially rewarded with a governor generalship of the Philippines.

[40] Foreword to Proceedings of the Institute on Federal Rules, Cleveland, Ohio, July 1938, 2 *LegHist*, (n 7), iii–iv; J Crowe, *Building the Judiciary* (n 14), 217).

[41] BD Coleman, 'Recovering Access' (n 29), 274, deals with technocratic bureaucracy.

[42] H Cummings, *Selected Papers of Homer Cummings: AG of the United States 1933–1939*, vol 1 (ed Carl Brent Swisher) (New York, C Scribner's Sons, 1939) (hereinafter '*CsSelP*') 186.

[43] ibid, 182. An extract from the speech appars in Holt, n 20, 179–80.

[44] J Crowe, *Building the Judiciary* (n 14), 217. For Cummings' view of his own role, see Chicago Bar Association Address, 2 August 1938, in *CsSelP*, 187, where he said, 'there was a time when it was touch and go whether the rules would go through or not. I labored with the committee in the Senate and with the committee in the House, and finally by personal appeals, pathetic persuasion, and something approaching imprecations, had caused most of the opposition to dissolve. There was, however, in the House Committee of the Judiciary one recalcitrant person with whom I had extraordinary difficulty … The situation was such that only unanimous consent would permit it to pass, and one voice raised in opposition at that critical moment would have been fatal to the entire project. I labored with that man for hours, and finally we compromised. He agreed to adhere to his principles, and, in order that he might not forego them, further agreed to absent himself from the House when the matter came up.'

became law. Cummings undoubtedly experienced a personal triumph, but the Act of 1934 needs to be seen in context: FDR had majorities in both Houses; Congress in turn was keen to get on with necessary change, for the mid-term elections were looming.

Section 1 of the Rule Enabling Act of 19 June 1934[45] provided in the following terms:

> That the Supreme Court of the United States shall have the power to prescribe, by general rules, for the district courts of the United States and for the courts of the District of Columbia, the forms of process, writs, pleadings, and motions, and the practice and procedure in civil actions at law. Said rules shall neither abridge, enlarge, nor modify the substantive rights of any litigant ...[46]

Section 2, added after the bill was tabled,[47] stated:

> The court may at any time unite the general rules prescribed by it for cases in equity with those in actions at law so as to secure one form of civil action and procedure for both: Provided, however, That in such union of rules the right of trial by jury as at common law and declared by the seventh amendment to the Constitution shall be preserved to the parties inviolate. Such united rules shall not take effect until they shall have been reported to Congress by the Attorney General at the beginning of a regular session thereof and until after the close of such session.

D. Interposition

It is worth interposing here that Peter C Hoffer[48] argues that the process of rule-making was not always easy[49] and demonstrates the human drama of

[45] 19 June 1934, c 651, §§ 1, 2 (48 Stat 1064), USC Title 28, chs 732b and 732c. Since revoked and replaced – see D Marcus, 'Institutions and an Interpretive Methodology for the Federal Rules of Civil Procedure', *Utah Law Review* 927, 927–98 (2011). This was very much a federal-only process. The making of the FRCP is not reported in the *Handbooks of the National Conference of Commissioners on Uniform State Laws and Proceedings* (Baltimore, MD, Lord Baltimore Press) for 1935,1936,1937, or for 1938. In 1930 the ABA produced a bibliography of literature on the topic of the rule-making power: see 'The Rule-Making Power: a Bibliography', 16:3 *American Bar Association Journal* 199–200 (March 1930).

[46] Cited in Report of the Advisory Committee on Rules for Civil Procedure containing Proposed Rules (April 1937), 1 *LegHist* (n 7), ii.

[47] William D Mitchell said that the draft of s 2 had come from WH Taft. WD Mitchell, 'The Federal Rules of Civil Procedure' in *David Dudley Field Centenary Essays*, ed A Reppy (New York, New York University School of Law, 1949) 75–76.

[48] PC Hoffer, 'Text, Translation, Context and Conversation: Preliminary Notes for Decoding the Deliberations of the Advisory Committee', 37 *American Journal of Legal History* 409 (1993). P Johnston (see n 71), following Hoffer, is very careful to draw out the differing views represented on the Advisory Committee and on the Style Subcommittee. Hoffer's piece, written in 1993, reflects the move towards a postmodernist sensibility with its suspicion of grand narratives.

[49] Prior to his appointment, Mitchell was instrumental in steering the Supreme Court towards the merger of the administration of law and equity – see his letter of 9 February 1935 to CJ Hughes with its emphasis on simplicity and efficiency, reproduced in WD Mitchell, 'The Federal Rules' (n 47), 73–82.

law-making.[50] He looks at the differing versions of 'what happened' during the drafting of the Rules and warns against the danger of trying to find one single version of events that can be said to capture Clark's work. Nevertheless there is a story to be told: Hoffer is particularly good at reminding us that committees consist of people, and those people do not always agree or act in the most straightforward manner. He also draws Clark's personality and behaviour patterns with great care.[51] Nonetheless, we need consider the work of the Advisory Committee too.

It was conventional to portray the FRCP (1938) as the work of Charles E Clark (Dean of Yale Law School) and to see the FRCP's creation as the result of inevitable progress. The picture can now be drawn with more precision, thanks not least to the work of Stephen N Subrin, Brooke D Coleman, Peter C Hoffer and Patrick J Johnston. The FRCP were not Clark's rules, although he was the Reporter on the Committee. Clark did not chair the Committee, neither did he have the political clout of its Chair, William D Mitchell, nor the stellar reputation of his rival Edson R Sunderland, the expert on disclosure. Clark obtained the Reporter's role by nobbling two different candidates. It is worth noting that unlike in the case of the eponymous Woolf Reports, Clark was not in the driving seat in drafting the rules that were put forward. The members of the Advisory Committee worked together to produce a set of rules that had to be approved by Congress. Though Clark did much of the drafting, others were involved in the process and Clark did not always get his way.

The Advisory Committee was drawn from an extended circle whose members had knowledge of each other,[52] but not all of those on the Committee were friends of Clark.[53] The Advisory Committee was operating in an arena where the various interest groups were keeping an eye on the Committee,[54] so its members took care to communicate with a wide audience – they even attended conferences.[55]

The letter starts ibid, at 76. Further material on the use of uniform rules is contained in WD Mitchell, 'Attitude of Advisory Committee', 22 *American Bar Association Journal* 780 (1936).

[50] PC Hoffer, 'Text' (n 48), 431.

[51] For helpful biographical details on the members of the Advisory Committee, see J Resnik 'Failing Faith: Adjudicatory Procedure in Decline', 53 *University of Chicago Law Review* 494, 499, fn 24 and 498, fn 20 (1986). L Kalman's *Legal Realism at Yale 1927–1960* (Chapel Hill, North Carolina University of North Carolina Press, 1986, reprinted Union, NJ, by The Lawbook Exchange Ltd, 2001) contains good background material on Clark and his personality at 115–20, especially at 116 for a portrayal of a dull but ruthless and effective operator. NEH Hull, *Roscoe Pound and Karl Llewellyn: Searching for an American Jurisprudence* (Chicago Illinois, University of Chicago Press, 1997) 337–38 shows Clark's continuing interest in the impact of law. Clark comes out well for his defence of the role of lawyers even in unpopular causes: ibid, 320. KN Moore, 'The Supreme Court's Role in Interpreting the Federal Rules of Civil Procedure', 44 *Hastings Law Journal* 1039 (1990) is useful in reminding us of the various different players involved in the formulation and interpretation of the FRCP: the rule-drafters (the Committee), the rule-makers (the Supreme Court), the legislature (Congress) and the rule interpreters (the Supreme Court).

[52] PC Hoffer, 'Text' (n 48), 424.

[53] ibid, 423.

[54] ibid, 425.

[55] ibid, 426. It was Clark's claim that he had addressed over 5,000 American attorneys on the rules – CE Clark, *Fundamental Changes* (n 8), 551.

Clark personally lobbied for support for the Advisory Committee's work, yet not all judges were sympathetic: Justice Brandeis in the Supreme Court, for example, was not supportive.[56] There was a division on the Advisory Committee between practitioners and academics;[57] each group in turn had to relate to its professional peers outside the Committee. It is also worth noting that a number of the people involved had served in or been appointed by Republican Administrations,[58] so the effort was a remarkably bipartisan one.

Richard L Marcus refers to the origins of the FRCP as lying in the 'Golden Age of Rulemaking'.[59] It is into this age of gold that we must now venture.

E. Clark Cuts Loose: Choosing the Committee

Our story now brings us to the question of how the Civil Procedure Rules 1938 came to be written, and the positive and negative roles played by Charles E Clark. Under the 1934 Act, it was for the US Supreme Court to control the drafting of the new rules.[60] The Court exercised the new power given to it.[61] Chief Justice

[56] PC Hoffer, 'Text' (n 48), 426.

[57] ibid, 427.

[58] William D Mitchell had been Hoover's AG. Chief Justice Charles E Hughes had been appointed by President Taft and then by Hoover. Edgar B Tolman had been a special assistant to the AG of the United States.

[59] RL Marcus, 'Reform through Rulemaking', 80 *Washington University Law Quarterly* 901, 901 (2002), reviews the issues troubling American lawmakers in the early 21st century.

[60] The account in this part of the chapter simply seeks to set out the story of how the Advisory Committee came to be chosen and how the roles were allocated. It is drawn from the academic sources in the preceding footnotes, this footnote and the subsequent footnote. The intention is to make the process clear for readers in England who may not be familiar with events. The debt to Hoffer, Subrin, Crowe and others is acknowledged. For the background to the drafting and reception of the rules, see: CE Clark, 'Challenge of a New Federal Civil Procedure', 20 *Cornell Law Review* 443 (1935) (for interesting comments on wastage flowing from out-of-date practice, see 443); CE Clark and JW Moore, 'A New Federal Civil Procedure I', 44 *Yale Law Journal* 387 (1935); CE Clark and JW Moore, 'A New Federal Civil Procedure II', 44 *Yale Law Journal* 1291 (1935) (the background to these two jointly-drafted articles appears in SN Subrin, 'Charles E Clark' (n 24) at 120–31); *Report of the Advisory Committee on Rules for Civil Procedure containing Proposed Rules* (April 1937) 1 *LegHist* (n 7) (unpaginated); *Final Report of Advisory Committee on Rules for Civil Procedure* (November 1937), 1 *LegHist* (unpaginated); *Proceedings of the Institute on the Federal Rules of Civil Procedure held at Washington DC and Symposium at New York* (October 1938) (Chicago, IL, American Bar Association,1938) at 23–36; *Rules of Civil Procedure for the District Courts of the United States with Notes as prepared under the direction of the Advisory Committee* (July 1938) (Chicago, IL, American Bar Association, 1938); CE Clark, 'The Handmaid of Justice', 23 *Washington University Law Quarterly* 297 (1937–1938); CE Clark, 'Afterthoughts of the Institute on Federal Rules of Civil Procedure at Cleveland, July 1938', 14 *Notre Dame Lawyer* 103 (1938–1939); CE Clark, 'The Influence of Federal Procedural Reform', 13 *Law and Contemporary Problems* 144 (1948).

[61] For later comment, see CE Clark, 'Two Decades of the Federal Civil Rules', 58 *Columbia Law Review* 435 (1958). KN Moore, 'The Supreme Court's Role in Interpreting the Federal Rules of Civil Procedure', July 1993, 44 *Hastings Law Journal* 1039, helpfully covers the interpretation placed upon the Act and the background separation of powers issues. D Marcus, in 'Institutions' (n 45), 927–98, looks at the rule-making situs before dealing with approaches to interpretation. BD Coleman, 'Recovering Access' (n 29), 265–76, also covers, for our purposes, the history of the Rules Enabling Act. Note

Hughes looked at the existing procedure and consulted with the judiciary.[62] The Supreme Court appointed an Advisory Committee on the Rules by order of 3 June 1935. William D Mitchell, former AG in the Hoover Administration, became the Advisory Committee's chairman.[63] On 6 June 1935 the AG, Homer Cummings, was reporting[64] that CJ Hughes' objective was 'a simplified practice which will strip procedure of unnecessary forms, technicalities, and distinctions, and permit the advance of causes to *the decision of their merits with a minimum of procedural encumbrances*.'[65]

For how all this came about we need to look at Charles E Clark, Dean of Yale Law School, who may not have been a politician but who could scheme exceptionally well. A Washington outsider, he got what he wanted out of the Supreme Court. This part of Clark's career is one that shows him at his best and his worst. On the plus side, Clark pushed CJ Hughes into pursuing fusion and into appointing a really good rules committee. Against this we must set the fact that Clark set justices against each other, pushed Tolman out of his designated role as rule-writer and spiked Sunderland's guns, so preventing him from getting the post of Reporter. That was the post Clark himself coveted, for he thought that he should be drafting most of the rules. Clark actively sought the post of Reporter to the Advisory Committee, pushing behind the scenes to be made Reporter over the head of Edson R Sunderland, the acknowledged expert on disclosure. Clark ran him down behind his back in correspondence, and soothed Sunderland with the offer of a stipend.[66]

that members of the Rules Committee were discouraged from writing legal text-books on the Rules – see fn 165 in D Marcus, 'When Rules are Rules: The Federal Rules of Civil Procedure and Institutions in Legal interpretation', *Arizona Legal Studies Discussion Paper No 11-22* (2011). This paper appears to be a working draft of 'Institutions' (n 45). Judge Clark, it seems, was pretty consistent in his views – ME Smith, 'Judge Charles E Clark and the Federal Rules of Civil Procedure', 85 *Yale Law Journal* 914 (June 1976), analyses Clark's judicial record and shows how firmly Clark remained committed to his view of procedure. LJ Silberman et al, *Civil Procedure Theory and Practice* (New York, Walters Kluwer, 2009) offers broad descriptive text on the background to the FRCP at 461–65.

[62] William G Ross, *The Chief Justiceship of Charles Evans Hughes* (Columbia South Carolina, University of South Carolina Press, 2007) 235. The changes had been something of which Hughes approved.

[63] Hughes had gone back into practice in New York to make some money. He handled big-ticket legislation and acted, inter alia, for governments. Clark was appointed as a Reporter on the same day as Mitchell was appointed to the chair: PD Edmunds, *Federal Rules of Civil Procedure* (n 2), 6.

[64] The CJ's full speech appears at 21 *American Bar Association Journal* 340 (1935). Hughes addressed the question of the administration of law and equity. The speech concluded with an announcement of the intention to appoint an advisory committee in respect of the rules. The speech is also quoted in *CsSelP*, 191. Cummings was directly quoting the CJ. For details of Clark's background lobbying, see Subrin, '*Charles E Clark*' (n 24), 119–32.

[65] Emphasis added. This text appears in EM Morgan, 'Judicial Regulation' (n 23), 82. Biographical material on Clark appears in the article on him in RK Newman (ed), *Yale Biographical Dictionary* (n 2), 278–79. JF Simon, *FDR and Chief Justice Hughes: the President, the Supreme Court, and the Epic Battle Over the New Deal* (New York, Simon & Schuster, 2012) provides much more background.

[66] For this unedifying episode, see SN Subrin, 'Charles E Clark' (n 24) 132–37. Clark alluded to this episode, in rather misleading terms, in CE Clark, 'Edson Sunderland and the Federal Rules of Civil Procedure', 58 *Michigan Law Review* 6, 8–10 (1959–1960). Hoffer addresses the sticky question of a 'sweetener' in PC Hoffer et al, *The Federal Courts* (n 38), 489, fn [49].

Following the passing of the 1934 Act the Supreme Court took its time to consider. It is clear from what subsequently happened that either there was a genuine split of opinion between the justices, with the risk that matters would be sent back to Congress (AG Cummings' view), or that Hughes' plan did not enjoy his colleagues' full support. The number of Justices who subsequently supported Clark's position suggests that both possibilities may have arisen. On 28 September 1934, CJ Hughes met with the Judicial Conference and proposed the setting up of consultative committees. The AG subsequently wrote to the judiciary. By 8 October 1934, Clark was aware that fusion might not be pursued. He determined to do something about this.[67]

On 24 December 1934, as a first step, Clark sent AG Cummings a draft of the joint article ANFP1. This co-written article set out Clark's pro-fusion position. After Christmas 1934 Clark received a nasty shock. On 2 January 1935 he met Major Edgar B Tolman and discovered that Tolman had been asked to write the new rules and that fusion was not going to be pursued. Tolman was due in Washington on 14 January 1935 to meet with Cummings and Hughes. At some time during the autumn of 1934, unbeknown to Clark, Edgar B Tolman had been appointed as Cummings' special adviser on procedure.

Clark set to work to outmanoeuvre Tolman. On 4 January 1935, a note from Clark reached the AG asking him to look again at the fusion issue. On the same day Clark wrote to Tolman suggesting that he (Clark), Sunderland, Dobie and Morgan could all serve on the rules committee. Presumably Tolman went ahead with his meeting with the AG and the CJ on 14 January 1935 for, on 16 January 1935, Cummings wrote to Clark asking if he would serve on a rules committee that would deal with common law rules only. This was the AG's Consultative Committee, which it was intended that Tolman would chair. It included Edson R Sunderland, Roscoe Pound and Clark.[68]

Clark accepted the proposed appointment even though he was completely committed to fusion. He was just getting started. On 18 January 1935 Clark was complaining in correspondence about Tolman's being like 'a babe in the woods'. The end of January 1935 brought the publication of Clark's first article in the *Yale Law Journal*.[69] Publication was the occasion for Clark to get out his pen. On about 31 January 1935 he started writing to the judiciary and legal luminaries. He sent them a copy of his article and asked his recipients to act. At some point in early February 1935, Clark met up with the AG in Washington. Cummings warned that if the justices were unhappy and could not agree then the matter would end up back in Congress. Politically one can see that the

[67] HP Chandler, 'Some Major Advances in the Federal Judicial System 1922–1947', 31 *Federal Rules Decisions* 307 (1963) is very helpful here, especially at 488.

[68] The Committee never met. The existence of the Committee was referred to in 18 *Journal of the American Judicature Society* 163, 163 (1935) under the title 'Attorney General's Committee has golden opportunity'. Clark appears sixth in the list, below Sunderland and Pound.

[69] CE Clark and JW Moore, 'A New Federal Civil Procedure I', 44 *Yale Law Journal* 387 (1935).

Administration, having successfully got the bill through, was reluctant to give Congress a second look.

The correspondence continued. By 4 February 1935 Clark was complaining about Tolman's appointment, saying that made him 'quite sick'. The same day Justice Cardozo wrote to Clark to tell him no final decision had been made on appointing Tolman, nor about fusion. Unbeknown to Tolman, his star was on the wane. On 6 February 1935 Justice Stone advised Clark to keep fighting. Clark must have concluded he was making progress, for on 8 February 1935 he wrote to William D Mitchell (the former Republican AG) to tell him what was going on and to say that the older judges were getting in the way. This was an adroit move. Mitchell had himself despaired of bringing forward a bill whilst there was opposition to it and, significantly, many of the existing justices were Republican appointees. Mitchell's voice would therefore carry a lot of weight. Mitchell acted immediately. On 9 February 1935 he wrote to CJ Hughes (at Clark's request) to call for the uniting of common law and equity procedure. Tolman, presumably still in the dark, was writing on 12 February 1935, wondering about fusion's political feasibility. Clark's plan had been to get at the justices, and even as Tolman was writing, Clark was making progress for, the same day, Justice Van Devanter wrote to say that his mind was still open to fusion. The date 12 February 1935 was something of a red letter day for Clark. The CJ wrote to remind him that the decision was one for the court but indicating, significantly, that no decision had yet been made. The following day, 13 February 1935, Hughes wrote again to tell Clark that his views would be put before the whole court. Clark had already sent his view to the court's members and knew that support for fusion was growing. On 18 February 1935, Justice Butler encouraged Clark to keep agitating. The CJ had been outmanoeuvred: 7 March 1935 found him saying that he had been misunderstood. The CJ addressed the annual meeting of the ALI on 9 May 1935. He told them that fusion was to be pursued and that there was to be a rules committee – that set another of Clark's hares running. Clark had won the first two rounds, he now wanted the post of Reporter.

The rest of the month saw Clark in full Machiavellian mode. By 11 May 1935 he was aware that he and Mitchell would be on the Advisory Committee. He also knew who might make good committee members. On 13 May 1935 Mitchell asked Clark for suggestions for academics to go on the Committee. On 16 May 1935 Mitchell then wrote to Clark asking him for his suggestions as to who should be the Reporter, indicating that Clark and Sunderland were both under consideration, though Mitchell was worried that Clark would not have time to do the job. By return, on 17 May 1935, Clark told Mitchell of his own qualifications for the job and was less than complimentary about Sunderland, his rival, suggesting that Sunderland's prior work in the field of procedure pointed towards his holding views that would cut across Mitchell's. On 22 May 1935, Mitchell wrote back to tell Clark he was not sure what the problem was. In all probability Mitchell was not sufficiently familiar with Sunderland's work, but he was a quick study. By 23 May 1935 Mitchell had grasped Clark's point and wrote a critical letter to Sunderland.

Why was Mitchell so concerned? He had put his political and professional weight behind the 1934 Act and was now being asked to implement it. He could not afford for the proposed Advisory Committee to go off track. Mitchell may also have been embarrassed that he was not on top of all the facts, for by all accounts he prided himself on his command of detail.

The die was probably cast at that point so far as the Reporter's job was concerned, for on Friday, 24 May 1935, Mitchell wrote to Clark saying that Sunderland was 'entirely off the track'. He also wrote to the Court about matters concerning 'personnel and organization'. Sunderland had likely received Mitchell's letter that morning. It was probably the following day, Saturday, 25 May 1935, that Clark wrote to Sunderland suggesting that he might deal with summary judgment on the Committee and receive a weekly or monthly payment for this. Clark's action in writing this letter suggests that he was now confident who would get the Reporter's post. Sunderland must have wondered what to make of all this. He now needed to deal with Mitchell's concerns, and that would have taken time. It was only on Friday, 31 May 1935, that he wrote a letter to Mitchell defending himself. It was too late. On Monday, 3 June 1935, the Supreme Court published its Order naming Mitchell as the Chair and Clark as the Reporter. Clark maintained his position by suggesting an Agenda for the Committee on 14 June 1935.[70]

The remarkable thing about all this is that Clark was able to form good working relationships with both Mitchell and with Sunderland.

F. The Drafting of the Rules: The Evolution of Rule 1 FRCP (1938)

Of importance in helping us understand the process of the drafting of the FRCP is Patrick J Johnston's 'Problems in Raising Prayers to the Level of Rule'.[71] Johnston refers to the 'just, speedy, and inexpensive determination' formulation in Rule 1 as the trinity.[72]

The problems with which the Advisory Committee[73] and Clark[74] had to wrestle were as follows:

(a) there was concern that established patterns of statutory interpretation might require the rules to be interpreted in a restricted fashion; on the other hand,

[70] SN Subrin, 'Fishing Expeditions Allowed' (n 16), 712.

[71] P Johnston, 'Problems in Raising Prayers to the Level of Rule: The Example of Federal Rule of Procedure 1', 75 *Boston University Law Review* 1325 (1995).

[72] ibid, 1326. Contrast A Zuckerman, *Zuckerman on Civil Procedure: Principles of Practice* (hereinafter '*ZoCP*') (London, Sweet & Maxwell, 2013) para 1.21, the three-dimensional aspect of justice.

[73] Some of whose work was done by a subcommittee on form and style.

[74] For Clark's general philosophy, see D Marcus, 'The Federal Rules of Civil Procedure and Legal Realism as a Jurisprudence of Law Reform', 44 *Georgia Law Review* 433, 485 (2010). Marcus points to Clark's emphasis on functional interconnectedness (at 493), the method of discretion (at 499) and foundational purpose (at 501–02).

allowing a liberal construction might lead to inconsistency or to one party's being favoured;[75]

(b) there was debate about whether to lead with justice or some other set of values, and which values should be addressed apart from justice;

(c) there was debate, in the context of Rule 2, about the extent to which it was important to highlight that decisions should be on made on the merits;[76]

(d) there was doubt about whether admonitions in rules were appropriate in a legislative context and whether, in any event, their inclusion would work.[77]

At the June 1935 Advisory Committee meeting[78] there was preliminary discussion as to whether new or established terminology should be used, Clark preferred to avoid the old language (where it had been controversial), but the Committee preferred to use existing language to ease the reception of the Rules.[79]

It is significant how much toing-and-froing there was over the wording of what is now Rule 1. The attention given to it reflects, on the one hand, a wish to see aspirations realised and, on the other hand, a scepticism about the stated aspirations and concern as to where all this might lead. The Committee and Clark were not always fully in step.

i. *Tentative Draft I*

Clark's tentative first draft of Rule 1, delivered on 21 September 1935, provided that 'these rules shall be liberally construed for the purpose of effectuating a simple, uniform and efficient procedure'.[80] The purpose was expressed positively

[75] Clark was alive to this concern, seeing civil procedure as bringing regularity to the way in which litigation proceeds and as enabling equal treatment, even though that may be at the cost of a limited 'individualisation' of proceedings. Part of the difficulty arises from the sheer amount of litigation which passes through the court system: see CE Clark, 'The Handmaid of Justice' (n 60), 299–300. The Civil Procedure Rules 1998 (as amended) (CPR) strike a balance through having three tracks, which represents at least an attempt at offering a procedure that is appropriate to cases of differing size.

[76] See P Johnston, 'Problems in Raising Prayers' (n 71), 1342. As Johnston argues, some thought that references to 'the merits' and 'just determinations' were unnecessary – a distinct shade of the 'it goes without saying' school of thought in England: see *ZoCP* (2013) (n 72), para 1.32.

[77] See P Johnston, 'Problems in Raising Prayers' (n 71), 1337–38 and 1344. Edward M Morgan referred to the admonitions as 'a pious hope' and Senator Pepper to them as 'the bunk'. Significantly, Johnston (ibid, 1345) cites William D Mitchell as saying, 'The Committee is rather embarrassed by that statement [the trinity] because it sounds a little bit as if it would have that result. Of course we know better.' This statement has a Jacksonesque realism to it.

[78] Sadly the critical part of the Rule 1 discussion on 14 November 1935 is missing. The reason given is that the stenographer's notebook was misplaced (Advisory Committee on Uniform Rules of Civil Procedure, transcript of vol I for November 1935, 2–3a, available at www.uscourts.gov.

[79] Advisory Committee transcript of 20 June 1935, 152–57. See also P Johnston, 'Problems in Raising Prayers' (n 71), 1335.

[80] Uniform Rules of Civil Procedure for the District Courts of the United States and the Supreme Court of the District Columbia (hereinafter 'Uniform Rules'), Tentative Draft I, Part 1 dated 15 October 1935 (Papers of Charles Edward Clark, Yale University Library, MS 1344, Series IV Box 97) (copy on file).This draft contains a Rule 1 and an alternative Rule 1, both at 1. The relevant wording is the same in both the preferred and the alternative versions. The notes (at 2) make clear that the preferred version

as *effectuating*. But on 27 September 1935 the Committee was pushing for an 'interpretative rule which would state the objectives and purposes of the rules', which were, amongst other things, to 'prevent delay, uncertainty and expense in the administration of justice', 'permit the advance of causes to the decision of their merits with a minimum of procedural encumbrances' and, where there was doubt as to the meaning of rules or there were two possible interpretations of the rules, 'so as to most fully aid in the accomplishment of the objectives above set forth'.[81] Notwithstanding the Committee's raising of the question of prevention (a negative formulation), the positive expression of purpose would continue.

ii. Tentative Draft II

A November 1935 Committee meeting led to the production of a Tentative Draft II on 26 December 1935.[82] The position of the rule was changed and the wording now provided the term 'practice' as an alternative to 'procedure'.[83]

Tentative Draft II also produced a rule that is interesting from the standpoint of relief from sanctions. Rule 2 read, 'At any stage of the proceedings when the ends of justice so require, the court on such terms as may be just, shall: relieve a party from the results of accident, surprise, misfortune or excusable neglect,' upon the basis that this was 'to the end that the decision shall be on the merits'.[84]

iii. Tentative Draft III

A draft of Rule 2 dated 12 March 1936 provided:

> These rules shall be liberally construed for the purpose of effectuating a simple, uniform, and efficient procedure to the end that decisions shall be on the merits. The courts at every stage of the proceeding must disregard any error, defect or irregularity therein which does not affect the substantial rights of the parties; and shall, when the ends of justice so require, relieve a party from the results of accident, mistake, surprise, or inadvertence on his part ...[85]

simply follows 'the general and inclusive wording of the Act; in the second, details are spelled out'. See also P Johnston, 'Problems in Raising Prayers' (n 71), 1337.

[81] P Johnston, 'Problems in Raising Prayers' (n 71), 1336. From Memorandum from Edgar Tolman to Clark, 27 September 1935. Tolman was the Committee's secretary.

[82] Uniform Rules (n 80), Tentative Draft II, 26 December 1935 (Papers of Charles Edward Clark, Yale University Library, MS 1344, Series IV Box 98) (copy on file).The rule is now found in section X 'Applicability of the Rules' as Rule A.36, although the pencil markings indicate the number A.78.

[83] ibid, p 1 of that rule. This draft shows the draftsman considering alternative titles for the rules. Page 4 of this draft discusses whether the term 'practice' or 'procedure' was a more appropriate title. See also P Johnston, 'Problems in Raising Prayers' (n 71), 1338. Note that the merits are not mentioned. Clark's solution was directed towards simplicity, uniformity and efficiency.

[84] P Johnston, 'Problems in Raising Prayers' (n 71), 1338, document of 23 December 1935. Contrast RSC (1883) Ord 70, r 1, RSC (1965) Ord 2, r 1; and CPR 3.10 and CPR 3.8 and 3.9.

[85] P Johnston, 'Problems in Raising Prayers' (n 71), 1339.

As Johnston points out,[86] the draft of Rule 2 in Tentative Draft III[87] was changed by Clark on 24 March 1936 to heighten the emphasis on justice and downplay the emphasis on efficiency, providing:

> Rule 2. Decisions to be made on the merits.
>
> These rules shall be liberally construed for the purpose of securing the just determination of every case upon its merits as speedily and inexpensively as possible. The court must, therefore, at every stage of the proceedings disregard any error, defect or irregularity which does not prejudice substantial rights; and shall, when the ends of justice so require, relieve a party from the results of accident, mistake, surprise, or inadvertence on his part, and from the results of fraud, misrepresentation or other misconduct of an adverse party.[88]

Notes to this rule made two points:

(a) 'It was thought advisable … to retain here a general admonition, to give tone and color to the rules … This was left to the draftsman and the Committee on style.'

(b) 'A general admonition such as this performs a useful function, in changing "the rule of the common law, that statutes in derogation thereof are to be strictly construed."'[89]

iv. *Preliminary Draft I*

In April 1936 the rules were before the subcommittee on form and style.[90] The subcommittee produced its own draft.[91] The new Rule 1 of the 'Rules of Civil Procedure' provided as follows:

> Rule 1. Scope of Rules
>
> These rules shall govern the procedure in the district courts of the United States and in the Supreme Court of the District of Columbia in all civil cases wherein it is sought to obtain the relief previously obtainable by actions at law and suits in equity. They are to

[86] ibid, 1340.

[87] Uniform Rules (n 80), Tentative Draft III, March 1936 (Papers of Charles Edward Clark, Yale University Library, MS 1344, Series IV Box 98, Vol III) (copy on file).

[88] ibid, p 1 of Rule 2.

[89] Noting the existence of 'general provision(s) of similar substance', the draftsman pointed, inter alia, to s 452 of the California Code of Civil Procedure of 1931: ibid, p 1 of Rule 2. The existence of 'English Rules under the Judicature Act (1935) O.70, r.1' is noted. RSC (1883) Ord 70, r 1 provided that proceedings were not rendered void by non-compliance. It contained no equivalent interpretation clause.

[90] It was asked to provide a 'general admonition at the appropriate place'. P Johnston, 'Problems in Raising Prayers' (n 71), 1339.

[91] This is almost certainly the 'Preliminary Draft of Advisory Committee' dated April 1936, entitled 'Rules of Civil Procedure' (Papers of Charles Edward Clark, Yale University Library, MS 1344, Series IV Box 99, Vol IV, *Preliminary Draft I*). See also P Johnston, 'Problems in Raising Prayers' (n 71), 1341. The subcommittee moved Rule 2 to Rule 1.

> be construed in all particulars so as to further and secure as speedily, simply, and inexpensively as possible the just determination of every action.[92]

The word 'just' was now placed after the phrase 'speedily, simply, and inexpensively'. But as one Committee member, Warren Olney, wrote, 'What is really meant is that the rules are to be construed in all particulars in furtherance of the end of securing a just decision.'[93] Justice on the merits was still firmly in the driving seat.

Of the effect of Rule 1 Johnston says this:

> Although the rules permit some discretion by design and cannot avoid discretionary application in practice it was never intended for any Rule to provide a source of unbounded judicial restraint.[94]

The draft rules were sent by Mitchell to Hughes under cover of a letter of 1 May 1936.[95] Hughes approved the draft rules for circulation on 5 May 1936.[96] He wanted professional engagement, so he addressed the annual meeting of the ALI in Washington, DC on 7–9 May 1936,[97] and commended the work of the Advisory Committee for critical assessment by the ALI. He said, '[give us] the benefit of your seasoned judgment'. There was an open forum session in Boston on 24 May 1936. By the middle of August 1936 it was clear that the Advisory Committee would not be in a position to publish Proposed Rules within its envisaged timeframe, so Hughes advised Mitchell that the Committee should be seen to make an effort in order to avoid being blamed for being tardy. In the event, the rules were not available before the Presidential election of November 1938.

G. The Promulgation of the Rules

The years 1935–38 were a busy period in American politics. Roosevelt launched the second wave of his New Deal reforms and encountered increasing difficulty with the Supreme Court. He ran for re-election against Alfred Landon in November 1938 and won a second term. Roosevelt's legislation was now receiving the punishing attention of the Supreme Court, and he responded with the Judicial Procedures Reform Bill of 1937, which would have increased the number of Supreme Court judges. The bill failed, not least because of opposition from the

[92] 'Rules of Civil Procedure' Preliminary Draft I, (n 91), 1. Note that in February 1937 the Committee decided to remove the words 'to further' from the rule. P Johnston, 'Problems in Raising Prayers' (n 71), 1343.

[93] P Johnston, 'Problems in Raising Prayers' (n 71), 1341. The parallel language with CPR 1.1 is intriguing, 'to further the overriding objective'.

[94] P Johnston, 'Problems in Raising Prayers' (n 71), 1393–94.

[95] This appears as an appendix to the Introduction to Preliminary Draft Rules (see n 96) viii.

[96] This also appears in the Introduction: see *Preliminary Draft of Rules of Civil Procedure for the District Courts of the US* (Washington, DC, Advisory Committee on Rules for Civil Procedure, 1936). in 1 *LegHist* (n 7) xix.

[97] *American Law Institute Proceedings*, vol 13 (Philadelphia, PA, American Law Institute, 1936) 63–64. Moore says that the speech was made on 9 May 1936 – James W Moore et al, *Moore's Federal Practice*, 2nd edn (Albany, NY, Matthew Bender & Co, 1993 (updated from 1948)) vol 2, 1–13.

Democrats, FDR's own party. Worse, CJ Hughes publicly opposed the Bill. By July 1937 FDR no longer had the support for the Bill that he needed in Congress. Coincidentally, 1937 seems to have marked a turning point in the Supreme Court's attitude to New Deal legislation. This, then, was the divisive atmosphere into which the proposed FRCP emerged.[98]

The consultation draft of the proposed new rules was published in April 1937.[99] Hughes again addressed the ALI in May 1937.[100] There was an Open Forum session in Kansas City in October 1937, and the Advisory Committee met to put the finishing touches to its Final Report, which was produced in November 1937.[101] Chief Justice Hughes addressed the ALI again at its annual meeting in Washington DC, extolling the work done on the rules. On 20 December 1937 CJ Hughes gave AG Cummings notice of submittal of the rules. The submittal noted that Justice Brandeis did not approve.[102] Cummings' letter of transmittal to Congress, confirming adoption of the rules by Supreme Court, was sent on 3 January 1938. Congress was not completely content. There was a hearing before Congress on 1–4 March 1938.[103] As well as the making of an appearance by the AG, the Advisory Committee was able to help by fielding a strong team, comprising a former US AG, William D Mitchell, and a former Senator, Edgar B Tolman. In a successful defence of the proposed rules to the House Committee on the Judiciary, AG Cummings said:

> [T]he rules prescribe a *very simple* form of pleading practice and procedure … (whose aim) has been to reduce the matter to *simple and easily understood* terms, and to provide for the maintenance of the procedure in such a fashion that even a mind of moderate capacity would easily understand what the required course may be.[104]

[98] For the difficulties in relationships, see HP Chandler, 'Some Major Advances' (n 67), 373–74. The relationship between the CJ and AG Cummings had completely broken down. For comprehensive historical coverage of the relationship between FDR and CJ Hughes and the Administration and the Court, see JF Simon, *FDR and Chief Justice Hughes* (n 65). For general background, see B Schwartz, *A History of the Supreme Court* (Oxford, Oxford University Press, 1993) ch 10; and PC Hoffer et al, *The Supreme Court: An Essential History* (Lawrence, KS, University Press of Kansas, 2007) ch 10. The Court packing plan was tabled on 5 February 1937, and was in the Senate in March 1937. CJ Hughes opposed the plan, but on 29 March 1937 changed judicial direction, upholding New Deal legislation in *West Coast Hotel Company v Parrish* 300 US 379 (1937). A more important decision in *National Labour Relations Board v Jones & Laughlin Steel Corp* 301 US 1 (1937) followed on 12 April 1937. The draft bill was rejected by the Senate Judiciary Committee on 18 May 1937 and the bill in its original form was effectively dead. It did not matter, for FDR's action had cleared the decks for New Deal legislation.

[99] Report of the Advisory Committee on Rules for Civil Procedure containing Proposed Rules of Civil Procedure for the District Courts of the United States (Washington DC, Advisory Committee on Rules for Civil Procedure, 1937) in 1 LegHist (n 7).

[100] 6–8 May 1937, Washington, DC. See *American Law Institute Proceedings*, vol 14 (Philadelphia, PA, American Law Institute, 1937) 36–38.

[101] Final Report of Advisory Committee on Rules for Civil Procedure (Washington, DC, Advisory Committee on Rules for Civil Procedure, 1937).

[102] Letter of Adoption of 20 December 1937 and Letter to Congress of 3 January 1938 (Hammond (ed), 1 *LegHist*, n 7).

[103] See PD Edmunds, *Federal Rules of Civil Procedure* (n 2), 7–8.

[104] *CsSelP*, 193. For a similar type of language, see Lord Woolf, *Access to Justice Interim Report* (London, HMSO, 1995) ch 17, paras 7–8, ch 26, paras 17, 28 and 29; and Lord Woolf, *Access to Justice Final Report* (London, HMSO, 1996) ch 20, para 13.

The opposition was led by Senator King. His witnesses were less impressive[105] and the objections went nowhere. Matters moved ahead. There were Institute meetings in Cleveland, Ohio, in July 1938 and, after the rules came into force, in Washington, DC and in New York, both in October 1938.

H. The Final Text of Rule 1

The final text of FRCP (1938) Rule 1, which came into force on 16 September 1938, was as follows:

> Rule 1 Scope of the Rules
>
> These rules govern the procedure in the district courts of the United States in all suits of a civil nature whether cognizable as cases at law or in equity, with the exceptions stated in Rule 81. They shall be construed to secure the just, speedy, and inexpensive determination of every action.

The Supreme Court's Order of 17 January 1938 noted that the FRCP had been submitted to Congress, and expressed the Court's appreciation of the Advisory Committee.[106]

I. The Wrap Up

Chief Justice Hughes was back at the ALI again in May 1938. There he praised[107] 'a series of outstanding efforts to remedy the defects in the law so far as these are responsible for unnecessary obstacles to obtaining as speedy justice as is consistent with a fair and full hearing'.

Speaking at an Institute conference in Washington on 6 October 1938, Edgar B Tolman[108] said:

> The general objective of these rules is a very old objective. Magna Charta declares 'to none will we sell, to no one will we deny or delay, right of justice' and *the objective of*

[105] PC Hoffer et al, *The Federal Courts* (n 38), 304.

[106] Order of 17 January 1938, 302 US 783–785. See CE Clark, 'The Influence of Federal Procedural Reform', *Law and Contemporary Problems*, vol 13 no 1, 'The Federal Courts' (Winter 1948) 144, 149; also CT Struve, 'The Paradox of Delegation: Interpreting the Federal Rules of Civil Procedure', 150 *University of Pennsylvania Law Review* 1099, 1105–06, fn 9 (2001–2002). The text of the Order is in Hammond (ed), 1 *LegHist* (n 7). The Court expressed its 'high appreciation' at p 3 of the Order.

[107] 12–14 May 1938, Annual Meeting, Washington, DC. *American Law Institute Proceedings*, vol 15 (American Law Institute, Philadelphia, PA, 1938) 34–35.

[108] For Tolman's own views, see EB Tolman, 'The Historical Beginnings of Procedural Reform Movement in This Country – Principles to be Observed in Making Rules', 22 *American Bar Association Journal* 783 (1936), which contained a useful review of three evils – delay, expense and uncertainty – at 785. This piece also offered photographs of Mitchell, Clark and Tolman.

> *these rules is that justice shall be administered without delay, without uncertainty, and with no avoidable expense.*[109]

He went on to refer to 'the *brevity and simplicity* which will enable any intelligent practitioner to try a case' as easily in the federal courts as in the court of his own State.[110]

Sunderland said that the purpose of the FRCP was both to remove 'the basis for technical objections' and 'to make litigation as inexpensive, as practicable and as convenient, as can be done'.[111]

Clark saw the FRCP as being 'but a means to an end', that end being 'the enforcement of substantive justice'.[112] James William Moore said that the FRCP 'epitomize the new objective of all procedure', which was that 'litigation ought to be settled on the merits and not upon some procedural ground'.[113]

In 1939, FDR called the Rules 'an outstanding milestone along the road of law reform'.[114]

So here in microcosm is what contemporaries practitioners thought the objectives of the proposed new Federal Procedural Rules were, and how successful they thought the reform project had been.

This History ends with Robert G Bone, who says that, in America, during the pre-FRCP period, the procedural reformers thought that

> The only proper function of procedure was to serve as a means to the end of enforcing the substantive law. For reformers, this meant that procedure was governed by instrumental values of good system design, such as simplicity, flexibility, and litigation efficiency ...[115]

The focus of chapter 1 is upon purpose and function in civil procedure, viewed as a matter of choice and principle.

[109] Emphasis added. Annual Meeting, Washington, DC (n 107), 31. Edgar Tolman was a member of the rule-making committee, see Report of the Advisory Committee (April 1937), n (46), iv.

[110] Emphasis added. Annual Meeting, Washington, DC (n 107), 32. Tolman is reported by Alexander Holtzoff as having described the effect of the rules thus: 'the effect of these rules is to take off all the labels, abolish all the different forms of actions, and thus clear the way for the joinder of legal with equitable claims'. A Holtzoff, 'Equitable and Legal Rights and Remedies Under the New Federal Procedure' (1943) 23(2) CLR 127, 127.

[111] ER Sunderland, 'The New Federal Rules', 45 *West Virginia Law Quarterly* 5, 30 (1938).

[112] CE Clark, 'Fundamental Changes' (n 8), 551.

[113] JW Moore, 'The New Federal Rules of Civil Procedure' 6 *Interstate Commerce Commission Practitioners' Journal* 41, 42 (1939).

[114] The President's letter of 4 May 1939 was sent to the Annual Meeting of the ALI held between 11 and 13 May 1938 in Washington, DC. *American Law Institute Proceedings*, vol 16 (American Law Institute, Philadelphia, PA, 1939) 19.

[115] RG Bone, 'Improving Rule 1: A Master Rule For The Federal Rules', 87:2 *Denver University Law Review* 287, 291–92 (2010). HP Chandler in 'Some Major Advances' (n 67), gives wider background on the promotion of efficiency (at 344) and expedition (at 346) from the perspective of judicial administration. AR Miller, 'Pleading and Pre-trial Motions – What Would Judge Clark Do?', Paper prepared for a 2010 conference at Duke Law School and subsequently revised, lists equality of treatment in the civil adjudication process (at 2) and the role of litigation in the enforcement of public policies (at 3) as being of importance. Available at www.uscourts.gov.

1

Purposes and Functions

I. The Need for Theory

It is a striking feature of the history of civil procedure in England and in America that disappointment in the process and its outcomes are writ large. The reality on the ground has failed to provide satisfaction, and that dissatisfaction has caused reformers, rule-makers and critics to consider what the civil justice system is supposed to be there to achieve. The Federal Civil Procedure Rules of 1938 (FCPR) were not a permanent fix. The Civil Procedure Rules 1998 (CPR) failed to achieve all that for which their promoters hoped.

Historically, there have been a number of attempts to describe what people thought they were doing in the field of civil justice: Pound notably criticised the lack of 'general ideas or legal philosophy'[1] in the procedure of the law. More recently in academia, it has become possible to talk of 'theories of justice'[2] covering procedural justice, comprising both 'Formalism' and 'Complete Justice';[3] the 'justice on the merits' approach;[4] 'and Woolf's 'new theory',[5] which was 'a theory of proportionate justice'.[6] Even the term 'hypothesis'[7] has been used. All of these point to a recognition that the civil justice system is there for a reason and has a purpose, and that it makes sense to consider whether that reason and purpose, and the procedures designed to achieve them, are constructively aligned. This alignment is not always an easy task, as history shows. It is for this reason that theories are needed.

[1] R Pound, 'The Causes of Popular Dissatisfaction with the Administration of Justice', 29 *Annual Report of the American Bar Association* 395, 407 (1906). It is a sad irony that the English reformers of the early 1850s had just such a general idea in mind.

[2] J Sorabji, *English Civil Justice after the Woolf and Jackson Reforms: A Critical Analysis* (Cambridge, Cambridge University Press, 2014) (hereinafter '*SorECJ*'), see the title to pt 1 at 7.

[3] ibid 34 et seq.

[4] A Zuckerman, *Zuckerman on Civil Procedure: Principles of Practice* (hereinafter '*ZoCP*') (London, Sweet & Maxwell, 2013) para 1.70. Zuckerman also uses the term 'philosophy' at para 1.71.

[5] *SorECJ* (n 2), 101, 107.

[6] ibid 197.

[7] J Jolowicz, *On Civil Procedure* (Cambridge, Cambridge University Press, 2000) 70.

II. Complexity and Intertwining

There are two issues here: procedural problems are more complex than they may first appear;[8] and the substantive and procedural are often intertwined.

Charles E Clark, writing in 1950,[9] is helpful on the topic of complexity. Clark was contrasting the care taken in approaching the substantive law with general attitudes towards procedural law. He said that

> a greater degree of legal sophistication is usually needed than in the substantive field to appreciate the subtle nuances of procedural causes and effects and their interpretation, yet the subject is often approached with a blitheness, indeed a naiveté, on the whole appalling.

It is fair to say that Clark overstated the position here, as we shall see in chapters 2 and 3, for he was the inheritor of a rich tradition of procedural reform. Nevertheless, reforming civil procedure is not an easy task, because reform is not just a matter of changing the process but of changing the behaviour and attitudes of people.

This reformation takes place at the border with the substantive law. The close cooperation required between the substantive law and the justice system is demonstrated by the American case of *Boddie v State of Connecticut*,[10] in which the claimants of welfare benefits were challenging a requirement that they pay court fees, which, they said, was restricting their right of access to the courts. In this passage Justice Harlan started with the substantive before moving to the procedural, saying:

> Perhaps no characteristic of an organized and cohesive society is more fundamental than its erection and enforcement of a system of rules defining the various rights and duties of its members, enabling them to govern their affairs and definitively settle their differences in an orderly, predictable manner. Without such a 'legal system' social organization and cohesion are virtually impossible; with the ability to seek regularized resolution of conflicts individuals are capable of interdependent action that enables them to strive for achievements without the anxieties that would beset them in a disorganized society.

Just a few years earlier in 1966, the basic purpose of the FRCP was considered in *Surowitz v Hilton Hotels Corp*, where it was said:

> The basic purpose of the Federal Rules is to administer justice through fair trials … If rules of procedure work … they not only permit, but should as nearly as possible

[8] See, eg, SC Yeazell, 'The Misunderstood Consequences of Modern Civil Process', 1994 *Wisconsin Law Review* 631, 676–77.

[9] Clark, 'Special Problems in 'Drafting and Interpreting Procedural Codes and Rules', 3 *Vanderbilt Law Review* 493, 496 (1950). This passage was cited in David M Roberts, 'The Myth of Uniformity in Federal Civil Procedure: Federal Civil Rule 83 and District Court Local Rulemaking Powers', 8 *University of Puget Sound Law Review* 537 (1985).

[10] *Boddie v State of Connecticut* 401 US 371 (1971).

> guarantee that bona fire complaints be carried to an adjudication on the merits. Rule 23(b) like the other civil rules, was written to further, not defeat the ends of justice.[11]

Given the difficulties with which civil procedure presents, three things are worth noting: civil procedure exists for a reason; the context of civil litigation is societal; and civil procedure is not an end in itself, although it ought to promote and satisfy certain process values.

III. The Function of Civil Procedure

We start with function, where Richard L Marcus[12] says, 'Without procedure there would be no guidelines as to what information is received by the decision-maker … [or] how the information is to be presented.' This points us towards one function of procedure. It is there to guide,[13] to set out the steps to be taken both at the specific level and at the general level.

The civil justice system exists to ensure that substantive justice is done and to give effect to the procedural rules that provide the platform for the dispensing and effectiveness of substantive justice. There are four aspects to this system:

(a) *The people who run it and engage with it.* Here we have the judges who are operators in individual cases or, in the case of appeal judges, operators at the system level. Apart from operators, there are direct users, the litigants, and indirect but repeat users, the practitioners. Litigants and practitioners are participants in the system.
(b) *The place.* This includes court rooms, judicial chambers and digital space where the activity is undertaken.
(c) *The large-scale processes.* These are the constituent parts that go to ensuring that a case is tried and that numerous cases can proceed at the same time.
(d) *The procedure to be followed.* Here we deal with individual acts directed by the rules or by court order to ensure that the constituent parts of the process are completed properly. We also have the acts to be done to achieve a particular result: for example, to have a case brought to an early close because it is a weak case, it is possible to make an application for summary judgment under CPR Part 24.

[11] *Surowitz v Hilton Hotels Corp* 383 US 363, 373 (1966). The case concerned an appeal in a derivative action. The decision of the Court was delivered by Black J, who was opposed to procedural 'booby traps'.

[12] RL Marcus et al, *Civil Procedure – A Modern Approach* (St Paul, MN, West Publishing, 1989) xxi and 1.

[13] See also M Hodson, *Civil Justice Review: Report of the Review Body on Civil Justice*, Cmnd 394 (London, HMSO, 1988) paras 220 and 221.

IV. Society and the Courts

Let us look at society and the courts. Society provides its citizens with a means of having their disputes resolved through authoritative means. The courts are not primarily there as symbols of justice, nor is their main role to develop the law, important though such roles are.[14] Rather, the courts are there to decide disputes according to the law, the outcome of which is justice according to the law. Not all disputes go to trial, many cases never even get as far as being issued. But the availability of trials, the laying out of specific court procedures and the use of pre-action protocols sets the context within which the disputants may come to terms; for even if a case does not come to trial, substantive justice will have been obtained if the case settles according to the substantive law.

The societal function of the courts, to dispense or facilitate substantive justice, can be disrupted, however, if the procedures provided to the parties do not work properly, so that a case proceeds too slowly or costs too much. In such circumstances one can see that there is a process and method aspect to justice, as well as a dispensing aspect.

The need for a specific goal for the rules by which the system operates follows on from the function the civil justice system plays within society. In *Mechanical Jurisprudence*,[15] Roscoe Pound argued as follows: 'Herein is the task of the sociological jurist … to secure for the *human factor* in experience the *central place* which belongs to it in our whole scheme of thought and action.'[16] Laws specify, control and trace the interrelationships between the citizenry and their relationships with the state. Such laws, which we call substantive, are particular to time and place. Thus, in England the judges take an oath in the following terms, 'I will do right to all manner of people after the laws and usages of this Realm'.[17] The laws and usages to be applied are those current in England when the dispute arose.

All of this highlights the importance of the substantive law. John Finnis argues[18] that the goal of the substantive law is 'a certain form or quality of communal life',[19] which includes individual autonomy.[20] But to return to our theme, the substantive law requires a system to make it effective when people are in dispute. This felt need for effective process goes deep in English and American culture. Magna Carta proclaimed, 'To no one will … we deny, or delay … justice.'[21]

[14] Though the symbolic role should affect the way in which the court goes about its business.

[15] R Pound, 'Mechanical Jurisprudence', 8 *Columbia Law Review* 605, 609 (1908) (emphasis added).

[16] Internal citations omitted.

[17] At http://www.judiciary.gov.uk.

[18] J Finnis, *Natural Law and Natural Rights* (Oxford, Oxford University Press, 1980) 261. He is arguing about criminal law, but the point is of wider application.

[19] ibid 261. See also Aristotle, *The Politics*, book III, ch 9, 1280b; and M Sandel, *Justice, What's the Right Thing to Do?* (London, Allen Lane, 2009) 192–95.

[20] J Finnis, *Natural Law and Natural Rights* (n 18) 261.

[21] Magna Carta (1215), cl 40.

Blackstone spoke of the citizen's right to apply to the court 'for redress of injuries', and said that the 'courts of justice must at all times be open to the subject, and the law be duly administered therein'.[22]

Finnis says that the substantive law has to be 'worked out' by a system of 'authoritative co-ordination',[23] which, he says, allows for both procedural fairness, being the due process of the law, and substantive fairness, relating to questions of deserving and to questions of proportionality.

If the due process[24] aspects of the system fail to operate properly then substantive justice remains out of the reach of the citizenry and, from the constitutional perspective, the judiciary will have failed to discharge its mandate.

V. The Social World

Just as individuals have a role to play in the social world, so do groups. In our context, groups are collections of people in similar circumstances – perhaps by choice, perhaps because it is required – who come together or work alongside each other, focusing on the same goal or task. Each group will have its own behavioural norms that become habitual. Individuals 'own' these norms because of what they can gain from compliance, because of their own moral commitments and because of what the group expects of them. The habituated norms can be passed on as a whole. So barristers will have their own culture – ways of behaving, dressing, speaking, eating, thinking and so forth. These sub-cultures encapsulate the world for the professional, to the extent that where changes in behaviour are required, it can seem as if the whole world, the group and the individual are threatened. So a required modification of behaviour may be resisted.

Further, if the habitual practice makes sense to those required to change, it will be defended. And one has to allow that people might genuinely think that an existing system is preferable to the proposed new one because of the loss of certainty, exposure to the unknown, and the learning and effort required to make the required change.[25] And the reason for change may be put across in such a way as to blame the proposed object of change, thus alienating its adherents. Woolf, in casting the blame on legal professionals, was not following the path

[22] W Blackstone, *Commentaries on the Laws of England*, vol 1 (Oxford, Clarendon Press, 1765–1769) book 1, at 140 and 137 respectively. These passages are cited in *ZoCP* (2013) (n 4) para 1.6.

[23] J Finnis, *Natural Law and Natural Rights* (n 18) 267. For Roscoe Pound's view from the US, see 'Some Principles of Procedural Reform', 4 *Illinois Law Review* 388, 407 (1909–1910).

[24] This is an old concern: see Sir Edward Coke, *Coke's Institutes of the Laws of England* (M Flesher and R Young, London, 1642) pt II, ch 29, 46.

[25] This, paradoxically, is the point that Woolf was making in his 1994 speech 'Access to Justice' in MDA Freeman (ed), *Current Legal Problems*, vol 47 (Oxford, Oxford University Press,1994) 341. See also Edmund Burke, *Reflections on the French Revolution* (London, JM Dent & Sons Ltd, 1910 edition reprinted 1953) 31, 55–59, 75–76 for this view in an overtly political context.

trodden when the FRCP (1938) were drafted.[26] And if, as Sorabji says, Woolf was proposing a new underlying philosophy, that would require a change of mentality. From the lawyer's perspective, the client's interests were to be subordinated to the process and to the needs of others. Worse, power was to be concentrated in judicial hands.

A. We Make Our World

The broad theory of social construction can be expressed in this way: we make the social world in which we live.[27]

Ian Haskins, in *The Social Construction of What?*,[28] reviews the structure of social construction theories. He points out that they are often used in the following manner: x is socially constructed, x is bad, we should therefore change x.[29] The argument of this book does not take this strong form. Rather it is argued that all systems of civil procedure are socially constructed; different systems will produce different results; it is possible to evaluate these results and then to change a system if it is insufficiently effective. This is true of the systems operating FRCP (1938), the RSC (1883), the RSC (1965) and the CPR. All of these systems were or are socially real. Civil procedural systems are operated by real people who live in the real world (ie the world of brute facts), so, on Christian Smith's argument,[30] the position stated here would be akin to a weak or realist one.

The argument here is not that all reality is socially constructed, for you can stub your toe upon a stone and definitely hurt yourself.[31] Nor is it the argument of this book that all reality is produced through rhetoric, or 'discourse' as it is technically termed. To say that everything is discourse-produced is to underdetermine.[32] Some social reality is clearly produced by rhetoric – Goebbels is a case in point – his propaganda influenced people's thinking and action. And some rhetoric can subtly function as an ideology aimed at lulling us into thinking that particular social facts are the natural order of things. But not all social reality is produced by rhetoric. It is neither necessary nor feasible to be suspicious of everything, nor to think that everything is a discourse of power. Rational reasonable thought is genuinely possible.

[26] Which is not to say that Woolf was wrong to be concerned at the cost of the established patterns of professional behaviour.

[27] See PC Berger and T Luckmann, *The Social Construction of Reality* (Harmondsworth, The Penguin Press, 1966) 65–85.

[28] I Haskins, *The Social Construction of What?* (Cambridge, MA, Harvard University Press, 1999).

[29] ibid 6–7.

[30] See C Smith, *What Is a Person: Rethinking Humanity, Social Life and the Moral Good From the Person Up* (Chicago, IL, University of Chicago Press, 2011) ch 3.

[31] See also D Elder-Vass, *The Reality of Social Construction* (Cambridge, Cambridge University Press, 2012) ch 12.

[32] ibid 125–29.

Dave Elder-Vass, in *The Reality of Social Construction*,[33] reminds us that it is important first to concentrate upon the basics and to ask 'what … is being constructed, what is it that is doing the constructing,' and what is the process through which this occurs. To answer each question in turn:

(a) It is the civil justice system that is socially constructed. It is created by people for people.
(b) Construction occurs through the reformers, the rule-makers and the rule-interpreters, but counter-construction occurs through those who do not agree with or buy into the process of change.
(c) The process of construction comprises established tradition and group behaviours, especially those clustered around adjudication, individual choices and preferences, the promise of reward (winning) and the threat of punishment (losing or facing sanctions), the granting or with holding of social approval (by judges or professional groupings, clients or society) and the making of rules of court.

Elder-Vass also tackles the question of whether 'the content of culture and rules exists in some sort of form' beyond the thoughts of individuals.[34] Following his argument closely, we can say as follows. The term 'culture' covers how people behave and the things they produce. Those things have physical reality, but they also carry meanings that can be decoded by other people. Behaviour is influenced by thoughts and beliefs. One can recognise thoughts and behaviours held and practised by more than one person at a time, and it is convenient to think of these as group thoughts and behaviours, which reside in the minds of anyone belonging to the group at any given point in time.

We also need to note two last things. First that the 'group' aspect of thought and behaviour is emergent, which is simply to say that the sum of the whole is greater than the sum of the parts; it has an effect, and that effect is recognisable.[35] Second, this group thought and behaviour is acquired by one individual from others, then is acted upon and transmitted on to others – so a parent teaches a child, who in due course teaches his or her own children. Margaret Archer calls this the 'morphogenetic cycle'.[36]

We return to the opening thought. We make the social world in which we live. That we can make, we can break and mend or change. And if we make the world, we can also see who wins and who loses by any particular social arrangement. Yet the social construction theory does not mean that these arrangements are

[33] D Elder-Vass, *The Reality of Social Construction* (n 31) 5–6.

[34] ibid 37–54.

[35] MS Archer, *Realist Social Theory: The Morphogenetic Cycle* (Cambridge, Cambridge University Press, 1995) 172–76. Which is not to say that there is 'out there' a body of thought or practices distinct from that contained in the heads of individuals.

[36] ibid 190–93. Archer is interested in how different groups work in strata of systems, organised groups, individuals and collectivities.

somehow not real.[37] The patterns of behaviour have social reality in that we participate in them and may have no choice about that. Further, the impacts of social facts are observable and may have significant consequences for those on the wrong side of an arrangement. A judgment of a court may just represent the decision of one person, but that decision is treated as a judgment which carries social consequences, whether in terms of execution, obligation or reputation. Because the social world is made by people, its constituent parts could be different. A different kind of people might have made a better world or a worse world. And successive generations may feel that their needs are different and require different solutions. Further, technology changes, as does the means of organisation, including ideas of how to manage or direct operations. And so a system that has processes *A*, *B* and *C* could instead contains processes *E*, *F* and *G*. If we look back, we can see that the system of common law civil procedure was capable of being changed to incorporate equity procedure, and the system of forms of action was capable of being replaced by a system allowing one form of action with variable remedies and claims.

Neither the substantive law nor procedure comes from above.[38] They are human creations and the product of their times. Thus they aim for the outcomes or use the means that were considered right at their point of origin. They incorporate or represent what was valued at a particular historical point in time and in a particular culture. That 'rightness' may not have worn well, for society changes, and an old system may no longer meet current needs. Further, what may once have seemed appropriate or desirable may not be so regarded in a contemporary setting. In law reform, as in politics, all ends in failure. And this causes difficulty for law, because lawyers see themselves, and the product of their work, as having a special role and a special status, which may cause them to hang on to things that others can see are outmoded.[39] Whether they express themselves

[37] Though social reality is not the same as the brute facts of physical existence, it is nonetheless real. See JR Searle, *The Social Construction of Reality* (Harmondsworth, Allen Lane, Penguin Press, 1995) 79–112. See also JR Searle, *Making the Social World: The Structure of Human Civilization* (Oxford, Oxford University Press, 2010) at 90–122.

[38] Though there is scope for argument about the source of law's authority. Even to make a claim to fundamental shared values such as human rights does not settle the question of authority – what was meant by liberty meant different things in different times and to different categories of people. Here one is content simply to note that English and American laws are created either by national politicians within their tradition of law-making, or by national judges within their tradition of law-making. See, eg, Lord Sumption, 'A Response' in *Lord Sumption and the Limits of the Law*, eds NW Barber et al (Oxford, Hart Publishing, 2016) at 213–14.

[39] In other eyes law may not seem as central to the scheme of things; it may simply be valued for what it does or what it should do. Much of the divide between politicians and judges over the Human Rights Act 1998 or over Brexit relates to how much power judges should have as the third arm of government. That in turn gives rise to the question of accountability. Politicians can be removed but judges cannot. There is an element here of judges creating their own social reality. Where it is effective, society benefits. Where it is ineffective, we simply experience another form of misgovernment. The rhetorical stance of promoters of the rule of law is protective – 'we will protect your rights' – but the rule of law is in truth also about government. One might add that we can enjoy all of our rights and liberties (see John Stewart Mill, *On Liberty*, 3rd edn (London, Longman, Green, Longman, Roberts & Green, 1864) ch 4, 134–67) and still be concerned about who draws the line about where judicial power ends.

in terms of justice or the rule of law, lawyers see themselves as the guardians of the values represented by these concepts,[40] even if the values are not always realised. There is a tendency to gloss over the time-conditioned nature of our values, such that it is easy to confuse the 'was good' with the 'currently good' and the 'currently good' with the 'always good'. The danger is that 'this is the law' is then taken to mean 'this is a good law' and that the law needs no further justification. Further, the act of eliding the 'currently good' and the 'always good' is bolstered by the growing up of schools of thought that over time harden into cultural traditions. Those following on inherit the traditions and their reasoning processes as a whole. In matters truly fundamental to the tradition it may be very difficult to formulate questions where the tradition offers a complete social world-view, albeit that the 'world' so covered is actually quite a small one, such as civil procedure in England.

Yet when a system fails to meet its social obligations and is operating in a way that is socially wasteful then it may be called upon to offer a justification for its existence. Where that justification is unconvincing then change may be forced upon the system and the people involved with it. When Sorabji speaks of paradigm change, he is speaking of it arising from conditions where justifications that were thought reasonable in 1880s (the 'was good'), and which still held sway even in the 1970s and 1980s (the 'currently good'), were considered unreasonable in the late 1990s.

Law delivers a particular good (or way of doing things) that the lawyers think is a good in itself. This, of course, is true not simply of lawyers and the law. People generally dislike change and prefer what is familiar. They get used to social arrangements. A person may not agree with a particular way of doing things, but she will have invested a large amount of intellectual capital in mastering a particular process or gaining the qualification that she needs to appear in a particular arena, or she may simply feel comfortable with how things are. And so a particular individual or group may resist change. And the arguments against change that people deploy may be arguments about the importance of established goals, or may work by linking the importance of the threatened activity in general with the particular local manifestation of it which is being challenged.

B. Rules and Culture

Rules are as much a cultural product as a product of particular historical circumstances. They may represent not just a particular pragmatic solution, but also a

[40] This is also true of writers about civil procedure – even academic writers. One writes that function and functionality matter because one thinks that they do. In critiquing system dysfunctionality, one does so from the assumption that dysfunctional systems are less likely to produce the outcomes one thinks are valuable and which one values. For a very clear view of the constitutional role of the court, see Lord Diplock in *Bremer v South India Shipping Co Ltd* [1981] AC 909, at 977. Lord Woolf used this passage in *WfIR*, ch 1, para 2.

way of doing things that may be well established within a group. Normally the cultural setting makes for progressive change. But sometimes radical change comes because the existing way of doing things no longer seems good enough. Society may have changed, or a system may become inefficient or defective. Both factors have driven legal reform.

If we recognise that social reality is made and therefore capable of being changed, we also need to take into account the fact that social facts are far less plastic than they might appear to the casual observer. In fact, the set of thoughts and behaviours we call 'culture' has tremendous strength and people are very attached to it. Culture helps us connect and communicate with others, and as such people can be very resistant to changes in culture – which is broadly a good thing. Our particular ways of being have been built up over time and handed on down the generations. Our culture represents the things that we value. But in the context of civil litigation reform culture has played a significant dampening role, as we shall see in chapter 4.

C. Roles

Part of a person's social reality relates to the role that she may play as, for example, a legal professional. This role carries particular social obligations, but also confers particular social rights. And the very complex nature of legal rules and processes means that it may take time to master them, and that those who perform a particular operation several times will become better at it. The professional therefore develops a rare skill and so has something saleable. The natural tendency is to work towards maximising profit.

D. Groups

As we engage with social reality, our own interests or group interests come into play, and those interests may well not necessarily serve the wider public interest. So a group may function to prevent competition or protect a particularly profitable way of doing things, or to protect its own existence. And as groups persist through time, a pattern of behaviour is established, indicating a right way of doing things or that a particular solution is preferable in a given set of circumstances. In a judicial context this can be by way of binding authorities imposed by a hierarchy (law), or established ways of doing things (practice) or particular steps that are to be taken in a specific order (procedure). All of these things are bolstered by the way in which the members of the judiciary will internalise values and behaviours – things like what the judiciary is for, and how a judge is supposed to behave in court.

E. Lawyers and Groups

Judges will have their own personal views of the role they occupy as dispensers and administrators of justice. These will impact how judges go about their task. There is also the group aspect to judicial work. There are some things that would be considered simply acceptable or unacceptable. In other cases there would be a range of views that would be recognisable as being appropriate. The same is true of legal practitioners: individual views as to the nature of justice and the role of the professional will fit into societal views about these things. Formal and ethical rules dictate lawyers' behaviour, but group expectations and peer pressure also have their effect. When all this works well this ensures that lawyers play by the rules and also in the spirit of the game. But when it does not work well, the rules can be flouted or the spirit of the game ignored. We shall encounter this in two contexts – attritional warfare in litigation, and judicial failure to fully support the Woolf Reforms.

VI. Pragmatism

John Dewey would have said that the utility of a theory lies in its problem-solving power. We have to be pragmatic: if procedure is to be a supportive vehicle for the administration of the substantive law then it must not be allowed to impede the progress of that which it is supposed to be facilitating.

Of course there is a need for minimum procedural standards and, indeed, for accuracy of outcome. But one also has to see things from the litigants' viewpoint. Where there is a dispute, it needs to be resolved. This requires the parties to come to terms, or for there to be a definitive ruling. In both cases the outcome is to be based on the substantive law. Settlement may offer scope for nuance, for the law is fact-dependent and no party can be wholly confident that it can establish all of its case. But it is the outcome that matters. How the dispute is resolved is, or ought to be, a secondary concern. Given that a dispute exists, any procedural theory has to concentrate on how the dispute may best be resolved, taking into account the resources any process will absorb and the ability of the users to afford or spare those resources. The constitutional context matters, but balancing it against socially wasteful activity is a tricky thing.

A. Absorbing Resources

From a pragmatic perspective there is little point to a process that absorbs so much resource that it makes the situation worse. The difficulty, as Bentham would have said, is that any process will inevitably absorb resources. So the question is how much resource should be absorbed. Some resource will have to be spent on meeting minimum procedural standards in all cases, but whether the highest standards are to be applied fully in every case is a matter on which opinions differ. Woolf's first answer was to try to level the playing field. He wanted to adapt the process to the parties. In this he ultimately failed: the process was adapted to the value of the case and not to the means of the parties. Woolf succeeded, however, in creating three case tracks, thus building in a degree of moderation at the lower levels of the system.

B. Four Factors

Given that there is a dispute and that it needs to be resolved, it is no answer for a party to say, 'I shall not engage for I have no resources'. Neither is a wealthy party entitled to say, 'I have more resources than you so I can exhaust you financially'. What is required is an acceptable means, taking into account the standards factor, the resource factor, the duration factor and the systemisation factor.

i. The Standards Factor

The standards factor includes notions of fair process and adequate process.[41] These are based upon the notions of which behaviour satisfies the criterion of fairness and what is the minimally acceptable interference by the state in the affairs of others. The amount of information required and the quality standards it has to meet ('information input') are currently set by lawyers. It is possible to conceive of making decisions based on a lower level of information input than is currently officially required. In this respect the pre-Woolf cards-on-the-table approach (more information) and the post-Woolf emphasis upon preparatory work (earlier preparation) have undermined the goal of lowering the cost of litigation. If the system operator, the judge, is known to want a high-quality information input then it is hardly surprising if the parties seek to deliver what is expected. There are difficult questions here: What is the threshold test the information input must meet? Perhaps proportionality offers a signpost to the future, but perhaps not. Lawyers make their decisions based on the information input. A truly proportionate approach would require a markedly lower information input for the fast track. This would mean judges would be operating with less information. They might not feel comfortable with this. One accepts that, had more information been available, this might well increase the incidence of decisions that would have

[41] The amount of information required and the quality standards it has to meet are currently set by lawyers. It is possible to conceive of making decisions based on less information or information of a lower quality than is currently officially required. One aspect of the fast-track ought to be to allow less information to be disclosed/prepared. CPR 31.5 appears to be moving us in this direction. The proposed Disclosure Pilot Scheme for the Business and Property Courts is another welcome step.

been decided the other way.[42] This would be a step worth taking if costs are to be controlled.

ii. The Resource Factor

The resource factor is principally financial, but also takes into account the fact that any dispute requires people to give time and attention to it that could be utilised elsewhere, so the cost of litigation is both financial and personal and social.

iii. The Duration Factor

The duration factor allows us to think of the time taken from the inception of a dispute to its resolution. One case may be more complex than another, and thus it is reasonable to expect it to take longer to conclude. Often it is easier to think of categories of case, and to do so by drawing some rough line of assumption of complexity, usually related to value. Categorisation also ensures consistency, which goes to the standards factor.

iv. The Systemisation Factor

The fourth factor is the systemisation factor. This term covers the processes set in motion by the administration of many cases required to be managed in a systematic fashion.

C. Efficiency

The current political intention is that parties should shoulder the cost of maintaining the civil justice system. The user pays – and where costs shifting applies, it is ultimately the loser who pays. It is in the overall interests of users if the system is organised efficiently so that the cost to them is no higher than it needs to be. And the first key to efficiency is an organisation premised on handling a bulk number of cases. This in return requires batching cases by value and by processing time. So a clear set of progression stages for cases is needed. There needs to be a limited number of options as to how a case is to be disposed of at each stage. The downside of this approach is the temptation to dispose of cases by genre, with the result that the treatment each case receives is, by and large, not personalised. It is proposed that the efficiency saving outweighs the loss of personal attention, and that here a pre-set level of care is the friend of efficiency and thus, ultimately, the litigants' friend. This of course raises the question of how much individual judicial

[42] See ch 6 for material on process costs and error costs.

attention a case should receive. Judicial attention is realised in terms of a judge giving individual attention to the case of a particular litigant. An efficient system will ration the amount of judicial time available – partly by penalising those who misuse judicial time. By percentage, most cases are small and should only require a minimum level of judicial involvement prior to trial.

VII. Management and Justice

As we shall see in chapter 2, there has been a great deal of thought given to the relationship between the management of litigation and the delivery of procedural justice. We deal here with the broader jurisprudential currents. John Finnis deals with the question of management. In speaking of the rule of law, of which we can take the civil justice system to be part, Finnis argues[43] that this constitutional feature is aimed at creating a 'certain quality of interaction between ruler and ruled, involving reciprocity and procedural fairness', which 'is very valuable for its own sake; it is not merely a means to other social ends, and may not lightly be sacrificed for other ends. It is not just a "management technique"'.

Having noted the point that procedural justice is not just a management technique, it is worth noting why there is such a focus upon management technique as a way of ensuring the delivery of the core purposes of the civil justice system. Civil procedure matters because it is the vehicle to get people to the point of judgment or settlement. The cost of this process, and the time that it takes, matters because people have limited amounts of money, litigation is a time sink, and a delayed result may both reduce the financial value of the outcome to the winners and make them lose faith in the availability of justice. Worse, expensive and time-consuming litigation may encourage those who expect a loss to play the system in the hoping of putting off the evil day.[44] The availability of justice is one of the pillars of a functioning democracy. It is also a core component of that set of political ideas called the rule of law.[45]

John Gardner has something to offer here. Although Gardner is working within a jurisprudential tradition different from that of Finnis,[46] he argues that Aristotle is not talking about mere forms when he speaks about justice but rather

[43] J Finnis, *Natural Law and Natural Rights* (n 18) 274.

[44] For a general American perspective, see SC Yeazell, 'Unspoken Truths and Misaligned Interests: Political Parties and the Two Cultures of Civil Litigation', 60 *UCLA Law Review* 1752, especially at 1765–72.

[45] Political in the sense of 'this is what our government should and shouldn't do' and 'this is how we should be treated'.

[46] Though going back to Aristotle, who is also the original source of Finnis's neo-thomistic jurisprudence. See also S Clark and R Jackson, *The Reform of Civil Litigation*, 2nd edn (London, Sweet & Maxwell, 2018) (hereinafter '*JnRef*') paras 1-001–1-006. Jackson makes the point that Aristotle is still relevant.

that he uses his conceptions of 'the just' and 'the unjust' to isolate the behaviour and concepts relating to justice[47] as opposed to, say, fortitude. It follows from this that the 'rational horizons' of justice are distinct from the rational horizons of other, distinct virtues,[48] and that, therefore, the object or mission of procedural justice is a distinct one, for 'the definitive adjudicative mission' is to be just.[49]

There is a rehearsal of this point in John Rawls's writing, where he says that 'the basic structure and the associations and social forms within it are each governed by distinct principles in view of their different aims and purposes and their peculiar nature and special requirements'.[50]

All of which give rise to the question, 'For whom does the civil justice system exist?' The short answer to this is 'not for the lawyers'.[51]

A. Peace, Order and Good Government

Society has an interest in its own harmony. This covers both the public interest, with which the state engages, and our interests as individual citizens and as members of the various groups which together make up civil society. The state, or at least some sort of authority, has to interfere to reach a solution and, if necessary, enforce it. Without this, either the parties will resort to self-help, or, more likely, one party will go without redress. Neither of these outcomes is socially beneficial. Public order, social arrangements, families and children, and the functioning of commerce all depend upon the availability of justice mechanisms.

B. Litigants and a Fair Hearing

The justice system may be there for society, but it is also there for the litigants using it at any point in time. The most difficult area comes, surely, in deciding how much information is to be presented to the court for it to base its individual decisions on, the procedural rules being largely oriented around this point. The more the information that is required, the higher the preparation costs. The higher the preparation costs, the less affordable justice is for the citizenry. The fewer the citizens who have real access to justice, the greater the risk of the judiciary's falling short in its higher-level duties.

[47] J Gardner, *Law as a Leap of Faith* (Oxford, Oxford University Press, 2012) 247. Gardner is closely followed at this point.

[48] ibid 242.

[49] ibid 257. These last two points track what will be said in ch 5.

[50] See J Rawls, *Justice as Fairness, a Restatement*, ed Erin Kelly (Cambridge, MA, The Belknap Press, 2001) 11.

[51] A point that emerges clearly from A Zuckerman, 'Litigation management under the CPR: a poorly-used management infrastructure' in D Dwyer (ed), *The Civil Procedure Rules Ten Years On* (Oxford, Oxford University Press, 2009) (hereinafter '*Ten Years*') 89.

The question then is the kind of process that will allow the parties to attempt self-resolution, for in alternative dispute resolution (ADR) the state disengages, or prepare for and attend trial where self-resolution fails, in which case the state is engaged. Substantially different levels of process are required in litigation. Each level must require a broadly right amount of preparation so that the standards factor, the resource factor and the duration factor are satisfied. Proportionate preparation is one of the golden keys. In smaller cases, which form the vast majority by number, it will be further standardised and embedded in the process. Such an approach would be focused upon the needs of users and society, and is the way to husband judicial time for those cases that need direct managerial input. To the extent that Woolf's case management and Jackson's proportionality were embedded in the lower tracks, this ought to be taken further.

Embedded proportionate preparation would satisfy lower minimum standards, impose no greater time or finance costs than are justifiable to achieve those standards, and provide a result or facilitate a settlement within an acceptable timeframe.

VIII. The Function of the English Civil Justice System

The broad current function of the English civil justice system is to:

(a) dispense justice;
(b) according to the law (ie substantive justice);
(c) in an individual case;
(d) with the official procedure working justly (ie procedural justice);
(e) both for the parties in that case; and
(f) for other users of the court system;
(g) so completing the system's required contribution to society at large.

Point (f) reflects the shift in emphasis envisaged, if imperfectly realised, by the CPR. Point (g) reflects the heightened attention given to the role of justice in underpinning society.

In order to discharge the system's function, the judges have to work to manage their caseloads in a hands-on manner so that the parties in each case work in an organised and efficient way.

Unless one understands the relative importance of the aims and nature of substantive justice, there is a danger of giving undue prominence to justice of the procedural kind. Rule 1.1 of the CPR has a narrower scope than the overall function of the civil justice system, dealing, as it does, with procedural justice and not substantive justice. It focuses upon what those applying the CPR, in any given case, can do with procedure as a means of delivering those outcomes at which the civil justice system as a whole aims. To that extent, the overriding objective is, in fact, subordinate to the system that gives it force and whose function it must help to fulfil.[52] The overriding objective plays an important but not solitary role in the delivery of substantive justice. This is an important issue, because it goes to the essence of the existence of the CPR. Whilst both procedure and matters of substance go together to make up the just outcome, there is an ever-present danger of the procedural tail wagging the substantive dog – which is what occurred when the RSC (1965) were in operation.

A. Three Core Purposes of the English Civil Justice System

We can highlight three core purposes[53] of the civil justice system as being:

(a) to provide litigants with substantive justice and the procedures that are a necessary preliminary to it;
(b) to provide concurrent litigants with substantive justice and the procedures that are a necessary preliminary to it;
(c) to aid the proper working of society.

We shall deal with each in turn, starting with individual litigants.

i. Core Purpose One: Litigants and the System

Let us look at things from the perspective of an individual litigant. As far as a typical claimant[54] is concerned, the purpose of the civil justice system is to deliver just results for that claimant in his or her particular case – that is, to give him or her justice according to law, win or lose. The claimant can achieve a just result either through a trial, or through an appropriate settlement before a trial. Ultimately, if the procedure works but the claimant does not get the correct result, that is, justice according to the law, then the civil justice system has not fulfilled its purpose for that particular claimant.[55] But, in like manner, if the system does not function effectively – because the procedure is used ineffectively or is diminished in its effects – then the value of the just result to the individual litigant is also diminished, if not altogether extinguished. If getting the correct answer costs too

[52] Hence the old use of 'the handmaid' or, in modern terms, the executive assistant. In *Re Coles v Ravenshear* [1907] 1 KB 1 (CA), 4, Lord Collins MR said, 'Although I agree that a Court cannot conduct its business without a code of procedure, I think that the relation of rules of practice to the work of justice is intended to be that of handmaid rather than mistress, and the Court ought not to be so far bound and tied by rules, which are after all only intended as general rules of procedure, as to be compelled to do what will cause injustice in the particular case.'

[53] This is not an exhaustive list.

[54] Of course a defendant may wish to avoid this outcome. See also Roscoe Pound, 'Some Principles of Procedural Reform', 4 *Illinois Law* Review 388, 394 (1909–1910).

[55] There is a live question here about the extent to which it is appropriate for all cases to be subjected to the full preparation process from their earliest stages.

much or takes too long[56] then the unfortunate litigant may be impoverished, or the just result may be stale, in that it no longer meets the needs of the moment.[57] So formal substantive justice is not enough; it must have the capacity to be effective. Civil procedure really matters: it is the primary means to transport the parties to the goal of justice according to law.

It follows that civil procedures need to be crafted with, and applied with, practical wisdom. There is a need to be aware and take account of the practicalities of time, money and effort.

ii. Core Purpose Two: Concurrent Litigants and the System

So much for the individual litigant. But, of course, any court will have many cases going through the preparatory stage at any one time. So delays or over-allocation of resources to one case will impact those other litigants who find themselves operating contemporaneously in the same system. If a person books a hospital appointment and then fails to turn up, someone else who could have had that slot has lost out. So the second core purpose of the civil justice system is to provide substantive justice via a civil justice system that works for all litigants within the system. The means by which this purpose is to be achieved is through case management, whether active, in the largest cases, or embedded, in most cases.

iii. Core Purpose Three: English Society and the System

But what about wider society? What stake does it have in ensuring that justice is administered in such a way that the dispensing of just outcomes can be a reality in a world where people do not always live up to their obligations, a world where agreement is not always possible?

In the British political tradition, John Locke[58] argued that the community has become the 'umpire' of our disputes because we have 'resigned' our natural power

[56] Pound said 'they lose sight of the end of procedure, they make scientific procedure an end of itself, and thus, in the result, make adjective law an agency for defeating or delaying substantive law and justice instead of one for enforcing and speeding them': R Pound, 'Mechanical Jurisprudence' (n 15) 617. For procedure as law enforcement, see A Zuckerman, 'Litigation management under the CPR' (n 51) at 90.

[57] A point not lost on the reformers of the 19th century: see, eg, the Second Report made to His Majesty by the Commissioners appointed to inquire into the Practice and Proceedings of the Superior Courts of the Common Law (London, House of Commons, 1830) 17–18, 20, 21, 25, 28–29, 31, 33, 45–46, 51; the Third Report made to His Majesty by the Commissioners appointed to inquire into the Practice and Proceedings of the Superior Courts of the Common Law (London, House of Commons, 1831) 13, 37–38; the Fifth Report made to His Majesty by the Commissioners appointed to inquire into the Practice and Proceedings of the Superior Courts of the Common Law (London, House of Commons, 1833) 8; the Second Report of Her Majesty's Commissioners for inquiring into the Process, Practice, and System of Pleading in the Superior Courts of Common Law (HMSO, London, 1853) 34–35. For a perceptive note on how litigation has changed (at least in the US), see RL Marcus, 'Looking Backward to 1938', 162 *University of Pennsylvania Law Review* 1691 (2014) especially at 1704–07.

[58] J Locke, *Two Treatises of Government*, book II: *Civil Government* (Dublin, J Shepphard and G Nugent, 1779), ch 7, 'Of Political or Civil Government', sec 87 at 212–14.

to the community so that we can appeal to it for protection by the law that it has established.

In the Continental radical tradition, Jean Jacques Rousseau[59] spoke of the social contract – whereby we pool our freedoms in return for protection. On the question of the law, Rousseau was very clear that the fundamental thing that makes the social contract function is that 'whoever refuses to obey the general will shall be constrained to do so by the whole body' of the other citizens. To do otherwise, says Rousseau, would lead to citizens' being exposed to 'vast abuses'.[60]

So the third core purpose of the civil justice system is to aid the working of society: a dysfunctional justice system cannot provide effective support to society. This would be true whether we viewed the issue from a social-contractarian aspect or from rights-orientated perspective. We think it helpful to highlight the social contract aspects, by way of metaphor,[61] to emphasise the social dimension of the interpretation and application of rules of court.

IX. Reading the Rules

With the overriding objective, under the CPR, it is perhaps best to think of it as normally taking effect through being embedded within the detail of the rules, in that the form of any particular procedure is designed to further the overriding objective. However, there are times where the court, for example at the directions stage, has a discretion and can make a series of choices. Here the court is able to have a relatively free, if principled, resort to the overriding object. This is because it is up to the individual judge to craft a solution that will deliver substantive and procedural justice using the available mechanisms of the CPR.

In reading the rules it is helpful for us to bear in mind the following:

(a) *Each rule is there for a reason.* Knowing the reason enables us to give an answer to the question, 'Why do we have this rule?' The broad reasoning underpinning most of the rules is that the case is to be properly prepared for trial so as to serve as the foundation for as accurate a decision as possible, given the restrictions or limitations inherent to the type of track to which a case may be allocated.[62] There is, however, more to each rule than a broad underpinning.

[59] JJ Rousseau, *The Social Contract*, book I, ed & tr Maurice Cranston (Harmondsworth, Penguin Books, 1968) ch VII, 64.

[60] This is an important justification for the imposition of sanctions in civil procedure. Pressure and punishment are a necessary component of a functioning justice system.

[61] There is of course no social contract in fact, but people may feel an obligation to a social group, and the group in turn may influence the way they behave. The idea of the social contract, or of duties or obligations, has the effect of modelling, instructing and shaping the behaviour of people and the group of which they are part. In an American context, the Constitution plays the same role.

[62] Exceptions would relate, eg, to reasoning that weak cases should not proceed to trial. Value is likely to be a significant factor in allocation to track, and is also likely to be a significant factor in indicating what is, and is not, proportionate in terms of case preparation.

Each rule is there for a reason: CPR 24.4 is there because weak cases need to be weeded out. At this level, reason can merge into function.

(b) *Each rule has a function.* Knowing the function of the rule enables us to give an answer to the question, 'What does this rule do?'

(c) *Each rule has a place in a sequence of actions.* Knowing the place in the process where it appropriate to use the particular rule of procedure enables us to give an answer to the question, 'When is this rule to be applied?'

A. Intention, Action and Outcome

Let us imagine a proceduralist who wishes to design a simple set of civil procedural rules, which will only ever be applied once by one judge in a case concerning two parties: the process is simplified so that the process can be seen clearly. Our proceduralist is faced with three constituent parts in the process of the design and operation of the procedural rules: *intention*, *action* and *outcome*.

The operation of our hypothetical rules requires us to understand the intention behind the rules, the action required to effect the purpose and the outcome to be achieved. Intention comprises both the goal chosen (what we want) and the reasons behind that choice (why we want it). Action, from the judicial perspective, involves both interpretation of the rules and the discretionary application of the rules, particularly in the context of case management (how we are going to get what we want). If intention and action are not in alignment then the outcome will not fulfil the purpose. Even where intention and action are in alignment, the desired outcome may still be frustrated.

The term 'outcome' covers the actual state of affairs that transpires, a state which may or may not align with the goal chosen at the stage of intention ('What happened?' and 'Is this what we wanted?').

Stating a specific goal should indicate, at the least, our hypothetical court's direction of travel in the one case before it. It should also help with any application of the rules that may be required. However, in practice, matters are not so simple, for purposes tend to be expressed generally without sufficient binding or guiding detail; the emphasis upon case management gives much scope for the general purpose to be defeated by the quantity or quality of the preparatory steps an individual judge may require; and the judge may bring to the exercise of interpretation and application an intention that is distinct from the intention behind the relevant set of rules.[63]

[63] See ch 3.

B. The Meaning of 'Philosophy'

In the curial realm, the Court of Appeal has spoken of 'the philosophy underlying this approach'.[64] The term 'philosophy' is a slippery one, and is capable of different meanings. It is helpful, therefore, to distinguish between the different ways in which the term 'philosophy' can be used. In normal usage, sometimes 'philosophy' can be used to mean 'the philosophy behind the rules' (ie what we want and why we want it). Here 'the philosophy behind the rules' is used in the sense of the specific intentions the rules were meant to achieve. The phrase covers both the end to which action is deliberately directed, namely some conception of justice, and the reason why one considers this to be desirable. As to the end, the system is there to deliver substantive justice – justice according to law. Why that end is desirable can be viewed from distinct positions – jurisprudential, political or social, to name but a few. Alternatively, 'philosophy' may be used in the sense of a 'guiding philosophy' (ie how we will get what we want). Here, 'guiding philosophy' refers to how people choose and use the means to an end, in a considered manner according to reason. It covers the sense of action stemming from a reasoned approach. Part of the reasoning process will include the consideration of procedural justice, a term that covers fairness, accuracy, speed, cost and accessibility, amongst other factors.

Having addressed intention and action, we come to outcome, to which people do not usually apply the term 'philosophy'. Outcome has a twofold aspect, as the state of affairs achieved has to satisfy two different tests: it must be just according to law, that is it must reflect the substantive law; and it must be just according to the secondary test of procedural justice.

Having a guiding philosophy is a good thing, for it gives meaning to action and should help in dealing with problems and the formulation of acceptable solutions. But the act of putting a guiding philosophy into practice, through the medium of procedural rules, might end up undermining the specific ends our hypothetical proceduralist had hoped to achieve. This is the problem that beset the courts under the RSC,[65] where the theory of justice on the merits sat uneasily with established views concerning party autonomy in litigation,[66] the cultural tendency to see litigation as being like a sport and the linked idea of the limited role of the judge as an umpire. This produced a result that is recognised as being unsatisfactory because of the financial cost, time cost and effort cost it imposed upon the parties.

[64] *Hytec Information Systems Ltd v Coventry City Council* [1997] 1 WLR 1666 (CA), per Ward LJ at 1674–75. Editorial note: in what follows, to speak of *intention*, *action* and *outcome* is to highlight only part of a process flow. If fully set out it would look something like *information*, *reflection*, *reason*, *intention*, *consultation*, *implementation*, *action*, *interaction* and *reaction*, *outcome*. We look here only at *intention*, *action* and *outcome*.

[65] See especially *SorECJ* (n 2) 56–74; and *ZoCP* (2013) (n 4) paras 1.68–1.96.

[66] Which in practice meant lawyer autonomy.

There is a further difficulty, in that it is not easy to simply disentangle reality from the concepts. Ultimately, such an exercise would be futile. Both procedural and substantive justice are abstract concepts that have to be realised in the social world, where the factors to be addressed in case management will vary in weight from case to case. Although questions of expedition, proportionality and cost fall to be addressed through the procedural rules, and thus naturally seem to fit within the rubric of procedural justice, there is also an argument that they are a necessary, if not sufficient, condition of substantive justice. A justice system dispensing legally and factually accurate decisions that are unaffordable or delivered too slowly is actually failing to deliver effective justice, even if it is delivering the formally 'correct' answer. Justice must mean more than that.[67]

C. Why Have A Specific Intention?

In practical terms, the act of specifying an intention (what we want) will do the following:

(a) it will force one to think about exactly what it is one is trying to achieve;
(b) it will enable one to think clearly about what steps need to be taken to realise the intention;
(c) it will give one the opportunity to think about the values inherent in both the end and the means, and enable one to tailor any particular steps to match one's values;
(d) it will enable one to judge against the intended goal the efficacy of all steps proposed.

Steps that might work to lead one astray from the main goal or to frustrate it altogether can thus be avoided, or their impact minimised.

D. Tension Between the General and the Specific

Nevertheless, the existence of a purpose clause can create a tension between the plain meaning of the words of a specific procedure and the wording of the purpose clause. The approach evidenced in the responses to FRCP 1 and CPR 1.1 suggests that the particular tends to triumph over the general, a situation that relates, in part, to the intention or underlying philosophy brought by the judge performing the task of interpretation. In America, the approach that was taken by Scalia J

[67] This is a complex issue: see, eg, *SorECJ* (n 2). Sorabji thinks that the substantive and the procedural aspects of justice are both covered by CPR 1.1 (ibid 146–47). On the other hand, he uses the terms 'justice's direct end' and 'justice's collateral ends' in the subheadings to chs 5 and 6 of his work, ibid 137 and 165. The collateral end point originated with Jeremy Bentham, in his *Introduction to the Rationale of Judicial Evidence, book II*, ed John Bowring (Edinburgh, William Tate, 1843) – see ibid ch 3, 286.

makes this difficulty very apparent.[68] In England, the epistemological variance between the judges' own intentions and the intentions of the CPR was such as to create difficulty under the early CPR, as Sorabji has shown.

The common approach of the courts in England and in the federal courts in the United States is to prefer the detailed language of specific rules over the more general language of the relevant purpose clause. In America, Scalia J exemplifies the narrow approach to construction. This approach proceeds upon on the basis that it is the job of a court to interpret the rules and not to infringe on the province of the legislator. In England, although, in theory, a court may choose to develop new procedure (which is subsequently adopted by the rules committee),[69] in practice it is for champions (such as Woolf and Jackson) to innovate and for the rules committee to implement whichever innovations it thinks appropriate.

In most cases, an intention or purpose clause functions by guiding the process of interpretation where the meaning of a rule is not clear. This is the course taken both in England under the CPR and in America under the FRCP (1938). There is a marked tendency on both sides of the Atlantic for the courts to be conservative in their handling of purpose clauses relating to civil procedure. In effect, this means that the specific detail of rules triumphs over the more general language of the purpose clause. In both England and America the judges may bring their own theories of justice to the interpretation of the rules in a way which may prevent the purpose of the rules from being realised effectively. Scalia J's approach to interpretation is based upon a theory of meaning that in turn is built upon a theory of the role of the judiciary. In England, the early reception of the CPR highlights the prevalence of the 'justice on the merits' theory, even when it had, officially at least, been rendered redundant. Current attempts to apply the rules are suggestive of a theory of accuracy that continues to impact not just the interpretation of the rules, but also the way in which they are applied.

The approach of this book is to look at the mechanics of justice in the context of the wider societies in which they are realised or fail to materialise. It is people who receive or fail to receive justice, and because this is a matter of social and political significance, this question has received sustained attention in the two common law jurisdictions we shall be considering – the United States and England.[70] In the case of the former, the political involvement has been overt, at least at the stage of naissance.

[68] For further analysis of Scalia J's general approach, see WN Eskridge Jr, 'The New Textualism' 37 *UCLA Law Review* 621 (1990), especially at 650–62.

[69] See Brooke LJ in *YD (Turkey) v Secretary of State for the Home Department* [2006] 1 WLR 1646, [22] (CA); and also H Brooke, 'Some thoughts on the first seven and a half years of the CPR' in *Ten Years* (n 51) 460.

[70] The US federal courts operate on the common law system, as do nearly all the courts of the separate constituent American States. Civil justice in Wales is not a devolved matter, although the move towards separating the one jurisdiction of England and Wales into two separate jurisdictions is gathering pace.

E. The Overriding Objective

We turn to look at the way in which the civil justice system in England operates. The current English civil justice system uses the CPR both as a necessary foundation for the achievement of justice according to law, and as an instrument[71] to try to achieve substantive justice through procedural means. The civil justice system can, at best, only deliver what it is designed to achieve. So if, for example, the mechanisms for promoting, protecting or ensuring speed or economy are not built into the system, the designers' intentions may never be realised.

There are, within the CPR, several interlocking procedures that, in theory, incorporate the values of the overriding objective. These are intended to promote the outcomes to which CPR 1.1 expressly looks. In other cases, the court has to use its discretion to further the overriding objective – case management is the example par excellence of this. As we shall see, there is no guarantee that the procedures, if properly applied, will work in a manner that delivers the outcomes envisaged by the overriding objective.

The current English high-level intention, set out in the overriding objective, is that cases should be dealt with justly and at proportionate cost. This intention needs to be delivered by a system that, in turn, needs the concerted work of a group of people, the judges, to implement the procedures in a patterned manner in such a way as to work towards the goal. But the current system and its procedures have a historical origin – that is, they were not completely new in 1998. And the system has to be operated in a refractory and complicated world where neither parties nor lawyers will, necessarily, see compliance or cooperation as a desirable thing.

Woolf made the overriding objective the first part of the rules the English reader encounters. Here, justice is conceived of as being concerned with the reaching of:

(a) a just and accurate[72] decision;
(b) based on the merits of the case; but
(c) in the context of this being accomplished in a timely and cost effective manner;
(d) with the needs of other court users being borne in mind.

Achieving the balance between (b) and (c) is not easy, as witness the difficulties with the old CPR 3.9 and the new CPR 3.9.[73]

The CPR's overriding objective of 'dealing with cases justly' and, later, 'dealing with cases justly and at proportionate cost' is not only party cognisant but system

[71] See *ZoCP* (2013) (n 4) para 1.2.

[72] Accuracy is unexpressed, but see *ZoCP* (2013) (n 4) paras 1.32–13.4. There is, further, scope for argument about whether 'deal … justly' relates to substantive justice, procedural justice or both.

[73] The 'old CPR 3.9' means the rule in force until 30 March 2013. The 'new CPR.3.9' means that rule in force from 1 April 2013.

Compliance is not an end in itself, even for procedure's collateral ends. Compliance is one of the means to deliver procedure's collateral aims.

cognisant too. System-level issues are given priority in the event of a party's failure to comply with a procedural obligation.

The overriding objective sets out the CPR's intention (in Rule 1.1(1)) and then illustrates this with some examples of action (Rule 1.1(2)) which are both specific enough to be realisable in their own right, and general enough to supplement our understanding of the meaning of CPR 1.1(1). This is helpful, not least because the more abstract the intention, the more difficult it is for the outcome to be realised through action. Rule 1.1(2) plays a valuable role in demonstrating what 'justly and at proportionate cost' looks like. Further, in the case of proportionality, CPR 1.1(2)(c) offers criteria for judging whether something is proportionate or not, thus rooting it within the world of application. Notably, neither 'justly' nor 'at proportionate cost' is defined further, although in the case of the latter some help can be gained from CPR 44.3(5) – the technical wording of which is noticeably more laboured than CPR 1.1, which is still recognisably in Woolf's plain language.[74] Perhaps the very simplicity and lack of particularisation in Rule 1.1 of the CPR is part of the enduring challenge here.

X. Conclusion

To recap, individual litigants, concurrent litigants and society as a whole, all have a real interest in the civil procedure system's functioning efficiently and effectively so that it produces substantive justice that operates individually, concurrently and corporately.

So civil procedure is a very important vehicle, yet it is not a direct end in itself. It follows that the organisation of the procedures must be such as to promote efficient handling,[75] with the minimum of diminution of the value of the final 'product' – justice according to the law. The term 'product' is not used here to denigrate that state of affairs which, if it is realised, we call justice. Rather, the term is used to denote the fact that justice according to law has to be 'produced' by the civil justice system. If the system misfires, it produces no 'product'. To speak of justice as a product is not to downgrade the public service or societal aspects of justice but to point to the fact that outcomes matter.

How the does the system get people to behave as the system requires? Perhaps you might hope to get them to the point where, like the functionaries in a bureaucracy, people do good because they see good in it.[76] But one has to make allowance for 'human recalcitrance',[77] which may arise for reasons that are selfish or reasons

[74] Jackson LJ worked hard at the new rule, see *JnRef* (2018) (n 46) para 5-008.

[75] For an American view on the justification for limiting party autonomy, see JM Glover, 'A Regulatory Theory of Legal Claims', 70 *Vanderbilt Law Review* 221, 258–82 (2017).

[76] J Finnis, *Natural Law and Natural Rights* (n 18) 266.

[77] ibid 260.

which are noble, or even for reasons that may simply be ill-founded. It is the struggle to get litigants and their representatives to engage with the system, in such a way as to ensure that they play their part in its operating effectively and efficiently, that has been the hallmark of civil litigation reform in recent times.

Having looked at the parties, concurrent litigants in the system and the system in its social context, we turn to consider the various theories and explanations used on both sides of the Atlantic when talking about civil justice, from the early twentieth century into our own era.

2

What is Civil Procedure For?

I. American Themes and Perspectives

A. Society and the Law

In 1905, Roscoe Pound considered the question of the need for a philosophy of law. He was not speaking about the particular content of common law but of its general epistemic traits. This is relevant for this enquiry, because the common law is never encountered by litigants in its general traits but in its particular content and effect. The common law is created by judges holding key offices at different points in history. Their work is often cumulative in effect. Save for rare cases, the common law is dispensed and not made by ordinary judges trying individual cases. The common law is administered by judges through the system of procedure contained in the procedural rules.

Pound wrote, 'To my mind, the real danger to the common law is in another quarter. Hitherto the people have been with it.' But, he went on,

> today the popular side is not that of the individual, but that of society … To-day, for the first time, the common law finds itself arrayed against the people; for the first time, instead of securing for them what they most prize, they know it chiefly as something that continually stands between them and what they desire.[1]

Pound noted that, of course, the view as to what is acceptable and desirable changes over time:

> Men have changed their views as to the relative importance of the individual and of society; but the common law has not … Today the isolated individual is no longer taken for the center of the universe … We no longer hold that society exists entirely for the sake of the individual. We recognize that society is in some wise a co-worker with each in what he is and in what he does …[2]

Pound thought that 'the spirit of the common law' was to be seen in

> a fundamental proposition that law exists for individuals, and hence is to deal with every question as a contest between individuals, is to decide it on its individual facts,

[1] R Pound, 'Do We Need a Philosophy of Law?' 5 *Columbia Law Review* 339, 344 (1905).
[2] ibid 346.

> not arbitrarily, but as like cases have been adjudged for others, and is to allow the parties to fight out the contest for themselves, and as much as possible in their own way.[3]

Which leads us on to the case of procedure.

Pound saw that the problem was an 'exaggerated respect for the individual', which manifested itself through the contentious process. He went on to cite two relatively contemporary writers, Pollock and Manson. Pollock had said:

> Litigation is a game, in which the court is umpire. The rules are in the knowledge of the court and will be declared and applied by it as required. It is for the parties to learn the rules and play the game correctly at their peril.[4]

More robustly, Manson put the issues thus:

> Law is in the nature of a cock-fight, and the litigant who wishes to succeed must try and get an advocate who is a game bird with the best pluck and the sharpest spurs.[5]

Pound could therefore say that 'the common-law theory of litigation is that of a fair fist fight, according to the canons of the manly art, with a court to see fair play and prevent interference'. He thought that Americans

> strive in every way to restrain the trial judge and to insure the individual litigants a fair fight, unhampered by mere considerations of justice. To give them this fair play, we sacrifice public time and money; incidentally also – for if all men are equal, their pocketbooks are not – giving certain litigants a conspicuous advantage in reality through a theoretical equality.[6]

As a result, the 'individual … gets so much fair play, that the public gets very little'.[7]

And even legal practitioners are a part of society:

> [I]t is because of the close connection of the lawyer with the vital machinery of our society. In view of his relation to a state wherein the most intimate problems of sociology and economics are tried in actions of trespass and suits to enjoin repeated trespasses, must not a philosophy of law founded on a sound knowledge of the elements of the social and political science of to-day form part – and a necessary part – of the equipment of the trained lawyer?[8]

[3] R Pound, 'Do We Need a Philosophy of Law?'(n 1)348–49.

[4] The citation is from F Pollock, *Expansion of the Common Law* (London, Steven & Sons Ltd, 1904) 32. Pollock was making the point both that the perils of pleading pre-1870 were a continuation of a longer pattern of behaviour and that the same pattern of party autonomy and responsibility was still alive in his day. Contrast *Davies v Eli Lilly & Co* [1987] 1 WLR 428 (CA), 431–32. This case concerned disclosure of confidential material.

[5] The citation is from E Manson, 'Cross-Examination: A Socratic Fragment' (1892) 8 *Law Quarterly Review* 160, 161. This is a spoof of a platonic dialogue leading to the conclusion cited by Pound.

[6] R Pound, 'Do We Need a Philosophy of Law?'(n 1) 347.

[7] ibid 348.

[8] R Pound, 'Do We Need a Philosophy of Law?' (n 1) 353.

B. The Administration of Justice

Given its importance and the unique quality of what it is trying to engineer, the effective administration of justice requires the application of methods of case management. Roscoe Pound[9] made this point as follows:

> [R]ules are not prescribed and administered for their own sake but to achieve social ends … the problem is not merely how … law administering functions are exercised, but how they may be exercised so as best to achieve their purpose, and what conception of these functions by those who perform them will best conduce thereto. The true juristic theory, the true juristic method is one that brings forth good works.

Pound reminds us that the administration of justice (civil procedure in our case) requires both the exercise of a method, and a theory[10] of what is being done, in order to achieve the desired result.[11]

C. Law and the Social World

Writing in 1924, John Dewey highlighted the importance of the law's keeping up with changes in social conditions. What he had to say related to the substantive law, but it is also of relevance to the question of legal procedure, because it, too, is bound by tradition and by rules.

> There is of course every reason why rules of law should be as regular and as definite as possible. But the amount and kind of antecedent assurance which is actually attainable is a matter of fact, not of form. It is large wherever social conditions are pretty uniform … It is much less wherever invention is active and when new devices … bring about new forms of human relationship … But statutes have never kept up with the variety and subtlety of social change … Hence to claim that old forms are ready at hand that cover every case and that may be applied by formal syllogizing is to pretend to a certainty and regularity which cannot exist in fact. The effect of the pretension is to increase practical uncertainty and social instability.[12]

And

> Here is where the great practical evil of the doctrine of immutable and necessary antecedent rules comes in. It sanctifies the old; adherence to it in practise constantly widens the gap between current social conditions and the principles used by the courts. The effect is to breed irritation, disrespect for law, together with virtual alliance between the judiciary and entrenched interests that correspond most nearly to the conditions under which the rules of law were previously laid down.[13]

[9] R Pound, 'The Scope and Purpose of Sociological Jurisprudence Pt 1', 24 *Harvard Law Review* 591, 598 (1911).

[10] What Pound calls a 'conception'.

[11] Pound calls this 'good works'. These are points that RG Bone explores in 'Making Effective Rules: The Need For a Procedure Theory', 61 *Oklahoma Law Review* 319 (2008).

[12] J Dewey, 'Logical Method and Law', 10 *Cornell Law Review* 17, 26 (1924). R Pound makes a similar argument in 'Do We Need a Philosophy of Law?' (n 1) 345–48.

[13] J Dewey, 'Logical Method and Law' (n 12) 26.

In *The Historic Background of Corporate Legal Personality*,[14] Dewey speaks of definitions that function by looking at consequences. With such definitions, 'a thing is – is defined as – what it does', the action/effect 'being stated in terms of specific effects extrinsically wrought in other things'. He argues that this is what Charles S Peirce called 'the pragmatistic rule', where we 'Consider what effects, which might conceivably have practical bearings, we conceive the object of our conception to have. Then, our conception of these effects is the whole of our conception of the object.'

D. Rules as a Means to an End

Edson R Sunderland was an important player in the formulation of the FRCP:[15] in the early 1920s he was arguing[16] that procedure should be taught as 'a mere mechanism designed to reach certain results. It is valuable solely as a means to an end.'[17] With that point in mind, the fundamental procedural principles would 'formulate themselves', and those same principles would be made 'available for the service of society'. Sunderland thought this point of such importance that he went as far as to argue that Law Schools should be teaching an iconoclasm that rejected respect for any procedural rule 'which is unable to prove its value as a convenient means to a legitimate end'.

Sunderland contrasted on the one hand the 'primary' role of substantive law, which constitutes society, and the 'secondary … derivative' and operative role of the procedural law. Sunderland argues that ultimately procedure could be changed 'without causing a tremor in the social structure', because procedure has no 'universal quality, save perhaps for its own flexibility'.

By 1938, Sunderland, had concluded that the purpose of the FRCP 'is to eliminate technical matters by removing the basis for technical objections … and to make litigation as inexpensive, as practicable and as convenient, as can be done'.[18]

Sunderland noted the tension between 'two theories' of rule drafting: first, 'to draw the rules so as to expressly lay down provisions covering all contingencies'; second, 'to cover the main features by explicit rules', leaving other matters for the discretion of the judge.[19] Whilst the text of FRCP(1938) Rule 1 was not explicitly addressed, Sunderland did talk about the difficulty in giving a 'connected

[14] J Dewey, 'The Historic Background of Corporate Legal Personality', 35 *Yale Law Journal* 660, 660–61 (1925–1926), internal references omitted.

[15] A survey of Sunderland's work can be found in 'Legal Writings of Edson R Sunderland', 58 *Michigan Law Review* 41 (1959–1960), a list created by his family for Sunderland's 84th birthday.

[16] ER Sunderland, 'Inquiry Concerning the Functions of Procedure in Legal Education', 21 *Michigan Law Review* 372 (1922–1923).

[17] ibid 379.

[18] ER Sunderland, 'The New Federal Rules', 45 *West Virginia Law Quarterly* 5, 30 (1938).

[19] ibid 6–7.

account' of the rules,[20] likening the process of setting out the rules to 'reading from a dictionary'.[21]

The next year (1939) Sunderland was referring to 'a certain economic extravagance' in the 'controlling principle' of civil procedure that parties should frame and present the controversy between them; this was coupled with the lack of control over the principal vehicle for the work of framing: originally the pleadings alone, and later the pleadings coupled with pre-trial procedure.[22]

The same year Charles E Clark, a significant contributor to the shaping of the FRCP (1938), speaking of the new rules, said 'procedural rules are but means to an end, means to the enforcement of substantive justice'.[23] With this is mind, and looking back from the vantage point of 1950, Clark argued that procedural rules should be seen 'as grants or creations of judicial power'[24] and, as such, rules needed to be 'stated in the terms of the functions they are to perform or the results they are to achieve',[25] so careful draftsmanship may require the spelling out of things that otherwise might seem obvious.[26] The functionalist nature of the rules meant that specialist expertise was required in judicial decision-making under them.[27] The purpose of the grant of power was to enable the court to engage in the 'effective and wise administration of court business',[28] or for 'effective judicial administration'.[29] Clark argued that the grant of power also carried with it the negation of old powers. The risk, therefore, was that old behaviours would reassert themselves under any new regime of rules,[30] because judges would 'stick to what they have known in the past'.[31] Further, because procedure in general would tend 'to harden and solidify', the reality was that any new system would become 'as hard and unyielding'[32] as the one that it replaced. Because of these things, rule-making would never be a complete success and reform would always be an ongoing process.[33]

[20] ER Sunderland, 'The New Federal Rules' (n 18) 5.

[21] ibid 30.

[22] ER Sunderland, 'Growth of Pre-Trial Procedure', 44 *Commercial Law Journal* 406, 406 (1939).This paper is a shortened version of 'Theory and Practice of Pre-trial Procedure' 36:2 *Michigan Law Review* 215 (December 1937).

[23] CE Clark, 'Fundamental Changes Effected by the New Federal Rules I', 15 *Tennessee Law Review* 551, 551 (1939). The article gives a useful review of the reform process from Clark's side. It also records that members of the Committee were encouraged not to write their own commentaries on the FRCP: ibid 555.

[24] CE Clark, 'Special Problems in Drafting and Interpreting Procedural Codes and Rules', 3 *Vanderbilt Law Review* 493, 493 (1950).

[25] ibid 493 and 499. Clark saw the Field Code's failure to take this road as part of the reason for its failure: ibid 499. Cf CPR 1.1.

[26] CE Clark, 'Special Problems (n 24) 497.

[27] ibid 496.

[28] CE Clark, 'Special Problems (n 24).

[29] ibid 495. Cf CPR 3.1.

[30] CE Clark, 'Special Problems (n 24) 497.

[31] ibid 501.

[32] CE Clark, 'Special Problems (n 24) 507.

[33] ibid 507–08. Cf S Clark and R Jackson, *The Reform of Civil Litigation*, 2nd edn (London, Sweet & Maxwell, 2018) (hereinafter '*JnRef*'), para 29-003.

E. What the Early Twentieth Century Law Reformers Wished to Achieve

As well as keeping up to date, it is necessary for a system to operate properly. And for that it needs a conceptual apparatus. But concepts can be difficult to apply with ease. Concepts are necessary for the conduct of civil litigation, but it is the consequences that matter.

Paul D Carrington offers the following explanation of the motivations of the law reform movement in the first third of the twentieth century: the law reform movement wanted to change the way that people behaved within litigation; Pound and other reformers sought the depoliticisation of court rule-making;[34] the reformers wanted to promote general simple rules that would not be distorted by special interest groups;[35] and the reformers wanted to promote understanding of 'coherence in rules'.[36]

Looking more specifically at the FRCP, David L Shapiro identifies the 1930s reformers as having three goals:[37]

(a) the goal of overall change: the detail of the rules would change the way in which the federal courts operated;[38]
(b) the goal of uniformity: they would achieve a higher uniformity of federal practice;[39] and
(c) the goal of flexibility: the reformers wanted to avoid rules that would be shaped by rigidity and technicality.[40] 'The key then was an increase in flexibility.'

Shapiro notes that there was 'some inconsistency between … the goal of uniformity and the goal of flexibility'.[41]

Judith Resnik, noting the increasing modern emphasis upon the use of ADR to try to settle cases, considers that it is possible that the 1930s reformers were at heart hostile 'towards procedure used as an obstacle to truth';[42] that the political culture of America in the 1930s may have been different and that civil reformers may have had a genuine belief in 'justice, truth, and the grand accomplishments of the legal profession'; that the historic reduction in the way that civil procedure

[34] PD Carrington, '"Substance" and "Procedure" in the Rules Enabling Act', 1989 *Duke Law Journal* 281, 301 (1989). Note that depoliticisation was a way of making sure that changes to the rules were actually made.

[35] ibid 302–04.

[36] PD Carrington, '"Substance"' (n 34) 307.

[37] DL Shapiro, 'Federal Rule 16: A Look at the Theory And Practice of Rulemaking', 137 *University of Pennsylvania Law Review* 1969 (1989).

[38] ibid 1972.

[39] DL Shapiro, 'Federal Rule 16', (n 37), 1973.

[40] ibid 1975.

[41] DL Shapiro, 'Federal Rule 16', (n 37), 1975. Shapiro confirms this position ibid 1993.

[42] J Resnik, 'Failing Faith: Adjudicatory Procedure in Decline', 53 *University of Chicago Law Review* 494, 540 (1986).

is valued may simply be 'based upon a realistic appraisal of its potential', which is to say that we are more realistic about what can be accomplished;[43] and, lastly, that people are only interested in results, that civil procedure 'is only a technique for establishing another agenda', being only 'a means to an end'.

F. Objectives and Systems: Bridging the Gap

We continue with an American perspective:[44]

> The first and chief function of the judicial department of government is to administer justice, that is, to determine and prevent controversies by applying substantive law through court proceedings. For the fair, orderly, and convenient administration of justice, it is necessary to have certain rules regulating pleading and practice (process, preliminaries other than pleading, trial, judgment, execution) in the courts of justice.

We pause to note that in England it would be conventional to refer to the independent judiciary rather than to emphasise the governmental nature of the law. Nevertheless, in English constitutional theory there is a separation of powers, viz the powers of government, so in this sense the power to make judgments is a governmental power. Further, at common law, judges make or develop law as much as they apply it. Making law is a governmental function.

Williams goes on to say that 'The second function of the judicial department is to administer fairly and intelligently these rules of procedure because substantive rights depend upon such administration of procedural rules.' The civil justice systems of the common law world are there to produce *outcomes*. It is to be hoped that those outcomes are the ones the designers of each system had wished to attain. If they are not then the system can be said to have failed to achieve its purpose.

In the modern era, the outcomes the civil justice system is producing have come under the microscope in common law jurisdictions, and where those outcomes and their consequent effects are seen to be undesirable, steps have been taken in an attempt to eliminate the undesirable outcomes and replace them with desirable ones. This has required reformers in the US and in England to consider the vexed question of what their civil justice system is for: a consideration that necessarily requires thought about the nature of procedural justice in particular.

This leads us on to consider Charles E Clark's 1950 paper on 'Special Problems'.

[43] ibid 541.

[44] T Williams, 'The Source of Authority for Rules of Court Affecting Procedure', 22 *Washington University Law Quarterly* 459, 471 (1937). (Much of Williams' discussion is based on the analysis of the separation of powers in the Supreme Court of Missouri's decision in *Clark v Austin*, 101 SW (2d) 977, 988–89 (Mo 1937). That case concerned disbarment of an attorney and is not directly on the point of our discussion.)

G. Charles E Clark: The Voice of Experience

Clark's starting point was apparently a straightforward version of the 'justice on the merits' theory: 'Procedure is a means to an end, not an end in itself ... its rules must be applied to do justice in the particular case.'[45]

This was not a new position, in 1933–34 Clark had said, 'While I have never claimed to be a functionalist ... I do not object to [the label] if by it [my critic] means one who tries to view the law in the light of its practical application and usefulness.' And:

> Court procedure, to be workable, must be treated as a means to an end, not an end in itself. Instead of being controlled by formidable rules whose arbitrary character is only concealed and tempered by their vagueness, it should be operated flexibly by wise administrators exercising wide discretion.[46]

Clark went on to say that procedural rules were to be seen as 'grants or creations of judicial power',[47] which should be given to the court to enable it to control the parties[48] and which were there 'for effective judicial administration' rather than just directed at individual litigants.[49] He also warned of 'the inveterate tendency of past dogmas to reassert themselves'.[50]

Clark noted that giving a court power did not guarantee that it would use it, for 'judicial inertia, precedent-mindedness' and 'love of technical niceties' could get in the way.[51] He observed that the new grant of a power might overturn previous negative rulings, and so some intellectual struggle could be expected. Such new grants might 'seem to be going too far in stating the obvious',[52] but many things needed to be spelled out for the avoidance of doubt because of the tendency of courts, 'left to their own devices, without any precise guide,' to 'stick to what they have known in the past'.[53] Draftsmen therefore, Clark warned, needed to be aware

[45] CE Clark, 'Special Problems' (n 24) 498.

[46] CE Clark, 'Cause of Action', 82 *University of Pennsylvania Law Review* 354, 360 and 362 (1933–1934). Clark was saying this in the context of an attack on his position by Dean Gavitt. The article is a good illustration of Clark's readiness to play hardball.

[47] CE Clark, 'Special Problems' (n 24) 493.

[48] ibid 495. Cf CPR 1.4.

[49] CE Clark, 'Special Problems' (n 24) 495. Cf CPR 1.1(2)(e).

[50] A point which is a key theme of J Sorabji, *English Civil Justice after the Woolf and Jackson Reforms: A Critical Analysis* (Cambridge, Cambridge University Press, 2014) (hereinafter '*SorECJ*').

[51] CE Clark, 'Special Problems' (n 24) 493.

[52] ibid 497. Contrast A Zuckerman, *Zuckerman on Civil Procedure: Principles of Practice* (hereinafter '*ZoCP*') (London, Sweet & Maxwell, 2013) para 1.32, 'it goes without saying'. Zuckerman's earlier works are A Zuckerman, *Civil Procedure* (London, Lexis Nexis Butterworths, 2003) and A Zuckerman, *Civil Procedure: Principles of Practice* (London, Sweet & Maxwell, 2006).

[53] CE Clark, 'Special Problems' (n 24) 401. Precisely the concerns behind Lord Woolf MR's statement in *Biguzzi v Rank Leisure plc* [1999] 1 WLR 1926 (CA), 1934, about old authorities not generally being of relevance. *ZoCP*, (2003) (n 5) para 1.49, was firmly of the view that it was folly to try to reinvent the procedural wheel. Here Zuckerman was following, more strongly, the line laid out in *Purdy v Cambran* [2000] CP Rep 67 (CA). Further comment is to be found from D Dwyer (ed), *The Civil Procedure Rules Ten Years On* (Oxford, Oxford University Press, 2009) (hereinafter '*Ten Years*') 67.

of the 'pulls, pressures and diverting principles',[54] and they needed to work in a way that looked 'at the problem as a whole' whilst trying to balance rights, as against a process that was workable.[55] Draftsmen needed to focus the rules upon achieving 'court functions and operations'[56] and ensure the rules gave 'instruction in the use of power';[57] thus rules needed to explain as well as to make grants of power.

In his paper, Clark argued that what was needed was a combination of subject expertise, poise and common sense. To this were to be added strong drafting skills.[58] Clark did not expect that all this would be found in one person, and pointed to the problems causes by appointing Stephen, an acknowledged expert on pleading, to draft the rules of Hilary Term 1934.[59]

H. Managerial Judges

Judith Resnik's 1982 paper 'Managerial Judges'[60] offers a useful overview of the positive and negative aspects of the rise of managerialism. On the positive side she noted that judicial concern to see cases settled meant that most cases never reached a trial. On the other hand she was worried about the constitutional and ethical issues this raised:[61] a judge might know too much about a case by virtue of carrying out pre-trial work.[62] Further, the existence of only limited rights of interlocutory appeal would mean that judges engaged in case management would 'enjoy unreviewable discretion'.[63] Resnik was also concerned that a judge's own personal prestige was engaged when he or she was trying to cause a case to settle.[64] The emphasis on 'speed, control and quantity' might overshadow the values and goals of 'due process': the accuracy of decision-making, the adequacy of the reasoning supporting the decision, the 'quality of the adjudication', 'efficacy' and human dignity.[65]

[54] CE Clark, 'Special Problems' (n 24) 493.

[55] ibid 506.

[56] CE Clark, 'Special Problems' (n 24) 493.

[57] ibid.

[58] CE Clark, 'Special Problems' (n 24) 499.

[59] ibid 499. For comment on this topic, see WS Holdsworth, 'The New Rules of Pleading of the Hilary Term 1834' (1923) 1 *Cambridge Law Journal* 261, showing how Stephen, one of the Common Law Commissioners, brought the other Commissioners around to his views, in the 2nd Report of 1830 (ibid 270). Holdsworth offers insight into how thinking from within a particular system, in this case that pleading is scientific, can blind a draftsman to much larger issues (ibid 271) – which reinforces the importance of Sorabji's point about the need for the occasional paradigm shift in thinking.

[60] J Resnik, 'Managerial Judges' 96 *Harvard Law Review* 374 (1982).

[61] ibid 380.

[62] J Resnik, 'Managerial Judges' (n 60) 408; with the consequent risk to impartiality, ibid 426–27.

[63] ibid 411. The exercise of discretion is currently under academic scrutiny in England: see Masood Ahmed, 'Procedural rules and judicial discretion: Cameron v Hussain [2017] EWCA Civ 366' 2018, 37(2) *Civil Justice Quarterly* 149. Ahmed is concerned that procedural justice is not being given sufficient weight: see ibid 157–58.

[64] J Resnik, 'Managerial Judges' (n 60) 427.

[65] ibid 430. Resnik also pointed to the paradox that judges were expected to take their time to deliberate. ibid 445.

More negatively Resnik noted that the change in the judicial role had an impact on the civil justice system as a whole and was causing an increase in judicial activism.[66] She considered that this might mean that 'standards of what constitutes rational, fair, and impartial adjudication' were being changed without proper discussion.[67]

Resnik said that the term 'adjudication' described a process in which 'judges employed by the government make decisions based upon information presented by the parties',[68] and 'in an adversarial system, the parties control the pace and shape of the litigation'.[69] She noted the American tendency to speak of 'party-presentation' and 'party-prosecution' as its 'two fundamental elements'.[70] Resnik noted the tension caused by 'contradictory mandates' when the FRCP's generous disclosure provisions were imposed in an area where the rules of adversarial proceduralism reigned, thus creating a situation where there were likely to be increasing disputes about disclosure that would require interlocutory resolution by a judge.[71] She traced the rise of managerialism to a combination of an increased need for judicial ruling, brought about by the increase in the overall volume of cases and the rise in the number of civil disputes requiring to be resolved through litigation.[72] She also noted that contemporary technology – the photocopier and the computer – meant that more information was being processed and stored, which meant that there was more information falling within the scope of disclosure.[73] This in turn was causing 'the perception that the courts were too slow, justice too expensive, and judges at least partly to blame'.[74] The problem was not just one for litigants, it affected the judges too,[75] as the 'delays and the absence of judicial accountability' were leading to talk of a crisis.[76] The search for a solution drew upon both organisational and utilitarian theory.[77] The conclusions reached were set out by Resnik and are reproduced here for the reader to see Woolf in early formulation:

- 'Court services … have become scarce commodities. A continually expanding number of consumers are seeking access to the courts, but are forced to wait.'
- The 'queue … the line created by claimants already waiting for judicial services' was to blame.

[66] J Resnik, 'Managerial Judges' (n 60) 380.
[67] ibid.
[68] J Resnik, 'Managerial Judges' (n 60) 378.
[69] ibid 380.
[70] J Resnik, 'Managerial Judges' (n 60) 380, fn 23. She notes RW Millar, 'The Formative Principles of Civil Procedure (Pt 1') 18 *Illinois Law Review* 1, 9–24 (1923).
[71] J Resnik, 'Managerial Judges' (n 60), 378–79 and 391.
[72] ibid 380.
[73] J Resnik, 'Managerial Judges' (n 60) 397.
[74] ibid 395. She also noted that Pound had expressed similar concerns prior to the FRCP 1938.
[75] J Resnik, 'Managerial Judges' (n 60) 395.
[76] ibid 398.
[77] J Resnik, 'Managerial Judges' (n 60) 414.

- 'A second cause comes from the some claimants … who … abuse their places … by monopolizing court time. Attorneys … seem to be the critical actors in the apparent misuse of court resources.'
- Judges were aware that they needed to consider those 'at the end of the queue and … the public, which benefits from and pays for the dispute resolution system'.
- What was required was that the judges take charge and 'allocate their time in a prudent, coherent, and fair manner'.
- Judges should 'speed cases at the head of the line and discipline litigants who waste resources'.[78]
- The proponents of case management claimed that it 'decreases delay, produces more dispositions, and reduces litigation costs'.[79]

As a consequence there was a turn to managerial thinking about efficiency and the rise of 'schemes for speeding the resolution of cases and for persuading litigants to settle rather than try cases'.[80] This thinking had such impact that Resnik was able to speak of managerial ideas having become pervasive.[81] And what was motivating judges in all this? Resnik suggests that there was disillusionment with the adversarial process and lawyers' part in that;[82] there was a belief that management increased the speed and quality of the litigation; and that in addition, the efficiency concerns of other judges or of the system itself might play an influential role.[83] Resnik noted that case management conferred 'vast new powers' upon procedural judges,[84] as well as undermining 'traditional constraints on the use of that power'.[85]

I. Federal Self-reflection

A Self-Study of Federal Judicial Rulemaking[86] helpfully shows that in America, during 1996, there was ongoing debate about how best to plan for the future at the federal level.[87] Significant in the context of Woolf's work in England was the section

[78] ibid 414–15.

[79] J Resnik, 'Managerial Judges' (n 60) 417.

[80] ibid 379. Resnik does not make clear at this point whether the intended chief beneficiary of the push for settlement was the litigants or the judges.

[81] J Resnik, 'Managerial Judges' (n 60) 399.

[82] For an extraordinary attempt at using social meetings to defuse tensions, see ibid 407, fn 135.

[83] J Resnik, 'Managerial Judges' (n 60) 404.

[84] ibid 425.

[85] J Resnik, 'Managerial Judges' (n 60) 425.

[86] *A Self-Study of Federal Judicial Rulemaking: A Report from the Subcommittee on Long Range Planning to the Committee on Rules of Practice, Procedure and Evidence of the Judicial Conference of the United States*, 10 May 1996, 168 Federal Rules Decisions 679.

[87] There had been dissatisfaction over the work of the Advisory Committee, which came to a head over a set of 1955 proposals the Supreme Court declined to pursue. There was then 'a void in rulemaking',

on evaluative norms.[88] The Report carefully drew out the 'competing conceptions of what justice requires'. The competition could be seen to arise between 'the primacy of fairness' and the 'primacy of efficiency'.[89] Fairness comprised fairness to the individual litigant in coming to an accurate decision relating to 'the merits', and tempering finality of decision-making with 'liberal opportunities' for righting wrongs. Efficiency related to 'equality and aggregate efficiency'. The Report noted that: concentration of resources on one case could deprive litigants in other cases; the governmental function extended beyond trials; that resources were limited; and that it was necessary to respect established rights and interests. Efficiency pointed in the direction of 'rigorous enforcement of procedural rules', 'expedited' decision-making and limiting the opportunities for appeal. All of this is very familiar to students of Woolf's work, and enables us to situate Woolf in the epistemological landscape of his day.

Lastly, the Report argued that when change was being mooted, there were 'five related norms' to consider. These were 'efficiency, fairness, simplicity, consensus and uniformity'.[90] The Report noted that while consensus usually favoured the established situation, it could also act as a constraint upon the rule-making power and as a guard against 'utopian reform by rulemakers detached from the realities of litigation'.[91]

The Report went on to advocate the use of empirical data – something both Woolf and Jackson did.[92]

On the question of style, the Report noted the drive for 'uniform, readable, rules consistent with modern legal usage'. But it warned of the risk of revision causing 'accidental changes in meaning',[93] and of the equal risk presented by a 'stated goal of preserving meaning', which might cause rule users to look back to old sets of rules.

J. The Process of Making Process

Finally we come to Robert G Bone. Writing in 1999 from an American perspective, he captures much of the intellectual ferment of Woolf's milieu.[94] Bone favoured

which led to the Judicial Conference's being given responsibility for advising the Supreme Court concerning a number of federal rules. Thereafter, in the period 1972–75, proposals made by an Advisory Committee on the Rules of Evidence were rejected and Congress stepped in to formulate its own rules: ibid 686–87. The Rules Enabling Act of 1988 imposed transparency requirements upon the process of rule-making and slowed the process down: *A Self-Study of Federal Judicial Rulemaking* (n 86) 678.

[88] ibid 692–93.

[89] *A Self-Study of Federal Judicial Rulemaking* (n 86) 692.

[90] ibid 693.

[91] *A Self-Study of Federal Judicial Rulemaking* (n 86) 695. The American rule-making process is very self-aware about the political nature of the work being done.

[92] See, eg. *JnRef* (2018) (n 33) para 28-008.

[93] *A Self-Study of Federal Judicial Rulemaking* (n 86) 704.

[94] RG Bone, 'The Process of Making Process: Court Rulemaking, Democratic Legitimacy, and the Procedural Efficacy', 87 *Georgetown Law Journal* 887 (1999).

Congressional restraint in rule-making.[95] He argued that a 'centralised, court based, and committee centred process' enabled engagement in a decision-making model akin to common law reasoning. It enabled the rule-makers to offer a 'principled account' of civil procedure through the rules that are created, and to create a general rules framework within which specific rules might be used to control 'costly strategic behaviour'.[96]

Bone argued that there were some common assumptions about rule-making shared by its advocates in the first three decades of the twentieth century. Procedure was a means to an end, it was 'distinct from and subordinate to substantive law'.[97] In contemporary thinking Bone noted two streams of thought, covering what he called substantive effects[98] and substantive justification.[99] Theories concerning '*substantive effects*' enabled people to concentrate upon the social outcomes – if a rule creates a wealth differential then those who lose from such a consequence should be heard in the process of rule-making in a way that makes the rule-making process democratically accountable. Theories concerning '*substantive justification*' concentrated upon the value choices made by the rule-makers. Bone noted how difficult it was to assign values at all, because the choice of a value inevitably required a controversial choice to be made.[100] Therefore, even to speak of a decision made on the merits, or of 'fair apportionment' was to put a value on accuracy and fairness respectively.[101] Bone argued that 'substantive value is central to measuring error costs, and error costs are critical to procedural analysis'.[102] He said that the primary purpose of civil procedure is 'to enforce the substantive law', which required the enforcement of the values the substantive law protects.[103]

Returning to the theme of substantive effects and substantive justification, Bone argued that the legitimacy of a process can be critiqued if it produces 'bad effects' (the substantive effects theories), or if it treats individuals unfairly 'by denying them voice, participation, power'[104] (substantive justification), that is, if it has an impact upon their rights. He also suggested that people's rights have a moral value, as opposed to an economic one,[105] and that this required addressing through democratic accountability.

The substantive effects approach here is interesting because it highlights the need for efficiency; the substantive justification approach because it highlights the

[95] ibid 890.
[96] RG Bone, 'The Process of Making Process' (n 94) 890.
[97] ibid 894.
[98] RG Bone, 'The Process of Making Process' (n 94) 909–10.
[99] ibid 910–14.
[100] RG Bone, 'The Process of Making Process' (n 94) 912.
[101] ibid 913.
[102] Error costs are revisited in ch 6.
[103] RG Bone, 'The Process of Making Process' (n 94) 913–14, fn 139.
[104] ibid 918–19.
[105] RG Bone, 'The Process of Making Process' (n 94) 933. Bone notes (ibid 934) that there are then two possible approaches to dealing with a failure to respect a particular procedural right: one does one's best and accepts the occasional lapse; or one sees a procedural right as a right 'to fair treatment, not to accurate outcomes'.

need to consider the degree, if any, of democratic accountability required in the rule-making process,[106] because ultimately which values the law should reflect is something that in a democracy should be the subject of input from the people. There are limits to this because procedural rule-making covers but a small domain in the overall territory of government, and some injustice will be inherent in any process chosen.[107] Perhaps the issue, then, is which form of injustice the rule-makers ought to eliminate.

Drawing on that legal economics thinking which bears on the question of efficiency, Bone made a number of points concerning efficiency: efficiency is a good because its goal is the minimisation of social costs;[108] but efficiency involves 'a trade-off between the costs of error and the costs of process to safeguard against error. The more protection is added by way of procedure, the greater the cost of avoiding the error.'[109]

Bone noted[110] that both the substantive effects and substantive justification approaches overlap in that they each see the value in 'distributive fairness':[111] error risks must be distributed fairly across cases and litigants. The question of distributive fairness bites upon the basic question of affordability and the philosophical point posed by Woodrow Wilson that, if you have to be rich to get justice then, because of the cost of the very process itself, there is no justice at all.[112] Woolf's approach of three tracks created a system where, put broadly, less preparatory work would be done for cases of the lowest value (the small claims track) or only modest value (the fast track). There are two effects of this: first, that the less work done the less information the court will have before it when it makes its decision; second, the reach of proportionality will restrict the recoverability of costs a party has incurred.

In advancing his own ideas, Bone thought that one should start with the existing hybrid metric that already exists within civil procedure,[113] even if it is not made explicit. He argued for a constructivist approach, where one starts from practice, clarifies the principles that are there and justifies a modified version that is a 'reasonably coherent and morally attractive whole'.[114]

Bone noted the difficulty in predicting whether 'major changes will actually realize their intended goal',[115] and argued that some weight should be given

[106] ibid 919. Though Bone appears to have been keen not to involve Congress.
[107] RG Bone, 'The Process of Making Process' (n 94) 948.
[108] ibid 919–20.
[109] RG Bone, 'The Process of Making Process' (n 94) 919–20.
[110] ibid 934.
[111] A point Bone applied from R Dworkin, *A Matter of Principle* (Oxford, Clarendon Press, 1986) 92–93.
[112] Report of the Committee on Uniform Judicial Procedure, 49 *Annual Report of the American Bar Association* 505 (1926) at 521.
[113] RG Bone, 'The Process of Making Process' (n 94) 940.
[114] ibid 941.
[115] RG Bone, 'The Process of Making Process' (n 94) 942. See also SC Yeazell, 'The Misunderstood Consequences of Modern Civil Process', 1994 *Wisconsin Law Review* 631, 631 (1994).

to a set of procedures that has stood the test of time.[116] He also notes the interdependence of the rules of procedure, which requires coordination and centralisation.[117]

II. English Themes and Perspectives

A. Jack Jacob

The Fabric of English Civil Justice was a landmark book, marking a serious effort by a well-respected member of the legal establishment to consider the nature and purpose of civil procedure. Jacob noted the move in terminology from 'civil procedure' to 'civil justice'.[118] We can see here an understanding that there is more to litigation than the process; there is the question of outcome to be taken into account. Jacob was also aware of the 'cultural, historical, moral, social, economic and administrative as well as legal' aspects of civil justice.[119] He spoke of the public dimension of civil justice. In Jacob's view, a right of action was a public right, and a public interest arose when proceedings were commenced. The state would take the claim under its control.[120] Part of the problem arose, thought Jacob, because the court's role was largely seen as comparable to that of an 'umpire'.[121] Whilst at trial the court might be 'dominating, positive and interventionist',[122] prior to that it was 'inactive, passive and non-interventionist'.[123] On the other hand, the parties had an active role to play in interlocutory matters. This manifested itself in the control of preparation – which he called 'party control'[124] – and in the control of the progress of the case to trial – called 'party prosecution'. Party prosecution was something of a misnomer. A key concern pre-Woolf was that parties were not prosecuting their cases with anything approaching diligence. This led to cases taking a long

[116] RG Bone, 'The Process of Making Process' (n 94) 942.

[117] ibid 946.

[118] Sir Jack IH Jacob, *The Fabric of English Civil Justice* (London, Stevens & Sons, 1987) (hereinafter '*JbFabr*') 2.

[119] ibid 3.

[120] *JbFabr* (n 118) 8.

[121] ibid 9.

[122] *JbFabr* (n 118) 12.

[123] ibid 9.

[124] *JbFabr* (n 118) 13. For a view of how parties did not always have control within Anglo-American civil procedure, see RG Bone's lengthy review essay about Stephen C Yeazell, 'Personal and Impersonal Litigative Forms: Reconceiving the History of Adjudicative Representation', 70 *Boston University Law Review* 213 (1990). Of interest in our context is how Rule 23 of the FRCP came out of a change in the way procedure was viewed. Pragmatic philosophy allowed one to consider what worked best, rather than be tied to the idea that particular adjudicative forms were linked to particular kinds of rights of action: Bone, 'Personal and Impersonal', 287–89. At root, then, the kind of process used is severable from the right, and this frees us to consider which process is most effective or desirable. So we can have theories of participation and see that court management is as possible as party control and party prosecution. This is precisely what Jacob was able to do.

time to get to trial, applications for strike out for want of prosecution and repeated applications for adjournments. Party control led to proceedings being influenced by tactical considerations.[125] The parties engaged in a 'battle of wits' like 'legal gladiators'.[126] Litigation was distorted by 'sportsmanship or gamesmanship'.[127] Jacob concluded that in truth the parties were not on equal terms, nor were all lawyers competent. 'The true casualties of the adversary system are the parties themselves,' he concluded.[128] It was for this reason that the question of civil justice was a matter of 'transcendent importance' for the public,[129] and why there was such a great need

> for a breath of fresh air to blow through the corridors of civil justice to de-mystify the process, to render it plain, simple and intelligible,[130] to enable … the man in the High Street to understand and appreciate its operation and in this way to bring justice closer to the common people.[131]

This coverage of Jacob ends with a longer extract[132] that could have come straight out of Woolf's reports, and which clearly shows that Woolf's solutions were firmly built upon Jacob's foundation:

> [O]nce the jurisdiction of the court has been invoked, the court should become invested with the public duty and interest to ensure the proper conduct, content and progress of the proceedings.[133] Such increased power of the court, to be more active and responsible,[134] would also help to promote equality in procedure, especially where one party is not legally or even competently represented. The active role of the court would enable it to monitor the progress of the proceedings, to control their future conduct,[135] to formulate the real issues or questions between the parties,[136] to determine that there has been full disclosure of documents between them,[137] to ensure the exchange of experts' reports[138] and … the exchange of the statements of the witnesses of the parties,[139] to increase the powers of the court to act of its own motion as, for example, to appoint a court expert[140] and to enable the trial court to call a witness not called by the parties. Above all, the court should be under a duty at all stages to endeavour by conciliation to promote the settlement or compromise of the proceedings.[141]

[125] *JbFabr* (n 118) 14.
[126] ibid 15.
[127] *JbFabr* (n 118) 16.
[128] ibid 16.
[129] *JbFabr* (n 118) 1.
[130] Cf Lord Woolf, *Access to Justice: Interim Report* (London, HMSO, 1995) (hereinafter '*WfIR*') ch 26, para 28.
[131] *JbFabr* (n 118) 3–4.
[132] ibid18–19.
[133] Cf *WfIR* (n 130) ch 1, paras 1–2; ch 4, para 2.
[134] Cf ibid ch 4, paras 2–3.
[135] Cf *WfIR* (n 130) ch 5, para 16.
[136] Cf ibid ch 5, para 11; ch 20, para 2.
[137] Cf *WfIR* (n 130) ch 21, para 22.
[138] Cf ibid ch 23. paras 3 and 5.
[139] Cf *WfIR* (n 130) ch 22, paras 11–12.
[140] Cf ibid ch 23, paras 20–23.
[141] Cf *WfIR* (n 130) ch 18, para 32.

B. The Civil Justice Review

The *Civil Justice Review* of 1987[142] recommended the fixing of periods for setting down trials, regular record checks and reminders, and power to strike out of the court's own motion.

The Report argued that 'In particular public policy requires that certain objectives be met, by virtue either of rules of court or of specific intervention by the court.' Those objectives were that: 'cases should be disposed of within a reasonable time'; 'full information' should be provided in order to assist settlement or preparation for trial; and 'there should be adequate preparation for trial; that cases should come on for trial once ready'. Trials were to be set down 'without delay', and any trials held should be both 'expeditious' and handled 'in as economical a manner as justice permits'.[143]

The Report envisaged that whilst primary responsibility for litigation lay with the parties, the court also had an interest in this.[144] Parties should try hard, the procedural rules could give guidance, but 'direct intervention by the court is also required'. The Report equivocated on whether all cases fitted into this category. Thus 'a general framework of court management is necessary, to be brought into play when required, but with minimum inconvenience to litigants and the court'. The phraseology is interesting in that 'court management' was seen as a potential inconvenience. This part of the Report therefore seems to respect not just party autonomy but judicial autonomy as well.

The focus of the Report was firmly on the question of delay[145] that undermined justice and resulted in procedural prejudice. Delay was recognised as having an impact on the ordinary user of the system. The Report recognised, however, that delay, cost and complexity were all playing a role.

Proportionality was treated as follows:

> The cost of litigation is often quite disproportionate to the amount involved in the claim. Thus the legal costs of both parties to a personal injury case which goes to trial often equal or exceed the damages recovered.[146]

Further,

> fear of costs is one of the greatest deterrents to using the courts. This fear is compounded by the fact that there is little or no chance of knowing beforehand what a case will cost or of making price comparisons.[147]

[142] M Hodson, *Civil Justice Review: Report of the Review Body on Civil Justice*, Cmnd 394 (London, HMSO, 1988) (hereinafter '*CivJ Rev*'). Lord Griffiths was a member of the *Review*'s committee.
[143] ibid para 220.
[144] *CivJ Rev* (n 142) paras 220 and 221.
[145] ibid paras 67–68.
[146] *CivJ Rev* (n 142) para 69.
[147] ibid para 70.

C. Judicial Recognition of the Problem

In *Westminster City Council v Clifford Culpin & Partners*, a want of prosecution case, Kerr LJ had said:

> [N]o changes in the organisation or administration of the courts would make any material difference to cases such as the present. By far the major part of all delays stems solely from the way in which litigation is conducted. In this connection our law needs to be changed, both in substance and procedurally … [T]he regime of *Birkett v James* should be replaced by a system of rules which are much stricter, more effective and simple to apply … The present system provides insufficient sanctions for those responsible for the dilatory and inefficient conduct of litigation, and it is frequently unfair to litigants.[148]

In 1989, in *Department of Transport v Chris Smaller (Transport) Ltd* [1989] AC 1197, Lord Griffiths addressed the question of case management:

> I believe that a far more radical approach is required to tackle the problems of delay in the litigation process than driving an individual plaintiff away from the courts when his culpable delay has caused no injustice to his opponent. I, for my part, recommend a radical overhaul of the whole civil procedural process and the introduction of court controlled case management techniques.[149]

D. Neil Andrews (1994)

In 1994, Neil Andrews' work *Principles of Civil Procedure*[150] was published. It marked an important stage in the evolution of the understanding of civil procedure in England. He first invited readers to consider the outsider's view: his criticisms related to the heavy role played by lawyers and the marginality of clients and courts; the cost of very technical procedure; the effect that precision had on preparatory costs; and the slowness and cost of litigation.

Andrews then went on to discuss the importance of principles: these he divided into nominate or recognised principles; half-articulated principles; and latent or disputable principles. Some principles were merely descriptive of what was done, other principles required to be put into practice. In defence of a principles-based approach, Andrews made the following points: that principles are 'general in their scope' and 'identify the connections between rules'; that they make the law easier to understand or communicate; that they advance comparative law insights; that they enable one to keep an eye on the big picture; and that they are capable of being weighed against each other. We might see Andrews as having collected and

[148] *Westminster City Council v Clifford Culpin & Partners* (Court of Appeal, 18 June 1987).

[149] *Department of Transport v Chris Smaller (Transport) Ltd* [1989] AC 1197, 1207. Lord Griffiths was referring to the *Civil Justice Review*.

[150] N Andrews, *Principles of Civil Procedure* (London, Sweet & Maxwell, 1994) (hereinafter '*AndPCP*').

catalogued a series of operative principles and principled reasons that explain both what is being done and the reasons for this. To this collection Andrews added some general ideas that he considered to be hard to achieve – the promotion of access to justice, the prevention of undue delay and the management of big-ticket litigation. In the last case Andrews distinguished between things that are necessarily complex and things that lawyers complicate. He also helpfully noted that the creation of new procedures also complicated matters. Andrews' solution was threefold: he advocated the removal of unnecessary procedure, restrictions being placed upon the way litigants use procedure, and encouraging the parties in the use of ADR. Andrews was not at all dewy-eyed about this. He closed his chapter on complexity with a quote from Dickens: 'The one great principle of the English law is to make business for itself.'

E. The Advent of Woolf

i. First Glimmerings

Woolf wanted to change things. The extent of Woolf's radicalism is hinted at in Jolowicz's *On Civil Procedure*:

> Lord Woolf himself is reported to have said ... that the White Book would be of 'historic interest' only, that looking back to old cases would, mislead rather than inform on the new position, and even that 'all learning should be forgotten.'[151]

The Woolf Reports did not appear out of nowhere. Aside from Woolf's own personal experiences and commitments, there had long been agitation for change in some legal circles. The year 1994 also fell within the era of the Citizen's Charter, pet project of John Major's premiership.[152] The emphasis there was very much upon delivering a service that met the needs of the client and not those of the provider. Woolf was speaking in a political atmosphere in which there was an appetite for change on both sides of the political divide.

Prior to his official appointment to enquire into access to justice, Lord Woolf delivered a speech to the Bentham Club Association entitled 'Access to Justice'.[153] Woolf started by arguing that two of Bentham's concepts would be of use: 'utilitarianism and ... the demystification of law'.[154] Having sketched out the positive side of English justice – high-quality judges and professionals – he then

[151] J Jolowicz, *On Civil Procedure* (Cambridge, Cambridge University Press, 2000) (hereinafter '*JoloCP*') ix, speech made in February 1999, reported by the *Law Society's Gazette* in the *Guardian* issue of 24 February 1999 at 4.

[152] See A Selden, *Major: A Political Life* (London, Weidenfeld & Nicolson, 1997) 187–95.

[153] H Woolf, 'Access to Justice' in MDA Freeman (ed), *Current Legal Problems*, vol 47 (Oxford, Oxford University Press,1994) 341. The concluding note confirms that the speech antedates Woolf's appointment (ibid 357).

[154] ibid 342.

adverted to the need for 'equality before the law'.[155] The reduction in legal aid meant that whilst one could receive medical treatment regardless of means, the same was not true of legal assistance.[156] If legal aid was to be targeted, how could others have 'accessible … and affordable'[157] access to litigation? One answer was to change the way litigation was conducted so that litigants in person could be involved.[158] Contemporary society needed something that worked for it. The consequence was that there needed to be 'a change of culture' and a departure from habituated and tradition-bound behaviours.[159] Changes might include a 'unified procedure' for the civil courts and a single 'concentrated' and plain language version of the rules. Woolf said that he would 'change the model' of the courts, slowly to be sure, but he thought that 'a radically different model' was required,[160] a user-friendly model.[161] Woolf had in mind a court that would 'take charge of litigation from the outset' and 'advise and instruct … and supervise and help'[162] litigants. Assistance in settling cases would need to be a priority. The judge would sometimes be the 'impartial adjudicator' and sometimes the inquisitor.[163] Woolf thought that sometimes an ombudsman could provide 'a perfectly adequate remedy'.[164] Drawing on his experience of conducting an inquiry, Woolf thought that it was possible to 'cut through the need for representation and expedite the process' and still meet 'the requirements of justice'.[165] He thought that this would be both effective and cut the cost to the Treasury.

ii. Woolf's Interim Report

Woolf's Interim Report is a very substantial report so it is necessary to select themes. We are looking here at the topics of the overriding objective and the sanctions regime, and why each was needed.

The starting points for Woolf's analysis was as follows. The law was requisite for the proper functioning of society.[166] This was so important that the court had a constitutional role[167] in guarding the right of access to a court. The basic requirements for any civil justice system to meet[168] were: ensuring just results; fairness

[155] H Woolf, 'Access to Justice' (n 153) 344.
[156] ibid.
[157] H Woolf, 'Access to Justice' (n 153) 345.
[158] ibid 346.
[159] H Woolf, 'Access to Justice' (n 153) 348.
[160] ibid 348–49.
[161] H Woolf, 'Access to Justice' (n 153) 349.
[162] ibid 349.
[163] H Woolf, 'Access to Justice' (n 153).
[164] ibid 351.
[165] H Woolf, 'Access to Justice' (n 153) 353.
[166] *WfIR* (n 130) ch 1, para 1.
[167] ibid ch 1, para 2.
[168] *WfIR* (n 130) ch.1, para 3; see also Lord Woolf, *Access to Justice: Final Report* (London, HMSO, 1996) (hereinafter '*WfFR*') ch 1, para 1.

in the way it handled cases;[169] and delivering all this by means of a proportionate procedure that operated at a reasonable speed. The procedure should be understandable by users and responsive;[170] it should offer a degree of certainty; and it should be 'effective: adequately resourced and organised'.[171]

Now it is significant for thinking about Sorabji's hypothesis about Woolf having a new theory of civil litigation to note what Woolf was not saying. He did not say, 'I want to depart from the justice on the merits theory', as if he thought that justice on the merits alone was the issue or the problem. Woolf took for granted that the bundle of values and outcomes offered in chapter 1 of the Interim Report was, or ought to be, a common factor in civil justice systems generally. Perhaps in putting just results first in his list he was blunting the impact of a genuinely radical theory of proportional justice, but it seems more likely that the general objective was not uppermost in Woolf's thinking when the report was written. It does not appear in chapters 1, 3 or 4 of Woolf's Interim Report, where one might most naturally find it, nor, significantly, is it mentioned in any of the recommendations at the close of that Report. There was no legerdemain about Woolf's formulation of the basic requirements, nor about his preferred solutions that follow. The proposals relating to personnel, court structure and the architecture of procedure fit together and work perfectly well without a general objective at all.

Returning to Woolf's basic requirements for civil justice, if these were Woolf's desiderata, the reality fell far short of this. Woolf recognised the key problems of 'cost, delay and complexity' that stemmed from 'the uncontrolled nature of the litigation process'.[172] As a result the 'worst excesses' of parties would go unchecked[173] and non-compliance was routine.[174] Skilled lawyers were able to outmanoeuvre the court,[175] and the very processes of the court were being used to defeat the purposes for which they were designed.[176]

Part of the issue was that English civil litigation was adversarial, which meant that what the parties gained in autonomy they lost in the cost of litigation as war.[177] Tactical jousting was common, for 'the litigation process is too often seen as a battlefield where no rules apply'.[178] The cost of all this to the parties was 'excessive, disproportionate and unpredictable'.[179] This also caused

[169] And fairness would be the context of the introduction of what became CPR 1.1: *WfIR* (n 130) ch 26, para 30.

[170] ibid ch 15, paras 1–2. The small claims procedure, the fast track and comprehensibility were key.

[171] *WfIR* (n 130) ch 1, para 3.

[172] ibid ch 3, para 1. See also *JoloCP* (n 151) 52 for the influence of the adversarial system. See also R Turner '"Actively": The Word that Changed the Civil Courts' in *Ten Years* (n 53) 78–79.

[173] *WfIR* (n 130) ch 3, para 5.

[174] 'Orders are flouted on a vast scale.' ibid ch, 3, para 6.

[175] *WfIR* (n 130) ch 3, para 7.

[176] ibid ch 3, paras 8–10.

[177] This is not a new point, see R Pound, 'The Causes of Popular Dissatisfaction with the Administration of Justice', 29 *Annual Report of the American Bar Association* 395 (1906).

[178] *WfIR* (n 130) ch, 3, para 4. For a similar view, see *JoloCP* (n 151) 395.

[179] *WfIR* (n 130) ch, 3, para 4. Woolf also said that he wanted to preserve the 'best features of adversarial litigation': ibid ch 5, para 15.

unreasonable delay.[180] The process of civil procedure too was complex and cumbersome.[181] As a result of all this, businesses and the public were either settling cases or not going to law,[182] and much time and effort was being expended wastefully on litigation.[183] In the case of business, the loss was being passed on to shareholders.[184]

One is immediately struck by the gravity of all the charges that Woolf made. So what did Woolf propose? He intended to focus on making procedure 'appropriate and proportionate' in nature, to establish equality of arms, to promote dispute resolution and to focus resources at the communal level rather than allowing individual parties to draw on resources as they chose.[185] He wanted 'a total change of philosophy'.[186] Autonomy was to be taken away from parties and the judiciary was to be given the power to control them.[187] This would require a 'radical change of culture' for judges, lawyers and litigants.[188] It would require them to take into account 'questions of cost and time' and the 'means of the parties'.[189] All this would need a system that promoted settlement[190] and then ensured that the litigation was focused on the important things.[191] Woolf proposed[192] that the small claims jurisdiction be increased,[193] and that there should be a fast track[194] and a multi-track. The fast track offered no-frills litigation and proportionate cost was built in.[195] That cost was to be predictable.[196] In larger cases, Woolf's intention was that there should dedicated appointments for case management. The multi-track exemplified this, with two appointments dedicated to case management.[197] Judges would manage cases:[198] this would mean their taking responsibility for

[180] Delay might cause the parties to lose heart but the lawyers were ahead of the game: *WfIR* (n 130) ch 3, paras 30–31.
[181] ibid ch 3, para 44. See also ibid ch 26, paras 6–24 and 31–36. Woolf wished to simplify procedure and the language in which it was expressed.
[182] *WfIR* (n 130) ch, 3, para 13.
[183] ibid ch 3, para 14.
[184] *WfIR* (n 130) ch 3, para 15.
[185] ibid ch 5, para 1.
[186] *WfIR* (n 130) ch 4, para 3. Note that the total change related to the judiciary's taking control and not to the introduction of proportionality per se.
[187] ibid ch 4, para 2. Woolf made clear he wanted to control behaviour (ibid ch 19, para 3) and so force the parties to behave better (ibid ch 19, para 1). This would include their being cooperative (ibid ch 19, paras 7–8, 11).
[188] *WfIR* (n 130) ch 4, para 4.
[189] ibid ch 4, para 6.
[190] ADR was dealt with at *WfIR* (n 130) ch 18.
[191] ibid ch 4, para 7.
[192] *WfIR* (n 130) ch 4, para 9.
[193] Material on small claims appears ibid ch 16.
[194] Albeit from £3,000 to only £10,000. Details of the fast track were set out in *WfIR* (n 130) ch 7.
[195] ibid ch 7, paras 1–2. The features of the track are at para 10 of the same chapter.
[196] *WfIR* (n 130) ch 7, paras 2, 16 and 17.
[197] ibid ch 8, paras 4–5.
[198] *WfIR* (n 130) ch 4, paras 10–11.

ensuring that cases did progress,[199] promoting settlement and getting unsettled cases to trial.[200]

It is worth noting that the rules were to have a general objective. Woolf's first version did not appear until chapter 26 of the Interim Report.[201] This is all rather strange if the general objective was to be at the heart of the project. Given that Woolf expressly said 'the general objective is to do justice but to achieve it by means which minimise cost and delay',[202] one might have expected Woolf to set out his stall earlier on. The general objective was, said Woolf, to be of 'fundamental importance in the managed system which I recommend'.[203]

Mentioned earlier was Woolf's call for a new philosophy that partly related to a move to place more power in judicial hands. This need not have been a sinister thing – clearly, party autonomy was a very expensive privilege. If it was not working, it made sense to try another approach. Also mentioned was the change of culture required from everyone in considering cost, speed and affordability. Unexpressed by Woolf at this point was the need for courts to go about the work of interpretation in a very different manner, namely the use of purposive interpretation.[204] The current English Supreme Court's very principle-led approach to solving problems is not reflective of the state of judicial practice in 1995, which took a conservative approach. Understanding of purposive construction was not firmly established at this point in time, and one can see that Woolf's proposal of this approach to interpretation, coupled with a belief in the power of principles, might have been something of a challenge for his colleagues. The judiciary must have been aware that political support for Convention law was gaining ground. In all of this, then, Woolf's choice to position his proposals as new, radical and absolutely the right way of doing applied jurisprudence must have struck a raw nerve or two. Woolf advanced three points: the judiciary was not there to project awe and majesty, it was there to serve the people;[205] the expertise required to navigate the current system was unnecessary and the system should be opened up to the non-technically minded (ie to laypeople);[206] and the current approach to interpreting

[199] ibid ch 5, para 16.

[200] Case management is explained at *WfIR* (n 130) ch 5, paras 16–20; ibid ch 6, especially paras 23 and 26.

[201] ibid ch 26, para 30.

[202] *WfIR* (n 130) ch 26, para 23.

[203] ibid ch 26, para 30.

[204] See *WfIR* (n 130) ch 26, paras 26–27. There Woolf expressly cites Lord Denning in *James Buchanan & Co v Babco Forwarding and Shipping (UK) Limited* [1977] QB 208 (CA), 213–14. There is some argument that s 2 of the Civil Procedure Act 1997, with its reference to civil justice being 'accessible, fair and efficient', would have validated this approach. However, there were other schools of thought: *Civil Procedure* vol 2 (London, Sweet & Maxwell) (hereinafter '*White Book*' plus year) (2017) para 11-7 refers to the cases on the risk of over-reliance on CPR 1.1. Para 12-38 of the same volume cites *Buchanan* and then skirts the issue. The topic of interpretation is revisited in ch 3.

[205] *WfIR* (n 130) ch 26, para 29. Woolf is not just speaking about process here. He is speaking to his colleagues about their role in a democratic society, see also ibid ch 1 para 2. The judges are there for the citizenry and not the other way round. Remoteness is the old way of doing things, conspicuous fairness is the way forward.

[206] ibid ch 26, para 28. This is a blatant argument for democratisation.

the rules was plain wrong. This last point is particularly significant. Any hardworking Court of Appeal judge who had contributed to the body of case law on the RSC, or been a supporter of previous rules changes, might have been forgiven for being taken aback by the severity of Woolf's criticism – broadly: '[T]he old way of doing things does not work so you must embrace a new method. The Europeans are doing it and so must we.' Small wonder that not everyone was convinced.

One wonders, too, about how comfortable judges would have been with Woolf's situational approach to procedural justice as exemplified by an overriding objective that was intended to be of 'fundamental importance' and later of paramount importance.

iii. Woolf's Final Report and the Draft Civil Proceedings Rules

Woolf's Final Report followed a period of intense consultation. He confirmed that he had offered 'a blueprint for reform'[207] based on a system where the courts would principally be responsible 'for the management of cases'.[208] Woolf was convinced that 'the landscape' of litigation would be 'fundamentally different'.[209] The features of this landscape would be:[210]

- the avoidance of litigation when this was possible;
- a greater emphasis on cooperation without removing the adversarial context;
- a simplification of litigation procedure;
- a shortening of timescales and a consequent increase in certainty;
- those of limited means would obtain an 'equal footing' within litigation;
- a change of internal judicial management structures;
- the provision of training to judges so they could do the work of case management;[211]
- a concentration of resources so that the needs of litigants would be met;
- continued accessibility and increased use of technology; and
- the system would be responsive to the needs of litigants.

Woolf said that the new landscape would be 'underpinned' by the new Rule 1, which would incorporate the overriding objective. This rule would 'define'[212] what

[207] Judith Resnik argued that the big questions relating to 'pace … allocation of authority' for that pace and the 'continued existence of the adversary process' were matters of constitutional and public importance: J Resnik, 'Managerial Judges' (n 60) 444.
[208] *WfFR* (n 168) s 1, para 3.
[209] ibid s 1, para 8.
[210] *WfFR* (n 168) s 1, para 9.
[211] See also ibid ch 1, paras 4–6.
[212] Presumably by inclusion or example.

was meant by 'justly' – a term 'embodying the principles of equality,[213] economy, proportionality[214] and expedition'.[215]

Lord Woolf had this to say about sanctions. He recognised that there was a problem to be faced in terms of non-compliance,[216] but he also had to accept that the County Court Rules' automatic striking out under Order 17, rule 11 had generated a great deal of satellite litigation[217] – a development largely triggered by practitioners making mistakes. Woolf concluded from this that ferocious sanctions alone without case management would not work. The obvious resort of requiring lawyers to bear the direct costs that they had wasted (wasted costs orders)[218] was, Woolf accepted, 'too cumbersome'[219] and could 'add to cost and delay'.[220] By the time of his Final Report, Woolf seems to have decided that there was an element of oppression in the way that non-compliance was operating against the compliant.[221] And non-compliance did not only consist of specific breaches of rules or orders; it could also, more insidiously, manifest itself in the way that litigation was conducted, if its cumulative effect was to prevent a case from receiving procedural justice.[222] All of this posed considerable difficulties in how to tackle non-compliant behaviour. Woolf went back to first principles.[223] He thought that the primary object of sanctions was 'prevention, not punishment', although this rather undercut his view that ferocious sanctions alone were not effective. Next, Woolf envisaged that the rules would provide for a sanction for their breach – the punishment would follow automatically on from non-compliance. To increase the weight of all this Woolf envisaged that all directions should provide for an 'automatic sanction' for breach unless time was extended in advance, and it should be for the party in default to seek relief from sanctions. In Woolf's view, sanctions would work preventatively where there was the threat of a 'prompt, relevant punishment'. Sanctions must be 'fair, relevant and simple to administer', and must not operate to cause further delay or cost for the compliant party. One is struck by how Woolf's Report presents all this as if it were a matter of common sense and simplicity. The Report was bold and confident, but implementation proved to be less simple.

Woolf was alive to the need for procedural fairness even in cases of non-compliance justice. He addressed this in chapter 6, paragraphs 10–11, where the

[213] See also *WfFR* (n 168) ch 2, para 30; ch 4, para 10;

[214] See also 'Proportionality underlies the whole concept of the fast track', ibid ch 2, para 19.

[215] *WfFR* (n 168) s 1, para 8.

[216] ibid ch 6, para 1 refers back to *WfIR* (n 130) ch 3, para 6.

[217] *WfFR* (n 168) ch 6, para 7.

[218] Senior Courts Act 1981, s 51(6)–(7). The present rule is CPR 46.8. The general case law is digested at para 46.8.17 of *White Book* (2017), vol 1. The irony of the problem is that lawyers also have rights to a fair hearing.

[219] *WfFR* (n 168) ch 6, para 8.

[220] Woolf did not propose the abolition of the Courts and Legal Services Act 1990.

[221] The term occurs in *WfFR* (n 168) ch 6, paras 2, 4 and 6.

[222] ibid ch 6, para 4.

[223] *WfFR* (n 168) ch 6, para 3.

emphasis was upon sanctions' being 'relevant and proportionate' and relating to a particular breach. Woolf also referred to the courts' being prepared to consider striking out – albeit that this was to be a 'draconian sanction' of last resort. Woolf was further alive to the possibility that a party might chose to suffer the lesser penalty of being unable to deploy documents in order to prevent those documents from coming into an opponent's hands, and thought that striking out might be appropriate where a final warning by order was given.[224]

Part 5 of the Draft Civil Proceedings Rules placed together general powers of case management;[225] powers relating to striking out (including non-compliance);[226] powers to specify consequences;[227] powers to give relief from sanctions;[228] and powers relating to errors of procedure.[229] Examples of the automatic sanctions Woolf envisaged appeared in relation to disclosure of documents,[230] witness statements[231] and experts reports.[232] The formula of words provided that the defaulter was prevented from utilising the missing document unless the court gave permission.

When it came to the rules themselves, Woolf published his Draft Rules at the same time as his Final Report. His ambitious plans had been to find the core of the rules, to offer procedures that were widely usable, to reduce the size of the rules, to make the rules 'simpler and plainer',[233] and to 'give effect' to his 'substantive reforms'.[234] This last point is the most important, yet it appears at the end of Woolf's list. Woolf's view was that the rules had become 'a tactical weapon' and 'a dead letter'. Part of the reason for this was that the language of the contemporary rules underpinned the attitudes and behaviour of those engaged in conducting litigation.[235] Woolf hoped that changing the language of the rules would be part of the process of change, but he also acknowledged that changes in the rules alone would not be enough.[236] There seems to be some greater sense also that involving non-lawyers might help to break the cycle of behaviour.[237] Woolf's preference for the avoidance of technical language and specialist procedures was part of a

[224] ibid ch 6, para 11. A carry-over of the old idea of an 'unless order'.

[225] Lord Woolf, *Access to Justice Draft Civil Proceedings Rules* (London, HMSO, 1996) (hereinafter '*WfDR*') 5.1, now CPR 3.1.

[226] *WfDR* (n 225) 5.2, now especially CPR 3.4 and CPR 46.8.

[227] ibid 5.3, now CPR 3.1(3)(b).

[228] *WfDR* (n 225) 5.4, now CPR 3.8 and 3.9.

[229] ibid 5.5, now CPR 3.10.

[230] *WfDR* (n 225) 27.21, now CPR 31.21.

[231] ibid 28.12, now CPR 32.10.

[232] *WfDR* (n 225) 32.12, now CPR 35.13.

[233] Woolf was aiming for the non-professionals: *WfFR* (n 168) ch 20, para 16. Robert Turner says that the Rules Committee was persuaded by civil servants 'to adopt a modern form of "plain English" … and to change the language of the Common Law': R Turner, '"Actively"' (n 172) 80–81.

[234] *WfFR* (n 168) ch 20, para 2. Compare with *WfIR* (n 130) ch 26, para 25.

[235] *WfFR* (n 168) ch 20, para 14.

[236] ibid ch 20, para 29.

[237] *WfFR* (n 168) ch 20, paras 3, 5, 15 and 23.

wider attitude that involved a preference for simplicity,[238] a system that was as user-friendly as possible, a system that could be understood and used by the many and not by the few. Each of these ideas creates its own tensions. A procedure might be complex because the things to be considered are themselves too complex to be handled with simplicity. The proliferation of rules and procedures post-1998 suggests that the pursuit of simplicity failed. On the question of user-friendliness, the language of the draft was indeed accessible, and the provisions for the small claims track[239] were straightforward and relatively self-contained. But whether even Woolf's Draft Rules as a whole were user-friendly, understandable[240] or usable by the many I would doubt, not least because many of the rules are to be read against the background of the law of evidence[241] and require the know-how that only comes from repeated exposure. To be sure, Woolf thought that advice services could bridge the gap,[242] but he was undoubtedly relying on ADR's acting as a by-pass around the new procedures.[243]

Given that Woolf wanted his rules to give effect to his overall plan, he had, he said, 'placed at the very beginning of the rules a statement of their overriding objective'.[244] This was intended to control the way the rules worked, assist the court as it made its choices, and cover the interpretation of the rules.[245] Part of the role of the overriding objective,[246] Woolf thought, was to fill the gaps left by the deliberate simplification of the rules. As there would be fewer rules, so the overriding objective would have to assist in filling in the gaps, or, as Woolf put it, the

[238] For the problems with achieving simplicity, see J Resnik, 'Managerial Judges' (n 60) 441: 'The variety and complexity of the civil docket would invite rulemakers to craft dozens of subrules. Yet [this] would in turn conflict with the premise … that a single framework can form the basis for litigating … myriad claims.'

[239] *WfDR* (n 225) 25.1 and Part 26.

[240] See, eg, *Barton v Wright Hassall LLP* [2018] UKSC 12 [18]–[19], per Lord Sumption, which appears to confirm the hardening of the position against litigants in person manifested in *R (Hysaj) v Secretary of State for the Home Department* [2014] EWCA Civ 1633, [2015] 1 WLR 2472 (CA) [44], per Moore-Bick LJ: 'I do not think that the court can or should accept that the mere fact of being unrepresented provides a good reason for not adhering to the rules'; and *Nata Lee Ltd v Abid* [2014] EWCA Civ 1652, [2015] 2 P&CR 3 (CA) [53], per Briggs LJ: 'I make it clear at the outset that, in my view, the fact that a party … is not professionally represented is not of itself a reason for the disapplication of rules … or for the disapplication of that part of the overriding objective which now places great value on the requirement that they be obeyed by litigants. In short, the CPR do not, at least at present, make specific or separate provision for litigants in person. There may be cases in which the fact that a party is a litigant in person has some consequence in the determination of applications for relief from sanctions, but this is likely to operate at the margins.' This post-Woolf change of tone is very much down to Jackson's emphasis on the importance of compliance by all. CPR 1.3A is supposed to ensure that the particular needs of litigants in person are taken into account. For consideration of the litigation in person issue, see A Zuckerman, 'No Justice Without Lawyers – The Myth of an Inquisitorial Solution' (2014) 33 *Civil Justice Quarterly* 355.

[241] eg ibid Part 27 (Disclosure), Parts 28, 30 and 31 (Evidence), and Part 32 (Experts).

[242] See *WfIR* (n 130) ch 17.

[243] See ibid ch 18. Note that this appears in the section on 'Assisting the Litigant'.

[244] See *WfDR* (n 225) 1.1.

[245] *WfFR* (n 168) ch 20, para 11.

[246] Called the 'overall objective' in the marginal note ibid ch 20, para 10.

overriding objective would 'provide a compass'[247] to guide the traveller across a landscape that would never be fully mapped because it would always change from case to case. This, coupled with the deliberate use of a purposive approach[248] and the utilisation of inexact or imprecise language,[249] was part of Woolf's intention. The overriding objective would have its own space.

If we start with the consolidation of judicial power, a good example is pre-action protocols.[250] Woolf's argument was as follows: most cases settle without a trial;[251] many cases settle before the commencement of proceedings, therefore pre-commencement settlement should be facilitated. Early settlement ought to be cheaper,[252] but an eye needed to be kept on ensuring that negotiations did not become protracted.[253] This could be achieved by the use of pre-action protocols, which would enable a court seised of the claim to look back at what happened before the commencement of proceedings.[254] The protocols would offer 'codes of sensible practice',[255] and the expectation would be that those familiar with particular kinds of work would be able to make an input.[256] Woolf was dismissive of the suggestion that because protocols would pull forward the occurrence of costs, they should not be used. He was firmly wedded to the notion that a case could not settle until 'sufficient information is available for a realistic commercial assessment of the value of the claim'.[257] This very much ties in with Woolf's belief that putting one's cards on the table at an early stage would encourage settlement.[258]

Woolf's belief was that the focus should no longer be upon the individual, not least because the right to a fair trial is held by the claimant and defendant indivisibly.[259] He thought that the court had a constitutional role to play. This required the design of a system of rules capable of enabling the court to deliver its constitutional mandate. Unfortunately any system needs to be implemented, and it is there that Sorabji locates the difficulty. In order to follow Sorabji's argument[260] we need to step back from details of the pre-CPR and early CPR case law and look at who was in the adoptionist and who in the rejectionist camp, and what views

[247] *WfFR* (n 168) ch 20, para 12.
[248] *WfIR* (n 130) ch 26, paras 26 and 27.
[249] *WfFR* (n 168) ch 20, para 10.
[250] ibid ch 10.
[251] *WfFR* (n 168) ch 10, para 2.
[252] ibid ch 10, para 3.
[253] *WfFR* (n 168) ch 10, para 4.
[254] ibid ch 10, para 5.
[255] *WfFR* (n 168) ch 10, para 6.
[256] ibid ch 10, para 13.
[257] *WfFR* (n 168) ch 10, para 16.
[258] *WfIR* (n 130) ch 3, paras 9 and 38; ch 4, para 7(a) and (b)(i); ch 5, paras 11(b) and 17(a); ch 19, paras 6 and 7; ch 20, paras 2 and 4; ch 22, para 10; ch 23, para 10. In this sense, Woolf here shows continuity with the thinking of the *CivJ Rev* (n 142). For comment on how the amount of information available to the judge was increasing, see *JoloCP* (n 151) 382.
[259] *SorECJ* (n 50) 165–66.
[260] Set out in great detail ibid chs 4–7. This account follows Sorabji closely at this point, but offers a more abstract approach, looking at timing, differing viewpoints and the individuals involved.

were expressed. If we do this we can see two lines of cases. The adoptionist cause suffered an early set-back in late 1996, had to take an ameliorating stance in 1997 and 1998, and was in eclipse by 1995. All in all, the new theory failed to ever gain critical mass.

iv. Woolf's View of His Own Work

In *A New Approach to Civil Justice*,[261] Lord Woolf explained and defended his work. He said that he had taken 'a new look at what should be the aims of the justice system',[262] and that the old controlling principles of civil litigation '[had] to give way' to his new principles.[263] He said that he had worked on the basis of five principles: the 'equality principle', the 'expense principle', the proportionality principle', the 'expedition principle' and the 'efficiency principle'.[264] On the question of proportionality, Woolf accepted that complex cases might need a complex solution but objected to 'taking a sledgehammer to crack a nut' in simple cases.[265] He reinforced this image by saying that he was not proposing to ditch the Rolls-Royce approach, but rather was saying that

> the Rolls is kept in the garage except when … a long journey justifies its use. For shorter journeys … the Mini will get you to the correct destination just as well if not quicker and certainly more cheaply. For even shorter journeys … it's possible to use a bike.[266]

v. Woolf and Pre-implementation (1996–97)

In a pre-CPR decision delivered in June 1996,[267] Lord Woolf had indicated the need to consider the administration of justice. He spoke of the point of view of both parties and the need 'to do justice between other parties as well'.[268] However, in November of the same year the Court of Appeal set out principles the Court

[261] H Woolf, 'A New Approach to Civil Justice' in *Law Lectures for Practitioners*, Hong Kong Law Journal special edn (Hong Kong, Sweet & Maxwell, 1996) 1–14. Woolf needed to defend his work. Michael Zander was a persistent critic: see eg M Zander, *The State of Justice*, Hamlyn Lectures 51st series (London, Sweet & Maxwell, 2000) 39–42. Another of Woolf's defences appears in H Woolf, 'Medics, Lawyers and the Courts' (1997) 16 (Oct) *Civil Justice Quarterly* 302: Woolf's comment about Zander, 'If you heard his lecture you would no doubt be impressed by his eloquence but you should not have been impressed by the content. It was not based on any relevant practical experience' (ibid at 307), and Woolf's sensitivity that 'in addition to being Canute like and indulging in scatter gun tactics' Zander said that he was' building castles on sand and proceeding like the Generals of the First World War, just thoughtlessly blundering ahead' (ibid at 310), give a good flavour of the heat being generated by the debate.

[262] H Woolf, 'A New Approach' (n 261) 3.

[263] ibid 9.

[264] H Woolf, 'A New Approach' (n 261) 5.

[265] ibid, 7.

[266] H Woolf, 'A New Approach' (n 261) 12.

[267] *Beachley Property Ltd v Edgar* [1997] PNLR 197 (CA).

[268] ibid 201.

said would govern how the rules were to be applied in the context of missed time limits.[269] Whilst Millett LJ emphasised the importance of keeping to time limits, identified how failure to keep time impacted the system, and also talked about upholding the sanctity of the trial date and the need to prevent parties from jockeying to gain a strategic advantage,[270] the decision heavily emphasised the need for party cooperation, and seemed to place less weight on Woolf's overall philosophy than Woolf did.

A number of points arise from this. Perhaps judges in the Court of Appeal were concerned that one could take active case management too far. Did they worry about the level of applications that would be made on points where agreement could otherwise be reached if the parties were left to their own devices as much as possible? What we can see is a recognition that there would be many cases where case management would not be active as it amounted to a ready acceptance of the parties' wishes. The emphasis on keeping the trial date seems to have been viewed as a principal means of case management, a curiously conservative form of it. This decision makes sense from a purely legalistic perspective, but the impact of pushing back the start date for implementing the new approach simply meant that the implementation of the CPR would mark a wholly new beginning in philosophical terms, thus reducing the new philosophy's chances of gaining a hold.

In December 1996 the Court of Appeal came back to the question of implementation in *Letpak v Harris*,[271] where Waller LJ said that the trial judge was wrongly 'persuaded that the wind of change which is blowing hard in the direction indicated by *Beachley* had in effect already changed the practice of the court from that laid down in *Costellow*'. It is not evident that at this point Waller LJ thought that the CPR's overriding objective would take priority as a matter of principle.[272] He was very careful to emphasise the approach taken in *Costellow*[273] in 1993, where Sir Thomas Bingham MR had said,

> this problem arises at the intersection of two principles, each in itself salutary. The first principle is that the rules of court and the associated rules of practice, devised in the public interest to promote the expeditious dispatch of litigation, must be observed. The prescribed time limits are not targets to be aimed at or expressions of pious hope but requirements to be met …

[269] *Mortgage Corporation v Sandoes* [1997] PNLR 263 (CA) 284 (Millett LJ). Curiously Woolf was said to have agreed to the decision. Part of the issue for the courts was when the new approach was to operate. It was decided that, however unsatisfactory the old system, the new approach had to await the new rules: *Grovit v Doctor* [1997] 1 WLR 640 (HL) (Lord Woolf MR) (where the knock-on effects of delay were considered); and *Arbuthnot Latham Bank Ltd v Trafalgar Holdings Ltd* [1998] 1 WLR 1426 (CA) (Lord Woolf MR).

[270] Similar solutions being discussed in *Mitchell v News Group Newspapers Ltd* [2013] EWCA Civ 1537 and *Denton v TH White Ltd* [2014] EWCA Civ 906.

[271] *Letpak v Harris* (Court of Appeal, 9 November 1996), TLR 6 December 1996 (Waller LJ).

[272] Waller LJ certainly later recognised the importance of the changes required: see Waller LJ's dicta in *Worldwide Corporation Ltd v GPT Ltd* (Court of Appeal, 2 December 1998) (amendment of pleadings); and *Woods v Chaleff & Ors* [1999] EWCA Civ 1522 (amendment of pleadings).

[273] *Costellow v Somerset County Council* [1993] 1 WLR 256 (CA), a pre-Woolf and pre-CPR case.

He went on to say that 'The second principle is that a plaintiff should not in the ordinary way be denied an adjudication of his claim on its merits because of procedural default, unless the default causes prejudice to his opponent for which an award of costs cannot compensate.' Before concluding, 'Neither of these principles is absolute.'[274]

vi. The Civil Procedure Act 1997

Section 1(1) of the Civil Procedure Act 1997 provided:

> There are to be rules of court (to be called 'Civil Procedure Rules') governing the practice and procedure [of the civil courts].[275]

Section 1(3) of the Act dealt with the objects at which the rule-makers were to aim 'with a view to securing' them. Two kinds of aims were identified: there were system-level aims and rules-level aims. The former aims were that 'the system of civil justice' be 'accessible, fair and efficient'.[276] Noteworthy here is the introduction of efficiency as a concept, yet one that comes third in the order of priority, after accessibility[277] and fairness.[278]

Schedule 1, paragraph 4 to the Civil Procedure Act 1997 dealt with the vexed question of the interface between the law of evidence (a matter of substance) and rules of court (a matter of the law of procedure). The provision allowed the CPR to 'modify rules of evidence as they apply to proceedings in any court within the scope of these rules'.[279] As it happened, this scope was of narrower application than its promoters expected, the view being taken that legal professional privilege was a matter of fundamental rights.[280]

vii. Woolf: Implementation and Eclipse

So much for the run up to implementation of the Woolf Reforms. Thereafter, during the CPR's early era, the Court of Appeal had a number of opportunities to articulate the radical nature of CPR 1.1. In *Biguzzi v Rank Leisure Plc*, Lord Woolf

[274] ibid 263–64.

[275] Section 1 of the 1997 Act replaced provisions in s 84 of what was then the Supreme Court Act 1982. Section 84 in turn is traceable to s 99 of the Judicature Act 1925. Neither provision set out the objectives it was intended to achieve.

[276] Civil Procedure Act 2007, s 1(3)(a). *ZoCP* (2003) (n 52) para 1.38, touched upon this.

[277] The title of Woolf's Reports was *Access to Justice*.

[278] *ZoCP* (2003) (n 52) was to say that the rules committee was required to take 'an integrated approach to all aspects of litigation': ibid 1.45.

[279] ibid.

[280] *General Mediterranean Holdings SA v Patel* [2000] 1 WLR 272 (QBD (Comm Ct)). In *R (ex p Morgan Grenfell & Co Ltd) v Special Commissioner of income Tax* [2002] UKHL 21, [7], Lord Hoffmann said that privilege is a human right. The Civil Procedure Act 1997 of course pre-dated the Human Rights Act 1998, but it is not possible to see civil procedure as existing in a hermetically sealed vacuum.

had placed emphasis on the punishment's fitting the CPR crime, as Sorabji puts it. Yet, Sorabji argues, the Court of Appeal missed the opportunity in 2000, 2001, 2002 and 2005[281] to articulate a philosophy in accordance with the adoptionist line, because key figures did not in fact accept the premise that the RSC's underlying theory had been replaced. The crowning glory of the rejectionist line came in 2005 when Lord Carswell directly criticised robust case management, saying that a judge had been 'over-influenced by the defects on the part of the solicitors in preparing the case and by the imperative of efficiency in managing a stream of actions for trial'.[282]

What emerges from Sorabji's account is that, as we might expect, the traditionalist view was firmly embedded in the judiciary prior to the commencement of the CPR; that the judiciary was not in one accord as to the 'new science' aspect of what Woolf was attempting; and that Woolf seems to have trimmed his sails prior to implementation[283] – even the CPR steering team suffered from the limited availability of Woolf himself. Brooke LJ felt that he was left with much responsibility.[284] Thus, just over 10 years from the inception of the CPR, Jackson LJ was able to note that courts had become too tolerant and that the 'balance therefore needs to be redressed.'[285]

Sorabji notes in his chapter 5 that the traffic was not all one way. In 2000, Jolowicz had noted the opportunity for 'a new legal culture' whilst asking about the 'general idea' underlying it.[286] In the same year Neuberger J had noted that need for a shift in thinking to serve the needs of contemporary civil justice system,[287] an approach recognised by May LJ and Ward LJ in two cases in 2000.[288] In 2002,

[281] *Hannigan v Hannigan* [2002] 2 FCR 650 (CA) (Brooke LJ); *Thurrock BC v Secretary of State for Environment, Transport & the Regions* [2001] CP Rep 55 (CA) (Brooke LJ); *Sayers v Clarke-Walker* [2002] 1 WLR 3095 (Brooke LJ); *B v B* [2005] EWCA Civ 237 (Longmore LJ with Brooke and Arden LJJ in agreement). To this list we can add the earlier views expressed by Millett LJ in both *Mortgage Corporation v Sandoes* [1997] PNLR 263 (CA) and *Gale v Superdrug Stores Plc* [1996] 1 WLR 1089, and the later cases of *Adoko v Jemal* (1999) *The Times*, 8 July (CA) (Laws LJ), *Holmes v SGB Services Plc* [2001] EWCA Civ 354 (Buxton LJ) and *Thomson v O' Connor* [2005] EWCA Civ 1533 (Brooke LJ).

[282] *Moy v Pettman Smith* [2005] 1 WLR 581 (HL), [42]. See *SorECJ* (n 50) 224, showing how this was a straightforward application of the principle in *Tildesley v Harper* (1876) 10 ChD 393 that costs would be the usual cure for a mistake. Carswell, of course, did not have to actively manage a first instance case-load.

[283] Perhaps hoping that implementation of the CPR would usher in a new dawn.

[284] Brooke LJ's view in *Southern & District Finance Plc v Turner* [2003] EWCA Civ 1574, (2003) 147 SJLB 136, [34], is representative of his approach to the application of the theory of proportionate justice. In *ZoCP* (2003) (n 52) ix, Brooke adverted to the difficulties in coordinating the Court of Appeal's response. He dealt further with his experiences in 'Some thoughts on the first seven and a half years of the CPR' in *Ten Years* (n 53) 455–56. Brooke's perception was that he had made a considerable input because the Master of the Rolls might be elsewhere or have additional responsibilities.

[285] R Jackson, *Review of Civil Litigation Costs: Final Report* (London, TSO, 2009) (hereinafter '*JnReview FR*') 397. Jackson's earlier report is R Jackson, Review of Civil Litigation Costs: Preliminary Report (London, TSO, 2009) (hereinafter '*JnReview PR*').

[286] *JoloCP* (n 151) 386–87.

[287] *Charlesworth v Relay Road Ltd* [2000] 1 WLR 230.

[288] *Purdy v Cambran* [2000] CP Rep 67 (May LJ); *Arrow Nominees Inc v Blackledge* [2000] CP Rep 59, [2001] BCC 591(CA) (Ward LJ).

Sir Anthony May had referred to 'a profound new philosophy'.[289] The House of Lords had addressed the matter in 2003,[290] referring to an 'important shift in judicial philosophy' away from 'the traditional philosophy'. Dyson LJ had expressed the view in 2004[291] that the CPR had brought in a new era where old practices were to be abandoned. In 2006, Lord Hoffmann noted the challenges of balancing substantive justice, proportionality in individual cases, access to justice and the costs of running the justice system as follows:

> The overriding objectives of the Civil Procedure Rules include achieving justice for both Claimants and Defendants and saving time and expense. These objectives sometimes conflict and compromises are required. It is not the case that the administration of justice, alone among the services provided by the state, is exempt from any considerations of cost. It is obvious that a trial of this action … would be an enormous and expensive undertaking. … That is a factor which, however unpalatable it may be to those who think that justice is priceless, must be taken into account … [W]hen one considers the scale and cost of a trial, the case for stopping the proceedings now appears to me to be overwhelming.[292]

Yet it is significant that Woolf, Dyson, May, Ward and Neuberger did not carry the day even with Lord Hoffmann's vocal support. One must conclude that the blame for the overall failure of the Court of Appeal to articulate support for the Woolf Reforms can be laid at the door of the concept of justice on the merits, a concept that clearly still had its attractions at the theoretical level, even when it was seen to fail at the practical level.[293]

F. Civil Procedure 1999: First Generation Commentary

We must get used to the idea that practitioner works can be captivated by a philosophy. Sorabji argues that from the earliest days of the CPR, the *White Book* took a traditional line concerning Woolf's new philosophy.[294] This will be dealt with, but first one might consider the difficulty faced by the commentators. They were writing for lawyers who needed guidance, yet anything they said might be second-guessed by a court. In the circumstances the standard editorial approach is to be conservative. Nevertheless, the traditional 'feel' to the commentators' approach is striking: there is a touch of *plus ça change plus c'est la même chose* about parts of the commentary. It is important not to over-state the case here.

[289] Cited in *SorECJ* (n 50) 136.

[290] *Three Rivers DC v Governor & Comp of the Bank of England (No 3)* [2001] UKHL 16, [92] and [106] (Lord Hope) and [153] Lord Hobhouse).

[291] *Hashtroodi v Hancock* [2004] 1 WLR 3206 (CA), [16] (Dyson LJ).

[292] *Sutradhar v National Environment Research Council Sutradhar v National Environment Research Council* [2006] UKHL 33, [2006] 4 All ER 490 (HL), [42].

[293] Sorabji notes the lack of a theory in *Woods v Chaleff & Ors* [1999] EWCA Civ 1522; *Adoko v Jemal* (1999) *The Times*, 8 July; and *UCB Corporate Services Ltd v Halifax (SW) Ltd* [1999] CPLR 691 (CA).

[294] *SorECJ* (n 50) 118.

The title of the book was changed, from *The Supreme Court Practice* to *Civil Procedure*, and new commentary had to be written. Even the nature of the book changed. The purposive construing of the rules required a distinct shift from description to explanation.[295]

The *White Book*'s 1999 paperback edition set out the text of the new CPR.[296] Master Turner's foreword[297] made clear that adding the wording 'a new procedural code' was intended to send a signal to those interpreting the rules. What is significant is that this is marked in terms of freedom from earlier precedent, rather than freedom to work out of the new philosophy. Master Turner also noted the appearance of proportionality within the rules, but did not explain why this was so important.

The Commentary on CPR 1.1 noted that the overriding objective mattered; its elaboration could not be 'treated as amounting merely to a set of pious aspirations'.[298] This of course is true; the aspirations needed to be worked out in practice. The commentators then picked out two of the aspirations and privileged them by connecting them with the 'handmaiden of justice' passage from *Re Coles and Ravenshear*.[299] The commentators ran together 'justly' from the entry line of CPR 1.1 and 'fairly' from CPR 1.1(d), and indicated that achieving justice and fairness was 'the fundamental purpose of civil procedure'.[300] Significantly, fairness was severed from expedition, and saving expense and proportionality were left out altogether. So much for 1999. Has this passage been extensively revised as thinking on this topic has developed? The answer to that question is 'no'. Even in the 2017 edition the basic introduction to this passage remains the same, with the addition of a Supreme Court decision favouring the *Coles* approach.[301]

[295] My colleague David Dixon would argue that the increasing number of practice directions has reduced the need for the old style of commentary.

[296] The CPR were made under s 2 of the Civil Procedure Act 1997 and published as the Civil Procedure Rules (SI 1998/3132). The SI was published on 10 December 1998 and came into force on 26 April 1999.

[297] *White Book* (Spring 1999) viii.

[298] ibid para 1.3.2.

[299] *Re Coles and Ravenshear* [1906] 1 KB 1 (CA), 4.

[300] *White Book* (Spring 1999), para 1.3.3.

[301] *White Book* (2017) vol 2, para 11-8. The case is *NML Capital Ltd v Republic of Argentina* [2011] UKSC 31, [74]. The *White Book* passage goes on to argue that rules reflect values, and that reasonable people may disagree on what is just and fair. Procedure has a fundamental role in ensuring that the court can carry out its constitutional role, but individual justice is not distinct from the kind of justice produced by the overriding objective. Here the commentators refer to *Mitchell v News Group Newspapers* [2013] EWCA 1537, [38]. The general status of early RSC (1883) case law on the 'justice on the merits' theory is not what it was. So the famous dictum of Bowen LJ concerning amendment of pleadings in *Cropper v Smith* (1884) 26 Ch D 700 (CA), 711, to the effect that 'I have found in my experience that there is one panacea which heals every sore in litigation, and that is costs. I have very seldom, if ever, been unfortunate enough to come across an instance … which has put the other side to such a disadvantage as that it cannot be cured by the application of that healing medicine', no longer holds good. In *Global Torch Ltd v Apex Global Management Ltd and others (No 2)* [2014] UKSC 64, [2014] 1 WLR 4495, Lord Neuberger said 'even more importantly, the approach laid down in *Cropper v Smith* has been overtaken by the CPR'.

In the next paragraph the commentators ran together 'saving expense' (CPR 1.1 (2)(b)) and 'expeditiously' (CPR 1.1(2)(b)), choosing to deal with them under the rubric 'cost and delay' and relating this to Woolf's Interim and Final Reports.[302] What is significant about this is the intellectual carry-over from the old system, going back even further than the RSC (1883). The concept of the twin evils of cost and delay has a lineage going back into the early nineteenth century. The RSC (1883) were aimed at taming both evils. That the old language was carried forward is significant. If there had been a Copernican revolution, it is not clear that the commentators had recognised this.

The commentators turned next to proportionality without trying to define it. Significantly, they saw proportionality not as a new concept but one dating back to at least the 1988 *Civil Justice Review*.[303] In the commentators' eyes, civil procedure had always tried to match the size of a case with an appropriate procedure, with a view to proportionality. What had gone wrong was that in increasing the jurisdictional limit of the county court, the courts had lost sight of the compressed nature of county court litigation. The solution was two levels of proportionality. Allocation to either of the two lower case tracks would itself ensure that proportionality was built in. On the multi-track, proportionality would be 'assured by the court's power to control the development of the case' – CPR 1.2 imposed a duty on the court to give effect to the overriding objective. The logic of the commentary's argument here is that in the smaller cases, little further needed to be done; and in the larger cases, active case management would deliver proportionality.

It must be said that the commentary did make the correct call on the rebalancing nature of the equal footing provision (CPR 1.1(2)(a))[304] and the question of allotment of the court's resources (CPR 1.1(2)(e)).[305]

G. *Blackstone's Guide* (1999): First Generation Commentary

The second edition of *Blackstone's Guide*[306] noted *Jones v Telford and Wrekin DC* as demonstrating that 'the primary concern of the court is to do justice'.[307] The commentary in chapter 1 was notably brief. However, emphasis was placed on proportionality and allocation of resources. The authors then noted the controversy over the inclusion of 'expense and resources, which has caused concern

[302] *White Book* (Spring 1999), para 1.3.4.

[303] ibid para 1.3.5. See *CivJ Rev*, Cmnd 394, 1988. One might say proportionality was there in a nutshell, but it is not a developed concept in anything like the Jacksonian sense. Further, in this passage, the commentators elide the questions of cost and complexity, which are treated as being distinct in the *Civil Justice Review's* report.

[304] *White Book* (Spring 1999), para 1.3.6.

[305] ibid para 1.3.7.

[306] Charles Plant et al, *Blackstone's Guide to the Civil Procedure Rules*, 2nd edn (London, Blackstone Press, 1999) (hereinafter '*Blackstone's Guide*').

[307] *Jones v Telford and Wrekin DC* (1999) *The Times*, 29 July 1999.

to purists who consider that the principle of justice implies and requires that it should be done without regard to the cost at which it is achieved'. The commentators noted that costs could exceed the value of the claim or 'be out of all proportion to the amount in issue'. The authors accepted that this was a 'radical reform of civil procedure' and that the new rules were an attempt to address longstanding concerns.

One of the principles identified was that 'the cost of litigation should be more affordable, more predictable and more proportionate to the value or complexity of their case'.[308] Here the authors noted the level playing field argument, the importance of civil trial centres and specialist judges, the need to prevent parties gaining tactical advantages, and the bringing into force of more effective sanctions.

H. Jolowicz: Looking Backwards

In *On Civil Procedure*, Jolowicz dealt with the question of 'the purposes of civil procedure law' (note the plural) as follows. The traditional view, said Jolowicz, had been to see the purpose of civil justice as the resolution of a dispute between a particular set of parties: which is to say that the focus had traditionally been upon the parties to a particular legal action.[309] Jolowicz said that this view failed to take account of the following wider societal effects:

(a) civil proceedings serve to demonstrate the effectiveness of the law; and
(b) civil proceedings enable judges to engage in the work of clarifying and developing the law.[310]

Although in terms of publication Jolowicz's book dates to 2000, it is in reality a work of an earlier age and so it is not to be counted as a first generational work. Most of its contents were written pre-Woolf, and it engages heavily with Jacob rather than Woolf. There are, it is true, some passages on Woolf,[311] but for the most part they set out Woolf's proposals without a great deal of analysis. Jolowicz was something of an evolutionist, believing in gradual change and as conscious of what might be lost as gained.[312]

We now turn to deal with two second generation commentators – Adrian Zuckerman and Neil Andrews – who were writing with the benefit of the unfolding domestic jurisprudence on the CPR, yet who were also writing at a time of uncertainty over the precise significance of CPR 1.1.

[308] *Blackstone's Guide* (n 306), Introduction, para 1.5.1.
[309] *Blackstone's Guide* (n 306) 69–70.
[310] ibid 71–77. In his 1980 work *Natural Law and Natural Rights* (Oxford, Clarendon Press,1980) 268, John Finnis had argued that society has a justice system that, like all legal creations, relies upon bringing 'definition, specificity, clarity, and thus predictability' into human relations through the administration of rules in such a manner as to lead to the delivery either of a just decision, or of a just settlement.
[311] *JoloCP* (n 151) ch 18 in a general way and ch 19 more specifically.
[312] ibid 7.

I. Adrian Zuckerman: Second Generation Commentary

Zuckerman on Civil Procedure is the pre-eminent academic treatment of the CPR. First published in 2003, it saw two further editions in 2006 and 2013. It therefore had followed developments in the field over a significant length of time. Here we look at the 2003 edition.

i. Zuckerman First Edition

Zuckerman had a very clear view of the significance of the CPR – they were transformative, amounting 'to a significant change' of the field.[313] The rules were 'founded upon three imperatives: reaching substantively correct decisions, by means of proportionate resources, and in a reasonable time'.[314] Zuckerman recognised that 'the principal goal of civil procedure' remained 'doing substantive justice'. But the CPR brought into effect 'a new procedural discipline designed to enable the court to do substantive justice'. This was to be achieved within 'a reasonable time' and with the use of 'proportionate resources'.[315] All this made perfect sense: the CPR were new and there were unfamiliar factors to be taken into account in interpreting and applying them. Yet there was another strand to Zuckerman's thinking. Rectitude of decision-making included 'doing justice on the merits'.[316] The use of this phrase echoes the ambiguity/conflict current in the case law of the period. Probably Zuckerman meant this as a synonym for substantive justice (including accuracy), that is, for the direct end of justice whilst allowing for the existence of collateral ends. However, as traditionally conceived, justice on the merits meant something different; the direct end was so important that it took precedence over and could cancel out collateral ends. The use of this term here is significant, especially when coupled with its use elsewhere.[317] Zuckerman conceives of justice on the merits as covering both outcome, that is rectitude of decision-making, and process, that is cases must be brought to trial on the merits, any procedural problems notwithstanding. The process point remained within the intellectual framework. Woolf had again failed to fully oust the RSC's theory.

It is significant that Zuckerman dealt with the matter of fair process before embarking upon an analysis of the overriding objective.[318] For him, procedural

[313] *ZoCP* (2003) (n 52) para 1.1.
[314] ibid para 1.2.
[315] *ZoCP* (2003) (n 52) para 1.2. See also ibid para 1.6. Note that the reference to 'proportionality' in the index to *ZoCP* (2003) refers only to paras 1.90–1.93. There are also significant passages to be found ibid paras 26.60–26.82.
[316] See ibid para 1.6, where 'doing justice on the merits' is equated to 'substantive justice'.
[317] *ZoCP* (2003) (n 52) para 1.33.
[318] ibid para 1.3a.

fairness involved different 'requirements of justice' from proportionality (including economy and efficiency) and 'expedition'.[319] Fair process was 'timeless and universal'; it required 'to be observed regardless of' proportionality and expedition.[320] The pre-eminency of fair process is marked.

Zuckerman's terminology in this work suggests that he was working with the following different categories, set out in order of importance:

(a) constitutional obligations;[321]
(b) fundamental rights;[322]
(c) fair process rights covering a fair trial and the need for procedural fairness;[323]
(d) the imperative of ascertaining the truth (accuracy);[324]
(e) the imperative of timely resolution of disputes (temporal);[325] and
(f) the imperative of proportionality (resources)[326] including accuracy.[327]

All this is indicative of Zuckerman's determination offer a distinct view of CPR, a mark of the second-generation works. Zuckerman's book is notable not simply for being a collection of gobbets from Woolf; it offers a clear vision of procedural justice, albeit firmly within the English tradition and placing greater emphasis upon fundamental rights, the wider aspect of fair process and rectitude of decision-making than did Woolf. Zuckerman, too, refused to simplify: chapter 1 of his 2003 edition is as much an exercise in problematisation as it is an explanation. On the one hand stood the problematic old system and Woolf's recommendations aimed at changing it, together with the ever-present risk of backsliding. On the other hand were questions of established and fundamental rights, the dangers of changing everything at once, the need to give precedence to the CPR's distinctive terminology over Woolf's reports and, lastly, Zuckerman's own particular views about accuracy of decision-making.[328] In the end, Zuckerman was walking something of a tightrope: he was writing for academics and practitioners. A practitioner reading chapter 1 might have been forgiven for thinking that Woolf had overstated both the scope and import of his reforms, something that would fit with the trend in contemporary case law.

Zuckerman recognised that CPR 1.1 was intended to be 'the interpretive machinery' for the CPR and that if it was not utilised, 'civil procedure could easily revert to the form it took under the old system',[329] which had been marked

[319] *ZoCP* (2003) (n 52) para 1.8.
[320] ibid para 1.8.
[321] *ZoCP* (2003) (n 52) para 1.13.
[322] ibid para 1.46.
[323] *ZoCP* (2003) (n 52) para 1.8.
[324] ibid paras 1.13–1.14.
[325] *ZoCP* (2003) (n 52) paras 1.21–1.31.
[326] ibid paras 1.15–1.20.
[327] *ZoCP* (2003) (n 52) para 1.20.
[328] Zuckerman was not alone – see *JoloCP* (n 151) 85–88 and 396.
[329] *ZoCP* (2003) (n 52) para 1.5. He also noted the open-ended nature of CPR 1.1.

by complexity, satellite litigation and costs that could not be predicted and were too high.[330] The rule set out management goals.[331] It was 'open-ended' and 'a practical tool designed to obtain practical results'.[332] As indicated, Zuckerman's approach to CPR 1.1 was to concentrate upon three imperatives.

The first imperative, accuracy, is described as 'reaching substantively correct outcomes'[333] and as 'rectitude of decision making'.[334] Zuckerman noted that a note to a draft of Rule 1.1 stated that 'seeking the truth is so obviously part of the court's role that it does not need to be stated expressly'.[335] Zuckerman drew on William Twining to go further and argue that seeking the truth was 'the court's basic constitutional purpose', an argument that allowed accuracy to sit both at the level of imperative and at the higher level of constitutional obligation. This may partly explain how Zuckerman's 'take' on CPR 1.1 is so different from Woolf's.

If Woolf's theory of proportionate justice was clearly articulated and embedded within CPR 1.1, one might have expected Zuckerman to have recognised this. Yet his treatment is more nuanced than this. Having grappled with whether there were technical and non-technical senses of proportionality, a question he answered in the negative,[336] Zuckerman went on to say that '[p]roportionality is a non technical concept, which expresses the idea of a reasonable correlation between process means and expected ends'.[337] Next, he situated his interpretation of CPR 1.1 in a political and social context. The logic of his argument was centred around the policy issues of the system's allocation of its own resources and the use of the parties' resources. It was for parliament to decide how to spend public funds. Any call for spending on civil justice would have to take its place amongst other calls upon the public finances. There would therefore be a limit on the amount of money available, which would limit the number of judges and the amount of time they could offer to litigants. No litigant had the right to dictate the share of the resource they were granted – to this extent Zuckerman saw clear limits to personal autonomy. It was fairer to give the most complex cases the largest share of resources, not least because of the accuracy imperative. Simpler cases could fairly receive a smaller resource share.[338] As to the resources of parties, they were not limited. The deployment of any procedure would involve a commitment of individual resources, which had to be proportionate to what was in dispute.[339]

[330] ibid para 1.1.
[331] *ZoCP* (2003) (n 52) paras 1.7 and 1.8.
[332] ibid para 1.8.
[333] *ZoCP* (2003)(n 52) para 1.2.
[334] ibid paras 1.6 and 1.10, the latter tracing the distinction in Bentham's thinking between the direct end and the collateral end of justice. See also ibid paras 1.13–1.14.
[335] *ZoCP* (2003) (n 52) para 1.13.
[336] ibid para 1.3. He also dealt with the cost-reducing impact of allocation to track (paras 1.96–1.97).
[337] *ZoCP* (2003) (n 52) para 1.93.
[338] ibid paras 1.15, 1.17, 1.20.
[339] *ZoCP* (2003) (n 52) paras 1.16, 1.18, 1.20.

The third imperative – timely resolution of disputes – need not detain us long. It is here that Woolf and Zuckerman were closest. The latter was fully supportive of the need for timetables,[340] and expressly linked English civil procedure with Article 6.[341]

Zuckerman was clear that the three imperatives were 'capable of pointing in different directions'.[342] Speed might be costly or under-cut accuracy. It is here that Zuckerman's approach was strained at the seams. He accepted that it was necessary for a balance to be struck, and that justice on the merits had previously taken precedence over 'time and resources'.[343]

ii. Ten Years On

Just as Jackson was at work on his *Review of Civil Litigation Costs*, Oxford University Press published *The Civil Procedure Rules Ten Years On*. Writing as one of a number of authors,[344] Zuckerman chose to focus upon litigation management, which he saw as having failed to grasp 'the management imperatives of public services'.[345] This piece contains an important statement of Zuckerman's views on the justice system as a public service. Sections B and C of this chapter largely followed what Zuckerman had said previously – civil justice was a law enforcement service[346] and it had to answer to three imperatives.[347] Zuckerman then went on to state that public services have to balance resources and the service they provide in order to provide a service that is optimally balanced. This was a matter of policy as to how resources were best to be spent, and of implementation via a 'coherent and robust strategy'.[348] The management objective was to ensure that the justice system 'operates satisfactorily overall' as well as operating properly for the parties in any particular case.[349] Zuckerman's conclusion was that one of the drivers of management failure was indifference to non-compliance[350] and/or a one dimensional approach to dispensing justice.[351] Zuckerman's

[340] ibid para 1.30.
[341] *ZoCP* (2003) (n 52) paras 1.25–1.31 Art 6 of the ECHR, given effect in English law by s 3 of the Human Rights Act 1998, provides for the right to a fair hearing.
[342] *ZoCP* (2003) (n 52) para 1.32.
[343] ibid para 1.33.
[344] A Zuckerman, 'Litigation management under the CPR: a poorly-used management infrastructure' in *Ten Years* (n 53) 89–106.
[345] ibid, 89.
[346] A Zuckerman, 'Litigation management' (n 344), 90.
[347] ibid 91–92.
[348] A Zuckerman, 'Litigation management' (n 344) 92. The comments on proportionality in *ZoCP* (2003) (n 52) paras 1.15–1.17 and 1.20 appeared in *ZoCP* (2006) (n 52) paras 1.17–1.19 and 1.21 (which has minor changes). Para 1.22 deals with the inter-party aspect of proportionality and is new.
[349] A Zuckerman, 'Litigation management' (n 344) 93. Zuckerman expressly noted the Thatcherite move to subject public services to prioritising managerialism. Such a comment would have been unexceptional in the years of Tony Blair's premiership, with its emphasis upon targets – ibid 103.
[350] *ZoCP* (2003) (n 52) para 1.72, spoke of 'degradation of time limits under the old system'. See also *ZoCP*, (2006) (n 52) para 1.68.
[351] A Zuckerman, 'Litigation management' (n 344) 95–102.

conclusion for this was that 'judges do not believe in the need for effective management of the litigation service'. Worse, he thought, 'judges believe in possessing a right to mismanage the law enforcement process'.[352] They had no right to do this and needed to allow outsiders to judge whether or not they were succeeding.[353] The courts had no special right to be free from accountability to the public. Firmly in Zuckerman's sight was the Court of Appeal's failure to use CPR 3.9 as a means of enforcing the rules.[354]

iii. Zuckerman Third Edition

By 2013, Zuckerman was of the view that the civil justice system was about law enforcement.[355] Upholding the rights of complainants was not just a private matter. Upholding private rights sent a public message and encouraged the overall smooth running of society. He said that this activity is 'a public service, delivered by a public authority, with the objective of redressing wrongs'.[356]

Further, there was the question of the amount of information upon which the decision is based. The more evidence that was required, the greater the cost to litigants and to the public purse.[357]

The question of proportionality[358] related to the public service theory that underlay Zuckerman's first chapter. The truth is that justice comes at a price,[359] and this is in a world where litigants and public services are constrained by questions of cost, as indeed are all but the very wealthiest individuals and corporations. The point is that public services are ultimately funded by the public by means of taxation. The question of what taxes should be levied is of course a political one – one that our political representatives make on our behalf. And decisions on taxation concern not just the question of what the public can afford to pay, but also what the public should pay and what it is feasible for the government to collect, in the case of multi-national companies for example. Zuckerman argued that no member of the public can claim a right to a public service that is unaffordable.[360] The question could then simply be 'What is affordable?'

Zuckerman said that the civil justice system is a public service.[361] That service has a constitutional role, and that is to deliver the enforcement of rights. The system is not, he said, the public equivalent of private dispute recognition services.[362]

[352] ibid 102.
[353] A Zuckerman, 'Litigation management' (n 344) 103.
[354] ibid 104.
[355] *ZoCP* (2013) (n 52) para 1.7.
[356] ibid. Echoing A Zuckerman, 'Litigation management' (n 344) 91.
[357] *ZoCP* (2013) (n 52) para 1.12.
[358] See *Campbell v MGN Ltd (No 2)* [2005] UKHL 61, [23] (Lord Hofmann).
[359] *ZoCP* (2013) (n 52) paras 1.10, 1.17, 1.29.
[360] ibid para 1.10. Here he appears to engage with R Dworkin's, *A Matter of Principle* (Oxford, Clarendon Press, 1986) 72–73 and 92–93.
[361] *ZoCP* (2013) (n 52) para 1.15 goes as far as referring to 'the litigation service'.
[362] ibid para 1.6.

The whole principle of the rule of law depends upon this. The courts uphold rights by offering a remedy for wrongs. Without such remedies there would be no rule of law. Zuckerman here was following the Blackstonian line on the role of the courts.[363] One is struck by a number of thoughts.

First, even though the system had gone badly wrong enough to require three major enquiries and concomitant rule changes in less than 50 years,[364] it seems wrong to argue that the rule of law was not operating properly during this period. Lord Bingham, for example, does not seem to suggest that the rule of law has not been achieved. Rather it is both a historical tradition, a present reality and, for him, a source of hope for the future.[365] So it might be possible to restate Zuckerman's argument in this way. The rule of law is optimised when the largest number of people have the right of access to a court, and where that right of access includes a service that is cost-effective and reasonably expeditious.

On the question of procedure, Adrian Zuckerman suggested that the function of the civil justice system is to deliver a public service for the enforcement of rights.[366] Other functions, such as dispute resolution and truth-finding, fit within the wider function of enabling the citizen to have his or her rights enforced.[367] Law enforcement is a 'transcendent' value that 'underwrites' the citizen's rights,[368] said Zuckerman, because 'the surest way of undermining good social order is to allow

[363] *ZoCP* (2013) (n 52) para 1.7. See also W Blackstone, *Commentaries on the Laws of England*, vol 1 (Oxford, Clarendon Press, 1765–69) 137 and 140, cited ibid.

[364] Civil Justice Review: Report of the Review Body on Civil Justice, Cmnd. 394 (London, HMSO, 1988); H Woolf, *Access to Justice: Interim Report* (London, HMSO, 1995); H Woolf, *Access to Justice: Final Report* (London, HMSO, 1996); R Jackson, *Review of Civil Litigation Costs: Preliminary Report* (London, TSO, 2009); and R Jackson, *Review of Civil Litigation Costs: Final Report* (London, TSO, 2009).

[365] See T Bingham, *The Rule of Law* (London, Allen Lane, 2010). To a large degree Bingham's is not a stand-alone theoretical work. He is theorising about constitutional law and practice in the light of a long political tradition of English politics – just as Montesquieu in *L'Espirit de Lois* was theorising about constitutional law and its nexus with politics: see C de Secondat (Baron Montesquieu), *The Spirit of the Laws*, tr T Nugent (New York, Hafner Press, 1949) chs 11 and 12. Bingham's is a book arguing for the importance of the judicial strand in English political life. Both it and H Woolf, *The Protection of the Public – A New Challenge*, Hamlyn Lectures 41st series (London, Stevens & Sons Ltd, 1990), and A Denning's *Freedom Under the Law*, Hamlyn Lectures 1st Series (London, Stevens & Sons Ltd, 1949), are of bigger import than simply being statements of what the law is or was.

[366] *ZoCP* (2013) (n 52) para 1.5. For an American view in the context of personal injury litigation, hypothesising that there are there two cultures of civil litigation (one of which does not view litigation as a public good) that are reflected in the political stances of parties, see SC Yeazell, 'Unspoken Truths and Misaligned Interests: Political Parties and the Two Cultures of Civil Litigation', 60 *UCLA Law Review* 1752, especially 1765–72. For partisan work on this topic, see WK Olson, *The Litigation Explosion* (New York, Truman Talley Books, 1991) 223–93; WK Olson, *The Rule of Lawyers* (New York, Truman Talley Books, 2003) 73–98; PW Huber, *Galileo's Revenge* (New York, Basic Books, 1991) 111–47. The standard scholarly survey is provided by W Haltom and M McCann, *Distorting the Law* (London, University of Chicago Press, 2004). I applied Haltom and McCann's approach in D De Saulles, 'Nought Plus Nought Plus Nought Equals Nought: Rhetoric and the Asbestos Wars' (2006) 4 *Journal of Personal Injury Law* 301.

[367] *ZoCP* (2013) (n 52) para 1.5.

[368] ibid para 1.7.

infringement to go without redress. Where there is no redress for wrongs there is no value to rights and no reason to behave according to law.'[369]

Having argued that the civil justice system is there to provide a public service, Zuckerman went on to argue that a public service requires management,[370] and that 'justice management' in particular requires the balancing of the cost to the taxpayer, with the risk and cost to which the litigants are exposed.[371]

J. Neil Andrews (2003)

In 2003, Neil Andrews noted that the Woolf Reforms represented 'the greatest shake-up in civil procedure since the 1870s'.[372] Andrews argued that Woolf's largest decision was the introduction of case management.[373] He also thought that the overriding objective, which he called 'a resonant preamble',[374] required the court to promote 'proportionality, procedural equality, speediness and efficiency'.[375] Andrews saw the overriding objective as 'guidance' aimed at the judiciary and the parties and their advisers, the last two categories being expected to change the way they had behaved in the past.[376]

Andrews revisited and developed his thinking on principles in chapter 3 of *English Civil Procedure*. He distinguished between 'fundamental procedural guarantees' (which had constitutional protection) and mere 'leading principles'.[377] It is not clear that Andrews bought the fundamental shift model.

[369] *ZoCP* (2013) (n 52) para 1.7.

[370] ibid para 1.8. See also A Zuckerman, 'The Challenge of Civil Justice Reform: Effective Court Management of Litigation' (2009) 1 *City University of Hong Kong Law Review* 49, 54.

[371] *ZoCP* (2013) (n 52) paras 1.10–1.13.

[372] N Andrews, *English Civil Procedure* (Oxford, Oxford University Press, 2003) para 2.04.

[373] ibid para 2.26.

[374] *AndECP* (n 372) para 2.28.

[375] ibid.

[376] *AndECP* (n 372) para 2.28.

[377] ibid para 3.01. Within the category of *fundamental procedural guarantees* Andrews placed his former principles of relating to the judiciary (ibid paras 4.02 and 4.28), publicity (ibid para 4.59) and due notice (ibid para 5.01) as fundamental procedural guarantees, and puts the giving of reasons (ibid para 5.41), the avoidance of delay (ibid para 5.70) and excusing the parties when the court has fallen short (ibid para 5.71) into the same category. In the *leading principle* category he placed access to justice (ibid para 6.03), the right to choose a lawyer (ibid para 6.04), the right to confidential legal consultation (ibid para 6.21), procedural equality (ibid para 6.26), protection against weak claims (ibid para 6.31), simplicity (ibid para 6.34), judicial control (ibid para 6.43), proportionality (ibid para 6.49), disclosure (ibid, para 6.52), orality (ibid para 6.55), procedural equity to deal with errors of procedure (ibid para 6.67), the promotion of settlement (ibid para 6.76), accuracy (ibid 6.81 133), fair play (ibid 6.136), protection of non-parties (ibid para 6.110), effectiveness (ibid para 6.116) and finality (ibid 6.122). He also noted (ibid paras 3.14–3.23) that principles could clash and that choices would have to be made. All of this is both exhaustive and exhausting. Looking back, one would have preferred Andrews to have used an arrangement similar to that later used in his *Andrews on Civil Processes*, vol 1 (Cambridge, Intersentia, 2013) (hereinafter '*AndoCP*'). In Andrews' defence, Woolf was similarly prolific with his spelling out of principles; it is just that one could navigate back to the overriding objective to give one perspective.

He did distinguish between the constitutional and the merely procedural, but his second account (*English Civil Procedure*) is less easy to follow than his first account or his third account of the topic.[378] The first account was premised on complete justice being a bundled set of principles. His second account had to take account of the overriding objective, yet seems not to fully engage with it. Perhaps Andrews' earlier scepticism about change accounts for this. Whatever may be the case, Andrews' *English Civil Procedure* offered no compelling rival to Woolf, though his book may have given intellectual support to the rejectionists. He made a respectable and principled case for all of his arguments. The only thing is, if there had been a Copernican change, Andrews account was inaccurate.

K. The Future of Civil Justice (2005)

The Association of District Judges published a report in 2005 that offers a useful indicator of progress.[379] The report noted that although the CPR had been a general success, cost, in particular, was a concern: '[W]e believe that Lord Woolf's hope that the new regime would reduce cost has not been met. The cost of civil litigation remains unreasonably high, and concerns about cost are widely expressed.'[380] Further, 'Legal costs, particularly in some smaller claims, have continued to increase, and are frequently out of all proportion to the amounts being claimed.'[381] This latter point is of interest given that Andrews' *Principles of Civil Procedure* had concentrated upon the complexity and cost of larger claims. The problem, it seems, had spread.

The Report was critical of recent rises in court fees and questioned why the cost of litigation should fall so heavily upon the litigants.[382] Overall the Report should be viewed as a principled defence of public funding coupled with heavily signalling that: ADR was to be a welcome part of the mix going forward;[383] investment was needed in technology;[384] the financial levels of the tracks were ripe for reconsideration;[385] and that the District Judges were willing to take on more complex cases.[386]

[378] *AndPCP* (n 150) and N Andrews, *English Civil Procedure* (n 372), respectively.

[379] D Oldman (ed), *The Future of Civil Justice: The Association's proposals for the future of the Civil Justice System* (London, Association of District Judges, 2005).

[380] ibid para 2.2.

[381] D Oldman, *The Future of Civil Justice* (n 379) para 4.1.

[382] ibid para 3.1.

[383] D Oldman, *The Future of Civil Justice* (n 379) paras 6.2–6.15; Early Neutral Evaluation was favoured (ibid Annex 1). See now CPR 3.1(2)(m), revised on 1 October 2015.

[384] D Oldman (ed), *The Future of Civil Justice* (n 379) paras 9.1–9.3.

[385] ibid paras 11.1–11.6

[386] D Oldman, *The Future of Civil Justice* (n 379) paras 12.1–12.6.

L. Jackson's Reports

i. Jackson on Costs

The Jackson Reports[387] were focused principally on the question of costs.[388] He noted that 'The issues upon which I am asked to report are both complex and intractable. They do not admit of simplistic answers.'[389]

His terms of reference were, 'To carry out an independent review of the rules and principles governing the costs of civil litigation and to make recommendations in order to promote access to justice at proportionate cost.'[390]

Jackson said, 'There is no doubt that litigation over costs has increased dramatically in recent years, and that this growth is one of the driving factors behind the present review.'[391] Note that the period covered was the period of the CPR, which were supposed to have eliminated the problem. It is notable also that chapter 3 of Jackson's *Preliminary Report* offered extensive coverage of the costs war over conditional fee agreements, before noting that the structure of the relevant legislation would have caused a costs war even without Woolf.[392]

Jackson expressly addressed the question of the purpose of the system. He said '[i]t is the role of the civil courts to resolve disputes between citizens, companies' and other bodies. Jackson thought that 'Dispute resolution by the courts means something more than finding a solution which everyone can live with or imposing a solution upon reluctant parties.' Rather, it involves the court in exercising five functions:

(i) receiving evidence on disputed matters and making necessary findings of fact;
(ii) identifying and applying the relevant legal rules or principles;
(iii) determining the issues fairly between the parties;
(iv) upholding the rights of parties;
(v) arriving at decisions which are in accordance with law and justice.[393]

This led on to a brief practical meditation on the nature of justice in England:

> This report is not the place for an essay on the nature of justice. Perhaps, however, it is legitimate to mention that the effective administration of justice, including civil justice, is vital to the well being of every community.[394]

[387] This book does not look at the other important aspects of Jackson such as qualified one-way costs shifting. The focus is upon proportionality and sanctions.

[388] Although this did not prevent him from also tackling CPR 3.9. See *JnReview FR* (n 285) ch 39. para [6.7].

[389] *JnReview PR* (n 285) (v). Jackson makes the same point in *JnRef* (2018) (n 33) para [28-001]. See also R Pound, 'Some Principles of Procedural Reform', 4 *Illinois Law Review* 388, 389 (1909–1910).

[390] *JnReview PR* (n 285) ch 1, para 1.

[391] ibid ch 3, para 5.1. For possible drivers of costs, see *ZoCP* (2013) (n 52) para 27.3, viz, 'economic activity follows the most rewarding path'; the legal market lacks 'transparency and competition'; and it is difficult for clients to quantify whether or not they are getting good value.

[392] *JnReview PR* (n 285) ch 3, paras 5.46–5.47.

[393] ibid ch 4, para 1.1.

[394] *JnReview PR* (n 285) ch 4, para 1.7. See also *JnRef* (2018) (n 33) paras 1-002–1-007.

The effective administration of justice requires consideration of questions of corrective justice and distributive justice, the practical issues involved in providing the legal architecture of society, the economic importance of being able to enforce agreements and the societal consequences that flow from people knowing that they need to keep to their obligations.[395] Jackson then moved on to discussing the benefits of ADR.[396] He concluded chapter 4 of the *Preliminary Report* by saying:

> If the civil courts are to perform their functions properly, one way or another, it is necessary that litigation costs should be contained within the means of all parties, namely claimants, defendants and all others brought into litigation.[397]

Jackson made clear that he was guided by two 'propositions':[398]

> First, the proper functioning of the civil courts is essential to the well being of society. Secondly, if the processes of the civil courts are so onerous that the parties cannot reasonably afford to litigate, then those courts are not functioning satisfactorily.[399]

Jackson argued that when thinking about the question of legal costs, there were two principles in play. First was the *principle of compensation*: 'a wrongdoer should restore the innocent party to the position in which he would have been, if the wrong had not occurred'.[400] This principle can be seen in the operation of what is now CPR 44.2(2)(a) – costs follow the event. It has the effect of shifting onto the unsuccessful party a good proportion of the legal costs incurred by the successful party. This is in addition to any question of compensation for the substantive breach or wrong. Second was the *principle of proportionality*. Broadly put:

> The essence of proportionality is that the ends do not necessarily justify the means. The law facilitates the pursuit of lawful objectives, but only to the extent that those objectives warrant the burdens thereby being imposed upon others.[401]

Put in a more focused manner, Jackson argued that 'the costs burden cast upon the other party should not be greater than the subject matter of the litigation warrants'.[402] This required that a balancing exercise be carried out. Jackson cited Adrian Zuckerman as highlighting the need 'to maintain a sensible correlation between costs, on the one hand, and the value of the case, its complexity and importance on the other hand'.[403] Jackson noted that proportionality was of narrower scope than necessity. It might be necessary to do something to win,

[395] *JnReview PR* (n 285) ch 4 paras 1.7–1.10.
[396] ibid ch 4, para 2.6.
[397] *JnReview PR* (n 285) ch 4, para 3.3.
[398] Compare *ZoCP* (2013) (n 52) para 27.2.
[399] *JnReview PR* (n 285) ch 4, para 3.3.
[400] *JnReview FR* (n 285) ch 3, paras 5.2 and 5.4.
[401] *JnRef* (2018) (n 33) para 5-014, says, 'Procedural requirements should be proportionate to the subject matter of the litigation.' J Tidmarsh, 'Realising the Promise of Costs Budgets: an Economic Analysis' (2016) 35(3) *Civil Justice Quarterly* 219, 225, refers to 'socially wasteful' expenditure. This phrase encapsulates that which proportionate costing is supposed to avoid.
[402] *JnReview FR* (n 285) ch 3, paras 5.3 and 5.4.
[403] ibid ch 3, para 5.8, citing *ZoCP* (2006) (n 52) para 26.38.

but it did not follow that it was proportionate to pass that particular cost on to the unsuccessful party.[404]

Jackson proposed the following new rule:

> Costs are proportionate if, and only if, the costs incurred bear a reasonable relationship to:
>
> (a) the sums in issue in the proceedings;
> (b) the value of any non-monetary relief in issue in the proceedings;
> (c) the complexity of the litigation;
> (d) any additional work generated by the conduct of the paying party; and
> (e) any wider factors involved in the proceedings, such as reputation or public importance.[405]

This proposed rule ultimately ended up in the new CPR 44.3(5), save that 'if and only if' became 'if'. There is surprisingly little judicial guidance on this rule. Jackson LJ has said:

> It was expected that there would be a cluster of test cases in which the Court of Appeal would apply the new rule to different scenarios. That has not happened. The profession is becoming impatient. The remedy lies in their own hands.[406]

Perhaps the most useful guidance has come from the Commercial Court, which has said that judges should look at the lowest reasonable amount that is required to have the case conducted proficiently.[407]

ii. Jackson on Sanctions

In his *Final Report*, Jackson LJ reach the following conclusion:

> [C]ourts at all levels have become too tolerant of delays and non-compliance with orders. In so doing they have lost sight of the damage which the culture of delay and non-compliance is inflicting upon the civil justice system. The balance therefore needs to be redressed.[408]

[404] For a viewpoint on some of the complex factors impinging upon proportionality, see G Simpson-Scott, 'Justice, proportionality and fixed costs in clinical negligence' (2017) 4 *Journal of Personal Injury Law* 249. Jackson understood the pull of the competing factors of compensation and proportionality: see *JnReview FR* (n 285) paras 5.1–5.13; and *JnRef* (2018) (n 33) para 5-028. There is the unresolved question of what 'proportionality' means. Vague language may invite satellite litigation, but so may a precise definition. Contrast *JnRef* (n 33) paras 5-038 and 5-039.

[405] *JnReview FR* (n 285) ch 3, para 5.15. For a thoughtful analysis of this, see A Higgins, 'Lord Justice Briggs' "SWOT" analysis underlines English law's troubled relationship with proportionate costs' (2017) 36(1) *Civil Justice Quarterly* 1. Noting the need for a functioning proportionality requirement, Higgins says, 'The English courts provide a Rolls Royce system of justice that works for a privileged few, and not the many'. The pre-2013 approach to proportionality was much hampered by the decision in *Lownds v Home Office* [2002] EWCA Civ 365: see, eg, *JnRef* (2018) (n 3) para 5-024. The effect of the post-Jackson rule changes was that 'proportionality should trump reasonableness': ibid paras 5-029–5-031.

[406] Lord Justice Jackson 'Was It All Worth It?', Lecture to the Cambridge Law Faculty on 5 March 2018, para 3.18.

[407] *Khazakstan Kagazy Plc v Zhunus* [2015] EWHC 404 (Comm), [13].

[408] *JnReview FR* (n 285) ch 39, para 6.5.

Jackson's proposal was to simplify CPR 3.9 by removing the nine separate factors, replacing them with '(a) the requirement that litigation should be conducted efficiently and at proportionate cost; and (b) the interests of justice in the particular case'. He went on to say that the proposal 'simplifies the rule and avoids the need for judges to embark upon a lengthy recitation of factors. It also signals the change of balance which I am advocating.'[409] He ended with the following recommendation 'The courts should be less tolerant than hitherto of unjustified delays and breaches of orders. This change of emphasis should be signalled by amendment of CPR rule 3.9.'[410]

Details of what transpired are set out in chapter 5. Suffice it to say that Jackson has, understandably, been quite circumspect about the decision in *Mitchell v News Group Newspapers Ltd* [2013] EWCA Civ 1537. The following comment sums up Jackson's overall public position: 'As a result of the decision in *Mitchell* ... for several months the courts went to the other extreme and imposed or maintained sanctions which were unduly tough'.[411]

Clark and Jackson's book, *The Reform of Civil Justice*, goes on to say that '[i]nitially the Court of Appeal took a very tough line ... The Court of Appeal took note of ... criticism and adopted a softer approach in *Denton*', a case which they said 'strikes roughly the right balance' and one which 'the courts have been following ... without particular problems or undue complaint'.[412]

M. Lord Neuberger and Lord Justice Peter Gross

We close the list on judicial statements by looking at two recent statements delivered extra-judicially. That context is important, because it is on such occasions that judges are more likely to express themselves in terms which may be accessible to the general public. Each statement pins its colours to the rule-of-law mast.

Lord Neuberger said, in the 2013 Tom Sargent Memorial Lecture:

> The rule of law requires that any persons with a bona fide reasonable legal claim must have an effective means of having that claim considered, and, if it is justified, being satisfied, and that any persons facing a claim must have an effective means of defending themselves. And the rule of law also requires that, save to the extent that it would involve a denial of justice, the determination of any such claim is carried out in public. So citizens must have access to the courts to have their claims, and their defences, determined by judges in public according to the law.[413]

[409] ibid.
[410] *JnReview FR* (n 285) ch 39, para 8.1(vi).
[411] *JnRef* (2018) (n 33) para 5-015.
[412] ibid para 13-034.
[413] D Neuberger, 'Justice in an Age of Austerity', Tom Sargent Memorial Lecture, 15 October 2013, para 23. Available at www.supremecourt.uk

And he continued:

> Access to justice has a number of components. First, a competent and impartial judiciary; secondly, accessible courts; thirdly, properly administered courts; fourthly, a competent and honest legal profession; fifthly, an effective procedure for getting a case before the court; sixthly, an effective legal process; seventhly effective execution; eighthly, affordable justice.[414]

In 2018, Peter Gross gave the Jonathan Hirst Lecture, where he said, 'If a State does not uphold law and justice, no other rights can be enforced or entitlements enjoyed', and '[t]he provision of civil justice by the State is an integral part of that … duty. The provision of civil justice is a public good, securing the rule of law, not simply another public service.'[415]

Dr John Sorabji was mentioned in each lecture, a fact that takes us on to Sorabji's understanding of Lord Woolf's theory.

N. Sorabji's Reading of Woolf

And what was this new theory? Sorabji called it 'proportionate justice', saying that it had four constituent parts:

(a) Ensuring access to justice for all by allowing 'an equitable distribution' of the court's resources, thus 'vindicating rights and upholding the rule of law'. The constitutional aspect is there and, from this, one could make the following case: it is the court's constitutional duty to deliver justice; if the court is to deliver justice then it must actively manage cases; the court does not have power to actively manage cases, so it must be given the requisite powers if it is to discharge its constitutional obligation. Sorabji emphasised the general vindication and enforcement of the rights of all as being the court's constitutional role.[416] He was, however, at pains to point out that he was not suggesting that individualistic substantive justice in individual cases was somehow excluded from the overriding objective. To the contrary, he said, substantive justice was included within the overriding objective and the general architecture of the rules was designed to deliver it, amongst other secondary aims.[417] So we may say that the constitutional aim was primary and the individualistic aim auxiliary to it.

(b) The delivery of substantive justice to individual litigants. This had been the primary aim of the 'justice on the merits' theory but was an auxiliary aim in Woolf's theory of procedural justice.

[414] ibid para 31.

[415] P Gross, 'Courts and Arbitration', The Jonathan Hirst QC Commercial Law Lecture (2018), available at www.judiciary.uk.

[416] *SorECJ*, (n 50) 143 and 169. The argument is based on Lord Woolf's comments in *WfIR* (n 130) 2.

[417] *SorECJ* (n 50) 142–44. 'Individualistic' appears at 161.

(c) Proportionality in how the case was prepared for trial. This was another auxiliary or secondary aim of equal importance in Woolf's theory.
(d) The minimisation of cost and delay for all litigants.[418]

Sorabji said that Woolf's theory was a distributive one,[419] which is to say it allocated goods in a proportional manner. This required taking into account, and balancing off against each other, the resources available and the demands for access to those resources.

O. What was Woolf Thinking?

As a preliminary to thinking about Woolf, there are a number of questions raised by Sorabji's account:

(a) *Whether Woolf really had a coherent theory at all?* Woolf did have a theory, and it was a general theory of procedural justice rather than a particular theory. It was general because it articulated the nature of procedural justice in a way that was potentially transubstantive and certainly transprocedural. The general theory was conceptually distinct from the particular local theories underlying the procedures that were to be used to deliver Woolf's vision.[420] In this sense Woolf went beyond Jack Jacob,[421] whose work offered great insight but no overarching new vision of civil procedure. Jacob was clearly concerned about the impact of litigation on the citizenry, but his work is conceptually located in the old procedural universe. Woolf also went beyond Neil Andrews,[422] who had presented a series of carefully worked out articulations of particular theory that demonstrate the effect to be achieved by particular rules and the procedural values which are to be served by proceeding in this fashion. There is, in Woolf, a distinction between the general and the particular, in the same way that Victorian civil procedure was able to distinguish between the particular procedure embedded in the forms of action and the general possibility of having a uniform originating process.[423]

Woolf was trying to do a great deal and the extent of his ambition exceeded the reach of his theory. The sheer number of actions required by Woolf's vision undoubtedly cut across the ability of the Woolf Reforms to succeed. The larger the number of actions required, the more difficult it was for any judge to link them to a general theory.

[418] Sorabji's order has been changed. See ibid 136–37.
[419] *SorECJ* (n 50) 224.
[420] *AndPCP* (n 150) convincingly demonstrated that each procedure had a function and that this function had a theoretical dimension.
[421] *JbFabr* (118).
[422] *AndPCP* (n 150).
[423] See the Uniformity of Process Act 1832, s 1; the Common Law Procedure Act 1852, s 2 and sch A no 1.

Woolf's theory is merged into the detail of his two Reports. With the benefit of hindsight, one can extract the parts of Woolf's Reports that amount to a general theory. One wonders whether it was so easy at the time to say what the theory was or, more importantly, how it would be applied. The high degree of 'misunderstanding' demonstrated by commentators should give us pause for thought here. The diffuse nature and structure of CPR 1.1 cannot have helped.

The detail itself of the Reports and the reforms proposed had to take account of existing personnel, structures and the procedural framework created by the RSC (1883). Woolf was not starting with a blank sheet. The system was already operational. Changes would have to be negotiated with the politicians and with the judiciary. Staff would need training, colleagues would doubtless carry on doing what they were used to. There was over a century of doing things the RSC way.

(b) *If Woolf did have a coherent theory, whether it was one of 'proportionate justice'?* This is a more difficult question. One wonders whether Woolf's theory was as fully worked out as Sorabji suggests.[424] The overriding objective looks like an attempt to inject some Article 6 thinking into English procedural law.[425] Woolf had a record here: his 1990 Hamlyn lectures displayed a distinct penchant for harmonising the Strasbourg and English jurisprudence on the topic of human rights.[426] Of proportionality there was no mention, but Woolf thought the common law capable of incorporating new ideas in a manner not dissimilar to that advocated by Lord Neuberger in his 2014 lecture in Melbourne.[427]

If Woolf did not have a fully articulated theory of proportionality, Jackson undoubtedly did have a theory of proportionate justice. He recognised the need to

[424] It can take time for legal ideas to sink in and for their implications to be worked out – see, eg, *R (Lumsdon) v Legal Services Board* [2015] UKSC 41, [23]–[39] (Lords Reed and Toulson) on a deeper understanding of what proportionality means; and *R v Horncastle* [2009] UKSC 14, [2010] 2 AC 373, [11] (Lord Phillips) on the flexibility available to the Supreme Court on questions of EU law. See also N Phillips, *Strasbourg Has Spoken* in *Judge and Jurist: Essays in Memory of Lord Rodger of Earlsferry*, eds A Burrows et al (Oxford, Oxford University Press, 2013) 111.

[425] Lord Woolf said that the CPR were intended to be Art 6 compliant, see *Daniels v Walker* [2000] 1 WLR 1382 (CA), 1386. By the stage of *Daniels* the courts were increasingly fed up with the citation of Convention law as if it offered a magic solution. One ventures to suggest that had proportionality been highlighted as of great significance in the early CPR days, it would have gone the same way as the level playing field – see *Maltez v Lewis* (1999) *The Times*, 4 May 1999 for an example of established theory and praxis trumping the new rules, a decision of Neuberger J. The principle expressed to be at stake was freedom of choice of counsel.

[426] H Woolf, *The Protection of the Public – A New Challenge*, Hamlyn Lectures 41st series (London, Stevens & Sons Ltd, 1990) 120–22.

[427] D Neuberger, 'The role of judges in human rights jurisprudence: a comparison of the Australian and UK experience', Supreme Court of Victoria, Melbourne, 8 August 2014, paras 29–30 (available at www.supremecourt.uk) – note Neuberger's distinctly Whiggish view of history. As it happened, of course, the common law did not adapt as Woolf had hoped and the Labour Party stepped in. The Human Rights Act 1998, a direct contemporary of the CPR, was the result. For brief comment, see Jack Straw, *Last Man Standing, Memoirs of a Political Survivor* (London, Pan Books, 2013) 270–71.

apply the proportionality brake to the ongoing rise in legal costs. Jackson's theory grew out of Woolf's and amounts to a practical outworking of it. If we look again at Sorabji's four constituent parts of proportionate justice, we can see the following:

(a) *Justice for all.* That this was undoubtedly Woolf's aim is most clearly manifested in the level playing field requirement in CPR 1.1(2).
(b) *Delivery of substantive justice.* This is another but weaker form of justice on the merits – here of the form 'justice on the merits through the operation of the system' rather than 'justice on the merits despite default', which was the approach taken under the RSC.
(c) *Proportionate preparation.* Notwithstanding the expressed aim of proportionality, the CPR as implemented contained insufficient controls to ensure that this was a likely or even feasible outcome.
(d) *The minimisation of cost and delay.* Woolf undoubtedly intended to reduce delays. He succeeded in this aim. The question of cost was addressed head-on in the Reports. Yet Woolf lacked a developed theory of proportionality of effort and cost. Woolf saw that management was part of the key, as was the use of tracks, yet there was no overall way of controlling effort if that could not be measured in terms of cost.

In conclusion, Jackson's theory was one of proportionate justice. Woolf's theory was one of managed justice. He trusted that this would deliver economy.

The next chapter looks at Anglo-American attempts to tackle problems within civil justice systems by looking at their intention (or object), the actions required to achieve the object and the outcomes that resulted.

3

Intention, Action and Outcome in Anglo-American Civil Procedure

I. The Rules of the Supreme Court (1883 and 1965)

A. The Role of the Court

The scholarly consensus is that under the Rules of the Supreme Court (RSC), the role of the Court was thought to be one of ensuring that procedure facilitated the reaching of a just and accurate decision based on the merits of the individual case. Thus intention was expected to produce action as expressed by the term 'complete justice'. The term is to be found in section 24(7) of the Judicature Act 1873. This provision permitted joinder where it was 'necessary or expedient to enable the court to do *complete justice*'.[1]

That this was the intention behind and the action required by the Rules is seen in *Cropper v Smith*,[2] to which Sorabji refers as proof of the RSC's theory of justice, where Bowen LJ said, '[n]ow, I think it is a well established principle that the object of Courts is to decide the rights of the parties, and not to punish them for mistakes they make in the conduct of their cases by deciding otherwise than in accordance with their rights' and 'Courts do not exist for the sake of discipline, but for the sake of deciding matters in controversy'.[3]

This classic statement of the justice on the merits theory's intention and action[4] defines it both negatively and positively. Put positively, Bowen LJ made clear that

[1] Emphasis added. In this chapter the 'old overriding objective' is used to refer to the rule as originally passed, and the 'new overriding objective' to refer to that in force from 1 April 2013.

[2] *Cropper v Smith* (1884) 26 ChD 700 (CA) (patent case, stay pending appeal). Michael Lobban sets out the background to English equity reform in M Lobban, 'Preparing for Fusion: Reforming the Nineteenth-Century Court of Chancery, Parts I and II' in 22:2 *Law and History Review* (Summer, 2004) 389, and 22:3 *Law and History Review* (Autumn, 2004) 565. *Cropper* is an interesting illustration of the use of ideas drawn from the law reform milieu. This utilisation has been very common under the CPR, and has extended as far as adopting the language of extra-judicial lectures.

[3] *Cropper* (n 2) at 710. Bowen LJ was in the minority. For a good discussion of the case law on this subject, see J Sorabji, *English Civil Justice after the Woolf and Jackson Reforms: A Critical Analysis* (Cambridge, Cambridge University Press, 2014) (hereinafter '*SorECJ*') 56–67.

[4] Other cases to cite would be *Poyser v Minors* (1881) LR 7 QBD 329 (CA), 333 (a pre-1883 case concerning county court non-suit), *Kurtz v Spence* (1887) LR 36 ChD 770 (CA), 776 (a patents case concerning striking out) and *Tildesley v Harper* (1878) 10 ChD 393 (CA) 396 (amendment of pleadings).

the prime function of a court of law was to decide the rights of the parties on the issues in dispute. Put negatively, the objective of the RSC (1883) and the Judicature Acts was not to punish parties for their mistakes, nor to enforce discipline, as had been the case prior to the Judicature Acts.[5] Bowen LJ was articulating a theory of justice that ran contrary to those which were dominant prior to the passing of the Judicature Acts. The positive goal was treated as being dominant. It was because this goal existed that the court must strive to avoid punishing parties.

As we shall see, in order to free the civil justice system from the captivity of the theory of justice articulated by Bowen LJ in *Cropper*, Woolf chose to specify new targets that the Civil Procedure Rules (CPR), and by extension the courts using them, were meant to hit. The CPR moved litigation away from the RSC's litigant-oriented *intention* and *action*; away from its theory of justice.

We should note that despite the work that has been done on identifying theories of justice or general ideas in relation to the RSC (1883), those Rules had no formally expressed goals on their face. The lack of effective reflection on this topic until the advent of the Woolf Reforms can be put down to a number of things:[6]

(a) the inherent reliance of substantive justice upon procedural justice. It took the Woolf Reports to really bring home to English lawyers the point that if the procedure does not work then people will not receive effective justice – either because they are put off litigating, or because the overall costs in time, money and effort are too high;
(b) the lack of a distinctly social aspect to the way that procedural justice was seen. It was only once it could be seen that delay in 'case 1' might have a knock-on effect for 'case 2' and 'case 3' that the social cost of dysfunction began to be articulated adequately;
(c) the lack of an adequate understanding of the complexity of processing large numbers of cases within the civil justice system;
(d) the lack of an adequate contemporary understanding of the need for judges to manage cases and to have the expertise to do this successfully;
(e) a belief in, or at least a respect for, party autonomy and a commitment to a self- denying ordinance on the question of the neutral role of the judge.

B. The Summons for Directions (1883 and 1965)

The RSC (1883) introduced what was known as the omnibus summons. Order 30, rule 1 provided that any party might take out 'one general summons for directions', which would cover the pleadings, disclosure, the taking of evidence,

[5] Judges really got their teeth into this post-1883.

[6] There are earlier meditations, but Woolf presented a sustained working out of a theory – managed justice.

and the mode and place of trial.[7] By 1965 the position of the summons for directions was pivotal.[8] Order 25, rule 1 provided that the summons for directions was to be a means of reviewing the preparation of the parties for trial. Interlocutory matters were to be dealt with as far as possible, and directions were to be given to 'secure the just, expeditious and economical disposal' of the action.[9] The summons was supposed to be truly comprehensive and to consider 'all the matters' that needed to be considered.[10] The court was supposed to try to secure admissions,[11] and parties were required 'to give all such information and produce all such documents' as might be required to help the court fulfil the mandate of the summons.[12]

The summons for directions was the procedural vehicle that most closely foreshadowed the move towards active case management under the CPR. That apart, the RSC did not contain any express statement of their intention or outcome. Nevertheless, the way that the Rules were operated can be seen to be underpinned by a general idea.[13]

C. The General Idea

The new 'Rules of the Supreme Court' came into force in 1883, against the background of a series of Commissions identifying problems with the operation of the civil justice system.[14] Broadly, the Commissioners saw what the problems were and favoured reform,[15] although it is questionable whether they conceptualised

[7] *White Book (1883–84)*, eds T Snow et al (London, William Maxwell & Son and Henry Sweet, 1883) at 311.The editors hoped that the omnibus summons might lead to fewer unnecessary applications.

[8] The Evershed Committee Final Report made proposals that are set out at section III, paras 77–80. See R Evershed, *The Final Report of the Committee on Supreme Court Practice and Procedure*, Cmd 8878 (London, HMSO, 1953).

[9] RSC (1965) Ord 25, r 1(1)(b). Cf Rule 1 of the FRCP (1938), 'the just, speedy, and inexpensive determination of every action'.

[10] RSC (1965) Ord 25, r 2(1).

[11] RSC (1965) Ord 25, r 4.

[12] RSC (1965) Ord 25, r 6(1).The closest equivalents under the CPR are allocation to track under CPR 26 and the Case Management Conference under CPR 29 and Practice Direction (PD) 29, para 5.

[13] This general idea was brought to the RSC (1883) by those who had to interpret them. They were very mindful of the formalistic nature of the system that had preceded the RSC (1883).

[14] The reforms are dealt with in ch 5 of RW Millar, *Civil Procedure of the Trial Court in Historical Perspective* (New York, Law Centre of New York University, 1952) at 43–51; B Odgers, 'Changes in Procedure and the Law of Evidence', in *A Century of Law Reform* (London, Macmillan & Co Ltd, 1901 at 203–40); and, *in extenso*, in S Rosenbaum, *The Rule-Making Authority in the English Supreme Court* (Boston, MA, Boston Book Company, 1917). Rosenbaum is particularly useful on the personalities involved, having had contact with important judicial figures in England during his stay here. P Polden, 'Mingling the Waters: Personalities, Politics and the Making of the Supreme Court of Judicature' (2002) 61 *Cambridge Law Journal* 575 deals with the passing of the Judicature Acts and the creation of the Supreme Court of Judicature. He is especially good on judicial resistance to change and on the failure arising from the sending of all the judges of the then Supreme Court (including those in the Court of Appeal) on circuit.

[15] Not all reports were equally enthusiastic about modernisation. For example, the *First Report of Her Majesty's Commissioners for Inquiring into the Process, Practice, and System of Pleading in the Superior Courts of Common Law* (London, HMSO, 1851) at 13, 34, was more enthusiastic than the *Third Report*

what they were doing in modern terms.[16] The RSC (1883) contained no statement of objectives[17] but the background was clear: the Common Law Procedure Act 1852 introduced the Writ of Summons, rendering the Forms of Action obsolete; the Judicature Act 1873 constituted a Supreme Court of Judicature,[18] incorporating the previously distinct Superior Courts of Common Law and Equity.[19] The same Act fused the administration of common law and equitable jurisdiction, procedure and remedies.[20]

Jolowicz argued that underlying the RSC (1883) and their successor Rules down to 1998 was a 'general idea' – that of 'complete justice'.[21] The phrase used by the Commissioners in 1853 had been, 'every court ought to possess within itself the means of administering complete justice within the scope of its jurisdiction'.[22] Jolowicz described the general idea as follows:

(a) the concepts of substantive and procedural justice became distinct;[23]
(b) there was a move towards fact pleading;[24]
(c) there was a clear understanding of the parties' autonomous role in 'fixing' the facts, that is in setting out the scope of the dispute;[25]
(d) the focus was upon the parties to the litigation, not upon the wider civil justice system or society.

made to His Majesty by the Commissioners appointed to inquire into the Practice and Proceedings of the Superior Courts of the Common Law (London, House of Commons,1831) at 6–7.

[16] The judges had power to change the rules: see, eg, the Rules of Hilary Term 1834. This is a point made by EM Morgan, 'Judicial Regulation of Court Procedure' 2 *Minnesota Law Review* 81 (1917–1918) at 82. It was established at common law that the English judiciary had this power – *Bartholomew v Carter*, 3 Manning & Granger, 133 ER 1083, 125 (1841). The case concerned a challenge to the 1833 Rules. The Court of Common Pleas held that the Rules were promulgated under the inherent jurisdiction rather than under s 3 of the Civil Procedure Act 1833 (3 & 4 Will IV, c 42).

[17] Although Zuckerman argues, in A Zuckerman, *Zuckerman on Civil Procedure: Principles of Practice* (hereinafter '*ZoCP*') (London, Sweet & Maxwell, 2013) para 1.71, that the RSC's philosophy was 'embedded' by virtue of RSC (1883) Ord 70, r.1 (non-compliance) and RSC (1883) Ord 64, r 7 (time).The 1883 Ord 70, r 1 can be traced back to 1875 (when it was Ord 59). Zuckerman's reference at para 1.71 must, anachronistically, be to RSC Ord 3, r 5 under the RSC (1965).

[18] Comprising what are now called the Senior Courts – namely the High Court and the Court of Appeal.

[19] Judicature Act 1873, s 3.

[20] Judicature Act 1873, s 24.

[21] J Jolowicz, '"General Ideas" and the reform of civil procedure' (1983) 3 *Legal Studies* 295, 297–98. As well as Jolowicz's work on this topic, Sorabji also makes the point that the Second Common Law Commission in 1853 adopted the concept of complete justice: *SorECJ* (n 3) 52–53. For a light-touch article written from the Michigan perspective, see WB Perkins, 'The English Judicature Act of 1873' 12:4 *Michigan Law Review* 277 (1914). We would want to leave open the questions of the exact interrelationship between *complete justice* and *justice on the merits*, and the wider question of whether the former is wider than the latter, or put another way, to recognise that the RSC's theory had a larger content than '*justice on the merits*' alone, albeit it was that which came to predominate.

[22] *Second Report of Her Majesty's Commissioners for inquiring into the Process, Practice, and System of Pleading in the Superior Courts of Common Law* (London, HMSO, 1853) 35. This passage appears in the context of an argument about the limited nature of the procedures available in the common law courts and the consequent need for reform (ibid at 34–36).

[23] J Jolowicz, '"General Ideas"' (n 21) 298, 300.

[24] ibid 300–01.

[25] J Jolowicz, '"General Ideas"' (n 21) 302.

Instead of referring to 'complete justice', Zuckerman refers to 'justice on the merits',[26] the latter being now more commonly used than the former.

In his recent book, Sorabji has argued forcefully for the general idea being, in fact, an underlying theory. He calls this theory both 'complete justice' and 'justice on the merits'. He also argues that English civil justice system has always tried to achieve substantive justice: prior to the 1870s it did so via formalism at common law and equity's complete justice;[27] from the 1870s (ie post fusion) it did so by applying the 'complete justice' approach to all cases,[28] and more latterly this has been replaced by the overriding objective's conception of justice.[29]

This author would be inclined to see 'complete justice' as describing equity's theory of how things should be done and why that approach was a good one. Complete justice was a theory of a dysfunctional system; the delays in equity cases were notorious. Yet the commitment to fusion and to the use of equity's best ideas[30] led to a new fusion procedure that could have worked. The sense that the old common law formalism had caused the rejection of meritorious cases led the RSC's early interpreters to push to prominence the theory of justice on the merits. This sowed the seeds for the RSC's eventual doom.[31]

So, justice on the merits can be seen as operating as both intention and action. It works to override all other procedural objectives of the justice system, but is subject to the limiting condition that the cost of rectifying mistakes be capable of being cured through the payment of costs by the party in breach. This sense of the meaning of 'overriding' is highlighted by Michael Legg.[32]

John Sorabji uses the analogy of science. Just as, from time to time, existing scientific theories prove inadequate and a paradigm shift is required in science, so, because civil justice reform had consistently failed, the Woolf Reforms ushered in a set of ideas and a new way of thinking.[33] As Sorabji points out, the civil justice system proved incapable of reforming itself by using 'known rules and procedures', as a result of which the 'normal science' of law reform 'went astray', leading to Woolf's 'extraordinary investigations', which led to 'a new set of commitments,

[26] *ZoCP* (2013) (n 17) para 1.70.

[27] *SorECJ* (n 3) 68.

[28] Sorabji deals with this topic in ch 2 of *SorECJ* (n 3). For an American view on this topic, see SN Subrin, 'How Equity Conquered the Common Law', 135 University of *Pennsylvania Law Review* 909 (1987) at 929–31, 942–43, 956–63.

[29] Sorabji traces the Benthamite roots of this approach in ch 3 of *SorECJ* (n 3), and the working out of Woolf's theory in chs 5 and 6 of the same work. In ch 4, Sorabji sets out the misunderstanding and misapplication of Woolf's theory post-1999.

[30] See here SN Subrin, 'How Equity Conquered the Common Law' (n 28).

[31] A good example of how the 'was-good' became the 'currently-good', with the background assumption that it was the 'always-good'.

[32] M Legg, 'Reconciling the Goals of Minimising Cost and Delay with the Principle of a Fair Trial in the Australian Civil Justice System' (2014) 33(2) *Civil Justice Quarterly* 157 at 162. Legg is referring to the Explanatory Memorandum, Access to Justice (Civil Litigation Reforms) Amendment Bill 2009 (see Legg's fn 30).

[33] *SorECJ* (n 3) from 21.

a new basis for the practice of science'.[34] The overriding objective encapsulates the new rules, that is it says what the new rules are for. Sorabji's application of the analogy to English civil litigation supports his insights into the purposive nature of the rules of civil procedure and the impact of theories on how civil justice systems operate.

A prefiguring of Sorabji's argument can be found in Jeffrey W Stempel's work.[35] Stempel writes about the moves towards civil procedural reform in the US in the 1980s and early 1990s, noting how politicised the question of reform had become. Significantly, for us, he applies Kuhn's ideas about the development of science to the development of the law. He notes that that instead of knowledge being immutable, it reflects the 'consensus of [a] profession's leadership'.[36] Stempel says that 'the open courts system came to face external events that it could not completely explain or neutralize'.[37] The fit is a good one for the pre-CPR and pre-Jackson English courts.

Stempel argues that lawyers have even more scope for invention than do scientists,[38] and that Kuhn's work provides 'an instructive analogy'.[39] This is because law has its own periods of stability and frenzy.[40]

Noting that the legal profession has more nominal opinion leaders than the scientific community, Stempel says that the reforms leading to the Federal Rules of Civil Procedure (FRCP) were driven by a relatively small group.[41] This is true of the Woolf and Jackson Reforms in their formulation (subject to revision by the Rules Committee). As to interpretation and implementation, Sorabji makes the point that the lack of support from key appellate judges was one of the causes of the problems that beset the CPR.[42]

We are assured that the FRCP 1938 are not the source of the overriding objective.[43] Yet there is a marked coincidence of ideas between the CPR in England and the FRCP in America, which, taken with the words of those who created or drafted them, is suggestive that there is at the very least an intellectual affinity between the two such as to be worthy of consideration.

[34] ibid 22, citing T Kuhn, *The Structure of Scientific Revolutions*, 3rd edn (Chicago, IL, University of Chicago Press, 1996) at 68ff. For further pressing into service of Kuhn, see P Ziegler, 'A General Theory of Law as a Paradigm for Legal Research' (1988) 51(5) *Modern Law Review* 569.

[35] JW Stempel, 'New Paradigm, Normal Science or Crumbling Construct? Trends in Adjudicatory Procedure and Litigation Reform', 59 *Brooklyn Law Review* 659 (1993).

[36] ibid 695–96.

[37] JW Stempel, 'New Paradigm' (n 35) 717.

[38] ibid 697.

[39] JW Stempel, 'New Paradigm' (n 35) 699.

[40] ibid 704.

[41] JW Stempel, 'New Paradigm' (n 35) 704–05. This is true of the Woolf and Jackson Reforms.

[42] This is addressed in ch 4.

[43] John Sorabji, in 'The Road to New Street Station: the Overriding Objective' [2012] *European Business Law Review* 77 at 79, cites R Turner, '"Actively": The Word that Changed the Civil Courts' in D Dwyer (ed), *The Civil Procedure Rules Ten Years On* (Oxford, Oxford University Press, 2009) (hereinafter '*Ten Years*') at 81. For further background, see D Dwyer, 'What is the Meaning of CPR r 1.1(1)?' in *Ten Years*, 66.

In a sense, English thinking on this topic was a relative latecomer. The Americans had been much more structured in their thinking at an earlier stage, and it is to this that we must now turn.

II. The Federal Rules of Civil Procedure (1938)

A. A Sense of Purpose

Speaking of early law reform movements in the US, Robert G Bone says that 'Each of the earlier movements had a strong sense of shared mission. Interest in reform peaked in large part because changes in ideas and beliefs about law and procedure made the existing system seem irrational.'[44] The point is the same as that made by Sorabji in his paradigm shift analogy.

Of the system today, Bone argues that 'we need a more rigorous approach to such fundamental questions as the purposes civil adjudication should serve … In short, it is not possible to choose good Federal Rules without knowing what makes a Federal Rule good.'[45] Bone's object of desire is the creation of 'principles that fit and justify the core features of litigation practice'.[46] This is not a new American concern, as the History has shown. The official formulation contained in FRCP Rule 1 is the subject of the next section.

B. Interpretation

As a reminder, Rule 1 read as follows:

> These rules govern the procedure in the district courts of the United States in all suits of a civil nature whether cognizable as cases at law or in equity, with the exceptions stated in Rule 81. They shall be construed to secure the just, speedy, and inexpensive determination of every action.[47]

[44] RG Bone, 'Making Effective Rules: The Need For a Procedure Theory', 61 *Oklahoma Law Review* 319 (2008) at 321.

[45] ibid 319–20.

[46] RG Bone, 'Making Effective Rules' (n 44) 328.

[47] For Rule 1, see CW Wheaton, 'Federal Rules of Civil Procedure Interpreted', 25 *Cornell Law Review* 28 (1939), which is notable (at 29) for citing the Rule without mentioning its interpretative role. The article is useful for reviewing literature prior to 1939. Rule 1 provides 'the basic philosophical principle for the construction of the rule'. See CA Wright and AR Miller, *Federal Practice and Procedure*, 3rd edn (Eagan, MN, West Group, 2002) section 1011 at para 60, Rule 12. The original Rule is cited in PD Edmunds, *Federal Rules of Civil Procedure*, vol 1 (Chicago, IL, Callaghan & Co, 1938) at 1; and JW Moore et al, *Moore's Federal Practice*, vol 2, 2nd edn (Albany, NY, Matthew Bender & Co, 1993 (updated from 1948)) at 1-1. See also PD Edmunds, 'Lecture Digest, The New Federal Rules of Civil Procedure' 4 *John Marshall Law Quarterly* 291 (1938).

The second sentence provides the basic guideline of construction to be used in applying the Rules; they are to be interpreted to secure 'the just, speedy, and inexpensive determination of every action'. James William Moore said that the second sentence 'states the guiding principle of interpretation for the Rules and insures their operation as a flexible and efficient instrument in the administration of justice'.[48] Moore made the point that the ordinary common law rules of strict interpretation were not to apply.

C. The Objective of the FRCP (1938)

Rule 1 of the FRCP expresses the objective of the Rules but in relation to an end to be achieved through interpretation – such a goal is internal to the rule system. Put in other language:

(a) the Rules are to be interpreted with the intention in mind;
(b) the court is mandated to 'construe' the Rules to achieve that intention; so
(c) where interpretation is required then an intention-directed interpretation is to be favoured.

A number of points arise here. First, the Rule sets out an action flowing from an intention. Robert G Bone makes the point,

> the critical sentence in Rule 1 is styled as a statement of interpretive method rather than general purpose. To be sure, it implies a purpose – 'to secure the just, speedy, and inexpensive determination of every action' – but it does so in the context of declaring how the Rules should be construed.[49]

It is correct that the intention of securing a certain type of determination of proceedings is mentioned only in the context of the interpretation of the Rules, a point to which we shall come, but it is nonetheless an explicated goal, and it is expressed in terms that the intention should be acted upon. We are not here dealing with an implicit theory in the form encountered in *Cropper v Smith*.[50]

Second, the goal is tripolar: speed and expense are as much goals as is justice. There is no sense here that the goal can be severed and one objective within the overall goal be treated as paramount, or even as first among equals.

[48] JW Moore et al, *Moore's Federal Practice* (n 47) vol 2 at 1–23. James William Moore became the Chief Research Assistant to the Advisory Committee and a member of the Committee in 1953 (ibid 1–13 to 1–14).

[49] RG Bone, 'Improving Rule 1: A Master Rule For The Federal Rules', 87(2) *Denver University Law Review* 287 (2010) at 292–93. Textual analysis can of course only carry one so far, but the words used may indicate what was important to the participants. Hoffer writes movingly of this in PC Hoffer, 'Text, Translation, Context and Conversation: Preliminary Notes for Decoding the Deliberations of the Advisory Committee', 37 *American Journal of Legal History* 409 (1993). This study is not limited to the wording chosen by the various participants. As SN Subrin says in 'On Thinking about Description of a Country's Civil Procedure', 7 *Tulane Journal of International & Comparative Law* 139 (1999) at 142, one also needs to look for the social, political and economic causes of reform.

[50] *Cropper* (n 2).

This non-differentiation is not without its problems for, third, the chosen goal reflects the values the draftsmen wished to be realised through the operation of the Rules. As Bone reminds us, the choice of rules is value-rich and subjective. Further, the act of choosing may lead to conflicts between distinct values, which in turn may require an element of compromise or the making of hard choices,[51] but the need for making such a choice may not have been apparent to the American law reformers.

Fourth, there is an apparent simplicity to the goal, which may be misleading. In 'The Federal Rules of Civil Settlement',[52] J Maria Glover argues:

> The 1938 reformers sought primarily to eliminate procedural technicalities that prevented cases from being resolved on their merits through the application of substantive law to the facts and that stood as an obstacle to justice for ordinary citizens. To achieve this goal, the Federal Rules embraced a relatively simple model of adjudication: Cases were to be resolved on their merits at trial.[53]

Yet as we have seen, the question of a meritorious disposal may not always sit easily with questions of time and economy.

Both Jolowicz and Zuckerman have highlighted the importance of the function of this concept of the merits within the interpretation of the RSC (1883),[54] Jolowicz referring to this as the 'general idea' and Zuckerman speaking of it as 'the justice on the merits approach'.

Fifth, where interpretation is required then an intention-informed interpretation is to be favoured. The object of interpretation – the just, speedy and inexpensive determination of proceedings – is to that extent an internal one – it relates back to the intention behind the rules.

Sixth, the just, speedy and inexpensive determination of proceedings is, at the same time, an external goal. The Rules as a whole are to be interpreted with the end in mind. That end relates to the people and the society for whom the FRCP exist. The interpreting court is mandated to construe the Rules to achieve the external goal.

Seventh, in the light of the statements made prior to the FRCP coming into force, it is the whole of the Rules in their detail, structure, procedure and sequencing that had the goal of merits-directed justice, speed and economy, and which were envisaged as being interpreted accordingly. As we shall see in discussing the 'narrow interpretation' approach exemplified by Scalia J in *Torres v Oakland Scavenger Company*,[55] this view is not shared universally.

[51] RG Bone, 'Improving Rule 1' (n 49) 292–93 and 301.

[52] JM Glover, 'The Federal Rules of Civil Settlement', 87 *New York University Law Review* 1713 (2012) at 1719.

[53] ibid.

[54] See J Jolowicz, '"General Ideas"' (n 21) 297–98; and *ZoCP* (2013) (n 17) para 1.70.

[55] *Torres v Oakland Scavenger Company* 487 US 312 (1988) at 318.

D. The Present-Day FRCP and Parallel Rules

We need to pause at this point to interpose within our study, for the sake of completeness, the current wording of Rule 1 of the FRCP and other State-level rules that run roughly parallel to it. The reception of the early FRCP Rule 1 is dealt with later in this chapter.

The current FRCP Rule 1[56] states that the Rules are to be 'be *construed, administered, and employed* by the court and the parties to secure the just, speedy, and inexpensive determination of every action'.[57] The current version provides that both the court and the parties are to be engaged in the process of construction, administration and use of the Rules to secure the goal.[58]

Turning to the State level, Rule 1 of the Massachusetts Code of Civil Procedure provides:

> These rules govern the procedure … in all suits of a civil nature whether cognizable as cases at law or in equity … They should be construed, administered, and employed by the court *and the parties* to secure the *just, speedy, and inexpensive determination* of every action and proceeding.[59]

Similar wording, with an important addition, is to be found in Rule 104 of the New York Code – Civil Practice Law and Rules – which provides that the 'civil practice law and rules shall be *liberally construed* to secure the *just, speedy and inexpensive* determination of every civil judicial proceeding'.[60] Here the emphasis shifts from interpretation and action to the ground of liberality of construction. The phrase 'liberally construed' will be encountered again when we look at the narrow approach to interpretation favoured by Scalia J.

We now address the question of how Rule 1 FRCP operates, in its old and new forms, and consider whether the language in which it is couched is of assistance.

E. Clarity and Opacity

Elizabeth G Porter[61] says that Rule 1 actually functions 'as the Rules equivalent of an agency's regulatory preamble – a statement of basis and purpose'.[62] Porter goes on to warn that due to a combination of 'cultural and semantic drift', Rule 1 may now have a meaning different from that which it originally had, or that at least the Rule gives us mixed messages. This is because the FRCP envisaged parties taking cases to trial, but the reality is that most cases now settle.[63]

[56] 2016 version.
[57] Emphasis added.
[58] It is interesting that Rule 1 FCPR 2016 uses the stronger term 'to secure' rather than the weaker term 'to further' used in CPR 1.1.
[59] Emphasis added. Reference to the obligations of the parties was added in 2016.
[60] Emphasis added.
[61] EG Porter, 'Pragmatism Rules', 101 *Cornell Law Review* 123 (2015).
[62] ibid 158.
[63] EG Porter, 'Pragmatism Rules' (n 61) at 160–61.

Porter goes on to mention the poetic 'irreducible opacity' of Rule 1.[64] This statement deals with a number of distinct issues:

(a) Rule 1 does not say when or how it is to function as a rule of construction.
(b) The Rule does not specify the weight to be given to the tripolar intention, as against the wording of specific procedural rules.
(c) The Rule does not indicate the range of discretion open to the court in applying any given discretion.
(d) The Rule does not say anything explicit about the goal of the Rules. It does not say 'because *x* is a reason therefore do *y* as an action' but rather 'do *y* as an action', leaving the reader to wonder whether '*y*' is both the action and its reason, or whether there is a distinct and unexpressed reason '*x*'.

The Rule is not quite as opaque as is suggested. The general drift is clear – justice, speed and economy are to be sought. To that extent, Porter's view that Rule 1 works like a statement of regulatory principle is closer to the mark. The difference is that Rule 1 is effect-directed (do action *y*) rather than cause-directed (because of *x* do action *y*), although the purpose behind the rule is very clear.

So here, paradoxically, intention, in the sense of purpose (the 'what we want') and action ('how we shall get what we want') begin to merge. Intention in the sense of reasons ('why we want it') remains unexpressed. We should not be surprised at the hazy boundary lines between intention and action, for life has a habit of falling short of the clarity with which we can think about it. The difficulties posed by the language used in Rule 1 can be illustrated by reference to an English statute drawing upon international thinking – the Arbitration Act 1996.

F. The Arbitration Act 1996

Rule 1 of the FRCP is less direct than section 1 of the Arbitration Act 1996. This Act was new law at the point when Woolf was considering access to justice.[65] Section 1 of the 1996 Act provides:

> 1. **General principles**
>
> The provisions of this Part are *founded on the following principles*, and shall be *construed* accordingly—
>
> (a) the *object* of arbitration is to obtain the fair resolution of disputes by an impartial tribunal without *unnecessary delay or expense*;

[64] ibid 163–64. The suggestion is that it is almost koan-like. As to koans, see AW Watts, *The Way of Zen* (Harmondsworth, Pelican Books, 1962) at 180–81.

[65] Woolf was appointed on 28 March 1994. H Woolf, *Access to Justice: Interim Report* (London, HMSO, 1995) was delivered in June 1995. A draft of an Arbitration Bill was published in July 1995 but without a purpose clause. This was added to the draft published in December 1995 (see R Merkin and L Flannery, *Arbitration Act 1996*, 4th edn (London, Informa, 2008) at 5–6). H Woolf, *Access to Justice: Final Report* (London, HMSO, 1996) (hereinafter '*WfFR*') was published in July 1996. See also J Sorabji, 'Prospects for Proportionality: Jackson Implementation' (2013) 32 *Civil Justice Quarterly* 213 at 221. Woolf's draft rules appeared at H Woolf, *Access to Justice Draft Civil Proceedings Rules* (London, HMSO, 1996) (hereinafter '*WfDR*').

(b) the parties should be free to agree how their disputes are resolved, *subject only to such safeguards* as are necessary in the public interest;
(c) in matters governed by this Part the court should not intervene except as provided by this Part.[66]

It is worth noting that in this section, as in Rule 1 of the FRCP, we find the combination of the statement of intention and the use of a construction rule. This is an opportunity to look more closely at this. If we were, as an exercise, to rewrite FRCP Rule 1 then it might look something like this:

(1) The provisions of the FRCP are founded on the following principles and shall be construed administered and employed by the court and by the parties accordingly.
(2) The object of these rules is to secure the just, speedy and inexpensive determination of every civil judicial proceeding.

So would such an approach, in expressing *intention* directly, make any difference? That would depend upon the approach taken to interpretation. Suffice it to say, at this stage, that if one construed the rules liberally then it might make a difference where it was possible to read the intention into a particular text so as to promote *action* without doing violence to the text. Further, our thought experiment allows us to see that our hypothetical rule might well encourage the action of the court in applying the rule dynamically when it came to the management of the case.

The benefit of the 1996 Act's approach to intention is set out in the non-technical explanation of section 1 of the Arbitration Act 1996. When the Bill was going through the UK Parliament, the Minister said,[67] 'Principles of fairness and impartiality are included in the general principles on which the Bill is based. They appear right at the start of the text so that users are left in no doubt about their importance.'[68]

But what we get from this kind of purpose clause is not confined to clarity of understanding alone. *Jowitt's Dictionary*[69] describes the work of purpose clauses as being 'to specify the purpose for which [the statute] has been enacted, so as to flavour the application and construction of the statute by the courts'. Daniel Greenberg, writing about purpose clauses, has this to say:

> The inclusion of purpose clauses is a matter of considerable debate at a theoretical level. Some … [believe] that they make it possible to reduce the overall length and complexity of legislation. Others believe that they are largely a distraction, creating possibilities of apparent contradiction and confusion as to what is meant by what is

[66] Emphasis added.

[67] The Uncitral Model Law 1985, as adopted by the United Nations Commission on International Trade Law on 21 June 1985, contains no purpose statement in ch 1, thus the inclusion of one in the 1996 Act is worthy of note.

[68] Per John Taylor, the Minister for Competition and Consumer Affairs, *Hansard*, HC Debs 2 May 1996, vol 276, col 1309.

[69] D Greenberg et al (eds), *Jowitt's Dictionary of English Law*, 4th edn (London, Sweet & Maxwell, 2015).

often relatively broad and imprecise language, at least compared with traditional 'black-letter' provisions.[70]

G. Rhetorical Function

The question of language leads us back to Porter's article and to her next point, where she notes the rhetorical function of Rule 1 FRCP.[71] A good example of this is offered by the judicial statement that Rule 1

> gives all the other rules life and meaning and timbre in the realist world of the trial court. It makes the rules useful tools for the trial of actual litigation instead of abstractions to be pontificated over in seminars by learned scholars of the law who have seen little or nothing of real litigation in the trial courts.[72]

Having looked at length about the interpretative challenges posed by FRCP Rule 1, it is time to consider how the federal courts dealt with the implementation of the FRCP 1938. After that will come Justice Scalia's interpretative approach by way of contrast.

H. Early Cases on the Meaning of Rule 1

We might start with Clark, by now Judge Clark.[73] *Arnstein v Porter*[74] gives us pause for thought. Ira Arnstein was a serial litigant. In this case he was suing Cole Porter for 'at least a million dollars' for breach of copyright. Songs said to be copied included 'Begin the Beguine' and 'Night and Day'. Porter obtained summary judgment so Arnstein appealed. He was successful in part. In his dissenting judgment, Judge Clark criticised interpretation as 'a novel method of amending rules of procedure'. He said that such an approach 'subverts the plans and hopes of the profession for careful, informed study', which ought to occur before the promulgation of new rules.[75]

In *Arnstein*, Richard L Marcus sees three points:[76]

(a) the objectives sought by judicial interpretation may depart from or contradict the objectives of the rule-makers;

[70] D Greenberg, *Westlaw Key Legal Concepts* (London, Westlaw online, Sweet & Maxwell, 2016).

[71] EG Porter, 'Pragmatism Rules' (n 61) at 158.

[72] *Re Paris Air Crash* (1975 CD Cal) 69 FRD 310 at 318. This was a very complex case dealing with an air disaster in 1974. Three hundred and forty-six people perished. The court was considering whether or not to have separate trials. An English case in similar circumstances would almost certainly be handled under CPR 19 by way of a Group Litigation Order, which can be made where there are 'common or related issues of law or fact'. See CPR 19.10.

[73] Charles E Clark was now sitting on the 2nd Circuit of the Federal District Court.

[74] *Arnstein v Porter* 154 F 2d 464 (2nd Cr 1946) at 479.

[75] ibid.

[76] RL Marcus, 'Reform through Rulemaking?' 80 *Washington University Law Quarterly* 901 (2002) at 924.

(b) revision through judicial interpretation opens the door to the danger of inconsistent practice on different circuits of the same court;
(c) a committee is more likely to be correct than a judge working alone.

It is worth bearing in mind that Clark knew broadly enough what the draftsmen had intended, even if he did not accept their reasoning. He was therefore well placed to spot departures from the intended scheme of things. It is interesting how supportive he remained of principled rule drafting rather than ad hoc development using the route of interpretation. In that sense he shares an affinity with Scalia J.

A look at the early case law on FRCP Rule 1 shows that the federal judiciary formulated the following principles to guide the court in its approach:

(a) the object of the FRCP was that decisions should be made on the merits;[77]
(b) the new system was intended to liberalise civil procedure and to avoid the harshness experienced under the former rules without causing a breakdown of the system;[78]
(c) the test of the validity of the Rules was whether they really worked in regulating procedure.[79] Validity is used here, by the US Supreme Court, in the sense of effectiveness and not vires;
(d) the intention behind the Rules was to achieve expedition in litigation, to save costs, avoid delay and to obtain the full disclosure of the truth;[80]
(e) the Rules were there to assist in the narrowing of the issues and to ensure that the parties were not taken by surprise;[81]
(f) the spirit of the Rules was to achieve the speedy adjudication of all the matters at issue between the parties[82] and, perhaps, to bring forward the making of decisions on disputed issues;[83]

[77] *Moore v Illinois Centre RR* 24 F Supp 731 (SD Miss, 1938) at 733–34.

[78] *Burke v Canfield* (1940) 72 App DC 127, 111 F2d 526 at 527.

[79] *Sibbach v Wilson & Co* 312 US 1 (1941) (Roberts J) at 14: 'The new policy envisaged in the enabling act of 1934 was that the whole field of court procedure be regulated in the interest of speedy, fair and exact determination of the truth. The challenged rules comport with this policy.' The proceedings concerned the need for examination by a medical expert in a personal injury case. In England, the rule established in *Edmeades v Thames Board Mills Ltd* [1969] 2 QB 67 (CA) and *Starr v National Coal Board* [1977] 1 WLR 63 (CA) would allow the court to stay proceedings until the examination was carried out. *Edmeades* firmed up the position taken in *Pickett v Bristol Aeroplane Co Ltd* (CA, 16 March 1961), relying upon CRN Winn, *Report of the Committee on Personal Injuries Litigation* (1968) Cmnd 3691. The tension between *Edmeades* and *Pickett* was resolved in *Murphy v Ford Motor Co Ltd* (1979) CA, Bar Library Transcript No 379 of 1970, and a workable test formulated in *Starr*.

[80] *Boysell & Co v Colonial Coverlet Co* 29 F Supp 122 (1939, DC Tenn) at 124.

[81] *Dill Mfg Co v Acme Air Appliance Co* 2 FRD 151 (1941, DC NY) at 153 and *Stark v American Dredging Co* 3 FRD 300 (1943 DC Pa) at 301, picking up Moore's reference to the spirit of the Rules.

[82] *John R Alley & Co v Federal National Bank* 124 F2d 995 (1942, CA 10 Okla) at 998.

[83] *Brewster v Technicolor Inc* 2 FRD 186 (1941, DC NY) at 188.

(g) a strictly technical interpretation of the Rules should be avoided where it might impose hardship on the litigants,[84] and the Rules should be reasonably and not technically construed;[85] however,
(h) the Rules should not be so construed as to destroy the distinction between pleading and proof, nor did Rule 1 have a 'magic' effect;[86]
(i) the Rules as a whole worked through setting out specified standards and procedures. Failure to observe these standards and procedures would defeat the purpose of the Rules.[87] That said, provided that the confines of the rules were not transgressed, the court was permitted to follow a liberal interpretation of the Rules.[88]

Apart from *Sibbach* (see point (c)), in the US Supreme Court, we find two other early cases touching upon FRCP 1938 Rule 1. *Ettelson v Metro Life Ins Co*[89] was a case concerning postponement of a jury trial, in which Rule 1 was cited but not explained.[90] In *City of Morganstown v Royal Ins Co*[91] the question concerned trial by jury. In both *Ettleson* and *Morganstown* the court was really directing its mind to Rule 2, not Rule 1. Neither case contributes to the other case law in this area.

What is notable in the early case law is:

(a) the approaches are not all reconcilable; but
(b) we can see the extent to which the courts were alive to the need to make the FRCP work so as to deliver justice, speed and economy whilst not wishing to substitute a general discretion in the place of the specifics of the rules.

I. The Narrow Interpretation: Scalia J

We turn now to the important concurring judgment of Scalia J in the US Supreme Court case of *Torres v Oakland Scavenger Company*.[92] The judgment exemplifies the narrow as opposed to liberal approach. *Torres* concerned an appellant whose

[84] *United States v One Ford Coupe* 26 F Supp 598 (1939, DC Pa) at 598. On the facts of the case strict interpretation was required as the Rule specified a time limit.

[85] *Caterpillar Tractor Co v International Harvester Co* 106 F2d 769 (1939 CA9 Cal) at 772.

[86] *Jessup & Moore Co v West Va Pulp & Paper Co* 25 F Supp 598 (1 Dec 1938, DC Del) at 599–600.

[87] *TSC Motor Freight Lines v Leonard Truck Lines Inc* 4 FRD 366 (1945, DC La) at 368.

[88] *Phillips v Baker* 121 F 2d 752 (CA 9) at 754 and *Land v Prudhomme Oil Co* 3 FRD 377 (1944, DC La). The latter case cites *Moore's Federal Practice* vol 1 at 662 and Cumulative Supplement at 654: 'It should be stated at the outset that it is in keeping with the spirit of the new Federal Rules to interpret them liberally, just so long as the confines of the Rules themselves are not transgressed.' The edition cited from is JW Moore et al, *Moore's Federal Practice: a treatise on the Federal rules of civil procedure* (Albany, NY, Mathew Bender & Co, 1938).

[89] *Ettelson v Metro Life Ins Co* 317 US 188 (1942), see the judgment of Roberts J.

[90] ibid 190–91.

[91] *City of Morganstown v Royal Ins Co* 337 US 254 (1949) 257–58, judgment of Murphy J.

[92] *Torres v Oakland Scavenger Company* 487 US 312 (1988) at 318.

employment case was eventually dismissed by way of summary judgment because of a failure to give his details in a notice of appeal. The appellant lost his appeal against dismissal.

Justice Scalia, concurring with the majority judgment, said:[93]

> The principle that 'mere technicalities' should not stand in the way of deciding a case on the merits is more a prescription for ignoring the Federal Rules than a useful guide to their construction and application.[94]

He went on to say:[95]

> By definition all rules of procedure are technicalities; sanction for failure to comply with them always prevents the court from deciding where justice lies in the particular case, on the theory that securing a fair and orderly process enables more justice to be done in the totality of cases.

We pause to note that Scalia J has elided the concept of 'mere technicality' with the concept of technical requirements. Not all technical requirements will be important, though some will be very important, and some may be sufficiently unimportant as to amount to a mere technicality.[96] Scalia J then said:[97]

> [W]e should seek to interpret the rules neither liberally nor stingily, but only, as best we can, according to their apparent intent. Where that intent is to provide leeway, a permissive construction is the right one; where it is to be strict, a permissive construction is wrong. Thus, the very first of the Rules of Civil Procedure does not prescribe that they are to be 'liberally construed,' but rather that they are to be 'construed to secure the just, speedy, and inexpensive determination of every action.

Scalia then went on to mention his previous judgment in *Houston v Lack*.[98] There, he had cited the following passage from the earlier case of *Thompson v Immigration and Naturalization Service*,[99] a case which had held:

> Rules of procedure are a necessary part of an orderly system of justice. Their efficacy, however, depends upon the willingness of the courts to enforce them according to their terms. Changes in rules whose inflexibility has turned out to work hardship should be effected by the process of amendment, not by ad hoc relaxations by this Court in

[93] The passage is set out in full because of the clarity with which it addresses the issues. The English Court of Appeal can be seen grappling with similar challenges in *Vinos v Marks & Spencer Plc* [2001] 3 All ER 784 (CA).

[94] RM Cover, in 'For James W Moore: Some Reflections on a reading of the Rules', 84 *Yale Law Journal 718* (1975) at 731, notes the danger of purposeful manipulation of part of the Rule to undermine the Rule. In Scalia's case, he imports an external notion of what the Rules are for and then interprets them in the light of that notion.

[95] *Torres* (n 92) 319.

[96] Which is why proportionality of punishment has an important role to play in relief from sanctions applications under the new CPR 3.9.

[97] *Torres* (n 92) 319.

[98] *Houston v Lack* 87 US 266 (1988).

[99] *Thompson v Immigration and Naturalization Service* 375 US 384 (1964) at 390.

> particular cases. Such dispensations in the long run actually produce mischievous results, undermining the certainty of the rules.[100]

Scalia J went on to say in *Houston*:[101]

> That could not be more correct, nor more applicable to the present case. The filing rule the Court supports today seems to me a good one, but it is fully within our power to adopt it by an amendment of the Rules … It is hard to understand why the Court felt the need to short-circuit the orderly process of rule amendment in order to provide immediate relief in the present case.

It is worth noting that Scalia J's point was not that the proposed approach would necessarily be a bad idea but that to interpret the Rule in such a way amounted to a rewriting of it. Rewriting ought to be accomplished through the proper channels by way of a formal amendment to the FRCP.

Karen Nelson Moore notes[102] that Scalia J was not alone in using plain meaning analysis, also known as the textualist approach.[103] She says that the rationale for plain meaning analysis begins with the duty of the court when faced with a piece of legislation to interpret it. How is that interpretation to take place? If the meaning is plain then the court must give effect to it. In such circumstances, other aids or approaches to construction should be eschewed because they unnecessary. Moore objects that plain meaning analysis presents a number of problems, especially in the context of how the federal rules work.[104] First, it is not always clear what a rule means: there may be no plain meaning to which resort may be had. Second, a rule is an entity operating within a set of entities: interpretation requires consideration of all of the functions of a particular rule and the way in which the designated rule operates within the set of rules as a whole. Third, rules do not exist in a vacuum: the 'policies and purposes behind' a particular rule or set of rules should not be left out of account. Interpretation should aim at making the rules work; therefore courts have a 'responsibility to develop a cohesive civil procedure framework in order to achieve the systemic goals of fair, efficient and just litigation'.[105]

The narrow interpretation approach can be justified, at least in relation to first instance decisions, upon the following basis. Judges, says Bone,[106] need guidance

[100] *Mitchell v News Group Newspapers Ltd* [2013] EWCA Civ 1537 shows that there is a very fine line to be trodden between interpreting a rule to make it work and, in effect, amending the rule by judicial interpretation. In the latter case there is a risk that an important ingredient may be missed out.

[101] *Houston* (n 98) at 284.

[102] KN Moore, 'The Supreme Court's Role in Interpreting the Federal Rules of Civil Procedure' (1990) 44 *Hastings Law Journal* 1039.

[103] ibid 1074, and see fn 159 on that same page.

[104] KN Moore, 'The Supreme Court's Role' (n 102) 1084–85.

[105] Moore suggests four factors to be taken into account: consideration of the purpose of the rule and how that purpose may be realised most fruitfully; consideration of the historic and current policy behind the rule; whether particular problems thrown up by the operation of a rule should in fact be resolved; consideration of one rule's place both in the universe of the rule set and in the galaxy of the operation of the federal courts in America. KN Moore, 'The Supreme Court's Role' (n 102) at 1096.

[106] RG Bone, 'Improving Rule 1' (n 49) at 301.

and to be constrained, so as to reduce the risk of their coming to different conclusions according to the outcomes they think are important. This matters, says Bone, because to have differing decisions on the meaning of the same rules is undesirable.[107] Scalia J's argument is, likewise, a utilitarian one: if a strict approach is followed then more justice will be done.

This approach presents difficulty, particularly in the area of case management, and the narrow way has not been the English approach towards case management decisions. There, it is accepted that there is a range of potentially acceptable case management decisions in any given case and that the judge's decision is not one be interfered with lightly.[108] Case management often concerns matters of application and not interpretation. There is a range of interpretations and applications that are possible prior to the conclusion of the interpretive process. Further, interpretation and application are conceptually distinct. The conclusion of the interpretive process is marked by the finding of a single meaning. That meaning is, in its turn, capable of many different acceptable applications in widely differing factual scenarios. This suggests that there is a practical flexibility to all this. Even where there is an undisputed single-meaning interpretation, it is still the case that differing outcomes are both unavoidable and the very stuff of case management given the factual variance between proceedings. As has been said in a case on discretion, *G v G (Minors: Custody Appeal),*[109] per Lord Fraser,

> the appellate court should only interfere when they consider that the judge of first instance has not merely preferred an imperfect solution which is different from an alternative imperfect solution which the Court of Appeal might or would have adopted, but has exceeded the generous ambit within which a reasonable disagreement is possible.[110]

Like Scalia J, Bone favours using the rule-making process over a liberal approach to interpretation. He also says that the rule-making committee should be the one to decide which trade-offs are to be made, and that it should then issue guidance

[107] This has not been the English approach towards case management decisions. As noted below, in England, it is accepted that a range of case management decisions is possible in any given case.

[108] See eg *Mannion v Ginty* [2012] EWCA Civ 1667 at [18]; *Chartwell Estate Agents Ltd v Fergies Properties SA* [2014] EWCA Civ 506 at [63]; *Abdulle v Commissioner of Police of the Metropolis* [2015] EWCA Civ 1260 at paras [28]–[29]; *BPP Holdings Ltd v Revenue and Customs Commissioners* [2017] UKSC 55 at [33]. The advent of the new CPR 3.9 has reinforced for the Court of Appeal the importance of respecting first instance discretion-based decision-making. For the difficulties raised by CPR 3.9, see ch 5.

[109] *G v G (Minors: Custody Appeal)* [1985] 1 WLR 647 (HL) at 652. The reasoning was applied to civil cases in general by Brooke LJ in the early CPR case of *Tanfern Ltd v Cameron Macdonald* [2000] 1 WLR 1311 at para [32].

[110] The 'generous ambit', point is a direct echo of the words of Asquith LJ, in the earlier case of *Bellenden (formerly Satterthwaite) v Satterthwaite* [1948] 1 All ER 343 (CA) at 345, 'the generous ambit within which reasonable disagreement is possible'. This approach can, in turn, be traced back to *Charles Osenton & Co v Johnston* [1942] AC 130 (HL) at 138 and, prior to that, to *Evans v Bartlam* [1937] AC 473 (HL) at 480–81. This approach is thus well established and shows how pragmatic appeal courts in England are in restricting what may be controverted upon appeal.

to judges.[111] In England, this is achieved partly through the issuing of Practice Directions and partly through guidance given by judges, in particular within the Court of Appeal.

III. The Civil Procedure Rules 1998

A. The Civil Procedure Rules

We now turn from America back to England, to look at Woolf's attempt to cut the Gordian knot of the twin evils of delay and cost, through the introduction of a new set of rules.[112] Woolf did not operate in a vacuum. Amongst others, he met judges in America, or was provided with information by them.[113]

Woolf knew what the system's official interpretation was. The terms of reference given to him included improving access to justice and reducing the costs of litigation.[114] Woolf's intention was manifested in his reports and within the overriding objective.

[111] RG Bone, 'Improving Rule 1' (n 49) 301.

[112] For a view of the difficulties inherent in law reform, see S Clark and R Jackson, *The Reform of Civil Justice*, 2nd edn (London, Thomson Reuters (Professional) UK Ltd, 2018) (hereinafter 'JnRef') ch 28.

[113] *WfFR* (n 65) Annex 2, at 334 and 338. It is clear from PJ Johnston's 'Problems in Raising Prayers to the Level of Rule: The example of Federal Rule of Procedure 1', 75 *Boston University Law Review* 1325 (1995) at 1326, that the Civil Justice Reform Act 1990 (whose official title was the Judicial Improvements Act 1990) refers to 'civil justice expense and delay plans'. Note that the 1993 FRCP rule changes inserted into Rule 1 the words 'shall be construed *and administered* to secure the just, speedy and inexpensive determination of every action' (emphasis added). An early draft supporting note stated that it was not 'proper for the court to allow its scarce energies and resources to be wasted' (PJ Johnston, 'Problems in Raising Prayers' at 1329). The phrase 'and administered' was added, said the Advisory Committee on Civil Rules (in Proposed Amendments to the Federal Rules of Civil Procedure and the Federal Rules of Evidence Submitted to Standing Committee on Rules of Practice and Procedure, May 1992 and Attachment B, at 1) 'to recognise the affirmative duty of the court to exercise the authority conferred by these rules to assure that civil litigation is resolved not only fairly but without undue cost and delay' – 146 Federal Rules Decisions 535 (1993). So by 1993 in the US it was recognised that the FRCP Rule 1 trinity had to be both interpreted and given effect. The structure of justice, speed and expense provides a clear *avant la lettre* foundation for CPR 1.1. It is worth noting that Attachment B to the covering letter states (at 1) that 'A few expressed concern that the proposed amendment would increase judicial discretion and perhaps be misused by some judges. Some concern was also expressed that the Committee Notes, stating that attorneys share responsibility with the court for seeing that the rules are administered to secure the objectives stated in Rule 1, may infringe on the obligations of attorneys towards their clients.' For a helpful overview of the rulemaking process (including the 1993 revision), setting out how infrequently the Supreme Court or Congress intervenes, see CT Struve, 'The Paradox of Delegation: Interpreting the Federal Rules of Civil Procedure', 150 *University of Pennsylvania Law Review* 1099 (2001–2002).

[114] *WfIR* (n 65) Introduction. The terms were set by Lord Mackay of Clashfern, the Conservative Lord Chancellor. Lord Irvine, the Labour Lord Chancellor who took Mackay's position in May 1997, was the happy recipient of Mackay's initiative.

Adrian Zuckerman[115] argues that the CPR are 'driven by three imperatives'[116] or 'principal components':[117]

(a) 'that judgments follow from the correct application of the law to the true facts',[118] also called 'the imperative of ascertaining the truth';[119]
(b) 'that judgments are reached by means of proportionate resources',[120] also called 'the imperative of proportionality';[121] and
(c) 'that judgments are delivered in a reasonable time',[122] also called 'the imperative of timely resolution'.[123]

It is noteworthy that only one of these imperatives relates to the doing of justice per se. The second and third imperatives relate to the way in which the machinery of justice is mobilised to secure the result.

B. The Expressed Rationale of Reform

By 1994 there was grave concern that the English civil justice system was not meeting the needs of the public. Woolf was appointed to look into the whole system.[124] Woolf's Interim Report expressed concern about the corrosive effect of the adversarial system, saying 'the conduct of litigation … is adversarial' and 'the adversarial process is likely to encourage an adversarial culture and to degenerate into an environment in which the litigation process is too often seen as a battlefield where no rules apply'.[125] The Final Report said that litigation should be less adversarial and more cooperative.[126]

Woolf concluded that radical steps needed to be taken. To prevent his reforms being blown off course, he decided to include an express statement of purpose. In 1995, Woolf said that he hoped that this express statement, which he then

[115] *ZoCP* (2013) (n 17).
[116] ibid para 1.16.
[117] *ZoCP* (2013) (n 17) para 1.18.
[118] ibid para 1.17.
[119] *ZoCP* (2013) (n 17) para 1.32.
[120] *ZoCP* (2013) (n 17) para 1.17.
[121] ibid para 1.35.
[122] ZoCP (2013) (n 17) para 1.17.
[123] ibid para 1.48.
[124] For the literature on this process and the difficulties it raised, see J Jolowicz, 'On the Nature and Purposes of Civil Procedural Law' (1990) 9 *Civil Justice Quarterly* 262; J Jolowicz, 'The Woolf Report and the Adversary System' (1996) 15 *Civil Justice Quarterly* 198; A Zuckerman, 'Quality and Economy in Civil Procedure: The Case for Commuting Correct Judgments for Timely Judgments' (1994) 14(3) *Oxford Journal of Legal Studies* 353; A Zuckerman, 'A Reform of Civil Procedure – Rationing Procedure Rather Than Access to Justice' (1995) 22(2) *Journal of Law & Society* 155; A Zuckerman, 'The Second Great English Reform of Civil Justice – A Triumph of Hope Over Experience' (2000) 1(2) *Hibernian Law Journal* 178.
[125] See *WfIR* (n 65) ch 3, paras 3 and 4.
[126] *WfFR* (n 65) Overview, para 5.

called his 'general objective',[127] would be of 'fundamental importance' in the new 'managed system'[128] he was proposing. Woolf's proposals went out to consultation and re-emerged in his Final Report. Far from moderating his tone in the light of criticism received, by 1996 Woolf had renamed his 'general objective' as 'the overriding objective'.[129]

Woolf thought that effectiveness in litigation involved 'the spirit' in which 'technical steps' are implemented.[130] There was to be a requirement to further the overriding objective, which was to be built into the Draft Rules.[131]

C. Overview of Rule 1.1 of the CPR

Rule 1.1 of the CPR starts with a declaration and a statement of principle. It follows this with a definitional list, which works by inclusion. Part 1 of the CPR does the following:

(a) it sets out the novelty of the Rules, calling them 'a new procedural code',[132] thus suggesting a clean break with the past;

(b) it sets out the objective of the Rules, 'enabling the court to deal with cases justly';[133]
it sets out to whom the objective is principally directed: the wording speaks of 'enabling *the court* to deal';[134] and

(c) it imposes a requirement for the court to give effect to the overriding objective in:
   (i) exercising any Rule-conferred power,[135]
   (ii) interpreting any Rule,[136]
   (iii) actively managing cases;[137]

[127] *WfIR* (n 65) ch 26, para 23.

[128] *WfIR* (n 65) ch 26, para 30. For an American view questioning whether one system can meet all needs, see HH Koh, 'The Just, Speedy, and Inexpensive Determination of Every Action', 162 *University of Pennsylvania Law Review* 1525 (2014). The existence of three tracks and specialist business means that the CPR do in fact offer a degree of flexibility in England.

[129] The nomenclature stuck. It was used in *WfDR* 1.1 (n 65) and has appeared in the old and new versions of CPR 1.1.

[130] *WfFR* (n 65) ch 20, para 10. This may have underestimated what was culturally acceptable, see eg LN Brown, 'British and French Statutory Drafting: A Review Article' (1988) 37(3) *International and Comparative Law Quarterly* 698, arguing that the British are 'a nation of literalists at heart', in the sense of believing the individual should be controlled by the letter of the law rather than by the general principles indicating its spirit. For Pound's view on litigation culture, see R Pound, 'The Causes of Popular Dissatisfaction with the Administration of Justice', *Annual Report of the American Bar Association* 395 (1906) at 402–03. Pound thought English litigation was then in better shape than its American counterpart.

[131] *WfDR*, r 1.2 (n 65), which became CPR 1.3.

[132] CPR 1.1(1).

[133] CPR 1.1(1).

[134] Emphasis added.

[135] CPR 1.2 (a).

[136] CPR 1.2(b).

[137] CPR 1.4(1).

(d) it encapsulates a new theory of procedural justice – dealing with cases justly;
(e) it confers benefits on the parties[138] and the world at large;[139] and, in return,
(f) it imposes an obligation to help the court upon the parties to litigation.[140]

'Dealing with cases justly' (see (d)) is new terminology, presumably coined to make the point that there is a break with the past – the use of new wording is to be equated with a new meaning. However, the phrase is not defined as such. Instead an inclusive list is given: 'dealing with a case justly … includes'. At law, the term 'includes' could mean those matters expressly specified (so as to be read as 'means and includes'). In such a case, the meaning would be exhaustive. However, 'includes' could be taken more widely as meaning both those things said to be included together with those things commonly taken to fall within established notions of procedural justice.[141] The latter meaning is what is meant here.

D. The Overriding Objective

The competing ways of realising the overriding objective as envisaged by Woolf[142] are set out in CPR 1.1. The old overriding objective provided as follows:

> (1) These Rules are a new procedural code with the overriding objective of enabling the court to deal with cases justly.

Rule 1.1(2) started with 'Dealing with a case justly includes, so far as is practicable', before listing a number of steps:

(a) equality of arms steps;
(b) steps to promote fairness;
(c) steps to ensure a rationed access to justice;
(d) money-saving steps;
(e) a restriction of steps to what is proportionate;
(f) steps to speed up the progress of cases to trial;
(g) steps to ensure that the system gives a rationed access to justice to all users.

E. A New Approach

The new overriding objective said that the CPR comprised 'a new procedural code with the overriding objective of enabling the court to deal with cases justly'.[143]

[138] CPR 1.1(2)(a)–(d).
[139] CPR 1.1(2)(e).
[140] CPR 1.3.
[141] For these two approaches, see *Dilworth v Commr of Stamps* [1899] AC 105 at 106, per Lord Watson.
[142] *WfIR* (n 65) ch 26, para 30.
[143] CPR 1.1.

The language is rather terse, but it covers both the *intention* behind the writing of the rules and the *action*, in the sense of how the Rules are to operate.

So, for example, in *Clark v University of Lincolnshire and Humberside*,[144] Lord Woolf MR made the following point:

> [The] CPR are, as r 1.1(1) states, a new procedural code. Parliament recognised that the CPR would fundamentally change the approach to the manner in which litigation would be required to be conducted.

The designed nature of the Code is brought out in Lord Woolf MR's judgment in *Daniels v Walker*,[145] where, in the context of an Article 6 ECHR argument, he said:

> Article 6 could not possibly have anything to add to the issue on this appeal. The provisions of the Civil Procedure Rules, to which I have referred, make it clear that the obligation on the court is to deal with cases justly.

In other words, the Rules had been designed to take account of rights under Article 6 ECHR, and therefore the overriding objective and the Rules work in partnership with a view to achieving this.

Déidre Dwyer[146] notes the 'interlocking' nature of the requirement to give effect to the overriding objective,[147] with the requirement to actively manage cases,[148] the use of case management powers including sanctions and the behaviour of the parties.

In his Interim Report, Woolf himself said that the cue for how his new approach was to be implemented would be contained in

> the new rules themselves. The opening provision of the new code will set out the general objective of the rules. This statement, which will be of *fundamental importance* in the managed system which I recommend, will be on the following lines:
>
> - The general objective of these rules is to enable the court to deal with cases justly.
> - The court shall apply these rules so as to further the general objective.[149]

It is to be noted that the latter point, dealing with the application of the rules, was removed from the final CPR 1.1 and moved to CPR 1.2. No mention is made of a separate interpretive requirement.

[144] *Clark v University of Lincolnshire and Humberside* [2000] 1 WLR 1988 (CA) para [34].

[145] *Daniels v Walker* [2000] 1 WLR 1382 (CA) at 1386. This decision needs to be read in the context of the then growing judicial disquiet about human rights points being taken as makeweights.

[146] D Dwyer, 'The Interpretation of the English Civil Procedure Rules in the Context of Article 6 of the European Convention on Human Rights' in H Snidjers and S Vogenauer (eds), *Context and Meaning of National Law in the Context of Transnational Law* (Munich, Sellier European Law Publishers GmbH, 2009) 40–41. Dwyer sees difficulties with the decision in *Daniels* that are beyond the scope of this chapter.

[147] CPR 1.2.

[148] CPR 1.4.

[149] *WfJR* (n 65) ch 26, para 30 (emphasis added). It is a curious paradox that despite Woolf's wish for a fresh start, and despite early attempts being made to protect the new theory by restricting the use of pre-CPR authorities, the old theory of justice on the merits made the passage from the world of the RSC into the world of the CPR. See ch 4 for the reasons for this and the mechanisms that were at work.

The phrase, 'the court shall apply these rules' became 'the court must seek to give effect to the overriding objective when' exercising power or interpreting the Rules. The change, coupled with the inflation of language from 'general objective' to 'overriding objective', does appear to suggest a move towards the overriding objective's having some sort of meta status in the minds of Woolf, or the rule-makers or both.[150] If that was the intention, it was not realised. The overriding objective does not simply override all other rules.

The term 'code' in CPR 1.1 relates not to codification of already existing procedural rules but to the production of an integrated set of rules *de novo*.[151] Thus, the normal expectation is that specific Rules have been designed to work so as to give effect to the overriding objective, but that when a court is interpreting the wording of any specific Rule, 'the court must seek to give effect to the overriding objective when it … interprets any rule'.[152]

The overriding objective was said to do a number of different things:

(a) it was setting out what the civil justice system was trying to achieve[153] in order to deliver on 'the political will of the state'[154] and the citizen's constitutional rights;[155]
(b) it was giving a 'guide' to the interpretation of other rules[156] – a 'guide' because the practice of civil procedure involves not just rules but 'judgment and knowledge'. Woolf envisaged that rules, judgment and knowledge would come together in a dynamic way so as to make the Rules function in deployment and effect.

Woolf compared the Draft Rule 1 overriding objective to 'a compass to guide courts and litigants … as to their general course'.[157] To some extent, therefore, the overriding objective was always interpretative in intention, but at its revealing it was envisaged as having a greater role and was expected to be purposive in nature. Woolf cited *James Buchanan & Co Ltd v Babco Forwarding and Shipping (UK) Ltd*[158] as an illustration of the approach he expected to be taken. In *Buchanan*,

[150] The procedural reformers and the rule-makers had distinct roles and, at times, different aims.

[151] The early editors of the post-Woolf *White Book* would not have agreed with this. See eg *White Book* (Spring Edition, 2002) and the commentary in vol 1 at 1.3.9. For the role that the *White Book* played in the early interpretation of the CPR, see *SorECJ* (n 3) at 118. It is also worth saying that much of the structure of the CPR obviously follows that of their predecessor rules.

[152] CPR 1.2(b).

[153] *WfIR* (n 65) ch 26, para 30 and 'the fundamental purpose of the rules and of the underlying system of procedure'; *WfFR* (n 65) ch 20, para 11.

[154] *WfIR* (n 65) ch 1, para 1, citing J Jacob in *The Reform of the Procedural Law and Other Essays in Civil Procedure* (London, Sweet & Maxwell, 1982).

[155] *WfIR* (n 65) ch 1, para 2, cited *Bremer v South India Shipping Corporation Ltd* [1981] AC 909 at 917 (per Lord Diplock).

[156] *WfFR* (n 65) ch 20, para 11; *WfDR* (n 65), Part 1, para 1.1.

[157] *WfFR* (n 65) ch 20, para 12.

[158] *James Buchanan & Co Ltd v Babco Forwarding and Shipping (UK) Ltd* 1977 QB 208 (CA); see *WfIR* (n 65) ch 26, para 27.

Lord Denning MR was referring to the approach to interpretation that was taken by the then ECJ (now the CJEU). That approach is genuinely teleological in the sense of developing meanings beyond what may have been originally intended, by treating the text as a living instrument. The English approach has tended to the purposive, that is looking backwards for intention, rather than towards the teleological, looking to develop meaning in 'the now' by way of extensions of meaning into new areas. Whatever Woolf actually meant by reference to *Buchanan*, we do know that he would have been familiar with the established English purposive approach, and his comments are best read as meaning that the rules should be interpreted purposively, so as to protect what was originally intended, rather than being developed teleologically so as to create new meanings: a reading that would respect the role of the Civil Procedure Rules Committee in tending to old rules and shaping new ones. The occasional, but dynamic, role of the courts in developing their own practice by innovative design is best seen as a reaction to fresh circumstances rather than as an act of teleological interpretation.

The overriding objective of 'enabling the court to deal with cases justly'[159] contains several objectives, not one, and those objectives are both competing and incommensurable. Woolf himself had said that there were four fundamental principles:[160] equality, economy, proportionality and expedition.[161] Reference to proportionality was only added into the top line of CPR 1.1(1) with the advent of the new overriding objective. The principle of equality, which featured in CPR 1.1(2), still remains there, rather than having been promoted to the top line.

As for the judges, who were being told to actively manage their caseload, a lot was being asked of them. Woolf offered them a two-fold 'overall purpose'[162] with five specific objectives,[163] to be administered in a way that had five characteristics.[164] For the Final Report, Woolf identified seven elements of case management[165] and added seven case-management outcomes.[166]

In the face of such a wealth of statements, one can question to what extent the overriding objective is in fact only a statement of intention and action. Even if one thinks in terms of one overall intention, such as 'justly, and then several subordinate intentions,[167] such as 'expeditiously and fairly', some of CPR 1.1(2)

[159] Also called the 'general objective': *WfIR* (n 65) ch 26, para 23, and note para 30 'the general objective of these rules is'.

[160] The term can also be used of matters that might otherwise be described as fundamental rights: *JnRef* (2018) (n 112), para 5-011.

[161] *WfFR* (n 65) Overview, para 8. Cf *ZoCP* (2013) (n 17), para 1.16; also N Andrews, *Andrews on Civil Processes*, vol 1 (Cambridge, Intersentia, 2013) (hereinafter '*AndoCP*') at 686.

[162] *WfIR* (n 65) ch 5, para 16.

[163] ibid ch 5, para 17.

[164] WfIR (n 65) ch 5, para 20.

[165] *WfFR* (n 65) ch 1, para 16.

[166] *WfFR* (n 65) ch 5, para 11. *WfDR* (n 65) Part 25, paras 25.5 and 25.6 are notably lacking these outcomes.

[167] Which may even function as waymarks, or as necessary but not sufficient conditions.

looks much more like a setting forth of the operating principles of a properly functioning civil justice system rather than the setting out of intention and action alone. On this approach, CPR 1.1 would cover both intention and action. In this context, Neil Andrews' focus upon the operating principles rather than the express goals of procedure may well offer a basis for a richer understanding of the overriding objective.[168]

The intentions expressed by the overriding objective are constrained by the procedures that form the majority of the Rules. In this context one looks at all the Rules that together list the actions to be taken to perform the designated procedures.[169] These procedures have at least one function, underlying principle and procedural objective: thus, for example:

(a) summary judgment is there to weed out weak cases (function); because
(b) court time is valuable and should not be wasted (principle);
(c) the needs of other litigants with meritorious cases need to be taken into consideration (principle); and
(d) parties to an action should not be forced to take to trial or defend a claim that lacks substance (principle);
(e) so that weak cases are disposed of before trial (procedural objective).

So we have a number of things: CPR 1.1 contains both objectives and values, there is an obligation on the court to give the effect to the overriding objective (CPR 1.2, and CPR 3.1A(4)), by means of actively managing cases (CPR 1.4). For that reason, the court is given a wide range of general procedural powers (CPR 3.1), which are over and above the powers that the court would otherwise have.[170] Parties are also required to help the court further the overriding objective (CPR 1.3).[171]

[168] See, eg, *AndoCP* (n 161) paras 25.01–29.67. This book is the third of a trilogy that tracks the progress of civil litigation reform. See also N Andrews, *English Civil Procedure* (Oxford, Oxford University Press, 2003) ch 3. This was the second work in Andrews' trilogy. It was published shortly after the CPR came into force. Like all works of the period (including early commentary in the *White Book*), it was overtaken by the wealth of case law and the many changes made to the Rules. The earliest book in the series is N Andrews, *Principles of Civil Procedure* (London, Sweet & Maxwell, 1994) – see the very valuable ch 2 for Andrews' early view on the relationship of rules to their underlying principles. We do not count N Andrews, *The Three Paths of Justice* (London, Springer, 2012) as part of the series, although paras 2.35–2.36 and 2.38 set out 'four fundamental aims of civil justice'. Neil Andrews has a chapter, 'Embracing the Noble Quest for Transnational Procedural Principles' in M Adams et al (eds), *The Future of Transnational Commercial Litigation* (London, British Institute of International and Comparative Law, 2003, reprinted in 2006). Andrews was on the committee that produced the ALI/Unidroit, *Principles of Transnational Civil Procedure* (Cambridge, Cambridge University Press, 2007).

[169] *WfIR* (n 65) ch 26, para 26. In what follows, *function*, *principle* and *procedure objective* are used to refer to the way in which the mechanics of specific rules work within a system of rules.

[170] And distinct from powers that are vested in the court by its inherent jurisdiction.

[171] Compare this with the new Rule 1 of the FRCP, which says 'be construed, administered, and employed by the court and the parties to secure the just, speedy, and inexpensive determination of every action'.

F. The Challenge of Interpretation

Woolf envisaged that the CPR would require a particular method of interpretation: CPR 1.1 is goal-directed and is to be interpreted and applied accordingly. The CPR require the court to take seriously the intent behind the Rules.[172] *Bennion on Statutory Interpretation* says that purposive construction traditionally means 'promoting the remedy parliament has provided to cure a particular mischief'. Bennion goes on to make the point that purposive construction can be 'purposive and literal', that is following the literal meaning where that would be in accordance with the legislative purpose,[173] or 'purposive and strained' where the wording of the statute is stretched beyond its normal meaning in order to give effect to the legislative purpose.[174] Using Bennion's terminology, and picking up on what has been said previously, Woolf is to be taken as having had in mind a 'purposive and literal construction', but one which was to be operated bearing in mind the intention behind the CPR, that is, taking into account the intention of dealing justly with cases in the light of the reasons why such a manner of dealing is a desirable one.

As indicated, such an approach is not really teleological, at least as the CJEU would understand it. This can be put down to a mixture of the constitutionally constrained approach that English courts take to statutory interpretation, the existence of an active Civil Procedure Rules Committee and the ability of judges to develop new procedure as necessity demands.[175]

There is a tension here: on the one hand the court may wish to avoid 'slavish' application of individual rules where to do so might undermine the overriding objective;[176] on the other hand, the court cannot avoid the plain meaning of a particular rule[177] to give effect to the overriding objective, nor can it use the overriding objective as a way of creating a discretion it would otherwise not have,[178] or to support what would otherwise be an unsustainable conclusion.[179]

[172] CPR 1.2.

[173] See FAR Bennion, *Bennion on Statutory Interpretation*, 3rd edn (London, Butterworths, 1997). The quotations are taken from 731 in Section 303, and 737 in Section 305.

[174] The CJEU's approach might go even further, viewing EU law as a living instrument where interpretation is effectively adaptation – albeit that the adaptation is carried out in a principled manner, although political critics of the CJEU would argue that its living instrument approach (see *Tyrer v UK* (1979–80) 2 EHRR 1) was, in fact, unprincipled. For a common law world view, see B Hale, *Devolution and The Supreme Court – 20 Years On*, speech to the Scottish Public Law Group (14 June 2018), available at www.supremecourt.uk, where Lady Hale (at 15–16) cites *Edwards v Attorney General* [1930] AC 124. That Privy Council case referred to the Canadian Constitution as follows (at 136), '[t]he British North America Act planted in Canada a living tree capable of growth and expansion within its natural limits'. For the political implications of all this, see J Sumption, *The Limits of Law*, 27th Sultan Azlan Shah Lecture 2013, at 7–11, available at www.supremecourt.uk.

[175] For the latter point, see *YD (Turkey) v Secretary of State for the Home Department* [2006] EWCA Civ 52, later in this section.

[176] *Orange Personal Communications Services Ltd v Hoare Lea* [2008] EWHC 223 (TCC) at [31].

[177] See the two early cases of *Vinos v Marks & Spencer Plc* [2001] 3 All ER 784 (CA) at [26], and *Totty v Snowden* [2001] EWCA Civ 1415 at [34].

[178] *Tinkler v Elliott* [2012] EWCA Civ 1289 at [28].

[179] *Law v St Margarets Insurances Ltd* [2001] EWCA Civ 30 at [16].

The apparently comprehensive nature of the overriding objective does not, in fact, displace the court's obligation to act in a consistent way, according to the specific text of a particular rule or the specific texts that together set out a particular procedure. The tensions can be reconciled by noting the designers' intention to integrate the way the rules and procedures within the CPR, taken as a whole, would work together. This means that hard choices have to be made. In what follows we shall interweave the Court of Appeal's decision in *Holmes v SGB Services Ltd*[180] with the views of the then editors of the *White Book*.

In the case of *Holmes*, the judge had commented that, 'one of these days the Court of Appeal is going to have to face up to the fundamental question' of whether the old case law about costs being a sufficient cure for amendment or adjournment was to be followed or whether one should prefer CPR 1.1, 'which says that the overriding objective is to do justice, but then sets out a series of considerations from which you can always pick one or two which point in the direction which the party wants to point'.[181]

In that sense, the general approach of saying that the old case law was not of assistance closed off old and familiar pathways.[182] This had the potential to create two different effects. Negatively, it put early first instance judges in a position where they had no sure guide, but more positively, it should have prevented them from using case law that reflected a guiding philosophy distinct from that set out in the overriding objective.[183] The various 'considerations' are not necessarily compatible. This is a point made in the editorial comment in *Civil Procedure* (2002),[184] that 'these sentiments cannot be allowed to hide the fact that procedural rules are not value free'.

The *White Book* editors go on to say that:

(a) the CPR already reflect choices made between values. As a result of this selection, the Rules have contents that might have been different. The editors might have added to this, that the nature of the Rules requires that one must select between values, and that to do so usually requires a choice to be made – on the basis that one cannot have one's cake and eat it;
(b) favourable parts of the Rules may be used to one party's advantage. This is true of any rule, but a bright-line rule conferring the exercise of a limited discretion may offer less scope for argument than an open-textured rule. The latter can be construed by its relationship to broad values and treated as being adjustable for a multiplicity of factually variable situations;

[180] *Holmes v SGB Services Ltd* [2001] EWCA Civ 354.

[181] ibid at [33].

[182] See, eg, *Flynn v Scougall* (Practice Note) 2004 EWCA Civ 873 at [24]. In that case it was noted that the structure of the Rules had not really changed between the old and new regimes.

[183] Sorabji argues that the justice on the merits theory made the leap between the RSC and the CPR because a significant body of judges either did not accept the new guiding philosophy (Sorabji calls this 'Woolf's new theory of justice') or did not understand what it entailed: see *SorECJ* (n 3) ch 4.

[184] *White Book* (Spring 2002) vol 1, para 1.3.3.

(c) reasonable people may differ on what is just and fair. This final point gets to the nub of the attitude to be taken by appellate courts when reviewing the exercise of a discretion.[185]

Returning to *Holmes*, we find that the Court of Appeal thought that there was no real conflict between rules governing the maintenance of trial dates and the interests of justice involved in protecting the right to a fair trial. What was required was for the judge to balance all of the factors without giving any of them undue weight.[186]

Having considered pluralism within the overriding objective, we now consider the potential conflicts between that objective and the detail of the specific rules within the CPR that are contained outside Part 1 of those Rules.

In *Vinos v Marks & Spencer Plc*,[187] May LJ said, 'Interpretation to achieve the overriding objective does not enable the court to say that provisions which are quite plain mean what they do not mean, nor that the plain meaning should be ignored.'[188]

And Peter Gibson LJ said:

> The construction of the [CPR] requires the application of ordinary canons of construction, though the [CPR] … spell out in Part 1 the overriding objective of the new procedural code. The court must seek to give effect to that objective when it exercises any power given to it by the rules or interprets any rule. But the use in rule 1.1(2) of the word 'seek' acknowledges that the court can only do what is possible. The language of the rule to be interpreted may be so clear and jussive that the court may not be able to give effect to what it may otherwise consider to be the just way of dealing with the case, though in that context it should not be forgotten that the principal mischiefs which the Civil Procedure Rules were intended to counter were excessive costs and delays.[189]

The point in *Vinos* was developed by May LJ in *Godwin v Swindon Borough Council*.[190] There, the Court of Appeal accepted that if the Rules conferred no discretion upon the court then a judge could not resort to the overriding objective in its own right in order to find an independent basis for the exercise of a discretion. May LJ said:

> The new procedural code of the Civil Procedure Rules is positively packed with instances where the court has a wide discretion to manage cases to achieve substantial justice in accordance with the overriding objective. But there are some instances where the court has no discretion or only a limited discretion. It is not surprising if some of those … are rules which relate to statutory limitation.[191]

[185] The question of the appellate jurisdiction is dealt with in ch 6.

[186] In *Holmes*, the Court of Appeal was reviewing the first instance decision, not rehearing the application.

[187] *Vinos v Marks & Spencer Plc* [2001] 3 All ER 784 (CA).

[188] ibid at [20].

[189] *Vinos* (n 187) at [26].

[190] *Godwin v Swindon Borough Council* [2001] EWCA Civ 1478.

[191] ibid at [44].

In *Totty v Snowden*,[192] Kay LJ confirmed the need to have regard to the overriding objective. He cited *Vinos* as covering 'clear express words', noting that the presence of such words would mean that the court was restricted by the meaning of the words used. However, Kay LJ went on to say that where 'there are no express words, the court is bound to look at which interpretation would better reflect the overriding objective'.[193] And that 'if the court does have a discretion, the circumstances … will fall to be considered by the court when it considers whether to exercise its discretion since discretion must be exercised having regard to the overriding objective'.[194] Which was not to say that such an interpretation would necessarily favour one who had breached a Rule.

This restrained approach to interpretation shown by the Court of Appeal is particularly important in that it was exercised early in the reform process and shows a sensitivity towards balancing the overarching objective with specific procedures.

But what about circumstances where applying the exact wording of a Rule would produce results that no longer seem appropriate? In *YD (Turkey) v Secretary of State for the Home Department*,[195] the court was quite open to the possibility of innovation and evolution in the form and content of the Rules; with the rule – drafters following the lead of the court, rather than the other way around. Brooke LJ said:

> In my judgment, the enactment of the Civil Procedure Act 1997 and the introduction of the CPR 1998 have changed the landscape. Recent history has shown the beneficent effect of the judges initiating innovative ways of regulating procedure, followed swiftly by the Rules Committee codifying or extending the new procedures the judges have introduced.[196]

He then gave examples 'of desirable changes which would never have been made, or not made so swiftly, if the judges had not been ready to take the lead'.[197] The contrast with the views expressed in the US Supreme Court case of *Thompson* could not be more marked.[198]

G. Conclusion

The end of the civil justice system is to deliver just results. Ultimately, if the procedure works but the adjudication fails to come to an answer that is just according

[192] *Totty v Snowden* [2001] EWCA Civ 1415 at [34].
[193] *Totty* (n 192) at [34].
[194] ibid at [34].
[195] *YD (Turkey) v Secretary of State for the Home Department* [2006] EWCA Civ 52.
[196] ibid at [22].
[197] *YD (Turkey)* (n 195) at [22].
[198] *Thompson v Immigration and Naturalization Service* 375 US 384 (1964) (n 100). The English Court of Appeal also considers that there is an inherent jurisdiction to create rules where there are gaps to be filled – see *Bovale Ltd v Secretary of State for Communities and Local Government* [2009] EWCA Civ 171 at [39]–[41]. For a discussion of this case, see A Zuckerman, 'Rule Making and Precedent under the Civil Procedure Rules 1998 – Still an Unsettled Field' (2010) 29(1) *Civil Justice Quarterly* 1.

to the law, the civil justice system has not delivered. But likewise, if the system does not function effectively then the worth of the result is diminished, if not altogether extinguished. That worth is received both by the litigants and by wider society.

Civil procedure matters because it is the vehicle to get people to the point of judgment or settlement. So civil procedure is a very important vehicle, yet it is not an end in itself. People are the end and not the means. Procedure is the means that is there to serve the end: real people in the social world. It follows that the organisation of the procedures must be such as to promote efficient handling with the minimum of diminution of the value of the final 'product'.

This chapter has looked at the role of intention in Anglo-American civil litigation. Both CPR 1.1 and Rule 1 of the FRCP contain, either expressly or by implication, statements of the intention behind the Rules. The review has covered an examination of intention, action and outcome.

The expressed intention of the new overriding objective in England is that cases should be dealt with justly and at proportionate cost.[199] That intention was formed because, under the RSC, in its various forms, the theory of justice on the merits meant that questions of economy and speed took a back seat to keeping defaulters within the system, so that cases could be disposed of on their merits at trial or another suitable hearing of the merits. The focus upon the merits, under the RSC, is in turn explicable because the reforms leading to the making of the RSC (1883) were a reaction against a dominant formalism that favoured the correct selection and use of procedure over awarding judgment to those who were favoured by the substantive law. The old overriding objective gave insufficient prominence to proportionality, and costs rose more than expected. The new overriding objective therefore has a corrective and astringent intention.

Rule 1 of the FRCP does not in terms identify the objective of the FRCP, but the words laying down the 'just, speedy, and inexpensive determination of every action' as the obligation to interpret makes clear that the intention of the Rules, taken together, is that cases should be disposed of justly, speedily and economically. Some of this approach can be traced back to the Sutherland Bill of 1917, which had envisaged the promotion of 'the speedy determination of litigation on the merits'. This idea can in turn be traced back to David Dudley Field's rule 3 in the Field Code, which provided that the rules should be 'liberally construed' with a view to promoting their objects and assisting 'the parties in obtaining justice'.[200]

Moving from intention to action, we note that both FRCP Rule 1 and CPR 1.1 are approached at a considerable level of abstraction, though CPR 1.1(2) does provide some examples of what the abstractions would look like when realised in the social world. Rule 1 of the FRCP is not so detailed, but the difference is probably best explained by the different roles played by the two Rules.

[199] CPR 1.1(2)(f) also strengthens the court's hand on the question of non-compliance. See *JnRef* (2018) (n 112), para 5-020.

[200] Ch 379 of the Laws of New York 1848, *Laws of the State of New York*, 71st session (Albany, NY, Charles van Benthuysen, 1847) at 497.

Rule 1 of the FRCP gives the court guidance as to how the rest of the Rules are to be interpreted; CPR 1.1 goes further, in that it is a statement of intention, which is fulfilled by being an aid to construction and by its having a symbolic function to which the court can have resort when considering the detail of application (action). The issues of interpretation and application were felt particularly acutely in the early life of the CPR, although the early case law in both England and in America shows a marked clustering around the restricted space any common law court is prepared to give to general purposes[201] when weighing them against the function of specific procedures – functions that have to be described in the wording of particular Rules. In the end, in the common law world, the specific tends to triumph over the general: grand strategic objectives may be lost in the detail of low-level tactical operations.

Thus, in England, the approach to the working of specific Rules truly overrode the operation of the old CPR 1.1. It was necessary to rewrite the Rule to add reference to proportionality to the top line of CPR 1.1(1). Sorabji has highlighted the role that the survival of the theory of justice on the merits, and indeed its quiet triumph, had in restricting the success of the Woolf Reforms, although much of the blame can be laid at the door of the specific structures and detailing of the CPR procedures, which, even if they were aligned in intention with CPR 1.1, did not operate to fulfil it. Indeed, it is arguable that the unexpressed accuracy expectation,[202] coupled with the large number of permutations available to judges, simply increased the amount of preparation that was required.

In America, the tension between general procedural theory and the particulars of action is exemplified by the approach taken by Scalia J in the US Supreme Court. Scalia argues that it is for the Rules Committee, established by statute, to make and change the Rules. This is, of course, a form of *intentional* statement in its own right. Scalia J is arguing that the underlying philosophy of interpretation is this: 'the what' is to be found in the exact words used within the FRCP. The detail of the Rules, it is said, perfectly expresses the system's intention. 'The why' of interpretation is expressed in these terms: the greater good will be served by sticking to the wording of the Rules as expressed, and by allowing the Rules Committee to consider questions of improvement or reform. Thus Scalia J's underlying philosophy of interpretation is built upon an underlying philosophy of the role of the judge in a democracy where there is a separation of power between Congress, the judiciary, and the executive. For Scalia, the judge is there to interpret the rules that are made by Congress.[203] Questions of change are a matter for Congress and not the judiciary. The curious status conferred upon the rule-makers is treated as being equivalent to the status conferred upon Congress by the US Constitution. The rule-making power is delegated to the Supreme Court,

[201] As distinct from constitutional purposes.

[202] Although one might reasonably retort that the accuracy expectation is, in its own right, a matter of intention, ie of underlying philosophy, albeit a latent one.

[203] Although when considering the Constitution, Scalia would give priority to that over the wording of a Congressional statute. We are here considering only procedural matters.

subject to Congressional disapproval. The rule-interpreting power is vested in the judiciary. Consistent with this approach, Scalia J does not disparage the contents of any particular change, such as would have been involved in the approach he rejected in *Torres*. Rather, for him, the question is who has the power to make that change.

This sharp divide between rule-making, as the source of intention, and rule-interpreting is also quite pronounced in England. The Rules have a text that is both general in orientation yet particular in effect, and, subject to the reception question to which we shall come, the courts have tended to respect the particularity of procedures, even though at times this has undermined the success of the generality of former. The Civil Procedure Rules Committee has, it is true, made changes, but the driving force behind those changes has come from particular individuals – Woolf, Jackson and Briggs – who are appointed, effectively as champions, to push for and to push through change. The courts, particularly the Court of Appeal, recognise that they have a licence to innovate, but they have not used this licence as much as they might have done.

This brings us to the reception question. Sorabji has convincingly argued that the way in which new rules are received has a bearing upon the likelihood of their success. He also shows how a judge's own theory of civil justice will affect how he or she approaches the question of interpreting new rules. The scale of the failure or inhibition of the Woolf Reforms shows that the alignment of *intention* and *outcome* must pass through *action*. Such *action* includes the interpretation and discretionary application of the Rules by the judiciary. If the judiciary do not accept or understand the goal and its supporting justification, which emerges from the intention phase, then they are left free to interpret or apply the Rules in such a manner as to defeat the *intention* behind them. But if *intention* feeds forward into *action*, so *action* feeds back into *intention*. If, at the *intention* phase, insufficient thought is given to how it will be realised, the detailed procedures may either of themselves create too much work for participants in litigation, or confer to much discretion upon judges to pursue, unknowingly, the accuracy aim – an aim that may result in orders which require the carrying out of a disproportionate amount of work.

Judith Resnik concludes her article 'Failing Faith' as follows:

> I have painted a story with a very broad brush … I have oversimplified and overgeneralized. Counter-examples abound and the world is more complicated than this essay suggests. Granting all that, we must explore the value choices … to determine what kind of procedure to provide to those who seek judicial attention.[204]

This chapter falls into Resnik's category, yet the story needed telling, although simplification and generalisation are required in the telling of it. The next chapter looks at some possible causes of underperformance in the reform of civil procedure.

[204] J Resnik, 'Failing Faith: Adjudicatory Procedure in Decline', 53 *University of Chicago Law Review* 494 (1986) at 556.

4

Voyages in a New World: The Unanticipated Consequences of Civil Justice Reform

I. Introduction

This chapter looks at the Jackson and Woolf Reforms through the analysis of consequences offered by the sociologist RK Merton and the analysis of culture and law put forward by Pierre Legrand.

Merton's ideas, which are set out in section II B of this chapter, are straightforward. The sorts of causes of failure of which Merton speaks are commonplace, but his combination of them makes for a dynamic way of looking at the reforms. Merton's 1963 paper is justly celebrated, but he did not think it was the last word on the subject and no suggestion is made that his ideas are completely comprehensive. Merton's ideas were formulated in a different time (the 1930s) and a different place (America), so we can see that the ideas originate, as it were, in a place different from the world of civil litigation, and hence offer the possibility of an outside-in vantage point.

The Jackson Reforms and their predecessor, the Woolf Reforms, were primarily an historical event experienced by all those participating in the system at the relevant time. But they went wider than personal experience. They were caused by or recorded in a series of texts: reports and rules from the rule-makers and reformers, together with commentary by contemporary practitioners and academics.

For the purpose of this study, the fewer the variations in the factual matrix the better. Sorabji's account[1] is taken as representing the reforms in an accurate manner and Jackson's views as offering the *ex post facto* viewpoint of a reformer.[2]

As noted in chapter 3, Karen Nelson Moore has reminded us of the different agents who wrote, implemented and interpreted the Federal Rules of Civil

[1] J Sorabji, *English Civil Justice after the Woolf and Jackson Reforms: A Critical Analysis* (Cambridge, Cambridge University Press, 2014) (hereinafter '*SorECJ*').

[2] R Jackson, *The Reform of Civil Litigation*, 1st edn (London, Thomson Reuters (Professional) UK Ltd, 2016) and S Clark and R Jackson, *The Reform of Civil Procedure*, 2nd edn (London, Thomson Reuters (Professional) UK Ltd, 2018) (hereinafter '*JnRef*') offer a mix of personal reflection, the fruit of Jackson's experience, and a defence of the Jackson Reforms. H Woolf's *The Pursuit of Justice* (Oxford, Oxford University Press, 2008) lacks the same degree of reflection. The relevant portions are explanatory rather than reflective.

Procedure (FRCP): the rule-drafters (the Committee), the rule-makers (the Supreme Court), the legislature (Congress) and the rule interpreters (the Supreme Court). We shall look at English civil procedure through the lenses of the system, the ends, the means, the reports and draft rules, the rule-makers, and the social and political context. We start with the civil justice system.

A. The System

People organise for particular purposes. The system is just one particular type of purpose-driven grouping. It functions by providing a process that will result in settlement or a trial for those who litigate within the system.

The system is the product of the working together of a group of judges and officials according to a set of rules, procedures and practices that mark out the 'territory' of the system and set the requirements for entry, the terms of engagement and the rules for behaviour of the parties and their lawyers.

Writing in 1928, Charles E Clark was able to recognise that rules were 'instruments of social control of much wider import than merely as determinants of narrow disputes between individual litigants'.[3] The context of the control of litigation is a social one.

B. The Ends

An important part of the theory underlying the pre-1998 civil justice system was to treat each case in such a way that a case would usually be disposed of on its merits.[4] The system was thought to be there to give just decisions on the cases that had been entered into it. That justice might be delivered by way of a final decision, but there was provision for terminating the case early because the strength or weakness of one of the competing claims justified it. There was also provision to dispose of cases otherwise than on the merits because of a party's behaviour or presentation of the case, but such provision was very much secondary in importance to the theory of justice on the merits.

The issue of whether a case should be disposed of on the merits, or should suffer disposal for issues unrelated to the merits, goes to the heart of the problems experienced under both the Rules of the Supreme Court (RSC) and the early Civil Procedure Rules (CPR) – as Sorabji shows. The RSC's theory of justice on the merits encouraged judges to allow cases to proceed to trial where the default was

[3] CE Clark, 'Fact Research in Law Administration', 1 *Mississippi Law Journal* 324 (1928) at 324. This sentence is taken from the opening section of a paper in which Clark identifies a disconnection between law and social reality, reports on research conducted and concludes by suggesting that international comparative data would be of assistance.

[4] The complete underlying theory would be of 'complete justice', but justice on the merits became, for our purposes, the dominant part of that theory.

not egregious. The CPR's theory of dealing with cases justly required judges to think about the wider needs of the system and the litigants pursuing their cases within it. These two views on the objectives of civil procedure are very different – the former being party-centred and the latter being system-centred. One of the reasons why the Woolf Reforms failed to make the desired headway is because the new ideal did not gain widespread support within important groupings – the appellate judges, and practitioners.

C. The Means

To speak of the Jackson or Woolf Reforms is to refer to the combination of:

(a) the reports and draft rules produced by the reformers; and
(b) those ideas and procedures put in place by the CPR 1998 (as amended) and as interpreted by the judges in individual cases.[5]

As we shall see, Sorabji shows that the judges in the appellate courts, in particular, did not all share the same ideas about the fundamental philosophy underpinning the CPR. As a consequence, the appellate courts did not always assist in the early stages of reform.

D. The Reports and Draft Rules

The official reports, together with any draft rules, comprise the body of thought of the reformers acting in their official capacity. What might appear in the reports would not necessarily comprise the reformers' personal views, for the reports would have been written to reflect the needs of the system from the system's perspective, taking into account the official recollection of past successes and failures together with any assistance that the system could gain from knowledge and experience available in the wider world, from judicial management theory for example.

The reformers' reports would also be written in the knowledge of the constitutional, executive and political sides to the difficulties faced by the system.

E. The Reformers

The term 'reformers' covers Lord Woolf and Sir Rupert Jackson, who were each given the official role of identifying the problems of the system and making recommendations for changes to it.[6]

[5] The reforms were received and acted upon by participants in the civil justice system, especially practitioners.

[6] Neither individual worked alone, but it is convenient to refer to the individual officially given the task.

The reformers were not outside appointments. Each reformer was a member of the senior judiciary, a group who held a range of views[7] about the function and purposes of civil procedure, taking into account the judiciary's views on their constitutional role, that is, what the judges were there for. Each reformer would have been aware of the range of his colleagues' views concerning the function and purposes of civil procedure and the judiciary's role within the system, and would have taken his place within that spectrum even if he also drew on ideas from outside the group.

It is important to distinguish between the reformers, the rule-makers and the judiciary, for the tendency to name implemented reforms after the person who made proposals for reform has the effect of obscuring the very real difference between these roles, and allows rule-makers or judges to form their own view and then allow the blame for failure to fall upon the shoulders of the named reformer. The lack of collective responsibility is marked, the more so because of the lack of political accountability – in the event of failure, any other part of government could be called to Parliament to be examined by the elected politicians.

F. The Rule-Makers

By 'the rule-makers' is meant all those politicians, officials, judges and draftsmen whose efforts produced the CPR. Though part of the same system as the reformers, the rule-makers took the reformers' recommendations and tried to put them into operation, modifying them as they went. Some of the modifications were minor, some not.

It is worth noting that where changes were made by the rule-makers, they were advanced under the cover of the name of the reformers.[8] So when we talk about the 'Woolf Reforms', we are talking about the product of the rule-makers' work, which may or may not have been the same as the reformers' recommendations.

We now turn to look at the context in which civil justice reform occurred.

G. The Social and Political Context of Reform

The reformers were appointed by the system to propose changes. The consensus that change was needed did not guarantee that any specific changes would be welcomed by those involved.[9] The reformers would have expected to encounter inertia, vested interests and entrenched views, all of which would have to be

[7] The homogeneity of judicial backgrounds is a matter of political concern.

[8] Although Jackson does blur the distinction somewhat: *JnRef* (2018) (n 2) para 28-016.

[9] See eg ibid paras 17-012, 28-012, 28-015. In the context of prison reform, see H Woolf, *The Pursuit of Justice* (n 2) at 12–13.

overcome.[10] Success was not guaranteed, though you would not think that from reading the Woolf Reports in particular.[11] Jackson has been more circumspect in this regard.

The reformers always had to deal with the realm of the possible, which meant working within the boundaries of what was acceptable and what was achievable:

(a) *What was acceptable to the executive.* Woolf, in particular, was writing in the knowledge that a change of government was likely. His ideas had to command wide political acceptance. Jackson was writing in an era of financial stringency.
(b) *What was acceptable to the rule-makers.* The rule-makers had to decide which reforms to modify and which reforms to implement as proposed.
(c) *What was acceptable to the judiciary.* The first instance judges had to work the reforms into everyday practice. Appellate judges had intervene from time to time, and this intervention would be critical given the authoritative nature of appellate pronouncements.[12]
(d) *What practitioners would accept or, at least, implement.* Given the limited resources available to the judiciary, change would depend upon what practitioners did – whether they decided to participate with a view to making the changes a success, or whether they saw the changes as unwelcome and engaged with t*hem as little as possible.*
(e) *What stakeholders would accept.* In this context we should note that the stakeholders were not necessarily the same as actual court users at any point in time.[13] Repeat players, such as businesses or insurance companies, were stakeholders even if, in the latter case, they were not usually a party to the action. Stakeholders could influence the environment in which reform was taking place and could be effective lobbyists.
(f) *What was achievable in practical terms.* The enormous scope of Woolf's recommendations should be noted. The bigger the scheme, the more likely it was that something would go wrong. Jackson's work was less ambitious in scope.

[10] Stinchcombe speaks of the need for change-makers to be both agitators and teachers and for them to have control of the agenda or risk failing to change behaviour: AL Stinchcombe, *Constructing Social Theories* (New York, Harcourt Brace and & World Inc, 1968) at 247.

[11] H Woolf, *Access to Justice: Interim Report* (London, HMSO, 1995) (hereinafter '*WfIR*') and H Woolf, *Access to Justice: Final Report* (London, HMSO, 1996) (hereinafter '*WfFR*'), although Woolf's Reports may contain an element of rhetorical positioning aimed to make the case for reform seem as forceful as possible. Woolf does seem to have been genuinely optimistic that it was possible to bring about change in the areas in which he was given work to do. H Woolf, *The Pursuit of Justice* (n 2) at 13. Woolf's proposed rules are set out in H Woolf, *Access to Justice Draft Civil Proceedings Rules* (London, HMSO, 1996) (hereinafter '*WfDR*').

[12] Or perhaps over-authoritative: see *SorECJ* (n 1) at 224–25, speaking of Lord Carswell's impact following *Moy v Pettman Smith* [2005] UKHL 7. For Sir Henry Brooke's view of *Moy*, see H Brooke, 'Some Thoughts on the First Seven and a Half Years of the CPR' in D Dwyer (ed), *The Civil Procedure Rules Ten Years On* (Oxford, Oxford University Press, 2009) (hereinafter '*Ten Years*') at 459.

[13] This point is approached elsewhere (see section II C of this chapter), from the viewpoint of asking whether those litigating only occasionally could be considered to be part of a litigation culture.

Further, the reformers were limited in what they could say about why reform was needed. They could not easily criticise the courts (of which they were members), nor individuals (with whom they had to work in future, or who might be held in high regard by the reformers' peers).

II. History and a New Paradigm

The reformers had also take into account the fact that the system had a long history of only partially successful reform – a fact that both informed the things that the contemporary system operatives thought were important and set the parameters within which it was possible for a reformer to operate.[14]

Sorabji[15] draws an analogy with Kuhn's theory concerning paradigm shifts in science: when 'normal science' is seen to fail then 'extraordinary investigations' may open up fresh insight, which in turn may change the whole way that a scientific issue is viewed – the so-called 'paradigm shift'. This all involves a radical restructuring of ideas and practice, which, if misunderstood or imperfectly implemented, can lead to more failure – and, of course, to the discrediting of the new paradigm.[16]

It is thought that Sorabji's analogy is sound to this extent: both Jackson and Woolf as reformers had to address the failure of normal procedures, which, in both cases, required an examination of the fundamental purpose of civil procedure. Woolf had to reconceive the purpose in systemic rather than party-orientated terms, and that required a major move away from party autonomy towards court intervention in the process. As is clear from the need for the Jackson Reforms, 'control' is too strong a word for what had occurred in the way of active case management,[17] but the judges under the CPR were more interventionist than they were under the RSC.

What is intriguing[18] is that Jackson's work accepted Woolf's paradigm shift as its starting point. Woolf's reconceived purpose was to be given an extended life, even though one might have expected that the need for Jackson's involvement might suggest that the CPR's attempt to turn reform into normal science had failed significantly, a failure which might have called into question the result of Woolf's extraordinary investigations.

Woolf's reforming reconceptualisation of the purpose of civil procedure, then, needed to be cast in terms of practical proposals for change – including the

[14] See eg *JnRef* (2018) (n 2) ch 2 and paras 29-025–23-027.

[15] *SorECJ* (n 1) 22–24 and 27–28.

[16] Such change is not confined to scientific knowledge alone. Social groups can also change when their concepts change, or the meaning of social concepts can change as society changes. For the former, see K Mannheim, *Structures of Thinking*, eds D Kettler et al, trs JJ Shapiro and S Weber Nicholson (London, Routledge Kegan & Paul Ltd, 1982) at 220–21.

[17] *JnRef* (2018) (n 2) paras 13-007–13-008.

[18] Intriguing but, perhaps, not surprising in the light of ibid paras 29-025–29-027.

introduction of an overarching objective,[19] the old and new versions of Rule 1.1, which both stated and symbolised the new ideal.

A. Charles E Clark

Merton was writing in 1936, when Charles E Clark was engaged in helping to shape the new Federal Rules. Looking back in 1950, Clark had some pertinent things to say about the operation of rules of court.[20] He argued that the court's exercise of its powers had to take into account matters of policy, because 'much of interpretation is designed to prevent the acting parties from running wild, to either their own detriment or that of society generally'.[21] As a result, Clark thought, the court should use its powers when appropriate, rather than only being able to act when called upon by a party.[22]

Lastly, Clark warned that it was of the nature of judicial decisions, which are made in a particular case, to have an afterlife as rules of precedent, which will impact how other judges can interpret the rules.[23]

B. Unanticipated Consequences

What follows draws upon Robert K Merton's study concerning 'Unanticipated Consequences' (see further below). Merton's approach lends explanatory power: it helps us to understand why the civil justice reforms fell short at different times and in different ways.

In the case of the Woolf Reforms, time is on our side. We can look back and, with the benefit of hindsight, ask: What were the consequences? Were they unanticipated? And why did things work out in that way? In many cases, it is simply too early to know whether the Jackson Reforms as a whole will work – although in some cases, for example CPR 3.9, it is possible to comment. Where it is possible to comment sensibly on the Jackson Reforms, I do so.

The Woolf Reforms are now concluded. They promised much but failed to live up to their promise – hence the need for the appointment of Jackson to reform the reforms.

[19] I use this as a descriptive term for the overriding objective. It captures the sense of 'the paramount importance of reducing the cost and delay of civil litigation': see *Practice Direction (Civil Litigation: Case Management)* [1995] 1 WLR 262. *WfJR* (n 11) ch 26, para 30, refers to 'the general objective'.

[20] CE Clark, 'Special Problems in Drafting and Interpreting Procedural Codes and Rules', 3 *Vanderbilt Law Review* 493 (1950).

[21] ibid 494.

[22] Clark, 'Special Problems' (n 20) 495. Cf CPR 3.3.

[23] Clark, 'Special Problems' (n 20) 498. This follows from the nature of stare decisis. Clark's point shows why Woolf was concerned to make a fresh start – see *Biguzzi v Rank Leisure Plc* [1999] 1 WLR 1926 (CA) – and, more broadly, why judges found it so difficult to break the link with the notion of justice on the merits.

The following four categories are taken from Robert K Merton's 1936 paper, 'The Unanticipated Consequences of Purposive Social Action'.[24] That paper sets out the categories to be considered when looking at this topic. They are:

(a) the conduct of those involved;
(b) action and the question of rationality or irrationality;
(c) states of knowledge, decision making and attitudes to power[25] as sources of difficulty;
(d) the resources available.

The first two categories will be taken as primarily applying to those who were to be reformed (primarily lawyers,[26] but also the courts). The third category concerns the reformers (Jackson and Woolf). The fourth category concerns not the human factor but the economic one.

i. *Conduct*

In talking about people's conduct,[27] says Merton, we need to remember that acts involve a motive and a choice: that is, people behave in a certain manner because that is what they have chosen to do. And they choose to do so because they have a motive. We call this '*conduct by choice*'.

Merton also makes the point that habitual acts can also drive conduct. A person does what she has done before; the act then becomes habitual such that the actor may no longer be aware of making the choice or of why she made it. We call this '*habitual conduct*'.

One of the reasons for the failure of the Woolf Reforms was that the behaviour of lawyers, being habitual conduct, was deeply ingrained and could not simply be changed by mere fiat. This is also true of the position that Jackson inherited.

ii. *Action*

Moving on from conduct, we turn to action,[28] which, says Merton, can be rational or irrational – that is, it may concretely deviate from the rational. Merton is using these terms broadly to mean behaviour that is based on or in accordance with reason or logic.

As we have seen, the new view espoused by Woolf was an import generated by his extraordinary investigations. This new view was a rival to and supplanted the

[24] RK Merton, 'The Unanticipated Consequences of Purposive Social Action', 1 *American Sociological Review* 894 (1936). The list of categories is not comprehensive but it does offer a starting point for our study. Modifications to the scheme are indicated at the relevant point.

[25] Merton called these ignorance, error and imperiousness.

[26] On the difficulties in classifying the behaviour of individual litigants in the same way as that of practitioners see later in this chapter.

[27] RK Merton, 'Unanticipated Consequences' (n 24) 895–96.

[28] ibid 895–96.

system's old theory of justice on the merits. This change in the system's rationality took place after Woolf's proposals had been adopted by the rule-makers. Part of the difficulty for civil justice reform was that the system's rationality was new to it in 1998 and therefore, aside from any question or individual or group reaction to the novel way of thinking and behaving, this new rationality was not culturally established when the CPR came into force. Rather, the system's rationality offered a completely new world, which was unfamiliar to practitioners and of which they were not part.[29] This new rationality had the capacity to supplant the old legal culture, but at the outset it was the old culture that was dominant. The old philosophy and the old culture were intertwined. The old culture was partly a carry-over from prior to 1883. It survived because the 1883 system applied insufficient sanctions to defaulters. The system's new rationality would require a new mind-set and a new culture.[30]

We turn now to irrationality, which amounts to an irrational use of the system. Where the behaviour of system users does not accord with the system's logic, it can be said to have concretely deviated from the gold standard of rational behaviour. For example, the court has power to make civil restraint orders[31] against vexatious litigants.[32]

So we have the system's rationality and possible irrational use of the system, but it is not right to explain post-1998 judicial and practitioner behaviour as irrational in that sense. For it may be that one's behaviour makes no rational sense when looked at by the system (objectively) but is perfectly rational when judged from the perspective of the actor or group, that is when viewed subjectively.[33] Here we have what Pierre Legrand, whom we shall encounter later, calls legal *mentalité* ('mentality'), which is formed by what is learned by individuals of the rules and behaviour appropriate to their situation – in this case the rules and behaviour appropriate to civil procedure in England and Wales. The legal mentality that had been established over time was part of the legal culture of this group, and until 1998 also aligned with the system's rationality. It went from orthodoxy to heterodoxy when the CPR came into force. The existing legal mentality presented a significant challenge to the success of the reforms, for the system had to deal with a group of people, for example practitioners, inclined to behave in a fashion that made perfect sense[34] to them even if, to the system's Olympian and utilitarian

[29] In a very real sense, everyone was an outsider, for judges and practitioners had to make a fresh start.

[30] Robert Turner thought that the Queen's Bench Masters had successfully moved on: see R Turner, '"Actively": The Word that Changed the Civil Courts' in *Ten Years* (n 12) at 82.

[31] CPR 3.11, which came into effect on 1 October 2004 following the decision in *Bhamjee v Fosdick (Practice Note)* [2003] EWCA Civ 1113.

[32] See *White Book* (2004) vol 1, paras 3.1.12 to 3.1.15. For a clear statement of what makes a vexatious litigant, see the judgment of Lord Bingham CJ in *AG v Barker* [2000] 1 FLR 759 DC at [19] and [22], cited in *White Book* (2004) vol 1, paras 3.1.13 to 3.13.14.

[33] Merton speaks of basic values: RK Merton, 'Unanticipated Consequences' (n 24) at 903.

[34] There is a separate comment on the study of mentalities to be found in the Endnote to this book.

eye, the behaviour deviated from the way the rational person ought to behave and, indeed, *must* behave if the system was to function effectively.

iii. Limitations

From action we move on to our third category: the limitations under which any reformer might be labouring: states of knowledge (ignorance), decision making (error) or attitudes towards power (imperiousness).[35]

Ignorance is a rather harsh word and 'states of knowledge' is the preferable locution: 'Known unknowns and unknown unknowns' captures Merton's spirit here.[36] Anyone who has to make a decision has to do so without all the necessary information: in the context of civil justice reform, the reformers did not know which, if any, of their recommendations would be rejected;[37] which would be modified;[38] which would be implemented in full; who would openly oppose the recommendations;[39] and who would openly support the reforms but implement them in the wrong manner.[40]

Merton follows with errors in decision making. To what extent might a person be in error? We can think of the following, non-exhaustive examples: one's assumptions might be flawed; one's data could have been misinterpreted, and one's expectations about the capacity of any culture or system to respond might turn out to have been misjudged, or perhaps merely over-ambitious.[41]

And lastly we come to attitudes towards power, which Merton calls imperiousness.[42] This is a concept that may be interpreted as shading from error

[35] RK Merton, 'Unanticipated Consequences' (n 24) 898–901. Merton's list is not necessarily exhaustive. He was painting on a small canvass.

[36] See *JnRef* (2018) (n 2) para 6-012 on the wide constituencies to be satisfied.

[37] For example, recommendation 95 on the use of witness summaries (rather than witness statements) on the fast track (see also *WfIR* (n 11) ch 22, para 14) was not implemented. The firmness of the interim recommendation 95 became a mere admonition to brevity in final recommendation 151, and the intentions were glossed over in *WfFR* (n 11) ch 12, paras 56–59. *WfDR* (n 11) Part 28.5(1) and *WfDR* 28.6(1) are reflected in the current CPR 32.4(1) and 32.5(1). The term 'witness summary' lives on in the current CPR 32.9, but these documents do not fulfil Woolf's originally intended purpose. For a useful summary of the earlier history of this, see J Thomas, 'Cutting the cloth to fit the dispute: Steps towards better procedures across the jurisdictions'. Singapore Academy of Law Annual Lecture 2016, at para 40, available at www.judiciary.uk.

[38] Draft r 5.4 became CPR 3.9, a vastly different rule and a catastrophic departure from Woolf's intention. The change took the teeth out of the reforms.

[39] See *SorECJ* (n 1) 223–29. Although, interestingly, Sorabji only puts forward Peter Smith J as being in the rejectionist camp at first instance.

[40] See ibid 119–30.

[41] Some of Woolf's views look positively utopian in hindsight, eg on the matter of compliance. Jackson is much more of a realist – see *JnRef* (2018) (n 2) paras 29-025 to 29-027. For a contrasting viewpoint, advocating one core set of rules without case law incrustation, see J Thomas, 'Cutting the cloth' (n 37) paras16–17 and 42.

[42] Merton refers to this in such a way as to suggest that one can be blinded by immediate consequences to subsequent consequences. It is perhaps better to treat imperiousness as relating to taking insufficient account of the interests of others. That insufficiency may be a deficit of pragmatics or

all the way into official hubris – the line is not always easy to draw. In this context it has to do with the extent to which the official position unnecessarily overrides the interests of others (those operating within the system)[43] or does not take sufficient account of the reformers' views – an outcome that may actually undermine the good the system has said it wishes to achieve.

Paradoxically, Woolf was commissioned by a dysfunctional system to cure its dysfunction. But because the system was, in Woolf's eyes, effectively captured by practitioners, the changes he proposed had to come from the outside and be adopted by the system. So the Woolf Reforms became the system's new rationality and new mechanics, which in turn would need to give rise to a new legal mentality and a new legal culture.

The practitioners wished to do their job (maximising gains or minimising losses for their clients). They had done so for more than a century according to their professional culture, in the knowledge that non-compliance was effectively tolerated. They were told their culture and mentality were no longer acceptable and must change – for good reason of course.

But if the success of the reforms would depend upon thousands of little decisions made every day by many different operators and participants[44] then an imperious imposition could lead to minimal compliance or, perhaps, even to secretly non-compliant behaviour, with consequent chaos. And if many saw continued benefit in non-compliance then there was scope for those practitioners to become 'the Resistance', as it were.[45]

iv. Economic Resources

Lastly we come to the problem of economic resources.[46] A reformer can recommend official action, the rule-makers can decree it, but if the state does not provide the expected resources then the hoped-for benefits may simply never materialise.[47]

We now move on to the application of Merton's ideas in the context of the Woolf Reforms. In what follows, we place each of the four categories with the factors relating to the politics and practicalities of reform as set out in the original reform documents and as described in detail by Sorabji. When we come to look

appropriate sensitivity, depending upon the view one takes as to the merits of the old philosophy and those who practised under it.

[43] This author would not follow Legrand as to the degree of understanding and acceptance that ought to be offered by officialdom towards those operating in a system beset by substantial defects.

[44] Genn makes this point in H Genn, 'Understanding Civil Justice' in M Freeman (ed), *Law and Public Opinion in the 20th Century, Current Legal Problems*, vol 50 (Oxford, Oxford University Press, 1997) 155 at 171.

[45] The labelling of deviant behaviour is a marked feature of the reform process.

[46] RK Merton, 'Unanticipated Consequences' (n 24) at 900.

[47] See *JnRef* (2018) (n 2) paras 13-010,13-037; and *JnRef* (2016) (n 2) para 14-054. See also R Turner '"Actively"' (n 30) at 85–86. Lord Woolf's Comments appear in *Ten Years* (n 12) at vi; see also I Burnett, 'The Age of Reform', the Sir Henry Brooke Annual Lecture 2018, at paras 9–10, available at www.judiciary.uk

at the question of legal culture and legal mentality, we shall turn to the work of Legrand.[48]

C. Why Did the Woolf Reforms Not Succeed as Expected?

i. Woolf Introduced a New Theory to Cause Behavioural Change

We might have used the term 'ideal' here, rather than 'philosophy' or 'theory',[49] because that term captures the morally expansive flavour of what Woolf wanted to do. Woolf wanted to change people's behaviour to achieve a moral good: a justice system that delivered affordable and timely justice.[50] Yet there was more to what Woolf was doing than that. He wanted to introduce a largely modified objective for the system. This required new concepts, a new way of thinking and a change to familiar ways of working. 'New Theory' must be taken to cover all of these things.

ii. The New Theory Failed to Take Sufficient Account of the Functioning of the Adversarial System

Woolf's Interim Report expressed concern about the corrosive effect of the adversarial system and pointed to the advantages of alternative dispute resolution.[51] The Final Report also took the line that litigation should be less adversarial and more cooperative.[52] This approach was followed by Lord Woolf sitting in the Court of Appeal in 2002,[53] when he spoke of the 'paramount importance of avoiding litigation whenever this is possible'.[54] He went on to say:

> [T]he lawyers acting on both sides of a dispute of this sort[55] are under a heavy obligation to resort to litigation only if it is really unavoidable. If they cannot resolve the whole of the dispute by the use of the complaints procedure they should resolve the dispute so far as is practicable without involving litigation.[56]

Yet being appointed by the conflict system, Woolf was not able to consider addressing the continuing effect that the conflict system itself would have on participants' behaviour when the system was officially predicated on creating an

[48] See section II C of this chapter.
[49] Sorabji uses both terms.
[50] See, eg, H Woolf, *The Pursuit of Justice* (n 2) 300, 334–35.
[51] *WfIR* (n 11) ch 18, paras 1, 2 and 31.
[52] *WfFR* (n 11) ch 11, para 11.
[53] *R (Cowl) v Plymouth CC* [2001] EWCA 1935.
[54] ibid at [1]. There was also criticism of 'the unfortunate culture in litigation of this nature of over-judicialising the processes which are involved' (ibid at [25]) and concern to avoid 'an over confrontational approach to the litigation' (ibid at [3]).
[55] That is, judicial review proceedings.
[56] *Cowl* (n 53) at [27].

adversarial contest as a way of resolving the actual dispute.[57] It a curious feature of the Woolf Reforms that rather than promoting resolution within the system or forcing active cooperation between the parties, the Reforms envisaged outsourcing dispute resolution and largely avoided addressing the question of cooperation, because the system seemed to conceive of itself in terms of a conflict system rather than a conflict resolution system.[58] Either way, in Mertonian terms, there is either an error of omission or official imperiousness.

This fundamental point remains an issue that requires to be solved. How do you encourage cooperative behaviour in an essentially antagonistic situation?[59] Whilst CPR 1.3 requires the parties to help the court, it does not, in terms, require the parties to cooperate with each other. The obligation is always on the court to encourage cooperation.[60]

iii. Woolf Thought that Case Management Would Solve the Major Problems of the System

Woolf envisaged judicial team-working.[61] That takes sufficient resources, which, of course, costs money. Woolf was in error in thinking that the money would follow the reform.[62] Jackson experienced similar problems.[63]

Woolf was correct in thinking that case management was possible, for this approach was employed with apparent success elsewhere.[64] Woolf believed that the judges would manage cases actively,[65] that is, that they would say what people should do, when they should do it and how they should do it. But on the question

[57] Woolf alludes to this in H Woolf, *The Pursuit of Justice* (n 2) at 1.

[58] Further, cooperation might easily slip back toward party control, which the whole shift of power was designed to neutralise.

[59] *WfIR* (n 11) ch 9, recommendation 1 refers to cooperation *before*, not after, the commencement of proceedings.

[60] CPR 1.4(1)(a). See also H Genn, *Judging Civil Justice* (Cambridge, Cambridge University Press 2010) 173.

[61] *WfIR* (n 11) ch 6, para 30; *WfFR* (n 11) ch 8, paras 13 and 14.

[62] See, eg, *JnRef* (2018) (n 2) para 13-010; and I Burnett, 'The Age of Reform' (n 47).

[63] *JnRef* (2016) (n 2) para 14-054; and *JnRef* (2018) (n 2) paras 13-037–13-038.

[64] Woolf drew on the system of 'case flow management' from Ontario (*WfIR* (n 11) ch 5, para 18) and from Australia (*WfIR* (n 11) ch 5, para 19), and was clearly influenced by the US Federal Judicial Center's *Manual for Complex Litigation* (*WfIR* (n 11) ch 5, para 20). As a reformer, Woolf was not advocating an untried approach. Although he was coming into an area of some controversy within the US.

[65] Not all cases would have 'full hands-on judicial control'; some would have would have a 'more limited judicial case management' and some would 'operate under a standard timetable' (*WfIR* (n 11) ch 6, para 21). There was a span 'from light control to full judicial hands-on case management' (*WfFR* (n 11) ch 5, para 1, but Woolf was in no doubt as to the need for 'a managed system of dispute resolution': *WfFR* (n 11) ch 1, para 15). Examples of the extensive nature of case management include: 'a full management review of the action will take place' (*WfIR* (n 11) ch 8, para 6); 'a significant opportunity to take important decisions about a case' (*WfFR* (n 11) ch 5, para 13); 'the court should become more active in exercising control over the parties' (*WfIR* (n 11) ch 19, para 1); 'The responsibility to ensure that discovery is limited … The court has the ultimate responsibility' (*WfIR* (n 11) ch 21, paras 20 and 21); 'The procedural judge will take the lead' (WfIR (n 11) ch 23, para 18).

of whether case management as a whole would be effective,[66] he was in error. The managers did not always manage actively.[67] The participants did not always change their behaviour, and it was necessary for Jackson to be appointed.

iv. Woolf Did Not Have Sufficient Judicial Support at the Appellate Level

Lack of judicial support was to prove important, because key implementation decisions would be made by the appellate judges who, Sorabji notes, could be described as falling into two camps – traditionalists and rejectionists. To that must be added the reformers' camp and, presumably, those who did not feel strongly either way – the neutrals. It stretches credibility to think that all judges would have strong feelings for or against the principle of 'dealing with cases justly', particularly given the common law world's pride in its pragmatic rather than idealistic judiciary.[68]

The traditionalists[69] had the established legal mentality: they did not think that the purpose of litigation had changed,[70] and it was therefore perfectly reasonable for them to apply the old 'justice on the merits' approach in deciding cases under the CPR.[71] The rejectionists,[72] who also were working with the established legal mentality, knew that Woolf wanted to move the goalposts, and they wanted to stop him. They rejected his move away from the old to the new theory. The rejectionist camp comprised a rather unlikely bunch of counter-revolutionaries. Both the traditionalists and the rejectionists were behaving in this way out of choice: they knew what they were doing and why they were doing it.[73]

From the system's perspective neither camp was acting rationally. For who, acting rationally, would reject rational ideas – that is, ideas that incorporated the system's new rationality? Unfortunately the reforms were envisaged as a package. You could not have the theory without the mechanics; neither could you have the

[66] The term 'effectively' appears in *WfIR* (n 11) ch 5, para 20.

[67] *JnRef* (2018) (n 2) para 13-008. This was particularly important in the cases designated for 'hands-on' case management, namely those on the multi-track: H Woolf, *The Pursuit of Justice* (n 2) at 339.

[68] This spread of views demonstrates (with Legrand) not only that a legal mentality is not monolithic but capable of being the establishment viewpoint against which others must position themselves, but also, to go beyond Legrand, that some people may not be particularly committed to any particular point of view but just accept whatever the establishment view is from time to time. P Legrand 'Comparative Legal Studies and the Matter of Authenticity' (2006) 1 *Journal of Comparative Law* 365 at 381.

[69] See *SorECJ* (n 1) 119 –30.

[70] Lord Thomas LCJ's comment about birds continuing to fly along their original route, even though the geography of the land might have changed, is apposite here: see J Thomas, 'Cutting the cloth' (n 37) at para 5.

[71] Helpful here for comparison is P Polden, 'Mingling the Waters: Personalities, Politics and the Making of the Supreme Court of Judicature' (2002) 61 *Cambridge Law Journal* 575, which gives good insight into the difficulties experienced after the Judicature Acts.

[72] See *SorECJ* (n 1) 223-29.

[73] For an example of deliberate opposition (in this case by an academic) and the heated response that it drew from Woolf, see H Woolf, *The Pursuit of Justice* (n 2) ch 20.

mechanics without the theory. The two went together.[74] But once others became involved, the reforms were in a difficult situation. Some judges did not share the reformer's views, and consequently viewed the new mechanics in a different light.[75]

Jackson makes some helpful observations about the difficulties here: first, of the need to garner support for reform across a wide area;[76] second, that many views are possible and are often contradictory;[77] third, that groups of people may find it difficult to agree;[78] and, fourth, that therefore a core group of judges would be needed to assist in promoting consistency in seeing through the reforms.[79] Significantly, however, such a group, which existed from 2012,[80] neither produced unanimity[81] nor did it smooth the path of reform.[82] We can see the problem at work in *Mitchell v News Group Newspapers Ltd*.[83] Dyson LJ applied the new CPR 3.9 in a way that cut across both the original intention of the reformer and Jackson LJ's attempt to rescue something from the fire. That was a missed opportunity, with a significant knock-on detrimental effect, the paradox being that the judges who worked hard to apply *Mitchell* were left beached when the tide turned in *Denton v TH White Ltd*.[84]

v. Cultural Behaviour is Powerful: Delay and Disproportionate Behaviour Were the Cultural Norm

The view that there was a cultural problem was not new. The Heilbron/Hodge Report had picked up on this in 1993.[85] The Practice Direction of 1995[86] expressly made reference to a need for judges to take more control, and was announced as

[74] Jackson makes the general point about the interlocking nature of reforms at para 6-013 of *JnRef* (2018) (n 2).

[75] ibid para 11-036.

[76] *JnRef* (2018) (n 2) paras 6-012, 6-015, 28-012, 28-013.

[77] ibid para 28-003.

[78] *JnRef* (2018) (n 2) para 28-005. Jackson is speaking of committees, but the point is applicable to the group of judges comprising the Court of Appeal.

[79] ibid para 13-036. This is a very significant comment.

[80] *JnRef* (2018) (n 2) para 13-035. See also ibid para 5-015 on post-*Mitchell v News Group Newspapers Ltd* [2013] EWCA Civ 1537 confusion.

[81] See Jackson LJ's dissenting judgment in *Denton v TH White Ltd* [2014] EWCA Civ 906 commencing at [83].

[82] The key problems arose in relation to *Mitchell*.

[83] *Mitchell* (n 80).

[84] *Denton* (n 81). The extent of judicial 'misunderstanding' was not limited to courts of first instance – see *Michael Wilson & Partners Ltd v Sinclair* [2015] EWCA Civ 774 at [42], [47] and [53]–[54]. See also *JnRef* (2018) (n 2) para 5-015 on post-*Mitchell* (n 80) confusion, and para 13-034.

[85] H Heilbron and H Hodge, *Civil justice on trial – the case for change* (London, Bar Council and Law Society, 1993) at para 1.8. The proposed change would include using litigation to facilitate settlement, encouraging efficiency and speed, making things simpler and easier to understand, and judges being more interventionist.

[86] *Practice Direction (Civil Litigation: Case Management)* [1995] 1 WLR 262 (QBD).

having the aim of trying to 'change the whole culture, the ethos, applying in the field of civil litigation.'[87]

Woolf said that there had to be a 'radical change of culture',[88] with a 'fundamental shift of responsibility'[89] away from practitioners towards a new 'managed system'.[90] The appropriation of the term 'culture' can be a useful shorthand when trying to identify and describe a problem arising out of a pattern of behaviour. For example, 'compensation culture' carries with it a sense of behaviour that is widespread and entrenched without necessarily having the full pattern of cultural behaviour – behaviour that is to some sense engrained and habitual. It is an irony that Woolf had to deal with a genuine and longstanding culture, with all the resistance to change that this implied.

At this point we can turn to the comparative law approach for assistance. Studying the thought and action of people in another place carries with it the risk that we might misunderstand what is going on. In law, for example, we might misunderstand the technical detail and function of a particular law. But the problem goes deeper than that. We might wrongly assume that what looks like a similar law has a similar meaning or function. This issue is something that Pierre Legrand has considered when thinking about legal culture. His approach is to identify a number of points to apply when considering another legal culture. We take those insights and apply them domestically in the context of domestic civil procedure, as a way of creating a platform from which to look in from outside: that is, to give a distinct vantage point.

a. Method

Pierre Legrand says:

> Beyond technical clarity … there is an urgent need to understand how foreign legal communities think about the law, why they think about the law as they do, why they would find it difficult to think about the law in any other way and how their thought differs from ours.[91]

b. What is Legal Culture?

When Legrand speaks of law-as-culture, he means 'the framework of intangibles within which an ascertainable legal community … operates and which organises … the identity of legal community as legal community'.[92]

[87] Cited at *WfIR* (n 11) ch 2, para 10.
[88] *WfIR* (n 11) ch 4, para 2.
[89] *WfIR* (n 11) ch 5, para 2.
[90] *WfIR* (n 11) ch 26, para 26.
[91] P Legrand, 'Matter of Authenticity' (n 68) at 369.
[92] ibid at 374.

c. What is a Mentality?

Legrand says[93] that when comparative lawyers are considering a legal culture, they would do well to concentrate upon the 'cognitive structure' and its 'epistemological substratum', which comprises the 'shared mental programme'[94] that he calls the legal mentality. By this he means the 'assumptions, attitudes, aspirations and antipathies'[95] of the people who make up the culture. This legal mentality then works at the level of thinking, intuition and emotion,[96] so that it marks out for those in the culture what makes sense and what does not, and what is relevant and what is not, when discussing any particular topic. Legrand gives as an example any given legal culture's view of 'the function of the judge'.

d. 'Legal Artifacts'

Drawing attention to the 'situated local properties of knowledge',[97] Legrand speaks of 'legal artifacts' – in this case the RSC[98] and the CPR. He says that they are 'incorporative cultural forms which cannot be significantly detached from the world of meanings that fashions a law world'.[99] He goes on to make two points: that legal artifacts themselves come out of a situation that is historically formed; and that the assumptions of the culture are carried across into the relevant artifact, which is thus the bearer of moral and political meaning. As Legrand says, there 'is more to ruleness than a series of inscribed words', and a 'rule is necessarily an incorporative cultural form'.[100]

e. Changing the Culture

Of culture change, Legrand says that 'manners and customs cannot be changed by law, but have to undergo change themselves. This process takes time.'[101]

[93] See P Legrand 'Matter of Authenticity' (n 68) and also P Legrand, 'European legal systems are not converging' (1996) 45(1) *International and Comparative Law Quarterly* 52.

[94] P Legrand, 'Matter of Authenticity' (n 68) 381.

[95] P Legrand, 'European legal systems are not converging' (n 93) 60–61. Described elsewhere as 'an array of predispositions, predelictions, propensities, or inclinations', in P Legrand, 'Matter of Authenticity' (n 68) at 376.

[96] P Legrand, 'Matter of Authenticity' (n 68) 376–77.

[97] ibid 369.

[98] The CPR are still in the process of becoming a legal artifact, in the cultural sense.

[99] P Legrand, 'Matter of Authenticity' (n 68) 371.

[100] P Legrand, 'The Impossibility of "Legal Transplants"' (1997) 4 *Maastricht Journal of European & Comparative Law* 111 at 115–16.

[101] Pound would have shared this view: 'It is in human nature to accept most of the institutions with which one is familiar without much question. Hence we might reasonably expect that in any system of natural law nature would be found to dictate [ie would make seem perfectly natural] for the greater part, the institutions with which the individual jurist who interpreted nature was familiar and under which he had grown up.' R Pound, 'The Scope and Purpose of Sociological Jurisprudence, Pt 1' (1911) 24 *Harvard Law Review* 591 at 611. In the civil litigation context, see also J Peysner and M Seneviratne, *The management of civil cases: the courts and the post-Woolf landscape* (London, Department for Constitutional Affairs, 2005) at 10–11.

This is partly because the established legal mentality is the result of views of what is thought to be 'probable possible or impossible'. These views then become stabilised and persist through time, being 'internalised … through socialisation … and crystallise[d] into patterns of action'.[102] This stabilisation matters because it forms the basis for what people consider is 'possible' or even 'rhetorically convincing and morally acceptable'.[103] Elsewhere Legrand argues that 'thought is, therefore, culturally constituted in a very significant way'.[104] The consequence of this is that a legal mentality has an impact on the ability of lawyers to comprehend or support change.

f. Lawyers and Mentalities

The various approaches to mentalities are treated in Patrick H Hutton's article 'Mentalities'.[105] Hutton says (and here he is followed closely) that the study of mentalities is concentrated on the interplay of thought and emotion, focusing not just on attitudes but on manners customs and habits of mind too.

It can be argued that there is a legitimate distinction to be made between:

(a) a concept (such as procedural justice);
(b) how the concept is incarnated in a procedural process (the rules);
(c) how those operating the system (the judges) see their professional roles;
(d) how those using the system (the legal professionals) see their professional roles;
(e) how the different groups accumulate ways of thinking, expression and behaviour that have a cultural feel; and
(f) the inner life of the lawyers.

Certainly, the boundaries are not easy to delineate – all of these things will be found in a single practitioner or judge. Nevertheless, the inner life of the lawyer is not to be ignored.

Sorajbi's analysis of the difficulties Woolf faced offers a way into a rich seam of study of the theory of justice on the merits and its evolution, the practical working out of the theory in terms of the system's being operated, how the judges saw their role and how professionals saw their role (to the extent that this can be reconstructed from their non-compliance), and how groups of judges and practitioners have thought, spoken and behaved. The inner component (or the mentalities component) is another aspect of the friction inherent in the system.

[102] P Legrand, 'Matter of Authenticity' (n 68) 376.
[103] ibid at 383.
[104] P Legrand, 'Matter of Authenticity' (n 68) at 375.
[105] PH Hutton, 'Mentalities' in K Boyd (ed), *The Encyclopaedia of Historians and Historical Writing*, vol 2 (London, Fitzroy Dearborn Publishers, 1999) 800–03.

g. Changing People's Behaviour Takes Time

In all this talk of culture and mentalities, one does not need to go as far as saying that manners, customs and behaviour can never be changed by law. Changing the procedural law is a definite start, requiring, as it does, participants to do new things in new ways. Sanctions, too, have a role in raising standards, punishing non-compliance and making an example of those who do not comply. But the inelasticity of ideas, emotions and habit needs to be reckoned with over the longer term, and Jackson shows a marked realism in that regard. Woolf was more optimistic: even as late as 2008, his position was that 'there has been the change of culture which I hoped to achieve'.[106]

It should be no surprise that attitudes and behaviour have taken time to change. Legrand argues that change is accomplished by the dissemination of the new through education, 'observation, imitation, and communication'[107] – all of which require time.

The legal culture of practitioners and judges prior to 1998 included a legal mentality: a system of ideas about what justice was; what the role of the lawyer was in relation to the client; and what the role of the judge was in relation to the litigants. This mentality was expressed in the symbols of 'justice', 'justice on the merits', 'litigation as conflict' and 'doing the best for the client', which were communicated in training and perpetuated through everyday behaviour. It was this that formed practitioners' and judges' understanding of what they and the system were there for. Pre-1883 understanding and behaviour was passed on historically behind the 'new' symbol of justice on the merits – a passing-on that was so successful that the fusion of ideas became taken for granted – hence the need for Woolf's paradigm shift. The difficulty for Woolf was that the old theory justified even older forms of behaviour. Justice on the merits acted as a moral justification or explanation for the way things were prior to 1998.

So successful had this process become that the old theory had become entrenched in everyday thinking and behaviour, that is in legal mentality and legal culture. Woolf was in error in underestimating the difficulty of imposing a change of culture and mentality when seeking to change practitioners and the judges.

Of course the litigants also had a role to play in all this, but there is some difficulty in any event in describing litigants' behaviour as 'cultural' in the formal sense, given the fact that many litigants do not litigate repeatedly and that their action

[106] H Woolf, *The Pursuit of Justice* (n 2) at 14. Though, to be fair, there is material supportive of this view in Peysner and Senevirantne *The management of civil cases* (n 101) at 12–13. Contrast Pound's view: 'Escape from the past is always slow and difficult. This is true especially in law, which, from its very nature, must always to a greater extent than other institutions "formulate the rule of the dead over the living."' R Pound, 'Some Principles of Procedural Reform', 4 *Illinois Law Review* 388 (1909–1910) at 395.

[107] P Legrand, 'Matter of Authenticity' (n 68) at 386.

may be motivated by internal notions of what is in their best interests rather than by cultural forces. The distinction between litigants and their lawyers is often not made in Woolf's writing – perhaps because Woolf was emphasising the justice-seeking aspects of the litigant's role rather than the justice-evading aspect.[108] Woolf's view of unrepresented litigants tended towards the rose-tinted.

Changing a culture is not impossible. As Geertz reflects, the change in a social context of some key concepts may have unpredictable but definite effects that, though they might not change everything, can change a great deal in terms of the way people consequently behave.[109] That said, changing a culture of behaviour is not easy. Woolf then, needed the cooperation of the practitioners and the judges. The practitioners – to whom he referred as an inner circle of initiates – and those managing them – the judges. The established conduct of practitioners was habitual; and worse, that of the judges was split between the intentional (the opposition at the appellate level) and the habitual (the everyday judges).

If the old automatic striking-out procedure had run into difficulty because so many participants were non-compliant,[110] and if non-compliance was as culturally endemic as Woolf had said that it was, then a thoughtful reformer or rule-maker might have predicted that when the Woolf Reforms were implemented, many cases would be thrown out for non-compliance. Woolf himself was rather imprecise on this point. He seems to have assumed that the threat of sanctions would turn things around of itself. Woolf's Final Report placed the blame for the troubles arising from automatic striking out firmly at the door of errant practitioners, but then avoided drawing any lesson from this about the problems posed by automatic sanctions.[111] The best Woolf could say was 'effective management should avoid a situation to which Order 15 rule 11(9) applies arising'. This was an optimistic conclusion, given that his proposal was to have more automatic sanctions under the CPR, coupled with a severe rule against relief from sanctions.[112] It is, further, not easy to reconcile the fatalistic view about practitioners in Chapter 6, paragraph 7 of the Final Report, 'even the most severe sanction does not change practitioners' behaviour when it is delivered without adequate warning', with the

[108] Woolf did recognise that problems stemmed from the system as well as from practitioners: see H Woolf, *The Pursuit of Justice* (n 2) *at* 331.

[109] C Geertz, *The Interpretation of Cultures* (New York, Basic Books, 1973) 408–09. This cultural anthropological insight is applicable in the field of comparative law. Remo Caponi is working towards the application of Geertz in Italian civil procedure: see R Caponi, 'The Performance of the Italian Civil Justice System: An Empirical Assessment' (2016) 2(1) *The Italian Law Journal* 15. His principal interest appears to be in the cultural mind-set of those who commence litigation – a study in itself. More widely, he looks at the work practices of judges and lawyers, and at a system that applies insufficient filters and is insufficiently staffed: see especially ibid at 30. I am grateful to one of the anonymous reviewers for drawing Caponi to my attention.

[110] See H Woolf, *The Pursuit of Justice* (n 2) 332-33. See also B Vincent, 'Order 17 rule 11 – a retrospective' (1998) 95(26) *Law Society Gazette* 34.

[111] *WfFR* (n 11) ch 6, para 7.

[112] *WfDR* (n 11) 5.2 was never implemented. The original CPR 3.9 was more lax, thus avoiding an initial rush of parties' cases being penalised. That came with the implementation of the new CPR 3.9. It was only because Woolf's Draft Rule was not implemented that the day of reckoning was postponed.

statement in Chapter 6, paragraph 16, that 'in such a new climate, sanctions will be able to play their proper role which is prevention rather than punishment. What is needed is the threat of a prompt, relevant punishment to prevent the offence'. Woolf hoped that 'draconian sanctions' would be a last resort, due to the wide range of sanctions that would be available to an actively managing judge: so much so that he argued that sanctions would 'become unnecessary'.[113]

h. Capacity for Change was Limited

The available capacity for change was limited. This was for a number of reasons:

(a) practitioners had been trained in the sporting theory of litigation, and the system within which they operated was a conflict system;[114]
(b) practitioners had to do their best for their clients or face liability for negligence and loss of business;
(c) no practitioner could be confident that his opponent would be 'reform compliant'. It only needed a few people to escape the constraints of the new rules and compliant practitioners who were dealing with non-compliant ones would be at a tremendous disadvantage;[115]
(d) the external system of behaviour of lawyers had been internalised by individual lawyers. The individual practitioners had absorbed ways of behaving. Woolf was asking them to change both their external behaviour and their internal view of how they ought to behave. Changing a mentality and a culture is not easy and takes time.

vi. The Judges Were Faced with Having to Deny Old-Fashioned Justice to Individual Litigants

The new integrated sanctions network,[116] which was supposed to deliver help in the achievement of the overriding objective, meant that judges who were used to applying the theory of justice on the merits were having to make decisions that would result in outcomes that failed to deliver this.

[113] H Woolf, *The Pursuit of Justice* (n 2) at 333. A rather utopian thought.

[114] For a wider view, see J Thomas, *Cutting the cloth* (n 37) at para 5.

[115] *WfIR* (n 11) ch 3, para 7 speaks of 'the powers of the courts' having 'fallen behind the more sophisticated and aggressive tactics of some litigators', and says that 'the main procedural tools for conducting litigation efficiently have each become subverted from their proper purpose'(ibid ch 3, para 8). If that were the case under the old system, how could practitioners be confident that the new system would be any better? The problem has not gone away—*Kazakhstan Kagazy PLC v Zhunus* [2015] EWHC 404 (Comm) offers a good current example of 'what is often euphemistically described as "hard fought litigation" in which neither side shows any sense of moderation' (per Leggatt J at [12]). *Okpabi v Royal Dutch Shell Plc* [2017] EWHC 89 (TCC) at [9] and [10] illustrates how too much evidence can be 'self-defeating'.

[116] See ch 5 of this work.

That outcome, whilst desirable from the system's perspective, would confront judges with having to make decisions resulting in real people having their right to bring or defend a claim overridden.

The application of the new theory with its accompanying mechanics had real consequences, and went very much against the grain of the old system and theory under which judges had practised. One can only wonder how they would have felt in trying to come to terms with this. Though, doubtless, some judges may have thought that integrated sanctions were a price worth paying for an efficient system, the opposition at appellate level suggests that not all judges felt this way.

This issue was surely foreseeable, yet the rule-makers pressed ahead. If the problem was not anticipated, we have Mertonian ignorance; if it was anticipated but ignored then the system was behaving imperiously towards the people on whom it relied to implement the system's desires on a daily basis.[117]

vii. Woolf's New Theory was Not Articulated Clearly

It is notable how Woolf's plain and simple theory written in plain English was so widely misunderstood or doubted. One can see a number of issues here with CPR 1.1 mark I:

(a) the use of 'justly' was not a better choice than 'just'. It enabled the confusion between substantive justice and procedural justice to continue, and thus muddied the distinction between justice's direct end and justice's collateral ends;
(b) the use of 'deal' could be read entirely as relating to action (procedure) rather than to outcome (substantive decision);
(c) the use of 'overriding' was understandable but less clear than the alternative 'overarching' or 'paramount', if that is what Woolf meant, and significantly it was misleading because it covered three distinct things: the objective of the Rules taken as a whole;[118] the objective to be achieved through the discretionary exercise of case management powers; and the objectives fulfilled by use of the procedures laid down by the Rules. In the third case the overriding objective had no overriding function, merely an interpretive one;
(d) the matters included in CPR 1.1(2) were not a coherent set. They included matters formerly considered to be fundamental to procedure that had remained largely unarticulated, as well as factors new to the system;
(e) the use of 'equal footing' as the first example undercut the force of 'saving expense' which followed it;
(f) the splitting of 'saving expense' and 'ways which are proportionate' in a situation where balancing of requirements was acceptable allowed a false

[117] To be fair, the position may have been that the system had no option but to press ahead regardless – but the lack of official comment about the potential problems is striking.

[118] CPR 1.1 Mark I said, 'These rules are a new procedural code with [ie which have been made with] the overriding objective of enabling the court to deal with cases justly.'

distinction to be made between saving expense and behaving in a proportionate manner;

(g) the lack of mechanisms for fixing, capping or budgeting costs meant that the objective of 'saving expense' could be marginalised.

D. Conclusion

In this chapter we have applied Merton's and Legrand's ideas to the civil justice reforms. Officially, failure was not anticipated, at least by Woolf. Yet neither the Woolf Reforms nor the early Jackson Reforms were a complete success. Indeed in some senses they were a failure. We have the benefit of hindsight, the reformers did not. They were constrained by many factors, some of which cannot be seen by those outside the process. The application of the concept of unanticipated consequences gives us pause for thought when looking at the involvement of reformers, rule-makers, appellate judges, first instance judges and the practitioners.

The reforms did not take adequate account of the difficulties of changing a longstanding practitioner culture, nor of the importance and difficulty of winning over or coordinating the appellate judges; and that the failure of the rule-makers to follow the reformers' lead concerning relief from sanctions meant that reforms went in a direction different from that anticipated by Woolf and Jackson.

Reform of civil justice is a very big change project involving the behaviour of thousands of different people working in different situations. The recent history of reform shows just how difficult it is to predict how people will react and to craft solutions that will work across the board, and why further attention to the factors operating upon those involved in and under the reforms would be worthwhile.

5

Defending the Civil Justice System: The Function of Sanctions

I. Introduction

A. Introductory Thoughts

In the last chapter we looked at the difficulties experienced during the Woolf and early Jackson reforms.[1] For the court system to function correctly, the court has to manage each claim so that substantive justice is delivered in a particular case.[2] To do that, it has to actively manage[3] each case within the system so that substantive justice is delivered for all cases passing through the system at that particular time. As Andrew Higgins argues, 'The purpose of the civil court is to secure the overriding objective, and unless that objective is imperilled in the instant case or in other litigation, the court has no interest in imposing a sanction.'[4]

The court cannot control the influx of cases, but it has to manage the caseload that appears. The larger the caseload, the greater the need for order.

Sanctions support the functioning of the system. They are imposed when something has gone wrong, and are therefore a secondary mechanism that is deployed to help the system to function. They are intended to punish those who fail to comply with the rules. But that is not all, for the existence of any particular sanction-imposing rule is designed to encourage compliance (in that the rule sets out the standard of behaviour to be reached) and to deter would-be defaulters.

The perennial challenge for the civil justice system has been to get the parties, and their lawyers, to comply with their process obligations. Carrots are out of

[1] In this chapter John Sorabji's account of the battle of two theories of procedural justice – which appears in J Sorabji, *English Civil Justice after the Woolf and Jackson Reforms: A Critical Analysis* (Cambridge, Cambridge University Press, 2014) – has broadly been taken for granted. The term 'process obligations' is Zuckerman's and taken from A Zuckerman, 'The revised CPR 3.9: a coded message demanding articulation' (2013) 32(2) *Civil Justice Quarterly* 123 at 126. See also A Zuckerman, *Zuckerman on Civil Procedure: Principles of Practice* (London, Sweet & Maxwell, 2013) (hereinafter '*ZoCP*') para 11.7. Zuckerman's relevant earlier work is A Zuckerman, *Civil Procedure* (London, Lexis Nexis Butterworths, 2003). In this chapter the 'old CPR 3.9' means the rule in force until 30 March 2013. The 'new CPR.3.9' means that Rule in force from 1 April 2013.

[2] Civil Procedure Rule (CPR) 1.1.

[3] CPR 3.1.

[4] A Higgins, 'CPR 3.9: The Mitchell guidance, the Denton revision, and why coded messages don't make for good case management.' (2014) 33(4) *Civil Justice Quarterly* 379 at 388–89.

the question. You cannot reward people for doing what they ought to do anyway. Therefore you have to resort to the stick. But how much is the stick to be applied, and where do you stop? Offer too little stick and you seem tolerant of laxity and risk creating 'laissez-faire litigation, which leaves the parties to swirl around in uncontrolled litigation'.[5] This undermines the basic principle that 'those who would voluntarily obey shall not be sacrificed to those who do not. To obey without this, would be to risk going to the wall.'[6] When this happens, people will be encouraged to feel that non-compliance is worth the risk. Use too much stick and you risk punishing genuine slip-ups – precisely the formalist atmosphere away from which the Judicature Acts were supposed to have moved us.

It would be easy to be misled by the case law on relief from sanctions into thinking that everyone is in default. Non-compliance may be common but it is not universal – for if it was, the court system could not function.

The Rules of the Supreme Court (RSC) offered no single overall model for the imposition of sanctions. The approach to sanctions, as it were, amounted to a congeries of 'isolated dooms', each imposed for separate reasons.[7] In most cases under the RSC, the aggrieved party had to take steps itself to force action from the defaulter – and to the extent that the system took note of sanctions, it did so largely with a view to goading the non-compliant into action. Applications were made for an unless order or by way of seeking a strike-out, but parties might have had good reason for taking neither step.[8] The lack of an effective compliance regime was one of the issues that concerned Woolf. But under the CPR, with the new CPR 3.9, default is being tackled vigorously.

From the RSC 1883 until 1997, the approach to the imposition of sanctions was driven by the idea that people should have an opportunity to go to trial – the philosophy of justice on the merits.[9] After the publication of the Woolf Reports, but prior to the implementation of the CPR, the Court of Appeal changed its approach, at least in relation to unless orders.[10]

The CPR were supposed to bring about a step-change in the way that non-compliance was to be managed, through the creation of an integrated sanctions network. This had two aspects: sanctions would normally be imposed by operation of the Rules, rather than as a result of the application of a party; and the court was given specific power to control when relief from sanctions would be granted.

[5] R Jackson, *Reforms Implementation Programme: Lecture No 5. Achieving a Culture Change in Case Management* (November 2011) para 1.10, available at www.judiciary.uk.

[6] HLA Hart, *The Concept of Law*, 2nd edn (Oxford, Oxford University Press, 1994) at 198. For similar comments more informally expressed, see J Finnis, *Natural Law and Natural Rights* (Oxford, Clarendon Press, 1980) at 262.

[7] BN Cardozo, *The Nature of the Judicial Process* (New Haven, CT, Yale University Press, 1921) at 126.

[8] See *Fitzpatrick v Batger & Co* [1967] 1 WLR 706 (CA), per Salmon LJ at 709–10; *Allen v Sir Alfred McAlpine & Sons Ltd* [1968] 2 WLR 366 (CA), per Diplock L.J at 257–58; and *Birkett v James* [1978] AC 297, per Lord Salmon at 325.

[9] Sorabji attributes this to the Equity's philosophy of 'complete justice': see *SorECJ* (n 1) 31–74.

[10] *Hytec Information Systems Ltd v Coventry City Council* [1997] 1 WLR 1666 (CA).

Under the CPR, the imposition of sanctions became largely automatic.[11] If a party broke a Rule then it would automatically reap its reward, for the event of default would trigger the sanction. This increased the need for applications for relief, because CPR 3.8 provided that all trigger events would now require an application for relief to be made if the punishment was to be reduced or avoided. The new approach was designed to allow the court to exercise more control, but it had the effect of using up more scarce court time in dealing with relief applications.

The CPR brought an integrated approach to the problem of default.[12] The key was to be CPR 3.8. It would control the way the court applied the grant of relief in all cases of relief from sanctions. The importance of CPR 3.8 became magnified once it was decided that a sanction could be either express or implied: CPR 3.8 was the gateway through which applications for relief must pass.

The introduction of the old CPR 3.9 did not create the expected benefits, because its multi-faceted test allowed individual courts to prioritise the merits of individual cases over the needs of the civil justice system.

Following the Jackson Review,[13] the new, stricter CPR 3.9 decreased the effectiveness of applications for relief – the clear intention was that fewer applications for relief would succeed. Prior to the introduction of the new CPR 3.9, there was a careful attempt to educate practitioners. The admonitions to change were followed by a deliberate assault on non-compliance. The first appellate approach[14] to the new CPR 3.9 proved too draconian and, subsequently, it became necessary for the Court of Appeal to 'restate' the position.[15] It was also recognised that CPR 3.9 was of very wide effect.[16] This has resulted in the imposition of extra hurdles to relief, for example in applications to set aside a default judgment, where the applicant has to satisfy both CPR 13.3 and CPR 3.9.[17] This extra hurdle did not exist under the RSC (1965).

There is ongoing controversy on the question of whether a CPR sanction is to be classified as being regulatory or punitive in nature,[18] the argument being that

[11] Adrian Zuckerman calls this a 'pre-determined consequence'. See *ZoCP* (2013) (n 1) para 11.98.

[12] Zuckerman, in *ZoCP* (2003) (n 1), spoke of 'pre-determined consequences' at para 10.74.

[13] R Jackson, *Review of Civil Litigation Costs: Preliminary Report* (London, TSO, 2009); and R Jackson, *Review of Civil Litigation Costs: Final Report* (London, TSO, 2009).

[14] *Mitchell v News Group Newspapers Ltd* [2013] EWCA Civ 1537.

[15] *Denton v TH White Ltd* [2014] EWCA Civ 906. For comment upon *Mitchell* and *Denton*, see A Higgins, 'CPR 3.9' (n 4) 379; JR Williams, '"Well, that's a relief (from sanctions)!" – Time to pause and take stock of CPR r.3.9 developments within a general theory of case management' (2014) 33(4) *Civil Justice Quarterly* 394; S Richards, 'The Mitchell/Denton line of cases: securing compliance with rules and court orders' (2015) 34(3) *Civil Justice Quarterly* 249; R Nayer, 'Post-Denton: an appraisal of Court of Appeal decisions on relief from sanctions' (2016) 35(2) *Civil Justice Quarterly* 97 (with a helpful typology); see also S Clark and R Jackson, *The Reform of Civil Justice*, 2nd edn (London, Thomson Reuters (Professional) UK Ltd, 2018) para 13-033.

[16] *Samara v MBI & Partners* [2014] EWHC 563 (QB).

[17] RSC (1965) Ord 13, r 9 and Ord 19, r 9.

[18] See S Sime, 'Lord Dyson and the Implied Sanctions doctrine' (2015) 34(3) *Civil Justice Quarterly* 267 at 271; and *ZoCP* (2013) (n 1) paras 11.13–11.19 and 11.136. Zuckerman has been consistent in arguing that exercising an elective choice will result in a 'consequence' rather than a sanction: see *ZoCP* (2003) (n 1) para 10.11.

if sanctions are regulatory then the court should be free to develop an integrated approach to sanctions. That the courts have now taken an integrated approach is clear. Rather than focusing upon the classification problem, the focus here is on the more general issues. We examine of the function of sanctions: what sanctions are for; how they operate and what impact they have. These functions are best viewed together.

For this we need to bear in mind some principles[19] concerning the function of sanctions:

(a) Sanctions are used as a regulatory mechanism so that the system can work efficiently.
(b) The object of a sanction is to control behaviour:
    (i) before the event, through setting standards (the positive side) and by providing a deterrent (the negative side); and
    (ii) after the event, by imposing a punishment that is both a specific punishment for the defaulter and an example, for others, of the consequences of default.

II. Systems

A. How Systems Work

Peter L Berger and Thomas Luckmann's classic work, *The Social Construction of Reality*[20] makes the following points of interest:

(a) The primary means of control lies in the existence of the system itself: there is a court and there are rules governing how the parties, their representatives and the court itself must behave.[21] The court has the sole right to make a final and binding decision about the dispute if alternative dispute resolution (ADR) (including arbitration) is not used.
(b) The system itself acts to restrict what the parties or their representatives can properly do. The very existence of the civil justice system pushes participants in a certain direction.[22] The Rules set out the system's chosen parameters for the way parties are to prepare and the case is to be tried. Case management limits parties' room for manoeuvre.[23]

[19] This puts us into the controversial territory of the punitive/regulatory debate concerning the classification of the treatment of defaults under the CPR. Such a question is beyond the scope of this chapter. We shall, however, consider the purpose and function of this treatment of CPR default events, which we shall call sanctions, whether properly so classified or not.

[20] PL Berger and T Luckmann, *The Social Construction of Reality: a Treatise In the Sociology of Knowledge* (Harmondsworth, The Penguin Press, 1966).

[21] ibid at 73.

[22] PL Berger and T Luckmann, *The Social Construction of Reality* (n 20) at 78.

[23] This is deliberate – see Lord Woolf, *Access to Justice: Interim Report* (London, HMSO, 1995) (hereinafter '*WfIR*') ch 3, para 4.

(c) It is only where a participant acts outside the limits set by the system that additional controls are required. Those additional controls are sanctions.[24] As we shall see, determined non-compliance undermines the court's ability to control people once they are within the system.

It is worth saying that, within the European Union, the Court of Justice sees itself as having a role in safeguarding the capacity of the Union to function and in using 'weapons for limited warfare' in that regard. This stance is primarily prophylactic rather than sanctioning, but the parallels are there.[25]

(d) It is unlikely that sanctions will be invoked continuously unless the system is itself in the course of disintegration. It is interesting that full relief under the new CPR 3.9 is being so frequently refused, because that is suggestive of the parlous situation in which the civil justice system now finds itself.
(e) Society has specific procedures for dealing with a breakdown in compliance. These can take the form of forceful defensive measures. The measures used will be, or should be, proportional to the threat felt.[26] Again, the stringent nature of the sanctions being applied is suggestive of the severity of the threat that the civil justice system considers is posed by non-compliance.

B. Participants in the Civil Justice System

So much for the system. But what about those caught up in the court process and those who advise them ('the participants'). Participants can engage with the procedural rules for a number of different reasons: (i) they can comply because they simply accept the Rules as setting the requisite standard of behaviour; (ii) they comply because they can see the need for the Rules, or the good that the Rules can achieve; (iii) participants may comply because they are motivated by the prospect of 'reward'[27] for compliance; (iv) they comply because they are motivated by the fear of punishment for non-compliance.

The reasons for non-compliance with the procedural rules may also be various: (i) the participants may be slow, forgetful or disorganised; (ii) the participants may not be able to respond to their procedural obligations (eg they have lost documents); (iii) the non-compliance may be tactical, in that participants hope to gain time or an advantage, or to shorten time or impose a disadvantage on the other side.

Some non-compliant behaviour makes sense if participants can see that it benefits them, but not all cases of non-compliance are deliberate. Nevertheless, there are sufficient non-compliant participants at any one time to cause the system

[24] PL Berger and T Luckmann, *The Social Construction of Reality* (n 20) at 73.
[25] H Kutscher, *Methods of Interpretation as seen by a Judge at the Court of Justice* (Luxembourg, Juridical and Academic Conference, 1976) at 42 and 46.
[26] PL Berger and T Luckmann, *The Social Construction of Reality* (n 20) at 176.
[27] The 'reward' is the smooth running of the process.

problems. Those problems have called forth a response in the form of the integrated sanctions network.

III. Analysis of Sanctions

A. The Dictionary Meaning of 'Sanctions'

'Sanction' may be a softer term than 'punishment' but it is capable of two distinct meanings,[28] which is particularly important in a context in which Woolf wanted to move from the dominant 'last chance' school of unless orders to the largely automatic punishment regime of the CPR. An ordinary language analysis of this term is justifiable in the light of Woolf's insistence on plain language,[29] and because it highlights the nature of the underlying change that occurred.

The term 'sanction' has two meanings. The primary dictionary meaning is not in common usage at all. The *Concise Oxford English Dictionary*[30] defines a sanction as 'a threatened[31] penalty for disobeying' a rule. In other words, people know that the punishment is there to take effect if they do not comply with the rule. The penalty is built into the system. Many sanctions[32] are triggered automatically by the failure to take a specific step. The risk of disobedience to the rule is known, or ought to be known, in advance.

It is the secondary dictionary meaning of 'sanction' that is the subject of everyday speech. The *Concise OED* definition goes on to speak of this secondary sense, describing 'measures taken by a state to coerce another to conform' to the norms of conduct in an international context. Both of these senses – a system that constrains people who have acted and a system that acts to coerce people – will be encountered later.

As commonly understood, a sanction is needed where one party has behaved in an undesirable way. Implicit in this understanding of sanctions is the hope that the miscreant will modify his or her undesired behaviour and move into compliance. If the bar for lifting a sanction is set too high then procedural clemency[33] is unlikely, and the possibility of redemption is heavily curtailed.

[28] The use of 'sanction' as permission is left aside in this chapter.

[29] *WfIR* (n 23) para 25(c) and para 36; H Woolf, *Access to Justice: Final Report* (London, HMSO, 1996) (hereinafter '*WfFR*') ch 20, para 13 and para 15.

[30] 10th ed, ed J Pearsall (Oxford, Oxford University Press, 2002).

[31] That a sanction ought to require a prior threat was one of the drivers behind the decision in *AG Trinidad & Tobago v Matthews* [2011] UKPC 38, para [15]. The idea is of long standing: see J Austin, *Lectures on Jurisprudence*, student edn ed Robert Campbell (London, John Murray, 1880). Lecture I at 13, 'a wish conceived … expressed … to another, with an evil to be inflicted … in case the wish be disregarded'.

[32] For example, CPR 31.21 (failure to disclose documents).

[33] N Andrews, *Andrews on Civil Processes*, vol 1 (Cambridge, Intersentia, 2013) at para 9.31. It is thought that 'clemency' is a good word here. It emphasises the fact that the applicant is reliant on the court's showing mercy. 'Relief from sanctions' is a rather colourless phrase.

As commonly used in an international context, there is usually some sense that sanctions will escalate if there is non-compliance. The old system of peremptory orders provided for such escalation. The use of sanctions following automatically upon default means that there is no scope for escalation: maximum force is used immediately. Automatic sanctions are more retributive and deterrent in effect than graduated or rehabilitative. The court, rather than acting in a graduated manner, now has only the option of de-escalation or the refusal of clemency, and can only do this after the event of default.

B. The CPR Meaning of 'Sanctions'

In *Summit Navigation Ltd v Generali Romania Asigurare Reasigurare SA*, Leggatt J, as he then was, said:

> The term 'sanction' seems to me apt to include any consequence adverse to the party to whom it applies … I interpret rule 3.8(3) and 3.8(1) as dealing with the same situation, in the one case before, and in the other case after, the time specified for doing an act has expired … It follows that any application to disapply a consequence specified in a court order for failing to do something within a time specified in the order is an application for relief from a 'sanction' within the meaning of these rules.[34]

Leggat J's comments show how much the term 'sanctions' has been stretched to cover sanctions detailed in advance and restrictions imposed *ex post facto* by way of punishment.

Some sanctions are clearly set out in advance in a rule that details the conditions to trigger the sanction, the effect of the sanction and the circumstances in which relief may be granted. It is worth noting that the allowance for discretionary relief from these sanctions is usually defeasible by discretion or variable by discretion. An example of such a sanctions-imposing rule is to be found in CPR 31.21.[35] This is a classic example of an express sanction: 'a party may not … [if] he fails to … unless the court gives permission'.

Automatic sanctions are a rather imprecise instrument. Whatever the degree of default, the sanction is the same. If no relief were possible then it would not be possible to vary the sanction in appropriate circumstances to produce a result that was proportionate to the gravity of the actual default. Under CPR 3.9, discretionary relief may be granted if the defaulter asks for it, and if it is appropriate. The review by the court, however, is carried out after the sanction has taken effect.

Some sanctions are set out in advance but operate conditionally, as they are designed to offer a last chance. This encourages compliance and deters default, as well as providing, in advance, for punishment where there is default. An unless

[34] *Summit Navigation Ltd v Generali Romania Asigurare Reasigurare SA* [2014] EWHC 398 (Comm) at [27].

[35] Failure to disclose documents.

order falls into the 'clear but conditional' category.[36] Even once an unless order has taken effect, it is possible for the defaulter to apply for relief, because the barring of a party's right to a fair hearing is the most significant sanction that a court can impose.[37]

Some sanctions are clearly not sanctions within the primary meaning of that term, as they are not clearly set out in advance. Instead they impinge as a consequence of the defaulter's needing the court's assistance to continue. We shall now concentrate on one example: setting aside a judgment in default. This type of sanction is secondary in intention and both contingent and restrictive in effect. It is secondary because the main purpose, for example, of the entry of a default judgment is to enable the claimant to obtain a court order. It is contingent because the sanctionable aspect of the entry of default judgment only operates if the defendant wishes to have it set it aside so as to proceed to trial.[38] It is at this point that the sanctionable aspect bites and the defaulter faces a restrictive test for relief. The interrelationship of CPR 13.3 and CPR 3.9 has a curious effect, for the defendant has to satisfy a double-barrelled test.

Looked at on its own, CPR 13.3 can be seen as prophylactic in design. The claimant has a regular judgment issued by a court. Neither should be troubled by applications where there is a very weak defence or, alternatively, a lack of a good reason for a trial, nor should either have to deal with stale applications. That CPR 13.3 is prophylactic means that it cannot truly be said to be aimed at the defendant; the defendant is the subject of the rule, not the object. The judgment is already in place, and it is the integrity of the judgment which the court looks to support.[39]

However, CPR 3.9 is primarily punitive rather than prophylactic in design. It functions by putting hurdles in the way of a defendant who has chosen, actually or by imputation, not to comply with the relevant order or rule. This position is defensible on the three distinct grounds of the autonomy of the individual, his or her obligations to society, and the responsibilities of the court.

A party is autonomous and can choose to engage, or not, with the court process as he or she wishes.[40] But that party cannot then complain if the court treats his or

[36] For the relationship between unless orders and CPR 3.9, see *British Gas Trading Ltd v Oak Cash & Carry Ltd* [2016] EWCA Civ 153 at [29]. The case is explained in *Suez Fortune Investments Ltd v Talbot Underwriting Ltd* [2016] EWHC 1085 (Comm).

[37] In the case of a claimant, he or she will be free to commence fresh proceedings, but may run up against the difficulty of any limitation defence and also the provisions of CPR 3.4(4) if the costs of the first proceedings have not been paid.

[38] The defendant may accept that he or she has no defence to the claim – that may be the reason for failing to file an acknowledgement of service or a defence in time – in which case the sanctionable aspect never takes effect.

[39] Ultimately, if there is a real prospect on the merits then the judgment, though regular, is not to be supported.

[40] See J Jolowicz, *On Civil Procedure* (Cambridge, Cambridge University Press, 2000) at 68 and 78–79. See also *Berowra Holdings Pty Ltd v Gordon* [2006] HCA 32 at [15]. Jolowicz is primarily thinking of pre-CPR freedoms, and it doubtful that such obligation-free liberty continues to exist in fact. What continues is the capacity to avoid engagement with the court system if the autonomous individual so chooses. The exercise of such autonomy is not, however, consequence free. Zuckerman touches upon the question of procedural autonomy in *ZoCP* (2013) (n 1) paras 11.9–11.20.

her non-engagement as a deliberate act. If a party wishes to resile from a position previously taken in exercise of his or her own freedom, it is proper that he or she should have to demonstrate the justice of his or her position. Justice here includes the questions of efficiency, proportionality and compliance, and the need to satisfy the wider concerns of the administration of justice so as to benefit society at large.

Turning to the question of obligation, we note that a party is not, in Michael Sandel's words, 'an unencumbered self'[41] but rather a participant in society, with the benefits that this brings (including the right to a fair trial). An obligation, if not a duty,[42] is imposed by CPR 1.3 on all parties to litigation.[43] Further, the Rule takes effect notwithstanding that it may fail to coincide with a party's own objectives. The Rule has a force that overrides the normal claims of reason.[44]

The source of the obligation imposed by the Rule is the need of society, in the sense of its members individually and together, to have a functioning court system. The obligation is to assist the court in fulfilling the overriding objective. Any failure by a party to fulfil the CPR 1.3 obligation may prevent the court from fulfilling its mission, and so justifies the imposition of a sanction: CPR 1.3 places an obligation on the parties to help the court in its mission. This obligation is owed to the court but relates to the wider social obligation of the parties to use only a fair share of resources, and in grounded in the wider social interests of all in living within a society where the court system functions effectively.[45]

As well as autonomy and obligation, there is the question of responsibility. Even if the parties were free to pursue their own interests without reference to the interests of others, CPR 1.1 recognises and reflects the paramount constitutional responsibility of the court to deal with all cases justly. The court is responsible to the parties; to other litigants within the system; to itself (to protect its own mission); and to society at large, which it is the court's mission to serve.

We now turn to consider the legal basis for express and implied sanctions.

C. Express and Implied Sanctions

The domestic case law establishes that CPR 3.8 covers two distinct types of situations, each of which is said to give rise to a sanction. These are situations

[41] M Sandel, 'The Procedural Republic and the Unencumbered Self' (1984) 12(1) *Political Theory* 81 at 86.

[42] *Davies v Forrett* [2015] EWHC 1761, per Edis J at [23]: 'CPR 1.3 … imposes a duty on the parties to help the court to further the overriding objective. This is a duty and not an exhortation. Breach of duty is a significant matter which is directly relevant to costs issues.' That CPR 1.3 may be said, at law, to be a duty does not answer the bigger classification question as to whether obligations under the CPR can be said to be duties (which tend to be thought of arising without choice) and obligations (where some sense of choice is involved). Certainly CPR 1.3 operates locally as a duty, even if it is not so classifiable.

[43] The claimant of course has chosen to accept that obligation, the defendant has not.

[44] J Raz's chapter on 'Authority and Justification' in J Raz (ed), *Authority* (Oxford, Basil Blackwell Ltd, 1990) at 124; and J Raz, *The Morality of Freedom* (Oxford, Clarendon Press, 1986) at 46.

[45] To pick up on the point made in ch 1, to say that the court has a responsibility is not to say that it is accountable. The two things are distinct.

where a sanction is expressly set out in a rule and situations where no sanction is set out in a rule. In the latter case, the sanctioning act has to be implied into the rule.[46]

Express and implied sanctions both fall to be treated under CPR 3.8, but implied sanctions may require the application of more than one test for relief.

There will be an express sanction where:

(a) a party fails to take a procedural step within the mandatory time limit prescribed by the Rules for the taking that step;
(b) the time limit has expired without that party making an application for an extension of time for the taking of the step;
(c) the rule expressly provides that the party is disabled from taking the relevant step;
(d) being placed under that disability is an adverse consequence for that party flowing from that failure to observe the rule. Such an adverse consequence is a sanction within the meaning of Rule 26.7.[47]

Moving on to implied sanctions, the emergence of the doctrine can probably be traced to *Sayers v Clarke Walker*, where Brooke LJ took the view that it was 'equally appropriate to have regard to the checklist in CPR r 3.9 when a court is considering an application for an extension of time for appealing in a case of any complexity'.[48] The court's reasoning was as follows:

(a) the defaulter had not complied with order giving him an extension of time; and
(b) although that rule did not expressly impose a sanction;
(c) a refusal to grant relief would have a consequence; and
(d) the consequence would be that the original order of the court would stand.[49]

The concept of sanctions has been expanded to cover situations where one party is given the right to take a step following default by the other party[50] – such as the entry of a default judgment. An order that is the outcome of such a step is

[46] For a careful review of the topic of implied sanctions, see S Sime, 'Lord Dyson and the implied sanctions doctrine' (2015) 34(3) *Civil Justice Quarterly* 267.

[47] Adapted from *AG v Matthews* [2011] UKPC 38 at [12].

[48] *Sayers v Clarke Walker* [2002] EWCA Civ 645 at [21]. As appears hereafter, the implied sanctions doctrine is now firmly established as part of the domestic law, and sanctions that are implied have all the bite of those which are express.

[49] In *Robert v Momentum Services Ltd* [2003] 1 WLR 1577 (CA), the Court of Appeal took the view that the implied sanction doctrine did not apply to cases where the application for an extension of time was being made before the original time period had expired. The implied sanctions doctrine was applied in *YD (Turkey) v Secretary of State for the Home Department* [2006] 1 WLR 1646 (CA), and in *Yeates v Aviva Insurance UK Ltd* [2012] EWCA Civ 634 and, post-*Mitchell*, in *Baho v Meerza* [2014] Costs LR 620 (CA) and, post-*Denton*, in *Altomart Ltd v Salford Estates (No 2) Ltd* [2014] EWCA Civ 1408.

[50] Adrian Zuckerman has argued that as many procedural requirement are neither obligations nor duties, so 'it is inaccurate to describe the consequences of procedural defaults as sanctions': *ZoCP* (2013) (n 1) para 11.19.

now classed as a sanction, because the right of the innocent party to take the step is conferred as a way of expressing the system's disapproval and is intended to punish the defaulting party. Whilst Lord Dyson in *AG Trinidad & Tobago v Matthews*[51] disapproved of the idea of implied sanctions, in *R (Hysaj) v Secretary of State for the Home Department*[52] the Court of Appeal confirmed that the implied sanctions rule was an established part of the domestic procedural jurisprudence, thus backing the integrated network approach to sanctions. So applications to set aside default judgment can be classed as dealing with relief from sanctions, thus engaging CPR 3.9 as well as CPR 13.3.[53]

D. The Purpose and Impact of Sanctions

There is nevertheless the question of the personal disadvantage that arises from the imposition of sanctions upon individuals. Someone is being punished and losing out on what they might otherwise have received. How can this be justified?

For convenience we return to what was said about John Gardner in chapter 1. In *Law as a Leap of Faith*,[54] John Gardner makes two important points that are of interest to us. First, the 'definitive adjudicative mission' is to be just.[55] For 'adjudicative institutions should be just above all'.[56] Second, courts are the 'lynchpin' of the legal system.[57] They are that point where law and justice come together.

Gardner goes on to make the point that the 'rational horizons'[58] of the virtue of justice are distinct from the 'rational horizons' of other virtues. He reminds us that Aristotle claimed that 'the just is a species of the proportionate',[59] and goes on to show that proportionality is *allocative*, that it is concerned to show that the right people get the right things for the right reason. What makes the virtue of justice distinct is that it approaches the dispute to be adjudicated with allocation in mind.[60]

In our context, a just procedural system has to take into account the varying needs of those using it, in relation to the case at hand, other cases in the system and other cases yet to be brought.

[51] *Trinidad & Tobago v Matthews* [2011] UKPC 38.

[52] *R (Hysaj) v Secretary of State for the Home Department* [2014] EWCA Civ 1633.

[53] *Samara v MBI & Partners Ltd* [2014] EWHC 563 (QB) at [34]–[39] was followed by *Regione Piemonte v Dexia Crediop SPA* [2014] EWCA Civ 1298 (obiter) at [58], then by *Blakemores LDP v Scott* [2015] EWCA Civ 999 at [58] and then by *Gentry v Miller* [2016] EWCA Civ 141 at [23]–[24].

[54] J Gardner, *Law as a Leap of Faith* (Oxford, Oxford University Press, 2012).

[55] ibid 258 n 28.

[56] J Gardner, *Law as a Leap of Faith* (n 54) 257.

[57] ibid 257.

[58] J Gardner, *Law as a Leap of Faith* (n 54) 242.

[59] Aristotle, *Nichomachean Ethics*, book V, ch 3, 1131a. For early CPR cases on proportionality, see *Biguzzi v Rank Leisure Plc* [1999] 1 WLR 1926 (CA) 1932–33; *Annodeus Entertainments Ltd v Gibson* (ChD, Neuberger J, 2 February 2000); and *Asiansky Television Plc v Bayer-Rosin* December 14, 2000 (QBD, Steel J, December 2000), this last decision itself being reversed on appeal.

[60] J Gardner, *Law as a Leap of Faith* (n 54) 246.

John Gardner further argues that the 'forms of law'[61] (in our context civil procedure) ought to be just because they 'purport to be just'. Put simply, if the claim of the law is that it is concerned with justice then, in order to live up to this distinct claim, it must operate the process of adjudication in a just manner. This is because what connects justice to law is adjudication, the business of the civil justice system.[62]

Having reviewed the wider philosophical case for sanctions, it is time to consider the practical and political logic of reform, which led to the creation of an integrated sanctions network.

IV. Reform of Sanctions

A. The Logic of Reform

The logic of reform operating behind the integrated sanctions network is as follows:

(a) party control[63] is associated with gamesmanship,[64] oppressive behaviour[65] and non-compliance;[66]
(b) non-compliance causes delay and increased expense for individual litigants;
(c) the same non-compliance causes the system to operate inefficiently;
(d) an inefficient system will not retain public confidence, a prerequisite for the curial system's being left to run itself without political interference;
(e) the use of case management (with the concomitant restriction on party autonomy) will reduce non-compliance;
(f) reduction of non-compliance will reduce delays and expense for individual litigants;
(g) the same reduction will cause the system to operate more efficiently; and
(h) an efficiently operated system will have the confidence of the public.

[61] ibid 251.

[62] For a judicial approach to this issue, see eg *Allen v Sir Alfred McAlpine & Sons Ltd* [1968] 2 WLR 366 (CA), per Lord Denning MR at 243 and 245–46, and per Diplock LJ at 254; *Birkett v James* [1978] AC 297, per Lord Diplock at 317–18. To say that process must be just does not answer the question as to what the content of a just process would be. The process chosen must reflect the intention of the rule-makers.

[63] The term 'party control' was used by Jack Jacob in *The Fabric of English Civil Justice* (London, Stevens & Sons, 1987) (hereinafter '*JbFabr*') at 13 and is set out clearly in N Andrews, *Principles of Civil Procedure* (London, Sweet & Maxwell, 1994) (hereinafter '*AndPCP*') at para 3-002. See also N Andrews, *English Civil Procedure: Fundamentals of the New Civil Justice System* (Oxford, Oxford University Press, 2003) at para 2.13. Zuckerman uses the term 'party autonomy' in *ZoCP* (2013) (n 1) at paras 11.9–11.12. As previously stated, in practice party control may have meant practitioner control.

[64] *JbFabr* (n 63) at 6.

[65] *WfIR* (n 23) ch 3 para 6; see *JbFabr* (n 63) at 14.

[66] *WfIR* (n 23) ch 5, paras 5–6.

This logic, of course, requires the judges to engage in a short-term crackdown – using even more precious judicial time – in the hope of gaining a long-term reduction in the number of defaulters.

B. Ways of Dealing with Non-Compliance

The RSC tackled non-compliance using a number of different methods. These will be set out according to their type.

Method A allowed the injured party to take the initiative in seeking the imposition by the court of an order providing for the deprivation of a right or the imposition of a restriction on a party's freedom of manoeuvre because of a default by that party, with such deprivation or restriction taking effect only after further default. Peremptory or unless orders played this role.

Method B imposed the sanction through rules that provided for an immediate and automatic imposition of a deprivation or restriction at the time of breach, with the onus put on the defaulting party to apply to the court for permission.[67] Method B utilised an automatic trigger for the sanction, a method that was to become the preferred way of dealing with the breach of key process obligations under the CPR.

Method C allowed the injured party to take a specific step, upon a party's having defaulted, to seek the imposition of a sanction that would bring the claim to an end, for example for a failure to serve a statement of claim,[68] to give discovery as required,[69] for a failure to take out a summons for directions,[70] for a failure to set the case down for trial,[71] or for failure to comply with a rule or court order under the originating summons procedure.[72]

Method D allowed the injured party to take a specific step to remedy a problem arising from a step taken by the other party, for example cases where there was no defence to the claim,[73] where the wrong party had been joined,[74] or where a pleading had been served but was defective or being used abusively,[75] or where the court had no jurisdiction.[76]

Method E covered the situation where a party had failed to engage with the claim at all, either by failing to acknowledge service[77] or by failing to serve

[67] RSC (1965) Ord 38, r 2A.
[68] RSC (1965) Ord 19, r 1.
[69] RSC (1965) Ord 24, r 16.
[70] RSC (1965) Ord 25, r 1.
[71] RSC (1965) Ord 34, r 2.
[72] RSC (1965) Ord 28, r 10.
[73] RSC (1965) Ord 14, r 1.
[74] RSC (1965) Ord 15, r 6.
[75] RSC (1965) Ord 18, r 19 or in reliance upon the inherent jurisdiction of the court to control its own process.
[76] RSC (1965) Ord 12, r 8.
[77] RSC (1965) Ord 13, r 1–6

a defence.[78] A default judgment could be entered. The entry of a default sanction is now treated as an implied sanction under the CPR.[79]

Method F dealt with situations where a stay of proceedings was required.[80] That is, where security for costs was sought and a stay of proceedings was granted that would remain in place until the required security was provided;[81] where a stay of proceedings was required on the basis that the proceedings as a whole were an abuse of the process of the court;[82] or where there had been a failure to disclose medical records[83] or to submit to a medical examination;[84] or where disclosure was required in Admiralty proceedings.[85]

Method G dealt with bars imposed for failure to take a required preliminary step.[86]

We shall now focus only upon two of these methods, starting with automatic sanctions (Method B), which have such importance under the CPR and give rise to the integrated sanctions network. The discussion then turns to unless orders (Method A), which have survived the transition from the RSC to the CPR and are now incorporated into the integrated sanctions network.

C. Automatic Sanctions and the Rule Restricting Relief

Method B imposes an automatic sanction and makes applications for clemency subject to a rule restricting relief.

The process obligations of the parties are backed by specific sanctions that come into force automatically upon breach, for example in relation to costs budgets (CPR 3.14), disclosure (CPR 31.21),[87] witness statements (CPR 32.10)[88] and expert reports (CPR 35.13).[89]

The integrated sanctions network means that CPR 3.9 works in tandem with whichever Rule triggered the sanction. In *Samara v MBI & Partners*, Silber J said,

[78] RSC (1965) Ord 19, rr 1–7.

[79] So that an application has to be made for the default judgment to be set aside and for the sanction to be lifted.

[80] The existence of the power was noted in s 49(3) of the Supreme Court Act 1981 and s 49 of the Civil Jurisdiction and Judgments Act 1982. The existence of such power was said in *Metropolitan Bank v Pooler* (1884–1885) LR 10 App Cas 210, per Lord Blackburn at 220–21, to derive from the inherent jurisdiction of the court to control its own process.

[81] RSC (1965) Ord 23, r1 and Practice Form 44.

[82] RSC (1965) Ord 18, r 19 or in reliance upon the inherent jurisdiction of the court to control its own process.

[83] *Dunn v British Coal Corp, The Times* (5 March 1993) (CA).

[84] *Jackson v Mirror Group Newspapers Limited, The Times* (29 March 1994) (CA).

[85] RSC (1965) Ord 72, r 10. The decision in *Probatina Shipping Co v Sun Insurance Office* [1974] QB 635 shows how flexible this sanction could be.

[86] RSC (1965) Ord 3, r 6, 'notice of intention to proceed after one year's delay'.

[87] Originating in Lord Woolf, *Access to Justice, Draft Civil Proceedings Rules* (London, HMSO, 1996) (hereinafter '*WfDR*') 27.21.

[88] Originating ibid 28.12.

[89] Originated in *WfDR* (n 87) 32.12.

'the new regime has universal application to all rules in the CPR. Indeed, it is based on and underpinned by the changes to the overriding objective which apply to all parts of the CPR.'[90]

The integrated approach means that once a sanction has been imposed, an effort is required to get it lifted. The universal approach means there is only limited scope for procedural clemency. Both Woolf's original Draft Rule 5.4 and the new CPR 3.9 (as interpreted by *Mitchell* and *Denton*) operate in a restrictive fashion. Woolf's Draft Rule 5.4 was not drafted in ignorance, for the old County Court Rules, Order 17, rule 11 had operated in the same way – see *Rastin v British Steel*.[91] It was the *Rastin* test Woolf used as the inspiration for his Draft Rule 5.4.[92]

D. The System's Assault on Non-Compliance

Woolf, the rigorist reformer, wanted sanctions to follow as a matter of course upon default, so as to make sanctions act more swiftly than the old system of peremptory orders. This was to have the effect of escalating the severity of all defaults. Woolf also wanted to make getting relief from sanctions rather difficult.[93]

The original CPR 3.9 moved away from Woolf's rigorist model and substituted a much more moderate checklist. This did not work, partly because CPR 3.9 offered too much flexibility. Relief from sanctions was perceived to be achievable with little difficulty, thus lessening the deterrent effect of the sanctions regime: the Editors of the *White Book* (2014) noted, 'there has been increasing concern about the incidence of parties ignoring rules … and it has been argued that the relief from sanctions provisions are too generous'.[94]

Jackson, setting his proposal in context of wider reform events in the common law world, proposed a more restrictive regime stopping short of full rigour. His proposal was only accepted in modified form. The new CPR 3.9 did not reflect exactly what Jackson wanted. The rigorists had won.

The test itself did not specify what weight was to be given to the particular as opposed to the general factors, but Zuckerman says it was intended to give the court a starting point and to free it from the shackles of the old CPR 3.9 factors.[95]

[90] *Samara v MBI & Partners* [2014] EWHC 563 (QB) at [36]. For the reach of this approach, see *BPP Holdings Ltd v Revenue and Customs Commissioners* [2017] UKSC 55 at [24], [26], [29] and [33].

[91] *Rastin v British Steel* [1994] 1 WLR 732 (CA).

[92] *WfFR* (n 29) ch 6, para 14; *WfDR* (n 87) 5.4.

[93] See *WfDR* (n 87) 5.4.

[94] *White Book* (2014) vol 1, para 3.9.2. Inbar Levy has shown us that the number of factors to be considered may make decision-making more difficult: I Levy, 'Lightening the Overload of CPR Rule 3.9' (2013) 32 *Civil Justice Quarterly* 139; and I Levy, 'Simplifying Legal Decisions: Factor Overload in Civil Procedure Rules' (2017) 41(2) *Melbourne University Law Review* 727.

[95] Zuckerman's 'justice on the merits' – see A Zuckerman, 'The revised CPR 3.9' (n 1) at 126–27.

In retrospect this can be seen to have been a mistake. Without a clear weighting, the proportionality aspects of 'all the circumstances' could be downplayed by the rigorist tendency, thus creating further problems.

In giving lectures on the implementation of the Jackson Reforms[96] Lord Dyson MR expressly pointed out that 'the individual justice of the case' was not 'an overarching consideration'.[97] Justice on the merits was not a trump card; rather it was the overriding objective that took priority,[98] because 'the relationship between justice and procedure has changed',[99] although it was claimed that compliance was not an end in itself and that the changes did not change rule compliance 'into tripwires'.[100]

One can compare the new CPR 3.9 with Rule 26.7 of the Civil Proceedings Rules 1998 (Trinidad and Tobago), which was the subject of *AG Trinidad & Tobago v Matthews*.[101] This Rule highlighted first the question of promptness, then the questions of whether the act was intentional, whether there was a good explanation for it and the defaulting party's history of compliance. The factors to be taken into account in reaching this decision were: the interests of the administration of justice; who was to blame for the default (the party or its lawyer); whether the default could be remedied; and whether the trial date could be kept.

The new CPR 3.9 was first tested in *Mitchell v News Group Newspapers Ltd*.[102] The Court of Appeal applied the Rule by asking:

(a) whether the breach was trivial and, if it was, whether the application for relief had been made promptly. In such cases a party could expect to gain relief from sanctions;[103]

but where this was not the case then the court was to go on to consider

(b) whether there was a good reason for the breach – the poorer the reason proffered, the less likely it was that the court would grant relief.[104]

[96] An ironic nomenclature in this context, given that Jackson's proposal for CPR 3.9 was not accepted.

[97] J Dyson, *Reforms Implementation Programme: Lecture No 18: The application of the amendments to the Civil Procedure Rules* (March 2013) (hereinafter '*Lecture 18*') para 25, available at www.judiciary.uk.

[98] The business case for this was made by Jackson LJ at para [90] of *Denton* (n 15), and verified in *Oak Cash & Carry* (n 36) at [35]–[36].

[99] J Dyson, *Lecture 18* (n 97) para 26.

[100] ibid, para 26. That the rule may not be designed to trip someone up does not render the impact of it innocuous. Surely here there is a deliberate echo of Jack Jacob's committee dissent, which appears in the Winn Report, *Report of the Committee on Personal Injury Litigation*, Cmnd 369 (1968), 151–52. Dyson was trying to de-fang Jacob at this point. Jacob argued two philosophical points: that the purpose of the courts was to dispense justice on the merits; and that costs rules were, by their nature, compensatory and not penal.

[101] *AG Trinidad & Tobago v Matthews* [2011] UKPC 38.

[102] *Mitchell* (n 14).

[103] ibid at [40].

[104] *Mitchell* (n 14) at [41].

In *Mitchell*, the Court of Appeal assigned a higher priority to the needs for efficiency, proportionate cost and enforcement of compliance than to any other factors comprising 'all the circumstances of the case'.[105] The Court further took the view that partial relief should be something of a rarity for fear of undermining the effectiveness of the sanctions regime.[106]

One of the unanticipated consequences of the decision in *Mitchell* was that parties saw the benefit in taking procedural points,[107] thus increasing the frequency and number of CPR 3.9 applications and the proportion of court time taken up in dealing with them.

The scene was set for a partial rethink disguised as a 'restatement'.[108] *Denton* provides that the court must consider:

- at stage 1, the seriousness and significance of the breach;[109]
- at stage 2, why the default occurred;[110] and
- at stage 3, all the circumstances of the case, including the need for efficiency and proportionate cost and the need to enforce compliance.[111]

Denton requires that the need for sanctions to be proportionate[112] is to be reflected in any alternative sanction imposed by the court, such as a conditional order.[113]

Jackson LJ, in a dissenting judgment, had a different slant on the third stage. He said:

> The rule does not require that factor (a) or factor (b) be given greater weight than other considerations. What the rule requires is that the two factors be specifically considered in every case. The weight to be attached … is a matter for the court.[114]

If this feels like a familiar philosophical divide, it is. The same divide existed as between Woolf's Draft Rule 5.4 and the original CPR 3.9, but the circumstances

[105] ibid at [36]–[37].

[106] *Mitchell* (n 14) at [58]. This rigorist approach was to undermine the effectiveness of the decision in *Mitchell*, as it did not allow for the graduated approach that would flow from proportionality.

[107] *Denton* (n 15) at [41]–[43]. As well they might, as *Mitchell's* all-or-nothing approach made procedural points worth taking.

[108] 'We propose to restate': *Denton* (n 15) at [24]. The Court in *Denton* criticised judges for failing to apply *Mitchell* correctly. Such 'failures' were widespread. See the sympathetic criticism of Lewison LJ in *Michael Wilson & Partners Ltd v Sinclair* [2015] EWCA Civ 774 at [42] and [47], [53]–[54], which is as close as the Court of Appeal has come to admitting that in *Mitchell* the law took 'a wrong turn', or rather that the judges got it wrong.

[109] *Denton* (n 15) at [25]–[28]: note the acrobatics required to equate 'triviality' with 'neither serious nor significant': ibid at [25]–[26]. In fairness it should be said that *Mitchell* (n 14) at [40] also speaks of 'no more than an insignificant failure' and 'insignificant', but this follows the definitional 'trivial'. The mention of 'insignificant' is intended to flesh out the content of triviality, not to stretch its scope.

[110] *Denton* (n 15) at [29]–[30] confirming the utility of *Mitchell* (n 14) [41].

[111] *Denton* (n 15) at [31]–[36], noting that Jackson's proposal in R Jackson, *Review of Civil Litigation Costs: Final Report* (London, TSO, 2009) para 6.7 had been rejected.

[112] *Denton* (n 15) at [65].

[113] See *White Book* (2017) vol 1, para 3.9.6.12 for the editor's commentary upon partial relief, which, whilst not expressly endorsed by *Denton*, would appear to be consistent with it.

[114] *Denton* (n 15) at [85].

here are reversed. Woolf wanted a very firm approach but received the old CPR 3.9. Jackson wanted some flexibility but received the new CPR 3.9, *Mitchell* and *Denton*. The distance between the reformers and the rule-makers remains.

The rule-makers and the judges hope to move system users from disengagement or opposition to compliance motivated by the threat of punishment and from there, perhaps, to compliance where the legitimacy and benefits of compliance are widely accepted. This last category ought to become largely self-policing.

E. Unless Orders

The unless order goes by a number of different names: it can be called a peremptory order,[115] a conditional order,[116] a self-executing order[117] or 'an anticipatory dismissal of the action'.[118]

Under the RSC, unless orders were normally imposed for failure to comply with a court order[119] and not for failure to comply with a rule per se. They were imposed with one eye on the risks of depriving a party of justice on the merits. For example, in *Haigh v Haigh*, the applicant applied to set aside judgment entered for wilful default of discovery. In considering the question of relief from sanctions, Pearson J made clear his support for the principle of justice on the merits, saying:

> I have the strongest disinclination, as I believe every other Judge has, that any case should be decided otherwise than upon its merits … So great was my anxiety to relieve this lady from the consequence of her wrongheadedness if, by any possibility, I could on proper terms, that I hesitated to refuse to make the order asked for, and I have looked into all the cases I could find on the subject to see what the practice of the Court has been.[120]

However, the applicant failed because the relevant rule[121] was designed to prevent parties causing delay through negligence or wilfulness, and the behaviour of the applicant fell into this category. Relief therefore was refused.

Samuels v Linzi Dresses Ltd[122] neatly sums up the pre-Woolf position on relief from sanctions imposed by peremptory orders. This was a case where a party had

[115] *Birkett v James* [1978] AC 297 at 321; see also *White Book* (1883–84), where the term is used at 291.

[116] J Jacob (ed), *Chitty and Jacob's Queen's Bench Forms* (20th edn) (London, Sweet & Maxwell, 1969) at 692–93.

[117] See *FJ Walker Limited v DA Hendy* [unreported] [Austlii No 219 of 1988], Supreme Court of the Northern Territory of Australia, per Kearney J at [27]: 'A self-executing order for conditional dismissal of an action precludes examination of the actual reasons for non-compliance; it is for that reason that such orders should not be made except where the circumstances so require'.

[118] *Albalian v Innous* [1936] 2 All ER, 834, per Greene LJ at 837.

[119] In many cases, it was not possible to move straight to an unless order. An intermediate step was required to obtain a further, final order requiring a party to act before an unless order was imposed. If the defaulting party complied with that final order or with the unless order itself, the only sanction it suffered was an adverse costs order.

[120] *Haigh v Haigh* (1885) 31 ChD 478 at 482.

[121] RSC (1883) Ord 26, r16.

[122] *Samuels v Linzi Dresses Ltd* [1981] QB 115 (CA).

failed to comply with an order made, on a summons for directions, to provide further and better particulars.[123] The defendant did not comply with the order, but subsequently made a retrospective application for an extension of time. The extension was granted in the form of an unless order, with which the defendant also failed to comply. The defendant applied for a further retrospective extension of time.[124] The Court of Appeal confirmed that an extension of time could be granted in the circumstances of the case.[125] Roskill LJ said that '[o]rders as to time, and in particular as to the time for delivery of pleadings and particulars are made not to be ignored but to be complied with',[126] but that

> the law today is that a court has power to extend the time where an 'unless' order has been made but not been complied with;[127] but that it is a power which should be exercised cautiously and with due regard to the necessity for maintaining the principle that orders are made to be complied with and not to be ignored.[128]

Roskill LJ said that the matter was one for the judge's discretion.

Moving on in time, *Hytec Information Systems Ltd v Coventry City Council*[129] was decided when the Woolf Reforms were in gestation. It shows the hardening of judicial attitudes towards relief from sanctions. Ward LJ said that he wanted 'to try and encapsulate what I understand to be the philosophy underlying this approach'.[130] In this context, 'this approach' means a combination of the established philosophy of justice on the merits and the mooted ideal of dealing with cases justly.

Ward LJ made the following points:[131]

(a) As an unless order was a matter of last resort, there would have to be 'a history of failure to comply with other orders', for an unless order was 'the party's last chance to put his case in order'. (Under the CPR, one strike is enough.)
(b) An intentional or deliberate failure to comply with an unless order would be met with no mercy. (A position similar to that in *Mitchell* but not *Denton*, which has resort to the concept of proportionality of punishment.)
(c) Given the 'last chance nature of the sanction, non-compliance with it would 'ordinarily result in the sanction being imposed', that is, in the case being

[123] RSC (1965) Ord 18, r 12.

[124] Under RSC Ord 3, r 5.

[125] The case turned upon the question of whether the proceedings were or were not dead. The case is of interest for revealing the doubts that were held about the correctness of the decision in *Whistler v Hancock* (1878) 3 QBD 83.

[126] *Linzi Dresses* (n 122) at 126–27. That there was power to make an unless order was recognised at the highest level of authority in *Tolley v Morris* [1979] 1 WLR 592 (HL), at 603–04. The case concerned striking out for want of prosecution.

[127] That is, a retrospective extension of time: the current equivalent would be to seek relief from sanctions under the new CPR 3.9, together with permission (by way of an extension of time) to perform the act, default in which triggered the automatic sanction in the first place.

[128] *Linzi Dresses* (n 122) at 128.

[129] *Hytec* (n 10).

[130] ibid at 1674–75.

[131] *Hytec* (n 10) at 1674–75.

struck out. This would happen unless there was a compelling reason not to proceed with imposition. This would usually mean showing that what had happened was beyond the defaulter's control. (The CPR 3.9 position has evolved towards a strict test coupled with a proportionate outcome.)

(d) The justification for this approach was that an unless order was 'a necessary forensic weapon which the broader interests of the administration of justice require to be deployed'. (The language is striking: the public good justifies the use of a 'weapon' of punishment against an individual party.)

(e) 'The interests of justice' would require the 'injured party' to receive recompense for 'the procedural inefficiencies' visited on him or her by 'the twin scourges of delay and wasted costs'. (This is the standard Woolfian trope dealing with procedural justice. There were not only the interests of the injured party to be taken into account, but also 'the public interest in the administration of justice to contain those two blights upon it'. Avoiding injustice to the defaulting party was to be placed at the back of the queue.)

(f) Nevertheless, in exercising his discretion the judge was to consider 'the facts and circumstances of each case on its own merits', depending on 'the circumstances of that case; at the core is service to justice'. (The approach in *Hytec* struggles with the same sort of structural balancing difficulty observable in *Mitchell*. There is a wish to consider the circumstances of the case, so as to do justice in dealing with the default, but to give more weight to the fact of default and to its systemic consequences than to the individual circumstances of the defaulter. *Hytec* concerned an unless order where, by definition, a party had been given an extra chance and not taken it. *Mitchell* concerned a failure to serve a costs budget, which failure caused the automatic imposition of the sanction. The justification for the *Hytec* decision was therefore stronger than in *Mitchell*.)

F. Unless Orders and the CPR

The CPR could have abolished unless orders[132] and placed the emphasis on automatic sanctions. Yet they survived at the margins.[133] The clearest reference to

[132] Unusually, in *Summit Navigation Ltd v Generali Romania Asigurare Reasigurare SA* [2014] EWHC 398 (Comm), at [36], Leggatt J used the term 'unless order' to cover both unless orders proper and the automatic sanction imposed under CPR 3.14. He did this to distinguish the application of *Mitchell* (*Denton* not having been decided), arguing that stays that were not intended to be permanent were to be treated distinctly from other sanctions. *Summit Navigation* concerned stays in security for costs cases. *Michael Wilson & Partners Ltd v Sinclair* [2015] EWCA 774 at [33]–[35] suggests that there is an ascending hierarchy in relation to permanence of sanctions: from stays, to unless orders and then to striking out.

[133] The commentary at *White Book* (2017) vol 1, para 3.4.4.1, reads CPR 3.1(3) together with CPR 3.4(2)(c) and notes that the existence of a power to make unless orders is assumed by CPR 3.5 and 3.8. That unless orders were considered to be a form of conditional order prior to the CPR is clear from J Jacob (ed) (n 116), see Form nos 1083 and 1085 at 692–93.

unless orders is in CPR 3.5 and Practice Direction 40B, paragraph 8.[134] Despite their apparently marginal status, unless orders have an important part to play under the CPR. As we shall see:

(a) an unless order can be fitted into the category of a conditional order;[135]
(b) to impose an unless order is to impose a sanction;
(c) unless orders should only be imposed when it is appropriate and proportionate to do so;
(d) where an unless order is imposed, a party is not free to re-argue the point when judgment is being entered;[136]
(e) granting relief from the sanction of an unless order, where it has taken effect, requires an application to be made under CPR 3.6 and CPR 3.9.[137]

The effect of the last two points is that unless orders have been fully incorporated into the integrated sanctions network.

G. Unless Orders and the New CPR 3.9

Unless orders have recently been described thus:

> The court usually only makes an unless order against a party which is already in breach. The unless order gives that party additional time for compliance with the original obligation and specifies an automatic sanction in default of compliance. It is not possible to look at an unless order in isolation. A party who fails to comply with an unless order is normally in breach of an original order or rule as well as the unless order.[138]

An unless order is intended to 'mark the end of the line for a party who has failed to comply with it',[139] being 'an order of last resort', which is 'not made unless there is a history of failure to comply with other orders'.[140] Put at greater length:

> Final, peremptory or unless orders are only made by a court when the party in default has already failed to comply with a requirement of the rules or an order, and the court is satisfied that the time already allowed has been sufficient in the circumstances of the case, and the failure of the party to comply with the order is inexcusable.[141]

[134] Orders requiring an act to be done.
[135] See the commentary at *White Book* (2017) vol 1, para 3.4.4.1.
[136] *Marcan Shipping (London) Ltd v Kefalas* [2007] EWCA Civ 463.
[137] *Oak Cash & Carry* (n 98) at [29] applies *Mitchell/Denton* to unless orders. The basis of such an order is set out in *Suez Fortune* (n 36).
[138] *Oak Cash & Carry* (n 98) per Jackson LJ at [38].
[139] *Hytec* (n 10) per Auld LJ at 1676.
[140] ibid per Ward LJ at 1674. See also *Apex Global Management Ltd v FI Call Ltd* [2013] EWHC 2818 (Ch) at [15]; and *Global Torch Ltd v Apex Global Management Ltd and others (No 2)* [2014] UKSC 64, at [16]–[18] and [23].
[141] Per Beldam LJ in *Caribbean General Insurance Ltd v Frizzell Insurance Brokers Ltd* [1994] 2 Lloyd's Rep 32, at 40.

With an unless order, if a defaulter fails to comply with it then his or her case is struck out – the gravest sanction of all. The sanction has the effect of a punishment. Automatic sanctions[142] are clustered around key or strategic points in the litigation: they do not result in striking out but merely restrict the defaulter's options, although the imposition of those restrictions might prove to be fatal to the conduct of the case. A party might still wish to apply for an unless order to force the issue against the defaulter.

The common practice is that the court first orders a person to do something. Assuming that it is a not a 'key stage' order[143] then a party may comply or not without immediate difficulty. The innocent party has to make an application to the court for the court to specify a further date by which something must be done. Such an application will often be met with a further application, made by the defaulting party, for an extension of time. In cases of minor breach, where the breach is or has been remedied, time is usually extended upon payment of costs.[144] But in more serious cases the extension of time is described as being a 'final order'.[145] It is unusual for the court to make an unless order on first application, the logic being that the imposition of an unless order amounts to the imposition of a sanction, albeit subject to a condition.

In *British Gas Trading Limited v Oak Cash & Carry Limited*,[146] Jackson LJ said:

> In order to assess the seriousness and significance of a breach of an unless order, it is necessary also to look at the underlying breach. The court must look at what X failed to do in the first place, when assessing X's failure to take advantage of the second chance which he was given.[147]

And:

> The very fact that X has failed to comply with an unless order (as opposed to an 'ordinary' order) is undoubtedly a pointer towards seriousness and significance. This is for two reasons. First, X is in breach of two successive obligations to do the same thing. Secondly, the court has underlined the importance of doing that thing by specifying an automatic sanction in default (in this case the Draconian sanction of strike out).[148]

Jackson LJ noted that 'not every breach of an unless order is serious or significant'. He contrasted a 45-minute delay (not serious or significant) with the multiple breaches in *Oak Cash & Carry*.[149]

[142] That is, one where default automatically triggers a restrictive sanction because of the seriousness of the default.

[143] That is, one where default automatically triggers a restrictive sanction.

[144] *Colliers International Property Consultants v Colliers Jordan Lee Jafaar Sdn Bhd* [2008] EWHC 1524 (Comm) at [35].

[145] *Sports Network Ltd v Calzaghe* [2008] EWHC 2566 (QB) at [113]–[114].

[146] *Oak Cash & Carry* (n 98).

[147] ibid at [39].

[148] *Oak Cash & Carry* (n 98) at [41].

[149] ibid at [42]–[43].

In *Suez Fortune Investments Ltd v Talbot Underwriting Ltd*, Flaux J said:

> the necessary underlying assumption in *Denton v White* is that relief may be granted if either
>
> (i) the relevant default has been cured (in other words, the rule, practice direction or Order has been complied with or is about to be complied with) or
>
> (ii) that compliance can somehow be dispensed with, perhaps on terms, without doing injustice between the parties.[150]

He went on to say that the court was unlikely to dispense with compliance in the case of an unless order.

H. Conclusion

We have looked at the following matters:

(a) How the civil justice system has two ways of controlling those who operate within it. It can control the types of cases that enter the system and it can impose sanctions upon those who are in the system.

(b) Sanctions can be applied gradually or automatically. Once a sanction is applied, it can be relatively easy or difficult to have the sanction changed, depending upon the sanctions regime.

(c) The sanctions regime under the RSC largely applied sanctions gradually and made changing any sanction imposed relatively easy, although the prospect of the implementation of the CPR resulted in a tightening of the approach.

(d) By and large the RSC's approach to sanctions was not integrated.

(e) Woolf wanted a sanctions regime weighted towards automatic sanctions that would work in an integrated fashion, and a regime for relief where it would be difficult to have the sanction changed.

(f) Woolf achieved the automatic sanctions regime and introduced a rule (CPR 3.8) that, by its express wording and by some judicious stretching of the term 'sanctions', was able to act as the centre for the integrated sanctions network; but he only achieved a weak approach to relief (the original CPR 3.9). This was because the reformers and the rule-makers wanted different things.

(g) The pattern of non-compliance could therefore continue. Worse, the automatic imposition of sanctions meant that more people would be caught by them, and so more people would need to apply for relief thus creating more work for the courts.

(h) Jackson recognised that something more needed to be done. An attack would have to be made on non-compliant behaviour by making it more difficult to have sanctions changed once they had been imposed. This was effected to

[150] *Suez Fortune* (n 36) at [50]–[51].

defend the civil justice system. The harshness of this approach indicates the severity of the threat non-compliance posed and poses to the system.

(i) This attack would require a consistent and deliberate coordination of approaches, at first instance and on appeal, which would absorb judicial time. It was worthwhile for the civil justice system to invest judicial time in this compliance exercise if it resulted in a change of behaviour by court users.

(j) Jackson proposed simplifying CPR 3.9, but in a manner that would still allow for the individual idiosyncrasies of a case to be taken into account. This was Jackson's way of steering between the dangers of too much court interference and too little. Jackson got a new CPR 3.9, but not the one he proposed. This was because the reformers and the rule-makers wanted different things.

(k) The new CPR 3.9 was given a rigorist interpretation in *Mitchell*. By making the lifting of a sanction difficult, and in closing the door to proportionality, the Court of Appeal in *Mitchell* created a situation where many more cases would be appealed because of the nature of what was at stake when relief from sanctions was refused.

(l) The Court of Appeal took a second look at CPR 3.9 in *Denton* and, without admitting it, changed its approach. That approach allows for harsh sanctions to be softened where it is proportionate to do so.

(m) The Court of Appeal has continued to give a wide meaning to the term 'sanctions', so enabling the continuance of an integrated approach to the treatment of default.

Kant makes the point that out of the crooked timber of humanity, no straight thing was ever made. This is the reality with which the civil justice system has to deal. People will not always do what they are told. The issue of sanctions is therefore an important one, for sanctions keep people in line. Looking back, we can see that the civil justice system became ineffective without an effective compliance regime. The system neither tried to detect default, nor, when default was brought to its attention, did it seriously question the justice on the merits theory that informed its approach to dealing with default. This impacted both individual users of the system and the confidence of wider society in the system. The inability of the civil justice system to police itself might have led to the high levels of political involvement that characterised the pre-1883 curial world.

Both Woolf and Jackson tried to find a way of forcing people to comply with the rules. This required a break with a long history of widespread non-compliance.

It is correct to say that the 'justice on the merits' theory hampered judicial efforts at enforcing compliance, but this is not the only explanation for a situation that continued under the CPR, leading, in part, to the Jackson Reforms.

One cannot simply blame the philosophy of judicial passivity[151] for the long-term neglect of the proper imposition and enforcement of sanctions. It is the lack

[151] For this term see *AndPCP* (n 63) at paras 3-012–3-013. The old regime of party control has been replaced by the judicial control exercised under the CPR: see eg N Andrews, 'A New Civil Procedural Code for England: Party-Control – "Going, Going Gone"' (2000) 19 *Civil Justice Quarterly* 19.

of bite to the imposition of sanctions that provides another source of explanation. The historic inability of the civil justice system to control non-compliance is indicative of where power within the system truly lay. We can discern here a weak centre of control, with independent participants retaining the initiative to act. The Woolf Reforms moved power to the centre by creating the structure and powers for case management, without giving the centre the capacity to enforce its will – the multi-factoral original CPR 3.9 worked in the opposite direction. It was the Jackson Reforms that really gave the centre the capacity to attack non-compliance, although finding the balance between punishment and clemency has taken some time.

We can now ask, 'What are the implications of all this for the future?' The enforcement of sanctions will have to continue: we must be realistic. Even if the behaviour of court users changes, there will always be a level of non-compliance for various reasons and the system will have to continue to act against defaulters. The increase in the number of litigants in person may or may not change the dynamic. Certainly where there is default by litigants in person it will be obvious, for there will be no lawyers behind whom the litigants may shelter.

The continuing challenge for the civil justice system is to impose sanctions that are proportionate. It remains to be seen whether the *Denton* approach has got the balance right.

6

Process Costs and Error Costs: The Reform of Civil Appeals in Anglo-American Perspective

I. Introduction

A. Purposes, Proportionality and Preference

Lord Phillips PSC, in *R (Cart) v Upper Tribunal*,[1] set out the private and public purpose[2] of appeals as follows,[3] 'The private purpose was to correct … The public purpose was to ensure public confidence … and … to clarify and develop the law, … and to … maintain … standards'. He went on to highlight the need for a measured approach to dealing with appeals, saying, 'More than one level of appeal would not normally be justified unless an important point of principle or practice was involved.'[4]

This is a very different approach from that which might be preferred by some litigants. As Roscoe Pound noted, it is of the nature of the process that parties will want to appeal. Many of these cases will involve 'futile appeals raising questions which have been long or well settled but are earnestly argued, often in entire good faith by those who raise them'.[5]

[1] *R (Cart) v Upper Tribunal* [2011] UKSC 28.

[2] AA Samaha considers the constitutional aspects of this in 'Undue Process', 59 *Stanford Law Review* 601 (2006–2007) 603 at fn 7.

[3] Echoing Sir Jeffery Bowman in J Bowman, *Report to the Lord Chancellor: Review of the Court of Appeal (Civil Division)* (London, Lord Chancellor's Department, 1997) (hereinafter '*Bow Rep*') ch 2, para 12, which in turn echoes H Woolf, *Access to Justice: Final Report* (London, HMSO, 1996) (hereinafter '*WfFR*') ch 14, para 2. For comment on Bowman, see N Andrews, 'A New System of Civil Appeals and a New Set of Problems' (2000) 59:3 *Cambridge Law Journal* 464; JM Jacob, 'The Bowman Review of the Court of Appeal' (1998) 61 *Modern Law Review* 390; and S Clark and R Jackson, *The Reform of Civil Justice*, 2nd edn (London, Thomson Reuters (Professional) UK Ltd, 2018) para 17-002. H Woolf, *Access to Justice, Draft Civil Proceedings Rules* (London, HMSO, 1996) made no provision for appeals.

[4] *R (Cart)* (n 1) at [68].

[5] R Pound, *Appellate Procedure in Civil Cases* (Boston, MA, Little Brown & Company, 1941) at 379. See also *Tanfern Ltd v Cameron-Macdonald* [2000] 1 WLR 1311 (CA) at [43] for similar sentiments.

B. The Need for an Appeals Process

There is always the possibility of error in the decision of a court. The purpose of the appeals process is to allow the civil justice system to correct decisions that have been made wrongly[6] and to intervene where there has been an insufficiently fair process.[7] Where correctness is concerned, any one of three things may suffice to justify overturning a judicial decision on appeal, that is, the judge being (i) wrong on the facts, (ii) wrong in law or (iii) wrong in the way a discretion is exercised. Fairness is also important. The process has to be fair in terms of the court's own standards of procedural justice,[8] but must also have some relation to wider societal notions of procedural justice. There the worry is that people would lose faith in the civil justice system's ability to deliver justice as an outcome, with a consequent loss of standing for the system.

C. The Intractable Appeals Problem

The appeals problem is not new.[9] There have been distinct threads running through attempts at appellate reform: a worry about diluting the 'quality' of the court's work; an inherent conservatism about the role of an appeal court; and a tendency to confuse process that enhances quality with process that increases efficiency.

Sir Jack Jacob, in *The Fabric of English Civil Justice*,[10] noted that there was an inherent tension within the civil justice system because of the conflict between 'two distinct principles', namely that decisions should be both correct and just, and that decisions should be final. This tension has not disappeared over time, but the current reforms are driven primarily by a lack of money. There are currently insufficient judges in the Court of Appeal to deal with appeals in a timely manner: more parties are seeking to appeal; parties are disinclined to take 'no' for an answer; cases are becoming increasingly complex; and the way that appeals are advanced is

[6] Where, in the terminology of CPR 52.6, the decision is said to have been 'wrong'.

[7] In *Ponamma v Arumogan* [1905] AC 383 PC, Lord Davey said, at 390, 'the question is, whether the order of the court … was right on the materials which that court had before it'.

[8] A close cousin of the American due process of law. There, it is common to distinguish between procedural due process and substantive due process. Procedural due process is akin to our procedural fairness but is constitutionally embedded.

[9] See M Briggs, *Civil Courts Structure Review: Interim Report* (London, Judiciary of England and Wales, 2015) (hereinafter '*BriggsIR*') ch 9, para 9.36. The topic is also dealt with generally in ch 9 of M Briggs, *Civil Courts Structure Review: Final Report* (London, Judiciary of England and Wales, 2016) (hereinafter '*BriggsFR*'). See also section VIII of R Evershed, *The Final Report of the Committee on Supreme Court Practice and Procedure* (Cmd 8878, 1953). For an American view of this, see CE Clark, 'The Evershed Report and English Procedural Reforms', 29 *New York University Law Review* 1046 (1954).

[10] J Jacob, *The Fabric of English Civil Justice* (London, Stevens & Sons, 1987) (hereinafter '*JbFabr*') at 210.

complicated, making it difficult to see the real point.[11] Judges, absorbed in considering applications for permission, do not have time to identify the point in issue and focus the parties' attention accordingly.[12] As a result, the workload of the Court of Appeal has increased.

So how much time and effort should an appeal court allocate to a case? This is strictly a second order issue, because an appellant is now aggrieved with the judge over his decision, as well as being aggrieved with the other party.[13] The temptation, however, is to examine the whole case again, because failure here would challenge the system's very raison d'être. But perfection, even if achievable, would be unaffordable.[14] The resources to deal with appeals are very limited, so how best to use them? The answer is to filter out weak and unimportant cases. At the first level of appeals the threshold is set, largely, by a merits test. For second appeals it is set, largely, by reference to both merits and importance.[15]

D. Restriction, Protection and Finality

The search for a win (not 'justice'[16]) has a habit of driving people to take a case as far as it will go. Some people will not accept that they should have lost,[17] and a limit on appeals may be justified on the basis of protecting parties from themselves.[18] The CPR 52.6 threshold test (for first appeals) and the CPR 52.7 threshold test (for second appeals) can help here. These procedures should also help to control the person who has lost all objectivity and become the unreasonable litigant.[19]

[11] This is actually an efficiency issue – the process is complicating the judges' task of deciding appeals. A set word limit for skeletons and a limit on the number of documents presented might make a difference.

[12] For discussions, see *BriggsIR* (n 9) ch 9, paras 9.1–9.36; and S Sime, 'Appeals after the Civil Courts Structure Review' (2017) 36(1) *Civil Justice Quarterly* 51, passim.

[13] See JE Lobsenz, 'A Constitutional Right to an Appeal: Guarding Against Unacceptable Risks of Erroneous Conviction', 8 *Seattle University Law Review* 375 (1985) at 382. CB Robertson makes a similar point in 'The Right to Appeal', 91 *North Carolina Law Review* 1219 (2013) at 1274.

[14] Whether the civil justice system's funding ought to be increased is a different question.

[15] Second appeals from the county court will be heard in the Court of Appeal. Second appeals from Masters will be heard by the Court of Appeal. Second appeals from High Court judges will go to the Supreme Court and be subjected to the threshold test of that Court.

[16] What a litigant thinks is justice may not be justice according to the law. No lower court decision can be said to be the final word on what is just. The Supreme Court may rely upon the Practice Statement of 26 July 1966 (*Practice Statement (Judicial Precedent)* [1966] 1 WLR 1234 – see *Austin v Mayor etc of LB of Southwark* [2010] UKSC 28 at [24]–[25]).

[17] See R Pound, *Appellate Procedure* (n 5) at 379.

[18] See Lord Hoffmann on killing the parties with kindness, in *Piglowska v Piglowski* [1999] 1 WLR 1360 (HL) at 1373. Notably absent from Lord Hoffmann's dicta is the process cost to the system of allowing the appeal to reach such a high level. But see SC Yeazell, 'The Misunderstood Consequences of Modern Civil Process', 1994 *Wisconsin Law Review* 631 (1994) 631–32 for an awareness of the dangers of concentrating adjudication at the lower levels of the system.

[19] This is nothing new, see P Polden, 'The Courts of Appeal' in W Cornish et al (eds), *Oxford History of the Laws of England* (Oxford, Oxford University Press, 2010) vol XI, ch VIII at 816–17. The names are different but the stories are recognisable.

The appeal is aimed at depriving a respondent of the fruits of his judgment in which he has invested money, time and effort. This is where Jacob's principle of finality comes into play. Finality is seen as important because of the disruption that disputes are believed to cause within society. Disputes are seen as an 'evil', the adversarial system recognising the value of imposed peace. As Lord Simon said in *The Ampthill Peerage Case*, 'in the end you must accept what has been decided. Enough is enough.'[20]

E. Vertical and Horizontal Relationships

Richard Nobles and David Schiff[21] have noted that the appeals structure creates both a vertical[22] relationship and a horizontal[23] one. The appeal court supervises and holds the lower court to account.[24] But the appeal court has to show some deference to the lower court on account of its detailed role in fact finding. Restraint is required, for the appeal court is already busy enough, and if it intervenes too often, the trial risks becoming seen as a preliminary ruling rather than a final one.[25] The horizontal relationship refers to the need of appeal judges to respect the decisions of courts of coordinate jurisdiction.

F. The Pyramid of Appeals

Following a trial, most parties will accept the first instance decision. If a party is dissatisfied, he or she may seek permission for a first appeal.[26] To gain that permission, the aggrieved party must pass the threshold test, which comprises a merits test or, exceptionally, a compelling reason test. Where permission is granted and a first appeal is heard, most parties will accept that decision. It is only in those cases where the dispute remains contestable that a second appeal may be considered. Again, permission is needed,[27] but the threshold test is set at a higher level.[28]

[20] *The Ampthill Peerage* [1977] AC 547 at 576. Andrews opens his chapter on 'Finality' with an extensive citation from this case – N Andrews, *Principles of Civil Procedure* (London, Sweet & Maxwell, 1994) (hereinafter '*AndPCP*') at para 17-001.

[21] R Nobles and D Schiff, 'The Right to Appeal and Workable Systems of Justice' (2002) 65 *Modern Law Review* 676 at 676.

[22] ibid at 680.

[23] R Nobles and D Schiff, 'The Right to Appeal' (n 21) 683.

[24] See *Attorney General v Sillem* (1864) 11 ER 1200 (HL) at 1209, per Westbury LC. For early comment on the tension between the US Supreme Court and State level courts, see *Wetherbee v Johnson* (1817) 14 Mass 412 at 420, Parker CJ.

[25] R Nobles and D Schiff, 'The Right to Appeal' (n 21) at 685. A point also made in *Bow Rep* (n 3) at ch 2, para 4.

[26] CPR 52.6.

[27] CPR 52.7.

[28] The logic of narrowing the gate for second appeals is laid out clearly in *R (Sivasubramaniam) v Wandsworth County Court* [2003] 1 WLR 475 (CA) at [48] and [54].

Second appeals are subject to a combined merits and public importance test, although there is a compelling reason escape hatch.[29] The number of second appeals should be limited, because the court can reject cases that are insufficiently important. But the effectiveness of the combined threshold test will depend upon two things: a willingness to reject cases that lack sufficient public importance; and an austerity of approach to the use of the escape hatch. The civil justice system may now appreciate that it cannot eliminate all wrong decisions, but success here is reliant upon what is done by individual appeal judges.

G. The New Position

As a result of the new CPR 52[30] and the new Destination of Appeals Order,[31] multi-track cases in the county court are subject to a new regime. The first appeal for these cases will now be heard by a High Court judge and the Court of Appeal will now act as the second appeal court.[32] The role of circuit judges as the destination of appeal from fast-track cases remains, but the role of the High Court is greatly increased. Few second appeals from county court multi-track trials will pass over the raised second appeal threshold (CPR 52.7). The role of High Court judges in hearing appeals from multi-track cases is therefore going to be a significant one. As a general rule, only those cases that are both meritorious and of importance will pass over the threshold for second appeals.[33] Only exceptional cases will pass through the escape hatch.

H. Who are Appeals For?

The obvious beneficiary of an appeals process is the disappointed party. This will usually be the appellant alone, but sometimes the respondent may also wish to cross-appeal.[34] In the light of CPR 1.1(2)(e) we might also want to think about the impact of an appeal on other appellants. When cases are inappropriately admitted for appeal then waiting times may increase.[35] So a decision to give permission to appeal may have a real impact on other cases.[36]

[29] CPR 52.7(2)(b).

[30] In force 3 October 2016.

[31] Access to Justice Act 1999 (Destination of Appeals) Order 2016 (SI 2016/917), in force 3 October 2016.

[32] Under the Access to Justice Act 1999 (Destination of Appeals) Order 2000 (SI 2000/1071), county court multi-track appeals went straight to the Court of Appeal.

[33] CPR 52.7(2).

[34] CPR 52.13(2)(b).

[35] Waiting times can also increase if too many meritorious cases are admitted to the appeal list. Briggs has not been able eliminate this systemic vulnerability.

[36] See Briggs*IR* (n 9) at 106–13.

The appeal system also has to take into account the need for the civil justice system to stay within its budget and to fulfil its mission to do justice according to the law in a fair, timely and proportionate manner. A civil procedural reformer could legitimately hope that more money were available to pay for more appeal judges,[37] but there are many demands upon the exchequer, and formalised judicial independence means that the judiciary has forfeited what political influence it had with the executive.

Society also has a stake in this. It is in society's interest that: disputes are resolved; the system operates as efficiently as possible;[38] cases are processed; judges have the information they need;[39] and that justice is dispensed fairly. If this happens, there ought to be two benefits: reassurance of the public and a reduction in transaction costs. If the system works then people can be reassured that lawful behaviour pays, that unlawful behaviour costs and that wrongs are righted. The theory is that if law-abiding behaviour is encouraged, settled arrangements will be adhered to and the risks of commitment will be lowered.[40]

II. Policy, Practicality and Proportionality

A. Is There a Constitutional Context to Appeals?

In common law cases the appeal court makes law[41] in overturning or extending the existing case law. New principles emerge, or rather are developed by the judges.[42] Allowing for the fact that not all appeals will be of wider significance, a proportion of the first appeal court's work may and the majority of the Court of Appeal's work should involve important matters of principle or practice.

[37] ibid, paras 9.20 and 9.36 in particular.

[38] Efficiency is clearly not the main goal of the English civil justice system. It is doubtful whether it was even afforded the place in the hierarchy envisaged by s 1(3)(a) of the Civil Procedure Act 1997. This was because: proportionality was not pursued with sufficient vigour; accuracy was a latent but highly important goal; and technological change has been underfunded. BD Coleman, 'The Efficiency Norm', 56 *Boston College Law Review* 1777 (2015), argues that efficiency can be too narrowly defined (see ibid at 1778), which can lead to an over-privileging of that which can be measured in cash terms. This matters, he says, because the Federal Rules of Civil Procedure (FRCP) (ibid at 1938) aimed to cut down on administrative distraction, not simply to handle cases as cheaply as possible (see ibid at 1788). The focus on efficiency pushes case away from trial towards settlement (see ibid at 1779). Coleman would say that this undercuts the 'on the merits' ethos of FRCP Rule 1 and is of great jurisprudential significance, because cases are no longer being prepared for trial but for a settlement (see ibid at 1810). From the American perspective this matters because of the function that the court is supposed to exercise through the conduct of public trials (ibid at 1821–22) and the social implication of concentrating disposal in the hands of 'elite' lawyers (see ibid at 1822).

[39] This relates to the accuracy principle.

[40] Where the risk of default is lowered, the costs of commitment are also lowered.

[41] The judiciary is an arm of government. See, eg, T Bingham, *The Rule of Law* (London, Allen Lane, 2010) 45–46.

[42] See J Reid, 'The Judge as Lawmaker', (1972–73) 12 *Journal of the Society of Public Teachers of the Law* 22.

Harlon L Dalton reminds us that there is an important constitutional context to the appeal process. He makes three points. First, that appeals enable the governed to participate in the process of government through engaging the sovereign in the process and being engaged with the sovereign in that process.[43] Robertson adds that the appeal process goes to human dignity – concerning a litigant's experience of fairness, having a greater say in his or her destiny, and not having his or her fate decided by one judge.[44]

Dalton's second point is that appeals are important because of the values they uphold,[45] values which are 'external' to process and worthwhile in their own right. Duties and rights matter and the checking or corrective element of the appeals process reinforces that.

Lastly, Dalton says that the exercise of filtering out appeals is, in its own right, an exercise of state power. It is worth commenting that change is being driven by a lack of resources,[46] that is the executive has declined to increase the resources available to the judicial branch of the state.

B. What are Appeals For?

We start first with an American view. Roscoe Pound said[47] that the scope of appellate work covered a review of the lower court's work and an authoritative finding of the law which would have precedential value.[48]

In his book *Appellate Procedure in Civil Cases*,[49] Pound spoke of the need for the correction of mistakes, and for the prevention of error. Why should there be such a need? Pound cited Ulpian, who said, 'There is no-one who is not aware how frequently appeals are employed, and how necessary they are to correct the injustice or ignorance of judges.'[50] Pound then cited Blackstone, to show there had been a long-established policy of quieting claims and supporting the individual's right not to be vexed by repeated attacks.[51]

[43] HL Dalton, 'Taking the Right to Appeal (More or Less) Seriously', 95 *Yale Law Journal* 62 (1985–1986) at 70 n.31, 66–67 and 94–95.

[44] CB Robertson, 'The Right to Appeal' (n 13) 1271–73.

[45] HL Dalton, 'Taking the Right to Appeal' (n 43) at 97,101–02. He speaks of criminal appeals, but the point is of wider application. There are echoes here of Harlan J's concurring judgment in the case of *Re Winship* 397 US 358 (1970) at 372.

[46] See *BriggsFR* (n 9) para 9.6.

[47] R Pound, *Jurisprudence*, vol 5 (St Paul, MN, West Publishing, 1959) at 603.

[48] ibid at 607.

[49] R Pound, *Appellate Procedure* (n 5) at 3. Pound was clear that 'double appeals are to be avoided as far as possible': ibid at 392. Principle 27 in ALI/Unidroit, *Principles of Transnational Civil Procedure* (Cambridge, Cambridge University Press, 2007) does not address the 'why' question. The Principles and Commentary are at 51–98.

[50] Ulpian in *Justininian's Digest*, book 49, title 1.1, from SP Scott (tr), *Corpus Juris Civilis, the Civil Law* (Cincinnatti, OH, Central Trust Co, 1932, reprinted New York, AMS Press, 1973) at 137.

[51] W Blackstone, *Commentaries on the Laws of England* (Oxford, Clarendon Press, 1765) book III, ch 10 at 182.

Pound went on to say that it is always necessary to be able to correct the unfairness or unskillfulness of those who judge.[52] This is true even at the higher levels, for even appellate courts are capable of making mistakes.[53]

Pound lastly says that the possibility of review offers 'prevention not cure' because it acts as a stimulus to thoroughness in the lower courts. Dalton points out that the way in which cases are handled can also 'foster party satisfaction'.[54] This matters, because the legitimacy of the court system depends, at least in part, upon the acceptance of its decisions. Dalton notes[55] the impact of the appeal system on judicial morale, and how, as a side benefit, an ambitious judge may benefit. In England, Neil Andrews has also noted that the existence of higher courts gives an ambitious judge a way of getting noticed.[56]

Similar views to those of Pound about error have been expressed in England. We look now at the correction of error from the English perspective.

C. On Being Wrong

In *Michalak v GMC*, Lord Kerr said:

> In its conventional connotation, an 'appeal' … is a procedure which entails a review of an original decision in all its aspects. Thus, an appeal body or court may examine the basis on which the original decision was made, assess the merits of the conclusions of the body or court from which the appeal was taken and, if it disagrees with those conclusions, substitute its own.[57]

Lord Kerr was comparing the concept of an appeal to the concept of judicial review.

In 1970 Lord Devlin said, 'We delude ourselves if we think that it always produces the right judgment. Every system contains a percentage of error.'[58] The Briggs Interim Report[59] spoke of 'the inherent fallibility of human beings', which 'means that perfection can never be more than an aspiration'. A system is therefore required to correct mistakes. Finally we might cite *R (Cart) v Upper Tribunal*, where Lady Hale, accepting the reality of error, said, 'Clearly there should

[52] R Pound, *Jurisprudence* (n 47) 606–07. There is a similar passage in R Pound, *Appellate Procedure* (n 5) at 4.

[53] This latter point is of interest when considering the cost of limiting the number of appeals that may be brought.

[54] HL Dalton, 'Taking the Right to Appeal' (n 43) 66–67.

[55] ibid at 68.

[56] N Andrews, *Andrews on Civil Processes*, vol 1 (Cambridge, Intersentia, 2013) (hereinafter '*AndoCP*') at para 15.04.

[57] *Michalak v GMC* [2017] UKSC 71 at [20].

[58] The citation is from P Devlin, 'Who is at fault when injustice occurs?' in M Zander (ed), *What's Wrong with the Law* (London, BBC, 1970) 75. This influential argument features in H Woolf, *Access to Justice: Interim Report* (London, HMSO, 1995) ch 4, paras 5 and 6; and *Gregory v Turner* [2003] 1 WLR 1149 (CA) at [46].

[59] *BriggsIR* (n 9) at para 9.30. See also R Assy, 'Briggs' online court and the need for a paradigm shift' (2017) 36(1) *Civil Justice Quarterly* 70 at 82.

always be the possibility that another judge can look at the case and check for error.'[60]

Jacob's classic *The Fabric of English Civil Justice*[61] drew upon the work of Peter E Herzog and Delmar Karlen,[62] who made the point that 'Courts like all other human institutions, make mistakes. Such mistakes may occur with respect to the facts, or with the applicable substantive law, or with respect to the procedure for resolving issues of facts or law.'[63]

This statement of fundamentals is worth contrasting with the features noted by the editors of the *White Book*: '"wrong" presumably means that the court below (i) erred in law or (ii) erred in fact or (iii) erred in the exercise of its discretion.'[64] To this can be added the second limb of the new CPR 52.6 test,[65] injustice arising from procedural irregularity.[66]

Sime points out that the error may arise because an established principle was ignored, or because the principles that were applied were in need of development or extension.[67]

D. Judicial and Social Reasons

Jacob went on[68] to set out six core 'judicial and social reasons'[69] why an appellate procedure was required. Corrective steps were needed:

(a) to ameliorate an appellant's sense of grievance;[70]
(b) to avoid any widespread public feeling that the civil justice system was unjust or unfair.

Such steps worked to maintain public confidence. Herzog had warned of the risk that 'bad decisions' might 'fester in the minds … of those directly aggrieved'

[60] *Cart* (n 1) at [56]. For a review of *Cart*, see M Elliott and R Thomas, 'Tribunal Justice and Proportionate Dispute Resolution' (2012) 71 *Cambridge Law Journal* 297.

[61] *JbFabr* (n 10) at 211.

[62] PE Herzog and D Karlen, 'Attacks on Judicial Decisions' in PE Herzog and D Karlen (eds), *International Encyclopedia of Comparative Law*, vol 16 (Boston, MA, Martinus Nijhoff Publishers, 2014) ch 8.

[63] ibid at para 8-4. For reflection on error, see Lord Hoffmann, 'Fairchild and After' in A Burrows et al (eds), *Judge and Jurist: Essays in Memory of Lord Rodger of Earlsferry* (Oxford, Oxford University Press, 2013) at 63.

[64] *White Book* (2005) vol 1, para 52.11.3.

[65] Formerly CPR 52.11(3)(c).

[66] Which Sime takes as the final quarter of the traditional approach: see S Sime, 'Appeals after the Civil Courts Structure Review' (n 12) at 64.

[67] ibid at 65.

[68] *JbFabr* (n 10) 211–12. The importance of this list is taken as a starting point by G Drewry et al, *The Court of Appeal* (Oxford, Hart Publishing, 2007) at 20–21.

[69] Neil Andrews' helpful summary in *AndPCP* (n 20) para 13-034, is on much the same lines, as is CB Robertson, 'The Right to Appeal' (n 13) at 1225. CB Robertson deals with distributive aspects ibid 1264-267, and with expressive value ibid 1266–71. For a review of the social and political aspects of the appellate structure, see M Shapiro, 'Appeals', Law and Society Review 14 (1980) 629.

[70] Avant la lettre, see para 104 of O Franks, *Report of the Committee on Administrative Tribunals and Enquiries* (Cmnd 218, 1957).

and in the minds of 'those who merely observe ... creating resentment and insecurity'.[71]

Corrective steps were also required:

(c) to ensure that the outcome was both right and in accordance with justice;
(d) to require the judiciary to exercise care in the performance of its role, 'in a proper and not arbitrary way'.

Sime's insight is that the appeal process keeps the whole judicial system honest, for corrupt or biased decisions will be overruled.[72] Or, as the Franks Committee more prosaically put it, 'the existence of a right of appeal is salutary and makes for right adjudication'.[73]

Furthermore, corrective steps were necessary:

(e) to allow the appeal court to express the law, offering clarification where required, thus producing a socially responsive 'uniform system of law' developed in 'a harmonious and consistent manner'.[74] This is especially necessary because of the role that precedent plays in a common law system;
(f) to allow more judges of greater experience to focus upon the issue being appealed.

Here, Jacob followed Herzog and Karlen, who had talked of the appeal judges being 'more mature and more experienced' and having 'a narrower focus and function', being 'less pressed for time' and 'able to devote a greater amount of deliberation and reflection to critically important issues'.[75]

To this Dalton adds[76] the role that an appeal court plays in maintaining consistent practice amongst geographically dispersed courts and judges. The same point was made by Herzog, who spoke of 'some central body to expound, clarify and harmonize' the law.[77]

E. Does Procedural Fairness Require an Appeal?

In England and Wales the right to appeal is not constitutionally recognised but is conferred by statute (section III of this chapter). Article 6 of the European Convention on Human Rights 1950 does not require that an appeal be offered but says that if an appeal is offered, the process should comply with established

[71] PE Herzog and D Karlen, 'Attacks on Judicial Decisions' (n 62) at para 8-4.

[72] See S Sime, 'Appeals after the Review' (n 12) 51.

[73] O Franks, *Report* (n 70) para 104.

[74] 'Note: Securing Uniformity in National Law: A Proposal for National Stare Decisis in the Courts of Appeals', 87 *Yale Law Journal* 1219 (1977–1978) looks at the challenges to harmony and consistency in the context of appeals in the US.

[75] PE Herzog and D Karlen, 'Attacks on Judicial Decisions' (n 62) at para 8-4. See also JE Lobsenz, 'A Constitutional Right' (n 13) at 382–83.

[76] HL Dalton, 'Taking the Right to Appeal' (n 43) at 69.

[77] PE Herzog and D Karlen, 'Attacks on Judicial Decisions' (n 62) at para 8-5. A similar point is made at paras 104 and 115 of O Franks, *Report* (n 70).

procedural standards. As was said in *Delcourt v Belgium*,[78] 'the Convention does not … compel the Contracting States to set up courts of appeal'.[79] In the US, whilst it might be thought that the right of appeal has constitutional status, it is settled that it does not.[80] Nevertheless there seems to be a general sense that 'the right to appeal … is a fundamental element of procedural fairness'.[81] As Robert Leflar says,

> the right is a protection against error, prejudice, and human failings in general … Justice and good law are needed for little cases as well as for good ones … One appeal is enough, but one should be allowed in almost any case.[82]

Put another way, one might say that the appeal process is the guarantee that efforts will be made to deliver a party's Article 6 rights.[83]

F. Process Costs, Error Costs and Perfectionism

Is it appropriate to restrict rights of appeal? There are three supportive arguments in favour of the post-CPR reforms: that a reduction in cost justifies an increase in the error rate; that there is no absolute right to a correct outcome; and that, as perfection is unattainable, the proper question is what level of imperfection is to be tolerated.

It was Lord Devlin who said, 'Every system contains a percentage of error; and if by slightly increasing the percentage of error, we can substantially reduce the percentage of cost, it is only the idealist who will revolt.'[84]

The Briggs Interim Report[85] said:

> Rights of appeal are not necessarily to be equated with a right of a litigant to some theoretically correct outcome to their dispute … The perfect can be the enemy of the good, and theoretically perfect but very slow justice can be worse than timely, but slightly rough, justice for everyone.[86]

[78] *Delcourt v Belgium* [1970] ECHR 2689/65 at [25].

[79] The Court of Appeal referred to this point in *Ebert v Official Receiver (No 2)* [2001] EWCA Civ 340 at [12]. Buxton LJ went so far as to describe the legal point involved as being a trite one. A similar point was made in the US in *Griffin v Illinois* 351 US 12 (1956) 24–25 per Frankfurter J.

[80] See eg *Wiscart v D'Auchy* 3 US 321 (1796) per Elsworth CJ at 329; *McKane v Durston* 153 US 684 (1894) at 687; *Griffin v People of the State of Illinois* 351 US 12 (1956). For a view of and literature on this issue from a criminal perspective, see R Cavallaro, 'Better off Dead: Abatement, Innocence and the Evolving Right of Appeal', 73 University of *Colorado Law Review* 943 (2002).

[81] ABA Commission on Standards of Judicial Administration: Standards Relating to Appellate Courts, section 3.10 commentary at 12 (1977), cited in HL Dalton, 'Taking the Right to Appeal' (n 43) at 66.

[82] R Leflar, *Internal Operating Procedures of Appellate Courts* 4, 9–10 (Chicago, American Bar Foundation, 1976) cited in HL Dalton, 'Taking the Right to Appeal' (n 43) at 66.

[83] For a similar approach but with different language, see *Young v Konz* 88 Wash 2d 276 (1977) (Supreme Court of Washington) per Hunter J at 280.

[84] P Devlin, 'Who is at fault' (n 58). There is a useful discussion of where the line is to be drawn in R Dworkin, *A Matter of Principle* (Oxford, Clarendon Press, 1986) at 72–103.

[85] *BriggsIR* (n 9) para 9.30.

[86] AA Samaha 'Undue Process', 59 *Stanford Law Review* 601 (2006–2007) 603–04 makes similar points. Samaha variously refers to 'undue process' in the sense of too much process and 'optimal

In 2007, Jacob LJ touched upon the search for perfect justice:

> 'Perfect justice' in one sense involves a tribunal examining every conceivable aspect of a dispute. All relevant witness and all relevant documents need to be considered. And each party must be given a full opportunity of considering everything and challenging anything it wishes. No stone, however small, should remain unturned. Even the adversarial system at its most expensive in this country has not gone that far … But a system which sought such 'perfect justice' in every case would actually defeat justice. The cost and time involved would make it impossible to decide all but the most vastly funded cases. The cost of nearly every case would be greater than what it is about. Life is too short to investigate everything in that way. So a compromise is made: one makes do with a lesser procedure even though it may result in the justice being rougher. Putting it another way, better justice is achieved by risking a little bit of injustice.[87]

Briggs highlights the conceptual distinction between a right to seek correction by appeal, effectively a process entitlement, and a right to a correct outcome regardless of cost. Further, he notes the resource of impact of the latter. Picking up again on the question of perfectionism, Briggs also notes that 'there comes a point where the route towards supposed perfection becomes so demanding of resources that a line has to be drawn'.[88] The cost in money, time and effort of eliminating error imposes another cost, the process cost.[89] Only recently, Stuart Sime has said that 'Obviously the Court of Appeal aspires to the dispensing of perfect justice. Ultimately, however, when it comes to the deployment of resources a line does have to be drawn.'[90]

As Cass Sunstein says, 'Decision costs are the costs of reaching judgments. Human beings incur these costs in all contexts … In the legal setting decision costs are faced by both litigants and courts,'[91] to which I would add 'and by society'. In our context, the decision cost (called here the 'process cost') is the cost of dealing with an appeal.[92] The process cost is paid by all those participating in the litigation, including the court.

Put shortly, there is a danger of excessive process being imposed to avoid inadequate process.[93] What Briggs and Bowman were trying to achieve was to strike the balance between limiting the cost of error and limiting the costs of error

process', which he considers as 'an impractical goal' (ibid 647) and to cause unjustifiably high process costs (ibid 648). Samaha notes how the same procedure can be seen to add process safeguards at the same time as adding costs (ibid 649).

[87] *Nichia Corporation v Argos Limited* [2007] EWCA Civ 741 at [50]–[51], concerning disclosure in a patent case. The case was reported but not in the mainstream reports, but has recently resurfaced in *Triumph Controls UK Limited v Primus International Holding Co* [2018] EWHC 176 (TCC).

[88] *BriggsIR* (n 9) para 9.30.

[89] On this generally, see AA Samaha, 'Undue Process' (n 86).

[90] S Sime, 'Appeals after the Review' (n 12)' at 54.

[91] C Sunstein, 'Foreword: Leaving Things Undecided', 110 *Harvard Law Review* 4 (1996–1997) at 16.

[92] See AA Samaha, 'Undue Process' (n 86) at 616. In this chapter we have concentrated upon the process costs relating to the appeal process.

[93] ibid 605.

elimination through the appeals process. Samaha shows[94] how process drives cost: in our case, in terms of the parties, the material put before the court and the arguments advanced. Even the notion of what amounts to justice may be controversial, one person's search for justice being another person's financial burden.[95] Process-driven cost might mean that to cure a backlog of cases (where the process cost is a loss of time), it is necessary to employ more judges (where the process cost is a financial one).[96]

As a result of this, says Samaha, human dignity[97] issues can take second place to resource issues. Further, not making a decision on appeal may still have a cost, for where the court declines one case, it may 'export' decision costs to other people, including litigants and judges in subsequent cases.[98]

Devlin's view about the need to weigh up different kinds of cost was current not only in England and Wales. In the US case of *Matthews v Eldridge*,[99] the Supreme Court had to consider the ambit of the constitutional due process clause. Justice Powell laid down a three-stage test[100] requiring consideration of:

(a) the impact on the litigant;
(b) the balance of the risk against the protection offered; and
(c) the impact upon the public purse and public administration.[101]

However one looks at it, the appeals process has resource implications for the litigants, the system and for society.[102] Section III goes on to look at steps taken to promote efficiency in first appeals starting with the question of rerouting.

III. First Appeals – The New Regime

A. Rerouting of First Appeals

Section 56 of the Access to Justice Act 1999 allows the Lord Chancellor to specify alternative destinations for appeals. This is referred to as rerouting.[103]

[94] AA Samaha, 'Undue Process' (n 86) 616–17.
[95] ibid 618.
[96] AA Samaha, 'Undue Process' (n 86) at 620. See also *BriggsIR* (n 9) paras 9.10–9.11.
[97] Samaha describes this as participation, being heard and engagement with the state. See AA Samaha, 'Undue Process' (n 86) 652.
[98] C Sunstein, 'Foreword' (n 91) at 17.
[99] *Matthews v Eldridge*, 424 US 319 (1976). The case is discussed in JE Lobsenz, 'A Constitutional Right' (n 13) at 380; CB Robertson, 'The Right to Appeal' (n 13) at 1241–45; and AA Samaha, 'Undue Process' (n 86) at 642.
[100] *Matthews* (n 99) at 901.
[101] This kind of balancing of risk and reward will be familiar to common law tort lawyers from the test described in *Stokes v Guest, Keen and Nettlefold (Bolts & Nuts) Ltd* [1968] 1 WLR 1776 at 1783.
[102] CB Robertson, 'The Right to Appeal' (n 13) at 1243 would take a different view of where the balance ought to be struck.
[103] *Consultation Exercise – Appeals to the Court of Appeal: proposed amendments to Civil Procedure Rules and Practice Direction* (London, Civil Procedure Rules Committee, 2016) at 5.

Arrangements have been put in place to reroute first appeals from the county court to reduce the number of first appeals coming into the Court of Appeal.[104]

Rerouting has been accomplished via the Access to Justice Act 1999 (Destination of Appeals) Order 2016. Article 5 deals with appeals from the circuit judge in the county court, routing them away from the Court of Appeal and towards the High Court.

On the question of rerouting, the Court of Appeal's proposals in May 2016 had said that 'the emphasis in [the Court's] work should be upon providing guidance for lower courts and the public on issues of law, rather than simply determination of run-of-the-mill cases'.[105] The justification for this was that offering an appeal to the High Court would be proportionate in judicial resource and legal costs terms; and the case would have been checked by an appeal court, albeit not by the Court of Appeal.

B. Seeking Permission

Under the old and new CPR 52, permission to appeal was and is a pre-condition (the old CPR 52.3(6) and the new CPR 52.6 respectively). This approach filters out weak cases by subjecting them to an initial consideration or checking process. It is in this context that Woolf's suggestions in his Final Report make sense. He seems to have envisaged[106] that a party whose application for permission had been turned down by the appeal court ought to feel that his or her case had in fact been 'looked at', that is checked, by the appeal court, even if not subjected to a full review.

C. Practicalities of First Appeals

First appeals from multi-track county court trials will no longer go to the Court of Appeal. Those applications for permission that were formerly dealt with by a single Lord Justice of Appeal will now be considered by a High Court judge instead. This will cut the workload of the Court of Appeal,[107] given the amount of time spent by the judges of that Court in considering permission to appeal applications.[108]

[104] The relevant legislation governing appeals is to be found in different places: Access to Justice Act 1999, ss 54(1) and 55; Senior Courts Act 1981, s 16; and County Courts Act 1984, s 77.

[105] ibid 40–41. RJ Fallon Jr, 'Some Confusions about Due Process, Judicial Review, and Constitutional Remedies', 93 *Columbia Law Review* 309 (1993) at 369 notes the tendency of the appellate courts to concentrate upon cases that will have systemic effect due to the hierarchic nature of appeals.

[106] *WfFR* (n 3) ch 4, para 1. R Nobles and D Schiff, 'The Right to Appeal and Workable Systems of Justice' (2002) 65 *Modern Law Review* 676 bring this point out at 687.

[107] Although, curiously, the number of appeals in 2016 fell by 18% on the previous year: see *Civil Justice Statistics Quarterly, England and Wales, January to March 2017 (provisional) and Royal Courts of Justice 2016* (London, Ministry of Justice, 2017), available at www.gov.uk.

[108] See *BriggsIR* (n 9) paras 9.3 and 9.22.

The rerouting of appeals means that multi-track appeals from the county court will not enter the Court of Appeal's first appeal list at all, thus, it is hoped, reducing the waiting time for other cases – the current backlog.[109] At present, the number of appeals being handled by the High Court appears under control and so, at least initially, parties may expect to get a faster appeal hearing in the High Court. But the problem is simply being shifted from one court to another, and as more work goes into the High Court, the listing time for appeals may lengthen there.[110] Given that appealing to the High Court is likely to be less costly than to the Court of Appeal, parties may consider that it is worth at least applying for permission to appeal, or perhaps proceeding to a full appeal, in which case the number of applications for permission may continue to rise.[111]

IV. Second Appeals – The New Regime

A. Second Appeals

For the Court of Appeal, granting permission has been a major source of problems in its own right[112] because of an apparent lack of confidence in decisions made without a hearing by a single Lord Justice. Here the instinct for *en banc* procedure works against the Court.

Jack Jacob had thought[113] that the underlying logic of the system was parsimonious. Appeal courts should respect the trial process and preserve finality wherever possible. This view was somewhat at odds with reality, for, as late as December 1998, the Court of Appeal had a very generous admissions policy, taking into account the very low success threshold requirement and the multiple exceptions for weak cases. More impressive was Jacob's statement that parties should be content with a decision, because 'there is no social or political need to provide an open avenue' for appeals, 'except within somewhat strict limits'.

From 2 May 2000[114] there were specific requirements for permission for a second appeal, which were structured around questions of importance and compelling reasons.[115] Even the latest changes retain this broad basic structure, albeit that specific attention is now given to the reality of the prospects of success.[116]

[109] ibid para 9.22. The backlog is set out at *Consultation Exercise* (n 104) Annex, paras 10–12.

[110] Unless more work is pushed down to the county court in return.

[111] Given the historic rise in the volume of permission applications in the Court of Appeal, this has to be a reasonable prospect.

[112] See eg *BriggsIR* (n 9) paras 9.1, 9.3, 9.22–9.32.

[113] *JbFabr* (n 10) 231–32. Jacob also placed importance upon the deference the appeal court would display towards the factual findings of the trial judge.

[114] When CPR 52 came into force.

[115] The old CPR 52.13(2).

[116] The new CPR 52.7 failed to adopt the sterner test of a 'substantial prospect'. This was not the Court of Appeal's preferred approach.

B. Bowman and Before

In February 1997, Lord Woolf said that leave to appeal would only be refused if there was 'no realistic prospect' of success.[117] The use of the term 'realistic' here meant that 'a fanciful prospect or unrealistic argument' was not enough. But a party without a realistic prospect of success could be granted permission where it was 'in the public interest' to examine it, or where 'the law require[d] clarifying'.

In September 1997, Sir Jeffery Bowman's Committee[118] concluded that appeals should disposed of in a 'proportionate'[119] manner. The norm would be only one appeal, with exceptions where appropriate.[120] Such a restricted approach would meet the 'need for certainty, reasonable expense and proportionality',[121] and keep 'uncertainty and delay … to a minimum'.[122] Appeals were not 'an automatic further stage in a civil case'; it was for the trial judge 'to dispose of the action'.[123] Bowman proposed that 'the assumption should be that the court … has made the correct decision'.[124] But if there was to be no automatic right of appeal, a party should be able to have the case 'looked at by a higher court so that it can consider whether there appears to have been an injustice'.[125] Only if that court saw an appearance of injustice would an appeal be permitted. The permission stage therefore had the dual function of filtering and offering reassurance through the checking process.[126]

This was a significant step in the Court of Appeal's thinking, akin to the American approach of focusing attention 'on whether decision making structures are adequate to achieve, on average, a socially tolerable level of accuracy in the

[117] *Smith v Cosworth Casting Processes Ltd* [Practice Note] [1997] 1 WLR 1538 (CA) at 1538. The importance of this case is confirmed in *Bow Rep* (n 3) at paras 37 and 39. The evolution of this approach can be traced through *Practice Direction, Court of Appeal: Leave to Appeal and Skeleton Arguments)* [1999] 1 WLR 2 at para 10 and *Practice Direction, Court of Appeal (Civil Division)* [1999] 1 WLR 1027 (CA), paras 2.2.1 and 2.8.1. For the history of these changes, see I Scott's note, 'Permission to appeal in "second tier" appeals' (1999) 18 *Civil Justice Quarterly* 287.

[118] *Bow Rep* (n 3).

[119] ibid ch 2, para 14.

[120] *Bow Rep* (n 3) ch 4 para 6.

[121] ibid ch 2, para 15.

[122] *Bow Rep* (n 3) ch 2, para 7.

[123] Andrews puts it thus, 'Trial is a luxury … an appeal should be regarded as exceptional.' *AndoCP*, (n 56) from summary of ch 15 at 416.

[124] *Bow Rep* (n 3) ch 2, para 4.

[125] ibid ch 2, para 5. RJ Fallon Jr, 'Some Confusions' (n 105) at 330, notes a reverse approach in US substantive due process cases where a lack at the earlier stage of a process is supplied at the later stage. The overall point is that in the English jurisdiction there has to be both a sufficient quantity and quality of process. In most cases the trial before the lower court will meet this standard.

[126] Page 3 of Bowman's covering letter to the Report (dated September 1997 and written to the Lord Chancellor) in *Bow Rep* (n 3) makes the identical point. This check is an important if under-emphasised element of the process.

level of law to fact'.[127] The difficult question for Bowman was how 'searching' the appeal process should be.[128]

From 2 May 2000, Part 52 of the CPR was in force. Rule 52.3(6) introduced the familiar 'permission to appeal will only be given' formula in the distinct limbs of 'real prospect of success' or 'some other compelling reason'.

C. The Old CPR 52.13

Prior to 3 October 2016, the test for permission to get to the Court of Appeal on second appeals was set out in CPR 52.13(2). The Court of Appeal would not give permission[129] unless it considered that the appeal concerned 'an important point of principle or practice'; or that there was 'some other compelling reason' for the appeal to be heard.[130]

The background logic to the post-CPR introduction of CPR 52.13 was explained by Brooke LJ, in *Tanfern Ltd v Cameron-Macdonald*,[131] as being that it was for Parliament to provide resources. Parliament was entitled to control expenditure. Section 54 of the Access to Justice Act 1999 was intended to achieve what Parliament wanted.[132] Appeals would be rare, and judges would concentrate upon first appeals. Many appellants would have to accept that, ordinarily, 'no' at the first appeal hearing meant 'no'.[133]

The threshold test had two limbs: importance; and 'some other compelling reason'.

i. Importance

In *Eba v Advocate General for Scotland*,[134] Lord Hope PSC said that the importance test looked at what was of general importance. The important

[127] RJ Fallon Jr, 'Some Confusions' (n 105) at 311. The argument is that without some cut off, the volume of court work would be too great: ibid at 336.

[128] Bowman concluded that one level of appeal would allow for scrutiny of an appropriate depth. Availability under the current CPR 52 is impacted by the quality filters of CPR 52.6 and 52.7, which govern when it is appropriate to intervene. Fallon speaks of a 'minimally adequate availability … of review': RJ Fallon Jr, 'Some Confusions' (n 105) 336; and see ibid at 333.

[129] Refusal of permission to appeal is final – *Moyse v Regal Mortages Ltd Partnership* [2004] EWCA Civ 1269 at [23] and [31].

[130] This test replicates the provisions of s 55(1) of the Access to Justice Act 1999.

[131] *Tanfern Ltd v Cameron-Macdonald* [2000] 1 WLR 1311 (CA) [41]–[46]. Adrian Zuckerman's book *Zuckerman on Civil Procedure: Principles of Practice* (London, Sweet & Maxwell, 2013) is especially good on the permission test up to 2013. Paras 24.135–24.138 and 24.165–24.179 repay study.

[132] *Tanfern* (n 131) at [41]. Note here the financial subordination of the judicial arm to the executive arm of government, although the language refers to 'Parliament'. Jacob's parsimony principle has come back in a new form.

[133] In this context Brooke LJ was speaking, in particular, of litigants in person – *Tanfern* (n 131) at [43].

[134] *Eba v Advocate General for Scotland* [2011] UKSC 29 at [48].

point of principle or practice ought to be a new point and not an already established one.[135]

Lord Clarke said, in *R (Cart) v Upper Tribunal*,[136] that the test worked well, enabling the husbanding of resources but leaving the door open for when 'something has gone seriously wrong'.

ii. The Escape Hatch

If the case did not raise an important point of principle or practice then it was for the would-be appellant to show a compelling reason for a second appeal, and so use the escape hatch.[137] This excluded cases that were only 'properly arguable' or had only a 'real prospect'.[138]

Dyson LJ considered the meaning of 'some other compelling reason' in *Uphill v BRB Residuary*.[139] He said:

(a) the prospects would ordinarily need to be 'very high' as a necessary condition of granting permission; but
(b) a strong case was usually not a sufficient condition. There would still need to be a compelling reason.

He went on to say that very high prospects would not be required if the reason was compelling enough. The implications of all this were clear: a second appeal might be refused even if an appeal court concluded that the lower court was wrong, unless the threshold test was satisfied.[140]

Further guidance has been provided by the Supreme Court. In *Eba v AG for Scotland*,[141] Lord Hope PSC said that the term 'compelling' would 'include circumstances where it was clear that the decision was perverse or plainly wrong or where, due to some procedural irregularity, the [party] had not had a fair hearing at all'.

[135] *Uphill v BRB (Residuary) Ltd* [2005] EWCA 60 at [18] per Dyson LJ.

[136] *Cart* (n 1) at [104].

[137] Just as there was in CPR 24.2(b) and CPR 13.3 (b); the 'compelling reason' or 'good reason' tests respectively.

[138] *Tanfern* (n 131) at [42].

[139] *Uphill* (n 135) at [24]. *Uphill* was considered in *Esure Insurance Ltd v Direct Line Insurance Plc* [2008] EWCA Civ 842 at [35].

[140] The Court of Appeal had said that some flexibility was required in the way in which CPR 52.13(2) is interpreted – *Cramp v Hastings BC* [2005] EWCA Civ 1005 at [64]–[67]. In *Cramp* there appeared to be a developing practice of county court judges making decisions that did not take account of established authority. For comment on *Uphill* and *Cramp*, see T Jenns, 'Is it all Downhill for Second Appeals?' (2006) 25 *Civil Justice Quarterly* 439. Bowman had envisaged the grant of permission where temporary problems had arisen, or where case management guidance was required: see *Bow Rep* (n 3) ch 4, para 21.

[141] *Eba* (n 134) at [48], a Scottish case.

In *Cart*, Lord Dyson had said that 'the second limb of the test ("some other compelling reason") would enable the court to examine an arguable error of law … which cries out for consideration by the court'.[142]

Reluctant to be definitive in the face of potentially differing circumstances, Lord Dyson did highlight 'wholly exceptional' failures of procedural fairness and errors of law with 'truly drastic consequences'. Both of these indications need to be read in the light of *Cart*'s being a judicial review case.

Our review concludes by looking at the new CPR 52.7, which now governs second appeals to the Court of Appeal.

D. The New CPR 52.7

The changes to the Rules came into force on 3 October 2016.[143] The explanatory memorandum, curiously, refers neither to the Briggs proposal to insert a merits test, nor to the opposition to setting the level of that test as 'a substantial prospect'.[144]

The Draft Rules had provided that, for second appeals, permission would only be granted where 'the court considers that the appeal would have a substantial prospect of success'.[145] This was intended to mean that it is 'seriously arguable that an error has been made (and not merely arguable so that it cannot be said to be fanciful)'.[146] The rationale was to concentrate the Court of Appeal's 'resources … on the cases which most merit review at an appellate level'.[147] This would mean putting the resources into 'the cases where it really matters'.[148]

That proposal was not reflected in the new Rules – undoubtedly a significant opportunity missed, but perhaps a sensible compromise given that first appeals in the Court of Appeal would comprise High Court appeals – by definition not run-of-the-mill cases. Further, keeping the same basic wording for first and second appeals does, at least, allow for a consistent approach to be taken.

[142] *Cart* (n 1) at [131]. The boundaries of what might amount to a 'compelling reason' have not been fully sketched, although it can be said it must be compelling from a legal perspective – *PR (Sri Lanka) v Secretary of State for the Home Department* [2011] EWCA 988. The second quotation is from *Cart* (n 1) at [131], internal citation omitted.

[143] See Civil Procedure (Amendment No 3) Rules 2016 (SI 2016/788) and r 10 thereof.

[144] See *Consultation Exercise* (n 104) 5, 7, where it is said that 'the CA believes that …'. This is a very strong statement.

[145] ibid at 16, proposed CPR 52.3D.

[146] *Consultation Exercise* (n 104) at 7.

[147] ibid. As Blackstone says, it is appropriate to give more 'time and circumspection' in cases 'where the suitors have valuable and permanent rights to lose': W Blackstone (n 51) book III, 423. He equates speedy justice with autocratic rule. We might equate it with efficiency.

[148] *Consultation Exercise* (n 104) at 7.

The new Rule provides, at CPR 52.7(2):

> The Court of Appeal will not give permission unless it considers that—
>
> (a) the appeal would—
>
> (i) *have a real prospect of success*;[149] and
>
> (ii) raise an important point of principle or practice; or
>
> (b) there is some other compelling reason for the Court of Appeal to hear it.

The continuity with the escape-hatch wording from the old CPR 52.13 means, ordinarily, that the prospects will need to be 'very high' (*Uphill*) for the escape hatch to open.

E. Conclusion

Restricting the right to appeal may be justified as:

(a) weeding out weak claims;
(b) protecting people from themselves (the *Piglowska* approach);
(c) protecting the system from the people (the Bowman and Briggs approach); and
(d) protecting society from an overly demanding system.

Although this may seem harsh, the system, as it was, could not cope. An increase in demand, together with a lack of money for extra staff, has been the driving force behind the changes to CPR 52: the executive, by withholding extra funding, has effectively required the civil justice system to tolerate increasing delays or impose a rationed approach to appeals. There is some logic to this.[150] Demand for the services of appeal judges continues to rise. Public funds are limited. No branch of government is able to act outside the constraints of limited funding.[151] Therefore the civil justice system either has to meet increasing demand through increased efficiencies, or fall short of its aspirations by doing less. The Government might argue that these are exactly the sorts of tough decisions that managers in the Health Service take on a daily basis. Procedural justice is difficult to measure using the yardstick of money, but it costs real money to deliver it.

It is concluded that:

(a) an appeal court focuses upon what has gone wrong. It should have the time, expertise and experience to address the problem being scrutinised;

[149] Emphasis added. Emphasised words added by new CPR 52.7.

[150] The duty placed on the Lord Chancellor is not an absolute one: Constitutional Reform Act 2005, s 3(6)(b).

[151] This was precisely the point made by the Court of Appeal in *Uphill* (n 135).

(b) in the case of the Court of Appeal, it is able to bring at least two minds to bear on any particular problem;
(c) because error is always a possibility, it is appropriate to have some mechanism to attempt correction and so reduce error costs. In addition, the existence of an appeal process encourages the lower courts to be diligent and allows the system to police itself;
(d) but perfection is not possible because of the process cost of an appeal, and because judges may ultimately disagree about the correct answer;
(e) all aggrieved litigants may ask for a check to be carried out concerning the decision in their case;
(f) in the first place, that check amounts to a review of the papers;
(g) where the appeal court thinks that the limited check reveals that an appeal may have merit or that a full review is really needed then the case will proceed to a full appeal;
(h) a by-product of the availability of this process should be continued confidence in the civil justice system;
(i) the norm that 'one appeal is enough' will only be realised if second appeal courts apply the threshold test properly. The idea that only cases of importance should reach the top of the appeals pyramid is a corollary of the one appeal theory. Making this a norm will require a consistent hardening of judicial attitudes; an acceptance by all appeal judges that the checking process is a valuable justice-enabling provision in its own right; and a shared confidence within the lower and higher courts that a single appeal amounts to the completion of justice.[152] If this point is reached then cases that would have received permission previously will now be refused permission;
(j) the High Court will of necessity make the running in developing or applying the law for smaller cases, as permission for a second appeal will not readily be granted;
(k) the most important first appeals will emerge from the High Court and will continue to be deal with by the Court of Appeal. Hearing these kinds of appeals is a significant part of the Court of Appeal's work. As a consequence of rerouting, the volume of appeals in the Court of Appeal should therefore reduce;
(l) first appeals from circuit judges will now be heard by the High Court. The volume of appeals in the High Court will therefore increase substantially;
(m) multi-track appeals will be conducted in most cases by High Court or former High Court judges.[153] It remains unclear to what extent these appeals will be directed towards judges with relevant experience;

[152] One wonders to what extent this philosophy of appeals has the widespread acceptance that it will need to be effective.
[153] It seems unlikely that the Court of Appeal would release judges to hear cases which are now, by definition, insufficiently important to be heard by a Court of Appeal judge.

(n) the attenuated procedure available for first appeals in the county court and High Court is likely to encourage parties to see whether permission to appeal will be granted;

(o) all second appeals from the county court and the High Court will be heard by Court of Appeal, provided the threshold of importance and merits is crossed or the test of compelling reasons is met. It is envisaged that many cases will not satisfy either permission test;

(p) the Court of Appeal will continue to give guidance and make law in those second appeals that warrant it;

(q) appeal courts are empowered and constrained by the vertical nature of appeals. The vertical axis means that appeal courts both correct the errors of lower courts and have to show an appropriate degree of deference. Such deference operates to preserve the resources of the Court of Appeal for when they are needed.

BIBLIOGRAPHY

ALI/Unidroit, *Principles of Transnational Civil Procedure* (Cambridge, Cambridge University Press, 2007).

Anonymous, 'The Rule-Making Power: a Bibliography', 16(3) *American Bar Association Journal* 199 (1930).

——, 'Legal Writings of Edson R Sunderland', 58 *Michigan Law Review* 41 (1959–1960).

——, Securing Uniformity in National Law: A Proposal for National Stare Decisis in the Courts of Appeals, 87 *Yale Law Journal* 1219 (1977–1978).

Ahmed, M, 'Procedural rules and judicial discretion: *Cameron v Hussain* [2017] EWCA Civ 366' (2018) 37(2) *Civil Justice Quarterly* 149.

Andrews, N, *Principles of Civil Procedure* (London, Sweet & Maxwell, 1994).

——, 'A New Civil Procedural Code for England: Party-Control – "Going, Going Gone"' (2000) 19 *Civil Justice Quarterly* 19.

——, 'A New System of Civil Appeals and a New Set of Problems' [2000] 59:3 *Cambridge Law Journal* 421.

——, *English Civil Procedure* (Oxford, Oxford University Press, 2003).

——, 'Embracing the Noble Quest for Transnational Procedural Principles' in M Adams et al (eds), *The Future of Transnational Commercial Litigation* (London, British Institute of International and Comparative Law, 2003, reprinted in 2006).

——, *The Three Paths of Justice* (London, Springer, 2012).

——, *Andrews on Civil Processes*, vol 1 (Cambridge, Intersentia, 2013).

Archer, MS, *Realist Social Theory: The Morphogenetic Cycle* (Cambridge, Cambridge University Press, 1995).

Aristotle, *The Politics*, book III.

Assy, R, 'Briggs' online court and the need for a paradigm shift', *Civil Justice Quarterly* (2017), 36(1) 70.

Austin, J, *Lectures on Jurisprudence*, ed R Campbell, student edn (London, John Murray, 1880).

——, *Lectures on Jurisprudence or The Philosophy of Positive Law*, ed R Campbell, vol 2 (London, John Murray, 1885).

Bates, JL, *Senator Thomas J Walsh of Montana Law and Public Affairs, from TR to FDR* (Urbana, IL, University of Illinois Press (1999).

Bennion, FAR, *Bennion on Statutory Interpretation*, 3rd edn (London, Butterworths, 1997).

Bentham, J, *Introduction to the Rationale of Judicial Evidence Book II*, ed J Bowring (Edinburgh, William Tate, 1843).

Bingham, T, *The Rule of Law* (London, Allen Lane, 2010).

Blackstone, W, *Commentaries on the Laws of England*, books 1 and 3 (Oxford, Clarendon Press (1765–1769).

Berger, PC, and Luckmann, T, *The Social Construction of Reality* (Harmondsworth, The Penguin Press, 1966).

Bone, RG, 'Personal and Impersonal Litigative Forms: Reconceiving the History of Adjudicative Representation', 70 *Boston University Law Review* 213 (1990).

——, 'The Process of Making Process: Court Rulemaking, Democratic Legitimacy, and the Procedural Efficacy', 87 *Georgetown Law Journal* 887 (1999).

——, 'Making Effective Rules: The Need For a Procedure Theory', 61 *Oklahoma Law Review* 319 (2008).

——, 'Improving Rule 1: A Master Rule For The Federal Rules', 87(2) *Denver University Law Review* 287 (2010).

Brooke, H, 'Some thoughts on the first seven and a half years of the CPR' in D Dwyer (ed), *The Civil Procedure Rules Ten Years On* (Oxford, Oxford University Press, 2009).

Brooke, H et al (eds), *White Book (2004)* sub nom *Civil Procedure (2004)* (London, Sweet & Maxwell, 2004).

——, *White Book (2005)* sub nom *Civil Procedure (2005)* (London, Sweet & Maxwell, 2005).

Brown, LN, 'British and French Statutory Drafting: A Review Article' (1988) 37(3) *International and Comparative Law Quarterly* 698.

Bunker, RE, 'New Federal Equity Rules', 11 *Michigan Law Review* 435 (1912–1913).

Burbank, SB, 'The Rules Enabling Act of 1934', 130 *University of Pennsylvania Law Review* 1015 (1982).

Burke, E, *Reflections on the French Revolution* (London, JM Dent & Sons Ltd, 1910 edn, reprinted 1953).

Burnett, I, 'The Age Of Reform', The Sir Henry Brooke Annual Lecture 2018.

Burns, JMG, *Roosevelt: the Lion and the Fox* (New York, Harcourt, Brace & Co, reprint 1986).

Burns, KJ, 'Chief Justice as Chief Executive: Taft's Judicial Statesmanship', 43(1) *Journal of Supreme Court History* 47 (2018).

Caponi, R, 'The Performance of the Italian Civil Justice System: An Empirical Assessment' (2016) 2(1) *The Italian Law Journal* 15.

Cardozo, BN, *The Nature of the Judicial Process* (New Haven, CT, Yale University Press, 1921).

Carrington, PD, ' "Substance" and "Procedure" in the Rules Enabling Act', 1989 *Duke Law Journal* 281 (1989).

Chandler, HP, 'Some Major Advances in the Federal Judicial System 1922–1947', 31 *Federal Rules Decisions* 307 (1963).

Clark, CE, 'Fact Research in Law Administration', 1 *Mississipi Law Journal* 324 (1928).

——, 'Cause of Action', 82 *University of Pennsylvania Law Review* 354 (1933–1934).

——, 'Challenge of a New Federal Civil Procedure', 20 *Cornell Law Review* 443 (1935).

——, 'The Handmaid of Justice', 23 *Washington University Law Quarterly* 297 (1937–1938).

——, 'Afterthoughts of the Institute on Federal Rules of Civil Procedure at Cleveland, July 1938', 14 *Notre Dame Law Review* 103 (1938–1939).

——, 'Fundamental Changes Effected by the New Federal Rules I', 15 *Tennessee Law Review* 551 (1939).

——, 'The Influence of Federal Procedural Reform', 13 *Law and Contemporary Problems* 144 (1948).

——, 'Special Problems in Drafting and Interpreting Procedural Codes and Rules', 3 *Vanderbilt Law Review* 493 (1950).

——, 'The Evershed Report and English Procedural Reforms', 29 *New York University Law Review* 1046 (1954).

——, 'Two Decades of the Federal Civil Rules', 58 *Columbia Law Review* 435 (1958).

——, 'Edson Sunderland and the Federal Rules of Civil Procedure', 58 *Michigan Law Review* 6 (1959–1960).

—— and Moore, JW, 'A New Federal Civil Procedure I', 44 *Yale Law Journal* 387 (1935).

—— and——, 'A New Federal Civil Procedure II', 44 *Yale Law Journal* 1291 (1935).

Clark, H, 'The Federal Equity Rules of 1912', 7 *Maine Law Review* 260 (1914).

Clark, S and Jackson, R, *The Reform of Civil Justice*, 2nd edn (London, Thomson Reuters (Professional) UK Ltd, 2018).

Coke, E, *Coke's Institutes of the Laws of England* (London, M Flesher and R Young, 1642).

Coleman, BD, 'Recovering Access: Rethinking the Structure of Federal Civil Rulemaking', 39(2) *New Mexico Law Review* 261 (2009).

——, 'The Efficiency Norm', 56 *Boston College Law Review* 1777 (2015).

Crowe, J, *Building the Judiciary: Law, Courts, and the Politics of Institutional Development* (Princeton, NJ, Princeton University Press, 2012).

Cummings, H, *Selected Papers of Homer Cummings: AG of the United States 1933–1939*, ed Carl Brent Swisher, vol 1 (New York, C Scribner's Sons, 1939).

Dallek, R, *Franklin D Roosevelt* (Harmondsworth, Allen Lane, Penguin, 2018).

Dalton, HL, 'Taking the Right to Appeal (More or Less) Seriously', 95 *Yale Law Journal* 62 (1985–1986).

Denning, A, *Freedom Under the Law*, Hamlyn Lectures 1st Series (London, Stevens & Sons Ltd, 1949).
De Saulles, D, 'Nought Plus Nought Plus Nought Equals Nought: Rhetoric and the Asbestos Wars' (2006) 4 *Journal of Personal Injury Law* Issue 4/06 301.
de Secondat, C (Baron Montesquieu), *The Spirit of the Laws*, tr T Nugent (New York, Hafner Press, 1949).
Devlin, P, 'Who is at fault when injustice occurs?' in M Zander (ed), *What's Wrong with the Law?* (London, BBC, 1970).
Dewey, J, 'Logical Method and Law', 10 *Cornell Law Review* 17 (1924).
——, 'The Historic Background of Corporate Legal Personality', 35 *Yale Law Journal* 660 (1925–1926).
Drewry, G et al, *The Court of Appeal* (Oxford, Hart Publishing, 2007).
Dworkin, R, in *A Matter of Principle* (Oxford, Clarendon Press (1986).
Dwyer, D, 'The Interpretation of the English Civil Procedure Rules in the Context of Article 6 of the European Convention on Human Rights' in H Snidjers and S Vogenauer (eds), *Context and Meaning of National Law in the Context of Transnational Law* (Munich, Sellier European Law Publishers GmbH, 2009).
——, 'What is the Meaning of CPR r1.1(1)?' in D Dwyer (ed), *The Civil Procedure Rules Ten Years On* (Oxford, Oxford University Press, 2009).
Dyson, J, *Reforms Implementation Programme: Lecture No 18: The application of the amendments to the Civil Procedure Rules* (March 2013).
Edmunds, PD, *Federal Rules of Civil Procedure* (Chicago, IL, Callaghan & Co, 1938).
——, 'Lecture Digest, The New Federal Rules of Civil Procedure' 4 *John Marshall Law Quarterly* 291 (1938).
Elder-Vass, D, *The Reality of Social Construction* (Cambridge, Cambridge University Press, 2012).
Elliott, M and Thomas, R, 'Tribunal Justice and Proportionate Dispute Resolution' (2012) 71 *Cambridge Law Journal* 297.
Eskridge Jr, WN, 'The New Textualism' 37 *UCLA Law Review* 621 (1990).
Fallon Jr, RJ, 'Some Confusions about Due Process, Judicial Review, and Constitutional Remedies', 93 *Columbia Law Review* 309 (1993).
Finnis, J, *Natural Law and Natural Rights* (Oxford, Oxford University Press, 1980).
Fish, PG, *The Politics of Federal Judicial Administration* (Princeton, NJ, Princeton University Press, 1973).
Freund, PA, 'Charles Evans Hughes as Chief Justice', 81 *Harvard Law Review* 4 (1967).
Galbraith, JK, *The Great Crash 1929* (London, Hamish Hamilton, 1955, reprinted Harmondsworth, Penguin Books, 1966).
Gardner, J, *Law as a Leap of Faith* (Oxford, Oxford University Press, 2012).
Genn, H, 'Understanding Civil Justice' in M Freeman (ed), *Law and Public Opinion in the 20th Century*, Current Legal Problems vol 50 (Oxford, Oxford University, 1997).
Genn, H, *Judging Civil Justice* (Cambridge, Cambridge University Press 2010).
Glover, JM, 'The Federal Rules of Civil Settlement', 87 *New York University Law Review* 1713 (2012).
Glover, JM, 'A Regulatory Theory of Legal Claims', 70 *Vanderbilt Law Review* 221 (2017).
Greenberg, D et al (eds), *Jowitt's Dictionary of English Law*, 4th edn (London, Sweet & Maxwell, 2015).
Greenberg, D, *Westlaw Key Legal Concepts* (London, Westlaw Online, Sweet & Maxwell, 2016).
Gross, P, *Courts and Arbitration*, The Jonathan Hirst QC Commercial Law Lecture (2018) online at www.judiciary.uk.
Hale, B, *Devolution and The Supreme Court – 20 Years On*, speech to the Scottish Public Law Group (14 June 2018) online at www.supremecourt.uk.
Haltom, W and McCann, M, *Distorting the Law* (University of Chicago Press, London, 2004).
Hammond, EH (ed), *Legislative History of the Rules of Civil Procedure of the District Courts of the US*, vol 2 (Chicago, IL, American Bar Association, 1938).
Hart, HLA, *The Concept of Law*, 2nd edn (Oxford, Oxford University Press, 1994).

Haskins, I, *The Social Construction of What?* (Cambridge, MA, Harvard University Press, 1999).

Herzog, PE and Karlen, D, 'Attacks on Judicial Decisions' in PE Herzog and D Karlen (eds), *International Encyclopedia of Comparative Law*, vol 16 (Boston, MA, Martinus Nijhoff Publishers, 2014).

Higgins, A, 'CPR 3.9: The Mitchell guidance, the Denton revision, and why coded messages don't make for good case management' (2014) 33(4) *Civil Justice Quarterly* 379.

——, 'Lord Justice Briggs' "SWOT" analysis underlines English law's troubled relationship with proportionate costs' (2017) 36(1) *Civil Justice Quarterly* 1.

Hoffer, PC, 'Text, Translation, Context and Conversation: Preliminary Notes for Decoding the Deliberations of the Advisory Committee', 37 *American Journal of Legal History* 409 (1993).

—— et al, *The Supreme Court: An Essential History* (Lawrence, KS, University Press of Kansas, 2007).

—— et al, *The Federal Courts: An Essential History* (Oxford University Press, Oxford, 2016).

Hoffmann, L, 'Fairchild and After' in A Burrows et al (eds), *Judge and Jurist: Essays in Memory of Lord Rodger of Earlsferry* (Oxford, Oxford University Press, 2013).

Holt, DS, *Debates on the Federal Judiciary: A Documentary History*, vol II: *1875–1939* (Washington, DC, Federal Judicial Centre, 2013).

Holtzoff, A, 'Equitable and Legal Rights and Remedies Under the New Federal Procedure', 23(2) *California Law Review* 127 (1943).

Huber, PW, *Galileo's Revenge* (Basic Books, New York, 1991).

Hull, NEH, *Roscoe Pound and Karl Llewellyn: Searching for an American Jurisprudence* (Chicago, IL, University of Chicago Press, 1997).

Hutton, PH, 'Mentalities' in K Boyd (ed), *The Encyclopaedia of Historians and Historical Writing*, vol 2 (London, Fitzroy Dearborn Publishers, 1999).

Ilse, W, *Federal Rules of Civil Procedure* (St Paul, MN, West Publishing Co, rev edn 1944).

Jackson, R, *Reforms Implementation Programme: Lecture No 5. Achieving a Culture Change in Case Management* (November 2011) online at www.judiciary.uk.

——, *The Reform of Civil Litigation*, 1st edn (London, Thomson Reuters (Professional) UK Ltd, 2016).

——, *Was It All Worth It?*' Lecture to the Cambridge Law Faculty on 5 March 2018 online at www.judiciary.uk.

——, *The Fabric of English Civil Justice* (London, Stevens & Sons, 1987).

Jackson R et al (eds), *White Book (2017)* sub nom *Civil Procedure (2017)* (London, Sweet & Maxwell, 2017).

Jacob J, (ed), *Chitty and Jacob's Queen's Bench Forms*, 20th edn (London, Sweet & Maxwell, 1969).

Jacob, J, *The Reform of the Procedural Law and other Essays in Civil Procedure* (London, Sweet & Maxwell, 1982).

Jacob, JM, 'The Bowman Review of the Court of Appeal' (1998) 61 *Modern Law Review* 390.

Jenns, T, 'Is it all Downhill for Second Appeals?' (2006) 25 *Civil Justice Quarterly* 439.

Jolowicz, J, '"General Ideas" and the reform of civil procedure' (1983) 3 *Legal Studies* 295.

——, 'On the Nature and Purposes of Civil Procedural Law' (1990) 9 *Civil Justice Quarterly* 262.

——, 'The Woolf Report and the Adversary System' (1996) 15 *Civil Justice Quarterly* 198.

——, *On Civil Procedure* (Cambridge, Cambridge University Press, 2000).

Johnston, P, 'Problems in Raising Prayers to the Level of Rule: The example of Federal Rule of Procedure 1', 75 *Boston University Law Review* 1325 (1995).

Justininian's Digest, tr SP Scott, *Corpus Juris Civilis, the Civil Law* (Cincinnatti, OH, Central Trust Co, 1932; reprinted New York, AMS Press, 1973).

Kalman, L, *Legal Realism at Yale 1927–1960* (Chapel Hill, NC, University of North Carolina Press, 1986; reprinted Union, NJ, The Lawbook Exchange Ltd, 2001).

Koh, HH, 'The Just, Speedy, and Inexpensive Determination of Every Action', 162 *University of Pennsylvania Law Review* 1525 (2014).

Kuhn, T, *The Structure of Scientific Revolutions*, 3rd edn (Chicago, IL, University of Chicago Press, 1996).

Kutscher, H, *Methods of Interpretation as seen by a Judge at the Court of Justice* (Luxembourg, Juridical and Academic Conference, 1976).

Legg, M, 'Reconciling the Goals of Minimising Cost and Delay with the Principle of a Fair Trial in the Australian Civil Justice System' (2014) 33(2) *Civil Justice Quarterly* 157.

Legrand, P, 'European Legal Systems are not converging' (1996) 45(1) *International and Comparative Law Quarterly* 52.

——, 'The Impossibility of "Legal Transplants"' (1997) 4 *Maastricht Journal of European & Comparative Law* 111.

——, 'Comparative Legal Studies and the Matter of Authenticity' (2006) 1 *Journal of Comparative Law* 365.

Leuchtenburg, WE, *Franklin D Roosevelt and the New Deal: 1932–1940* (London, Harper & Row, 1963).

Levy, I, 'Lightening the Overload of CPR Rule 3.9' (2013) 32 *Civil Justice Quarterly* 139.

——, 'Simplifying Legal Decisions: Factor Overload in Civil Procedure Rules' (2017) 41(2) *Melbourne University Law Review* 727.

Lobban, M, 'Preparing for Fusion: Reforming the Nineteenth-Century Court of Chancery, Part I' in (2004) 22(2) *Law and History Review* 389.

——, 'Preparing for Fusion: Reforming the Nineteenth-Century Court of Chancery, Part II' (2004) 22(3) *Law and History Review* 565.

JE Lobsenz, 'A Constitutional Right to an Appeal: Guarding Against Unacceptable Risks of Erroneous Conviction', 8 *Seattle University Law Review* 375 (1985).

Locke, J, *Two Treatises of Government*, Book II: *Civil Government* (Dublin, J Shepphard and G Nugent, 1779).

Mannheim, K, *Structures of Thinking*, eds D Kettler et al, trs JJ Shapiro and SW Nicholson (London, Routledge Kegan & Paul Ltd, 1982).

Manson, E, 'Cross- Examination: A Socratic Fragment' (1892) 8 *Law Quarterly Review* 160.

Marcus, D, 'The Federal Rules of Civil Procedure and Legal Realism as a Jurisprudence of Law Reform', 44 *Georgia Law Review* 433 (2010).

——, 'Institutions and an Interpretive Methodology for the Federal Rules of Civil Procedure' 2011(3) *Utah Law Review* 927 (2011).

——, 'When Rules are Rules: The Federal Rules of Civil Procedure and Institutions in Legal interpretation', *Arizona Legal Studies Discussion Paper No 11-22* (2011) online at www.law.arizona.edu.

Marcus, RL 'Reform through Rulemaking?' 80 *Washington University Law Quarterly* 901 (2002).

——, "Looking Backward" to 1938', 162 *University of Pennsylvania Law Review* 1691 (2014).

—— et al, *Civil Procedure – A Modern Approach* (St Paul, MN, West Publishing, 1989).

May, A et al (eds), *White Book (2002)* sub nom *Civil Procedure (2002) Spring Edition* (London, Sweet & Maxwell, 2002).

Merkin, R and Flannery, L, *Arbitration Act 1996*, 4th edn (London, Informa, 2008).

Merton, RK, 'The Unanticipated Consequences of Purposive Social Action', 1 *American Sociological Review* 894 (1936).

Mill, JS, *On Liberty*, 3rd edn (London, Longman, Green, Longman, Roberts & Green, 1864).

Millar, RW, 'The Formative Principles of Civil Procedure (Pt 1)', 18 *Illinois Law Review* 1 (1923).

——, *Civil Procedure of the Trial Court in Historical Perspective* (New York, Law Centre of New York University, 1952).

Miller, AR, 'Pleading and Pre-trial Motions – What would Judge Clark do?', Paper prepared for a 2010 conference at Duke Law School and subsequently revised.

Mitchell, WD, 'Some of the Problems Confronting the Advisory Committee in Recent Months – Commencement of Actions – Effect of Findings of Fact in Cases Tried by Court instead of Jury, etc.' 23 *American Bar Association Journal* 966 (1937).

——, 'The Federal Rules of Civil Procedure' in A Reppy (ed), *David Dudley Field Centenary Essays* (New York, New York University School of Law, 1949).

Moore, JW, 'The New Federal Rules of Civil Procedure', 6 *Interstate Commerce Commission Practitioners' Journal* 41 (1939).

——, 'Address of Professor Moore', 44 *American Bar Association Journal* 44 (1958).

—— et al, *Moore's Federal Practice: a treatise on the Federal rules of civil procedure* (Albany, NY, Mathew Bender & Co, 1938).

—— et al, *Moore's Federal Practice*, 2nd edn (Albany, NY, Matthew Bender & Co, 1993 (updated from 1948)) vol 2.

Moore, KN, 'The Supreme Court's Role in Interpreting the Federal Rules of Civil Procedure', 44 *Hastings Law Journal* 1039 (1990).

Morgan, EM, 'Judicial Regulation of Court Procedure', 2 *Minnesota Law Review* 81 (1917–1918).

Nayer, R, 'Post-Denton: an appraisal of Court of Appeal decisions on relief from sanctions' (2016) 35(2) *Civil Justice Quarterly* 97.

Neuberger, D, *Justice in an Age of Austerity*, Tom Sargant Memorial Lecture, 15 October 2013 online at www.supremecourt.uk.

——, *The role of judges in human rights jurisprudence: a comparison of the Australian and UK experience*, Supreme Court of Victoria, Melbourne, 8 August 2014.

Newman, RK (ed), *The Yale Biographical Dictionary of American Law* (New Haven, CT, Yale University Press, 2009).

Nobles, R and Schiff, D, 'The Right to Appeal and Workable Systems of Justice' (2002) 65 *Modern Law Review* 676.

Odgers, B, 'Changes in Procedure and the Law of Evidence' in *A Century of Law Reform* (London, Macmillan & Co Ltd, 1901).

Olson, WK, *The Litigation Explosion* (Dutton, NY, Truman Talley Books, 1991).

——, *The Rule of Lawyers* (Dutton, NY, Truman Talley Books, 2003).

Perkins, WB, 'The English Judicature Act of 1873', 12(4) *Michigan Law Review* 277 (1914).

Peysner, J and Seneviratne, M, *The Management of Civil Cases: The Courts and the Post-Woolf Landscape* (London, Department for Constitutional Affairs, 2005).

Phillips, N, 'Strasbourg Has Spoken' in A Burrows et al (eds), *Judge and Jurist: Essays in Memory of Lord Rodger of Earlsferry* (Oxford, Oxford University Press, 2013).

Plant, C et al, *Blackstone's Guide to the Civil Procedure Rules*, 2nd edn (London, Blackstone Press Ltd, 1999).

Polden, P, 'Mingling the Waters: Personalities, Politics and the Making of the Supreme Court of Judicature' (2002) 61 *Cambridge Law Journal* 575.

——, 'The Courts of Appeal' in W Cornish et al (eds), *Oxford History of the Laws of England*, vol XI (Oxford, Oxford University Press, 2010) ch VIII.

Pollock, F, *Expansion of the Common Law* (London, Steven & Sons Ltd, 1904).

Porter, EG, 'Pragmatism Rules', 101 *Cornell Law Review* 123 (2015).

Post, R, 'Judicial Management and Judicial Disinterest: The Achievements and Perils of Chief Justice William Howard Taft', 23(1) *Journal of Supreme Court History* 50 (1998).

Pound, R, 'Do We Need a Philosophy of Law?' 5 *Columbia Law Review* 339 (1905).

——, 'The Causes of Popular Dissatisfaction with the Administration of Justice' 29 *Annual Report of the American Bar Association* 395 (1906).

——, 'Mechanical Jurisprudence', 8 *Columbia Law Review* 605 (1908).

——, 'Some Principles of Procedural Reform', 4 *Illinois Law Review* 388 (1909–1910).

——, 'The Scope and Purpose of Sociological Jurisprudence, Pt 1' 24 *Harvard Law Review* 140 (1911).

——, 'Senator Walsh on Rule Making Power on the Law Side of Federal Practice', 13 *American Bar Association Journal* 84 (1926).

——, *Appellate Procedure in Civil Cases* (Boston, MA, Little Brown & Company, 1941).

——, *Jurisprudence*, vol 5 (St Paul, MN, West Publishing, 1959).

Raz, J, *The Morality of Freedom* (Oxford, Clarendon Press, 1986).

——, 'Authority and Justification' in J Raz (ed), *Authority* (Oxford, Basil Blackwell Ltd, 1990).

Rawls, J, *Justice as Fairness, a Restatement*, ed E Kelly (Cambridge, MA, The Belknap Press, 2001).

Reid, J, 'The Judge as Lawmaker', 12 *Journal of the Society of Public Teachers of the Law* (1972–73) 22.

Renshaw, P, *Franklin D Roosevelt* (New York, Longman, 2004).

Resnik, J, 'Managerial Judges' 96 *Harvard Law Review* 374 (1982).

——, 'Failing Faith: Adjudicatory Procedure in Decline', 53 *The University of Chicago Law Review* 494 (1986).

Richards, S, 'The Mitchell/Denton line of cases: securing compliance with rules and court orders' (2015) 34(3) *Civil Justice Quarterly* 249.

Roberts, DM, 'The Myth of Uniformity in Federal Civil Procedure: Federal Civil Rule 83 and District Court Local Rulemaking Powers', 8 *University of Puget Sound Law Review* 537 (1985).

Robertson, CB, 'The Right to Appeal', 91 *North Carolina Law Review* 1219 (2013).

Rosenbaum, S, *The Rule-Making Authority in the English Supreme Court* (Boston, MA, Boston Book Company, 1917).

Ross, WG, *The Chief Justiceship of Charles Evans Hughes* (Columbia, SC, University of South Carolina Press, 2007).

Rousseau, JJ, *The Social Contract*, ed & tr M Cranston (Harmondsworth, Penguin Books, 1968).

Samaha, AA, 'Undue Process', 59 *Stanford Law Review* 601 (2006–2007).

Sandel, M, 'The Procedural Republic and the Unencumbered Self', 12(1) *Political Theory* 8 (1984).

——, *Justice, What's the Right Thing to Do?* (London, Allen Lane, 2009).

Schwartz, B, *A History of the Supreme Court* (Oxford, Oxford University Press, 1993) ch 10.

Scott, I, 'Permission to appeal in "second tier" appeals' (1999) 18 *Civil Justice Quarterly* 287.

Scott, R et al (eds), *White Book (1999)* sub nom *Civil Procedure (1999) Spring Edition* (London, Sweet & Maxwell, 1999).

Searle, JR, *The Social Construction of Reality* (Harmondsworth, Allen Lane, Penguin Press, 1995).

——, *Making the Social World: The Structure of Human Civilization* (Oxford, Oxford University Press, 2010).

Selden, A, *Major: A Political Life* (London, Weidenfeld & Nicolson, 1997).

Shapiro, DL, 'Federal Rule 16: A Look at the Theory and Practice of Rulemaking', 137 *University of Pennsylvania Law Review* 1969 (1989).

Shapiro, M, 'Appeals', *Law and Society Review* 14 (1980) 629.

Silberman, LJ et al, *Civil Procedure Theory and Practice* (New York, Walters Kluwer, 2009).

Sime, S, 'Lord Dyson and the Implied Sanctions doctrine' (2015) 34(3) *Civil Justice Quarterly* 267.

——, 'Appeals after the Civil Courts Structure Review' (2017) 36(1) *Civil Justice Quarterly* 51.

Simon, JF, *FDR and Chief Justice Hughes: the President, the Supreme Court, and the Epic Battle Over the New Deal* (New York, Simon & Schuster, 2012).

Simpson-Scott, G, 'Justice, proportionality and fixed costs in clinical negligence' (2017) 4 *Journal of Personal Injury Law* 249.

Smith, C, *What is a Person: Rethinking Humanity, Social Life and the Moral Good From the Person Up* (Chicago, IL, University of Chicago Press, 2011).

Smith, ME, 'Judge Charles E Clark and the Federal Rules of Civil Procedure', 85 *Yale Law Journal* 914 (1976).

Snow, T et al (eds), *White Book (1883–84)* sub nom *The Annual Practice (1883–84)* (London, William Maxwell & Son (1883).

Stinchcombe, AL, *Constructing Social Theories* (New York, Harcourt Brace and & World Inc, 1968).

Struve, CT, 'The Paradox of Delegation: Interpreting the Federal Rules of Civil Procedure', 150 *University of Pennsylvania Law Review* 1099 (2001–2002).

Sorabji, J, 'The Road to New Street Station: the Overriding Objective' (2012) 23 *European Business Law Review* 77.

——, 'Prospects for Proportionality: Jackson Implementation' (2013) 32 *Civil Justice Quarterly* 213.

——, *English Civil Justice after the Woolf and Jackson Reforms: A Critical Analysis* (Cambridge, Cambridge University Press, 2014).

Stempel, JW, 'New Paradigm, Normal Science or Crumbling Construct? Trends in Adjudicatory Procedure and Litigation Reform', 59 *Brooklyn Law Review* 659 (1993).

Straw, J, *Last Man Standing, Memoirs of a Political Survivor* (London, Pan Books, 2013).

Struve, CT, 'The Paradox of Delegation: Interpreting the Federal Rules of Civil Procedure', 150 *University of Pennsylvania Law Review* 1099 (2001–2002).

Subrin, SN, 'How Equity Conquered the Common Law', 135 *University of Pennsylvania Law Review* 909 (1987).

——, 'Federal Rules, Local Rules, and State Rules: Uniformity, Divergence, and Emerging Procedural Patterns', 137 *University of Pennsylvania Law Review* 2000 (1989).

——'Charles E Clark and His Procedural Outlook: The Disciplined Champion of Undisciplined Rules' in P Petruck (ed), *Judge Charles Edward Clark* (New York, Oceana Publications, 1991).

——, 'Fishing Expeditions Allowed: The Historical Background of the 1938 Federal Discovery Rules', 39(3) *Boston College Law Review* 691 (1998).

——, 'Clark, Charles' in RK Newman (ed), *The Yale Biographical Dictionary of American Law* (New Haven, CT, Yale University Press, 2009).

——, 'On Thinking about Description of a Country's Civil Procedure', 7 Tulane *Journal of International & Comparative Law* 139 (1999).

Sumption, J, *The Limits of Law*, 27th Sultan Azlan Shah Lecture 2013 online at www.supremecourt.uk.

——, 'A Response' in NW Barber et al (eds), *Lord Sumption and the Limits of the Law* (Oxford, Hart Publishing, 2016).

Sunderland, ER, 'Inquiry Concerning the Functions of Procedure in Legal Education', 21 *Michigan Law Review* 372 (1922–1923).

——, 'Theory and Practice of Pre-trial Procedure' 36(2) *Michigan Law Review* 215 (1937).

——, 'The New Federal Rules', 45 *West Virginia Law Quarterly* 5 (1938).

——, 'Growth of Pre-Trial Procedure', 44 *Commercial Law Journal* 406 (1939).

Sunstein, C, 'Foreword: Leaving Things Undecided', 110 *Harvard Law Review* 4 (1996–1997).

Taft, WH, 'The Attacks on the Courts and Legal procedure', 5:2 *Kentucky Law Journal* 3 (1916).

Thomas, J, 'Cutting the cloth to fit the dispute: Steps towards better procedures across the jurisdictions', Singapore Academy of Law Annual Lecture 2016 online at www.judiciary.uk.

Tidmarsh, J, 'Realising the Promise of Costs Budgets: an Economic Analysis' (2016) 35(3) *Civil Justice Quarterly* 219.

Tolman, EB, 'The Historical Beginnings of Procedural Reform Movement in This Country – Principles to be Observed in Making Rules', 22 *American Bar Association Journal* 783 (1936).

Turner, R, '"Actively": The Word that Changed the Civil Courts' in D Dwyer (ed), *The Civil Procedure Rules Ten Years On* (Oxford, Oxford University Press, 2009).

Vanderbilt, AT, *The Challenge of Law Reform* (Princeton, NJ, Princeton University Press, 1955, 2nd printing 1956).

Vincent, B, 'Order 17 rule 11 – a retrospective' (1998) 95(26) *Law Society Gazette* 34.

Watts, AW, *The Way of Zen* (Harmondsworth, Pelican Books, 1962).

Weinstein, JB, 'The Ghost of Process Past: The Fiftieth Anniversary of the Federal Rules of Civil Procedure and Erie', 54(1) *Brooklyn Law Review* 1 (1988).

Wheaton, CW, 'Federal Rules of Civil Procedure Interpreted', 25 *Cornell Law Review* 28 (1939).

Williams, JR, '"Well, that's a relief (from sanctions)!" – Time to pause and take stock of CPR r.3.9 developments within a general theory of case management' (2014) 33(4) *Civil Justice Quarterly* 394.

Williams, T, 'The Source of Authority for Rules of Court Affecting Procedure', 22 *Washington University Law Quarterly* 459 (1937).

Woolf, H, *The Protection of the Public – A New Challenge* (London, Stevens & Sons Ltd, 1990).

——, 'Access to Justice' in MDA Freeman (ed), *Current Legal Problems 1994*, vol 47 (Oxford, Oxford University Press 1994).

——, 'A New Approach to Civil Justice' in *Law Lectures for Practitioners, Hong Kong Law Journal* special edn (Hong Kong, Sweet & Maxwell, 1996).

——, 'Medics, Lawyers and the Courts' (1997) 16 *Civil Justice Quarterly* 302.

——, *The Pursuit of Justice* (Oxford, Oxford University Press, 2008).

Wright, CA and Miller, AR, *Federal Practice and Procedure*, 3rd edn (Eagan, MN, West Group, 2002).

Yeazell, SC, 'The Misunderstood Consequences of Modern Civil Process', 1994 *Wisconsin Law Review* 631 (1994).
——, 'Unspoken Truths and Misaligned Interests: Political Parties and the Two Cultures of Civil Litigation', 60 *UCLA Law Review* 1752 (2013).
Zander, M, *The State of Justice* (London, Sweet & Maxwell, 2000).
Ziegler, P, 'A General Theory of Law as a Paradigm for Legal Research' (1988) 51(5) *Modern Law Review* 569.
Zuckerman, A, 'Quality and Economy in Civil Procedure: The Case for Commuting Correct Judgments for Timely Judgments' (1994) 14(3) *Oxford Journal of Legal Studies* 353.
——, 'A Reform of Civil Procedure – Rationing Procedure Rather Than Access to Justice', (1995) 22(2) *Journal of Law & Society* 155.
——, 'The Second Great English Reform of Civil Justice – A Triumph of Hope Over Experience' (2000) 1(2) *Hibernian Law Journal* 178.
——, *Civil Procedure*, 1st edn (London, Lexis Nexis Butterworths, 2003).
——, *Civil Procedure: Principles of Practice*, 2nd edn (London, Sweet & Maxwell, 2006).
——, 'Litigation management under the CPR: a poorly-used management infrastructure' in D Dwyer (ed), *The Civil Procedure Rules Ten Years On* (Oxford, Oxford University Press, 2009).
——, 'The Challenge of Civil Justice Reform: Effective Court Management of Litigation' (2009) 1 *City University of Hong Kong Law Review* 49.
——, 'Rule Making and Precedent under the Civil Procedure Rules 1998 – Still an Unsettled Field' (2010) 29(1) *Civil Justice Quarterly* 1.
——, *Civil Procedure: Principles of Practice*, 3rd edn (London, Sweet & Maxwell, 2013).
——, 'The revised CPR 3.9: a coded message demanding articulation' (2013) 32 *Civil Justice Quarterly* 123.
——, 'No Justice Without Lawyers – The Myth of an Inquisitorial Solution' (2014) 33 *Civil Justice Quarterly* 355.

English Official Reports

Second Report made to His Majesty by the Commissioners appointed to inquire into the Practice and Proceedings of the Superior Courts of the Common Law (London, House of Commons, 1830).
Third Report made to His Majesty by the Commissioners appointed to inquire into the Practice and Proceedings of the Superior Courts of the Common Law (London, House of Commons, 1831).
Fifth Report made to His Majesty by the Commissioners appointed to inquire into the Practice and Proceedings of the Superior Courts of the Common Law (London, House of Commons, 1833).
First Report of Her Majesty's Commissioners for inquiring into the Process, Practice, and System of Pleading in the Superior Courts of Common Law (London, HMSO, 1851).
Second Report of Her Majesty's Commissioners for inquiring into the Process, Practice, and System of Pleading in the Superior Courts of Common Law (London, HMSO, 1853).
The Final Report of the Committee on Supreme Court Practice and Procedure (Cmd 8878, 1953) (Evershed Report).
Report of the Committee on Administrative Tribunals and Enquiries (Cmnd 218, 1957) (Franks Report).
Report of the Committee on Personal Injury Litigation (Cmnd 369, 1968) (Winn Report).
Civil Justice Review: Report of the Review Body on Civil Justice (Cmnd 394, 1988) (Civil Justice Review).
Civil justice on trial – the case for change (London, Bar Council and Law Society, 1993) (Heilbron and Hodge Report).
Woolf, H, *Access to Justice: Interim Report* (London, HMSO, 1995).
——, Access to Justice: Draft Civil Proceedings Rules (London, HMSO, 1996).
——, Access to Justice: Final Report (London, HMSO, 1996).
Bowman, J, *Report to the Lord Chancellor: Review of the Court of Appeal (Civil Division)* (London, Lord Chancellor's Department, 1997) (Bowman Report)).

Oldman, D (ed), *The Future of Civil Justice: The Association's proposals for the future of the Civil Justice System* (London, Association of District Judges, 2005).

Jackson, R, *Review of Civil Litigation Costs: Preliminary Report* (London, TSO, 2009).

——, *Review of Civil Litigation Costs: Final Report* (London, TSO, 2009).

Briggs, M, *Civil Courts Structure Review: Interim Report* (London, Judiciary of England and Wales, 2015).

——, *Civil Courts Structure Review: Final Report* (London, Judiciary of England and Wales, 2016).

Consultation Exercise – Appeals to the Court of Appeal: proposed amendments to Civil Procedure Rules and Practice Direction (London, Civil Procedure Rules Committee, 2016).

Civil Justice Statistics Quarterly, England and Wales, January to March 2017 (provisional) and Royal Courts of Justice 2016 (London, Ministry of Justice, 2017).

American Reports

Laws of the State of New York, 71st session (Albany New York, Charles van Benthuysen, 1847).

29 Annual Report of the American Bar Association (1906).

Report of 27th March 1914 of the Committee on the Judiciary, 63rd Congress, 2nd Session, Report No 462.

Report of the Committee on Uniform Judicial Procedure, 49 Annual Report of the American Bar Association (1926).

Handbook of the National Conference of Commissioners on Uniform State Laws and Proceedings (Baltimore, MD, Lord Baltimore Press, 1935).

Advisory Committee on Uniform Rules of Civil Procedure, transcript (Washington, DC, United States Courts, June 1935).

Advisory Committee on Uniform Rules of Civil Procedure, transcript June 1935 (United States Courts, November 1935) vol 1.

Uniform Rules of Civil Procedure for the District Courts of the United States and the Supreme Court of the District Columbia Tentative Draft I, Part 1 (15th October 1935). Copy in the papers of Charles Edward Clark, Yale University Library, MS 1344, Series IV Box 97.

Uniform Rules of Civil Procedure for the District Courts of the United States and the Supreme Court of the District Columbia, Tentative Draft II (26 December 1935). Copy is in the Papers of Charles Edward Clark, Yale University Library, MS 1344, Series IV Box 98.

Handbook of the National Conference of Commissioners on Uniform State Laws and Proceedings (Baltimore, MD, Lord Baltimore Press, 1936).

Uniform Rules of Civil Procedure for the District Courts of the United States and the Supreme Court of the District Columbia Tentative Draft III (March 1936). Copy in the Papers of Charles Edward Clark, Yale University Library, MS 1344, Series IV Box 98, vol III.

Preliminary Draft of Rules of Civil Procedure prepared by Advisory Committee (April 1936). Copy in the Papers of Charles Edward Clark, Yale University Library, MS 1344, Series IV Box 99, vol IV preliminary draft I.

Handbook of the National Conference of Commissioners on Uniform State Laws and Proceedings (Baltimore, MD, Lord Baltimore Press, 1937).

Report of the Advisory Committee on Rules for Civil Procedure Containing Proposed Rules of Civil Procedure for the District Courts of the United States (Washington, DC, Advisory Committee on Rules for Civil Procedure, 1937) in ED Hammond (ed), *Legislative History of the Rules of Civil Procedure of the District Courts of the US* (Chicago, IL, American Bar Association, 1938) vol 1.

American Law Institute Proceedings, vol 14 (Philadelphia, PA, American Law Institute, 1937).

Final Report of Advisory Committee on Rules for Civil Procedure (Washington, DC, Advisory Committee on Rules for Civil Procedure, 1937) in EH Hammond (ed), *Legislative History of the Rules of Civil Procedure of the District Courts of the US* (Chicago, IL, American Bar Association, 1938) vol 1.

Letter of Adoption of 20th December 1937 and Letter to Congress of 3rd January 1938 in EH Hammond (ed), *Legislative History of the Rules of Civil Procedure of the District Courts of the US* (Chicago, IL, American Bar Association, 1938) vol 1.

US Supreme Court's Order of 17th January 1938 in EH Hammond (ed), *Legislative History of the Rules of Civil Procedure of the District Courts of the US* (Chicago, IL, American Bar Association, 1938) vol 1.

Handbook of the National Conference of Commissioners on Uniform State Laws and Proceedings (Baltimore, MD, Lord Baltimore Press, 1938).

Proceedings of the Institute on Federal Rules, Cleveland, Ohio July 1938 in EH Hammond (ed), *Legislative History of the Rules of Civil Procedure of the District Courts of the US* (Chicago, IL, American Bar Association, 1938) vol 2.

Rules of Civil Procedure for the District Courts of the United States with Notes as prepared under the direction of the Advisory Committee (July 1938) in EH Hammond (ed), *Legislative History of the Rules of Civil Procedure of the District Courts of the US* (Chicago, IL, American Bar Association, 1938) vol 2.

Proceedings of the Institute on the Federal Rules of Civil Procedure held at Washington DC and Symposium at New York (October 1938) (Chicago, IL, American Bar Association, 1938).

American Law Institute Proceedings, vol 15 (Philadelphia, PA, American Law Institute, 1938).

American Law Institute Proceedings, vol 16 (Philadelphia, PA, American Law Institute, 1939).

A Self-Study of Federal Judicial Rulemaking: A Report from the Subcommittee on Long Range Planning to the Committee on Rules of Practice, Procedure and Evidence of the Judicial Conference of the United States, 10 May 1996, 168 Federal Rules Decisions 679.

Advisory Committee on Civil Rules in Proposed Amendments to the Federal Rules of Civil Procedure and the Federal Rules of Evidence Submitted to Standing Committee on Rules of Practice and Procedure, May 1992, 146 Federal Rules Decisions 535.

INDEX